C0-AKV-477

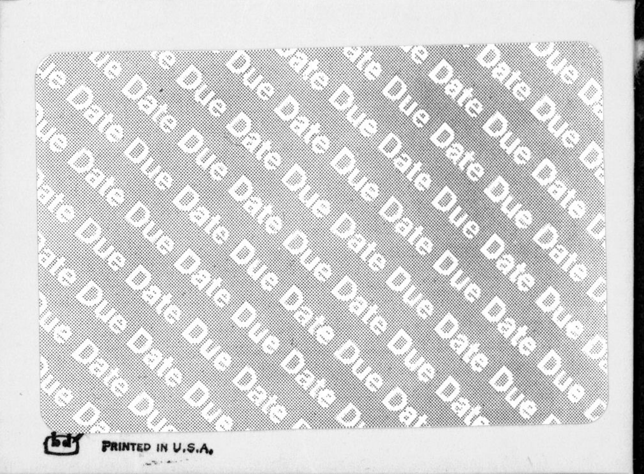

USAF HISTORICAL STUDIES

THE GERMAN AIR FORCE IN WORLD WAR II

LIST OF PUBLICATIONS AVAILABLE IN THE SERIES

HISTORICAL TURNING POINTS IN THE GERMAN AIR FORCE WAR EFFORT
by Richard Suchenwirth

THE GERMAN AIR FORCE VERSUS RUSSIA, 1941

THE GERMAN AIR FORCE VERSUS RUSSIA, 1942

THE GERMAN AIR FORCE VERSUS RUSSIA, 1943
by Generalleutnant Hermann Plocher

GERMAN AIR FORCE OPERATIONS IN SUPPORT OF THE ARMY
by General der Flieger a. D. Paul Deichmann

GERMAN AIR FORCE AIRLIFT OPERATION
by Generalmajor a. D. Fritz Morzik

THE GERMAN AIR FORCE GENERAL STAFF
by Generalleutnant Andreas Nielsen

THE RUSSIAN AIR FORCE IN THE EYES OF GERMAN COMMANDERS
by Generalleutnant a. D. Walter Schwabedissen

RUSSIAN REACTIONS TO GERMAN AIRPOWER IN WORLD WAR II
by Generalleutnant a. D. Klaus Uebe

AIRPOWER AND RUSSIAN PARTISAN WARFARE
by General der Flieger a. D. Karl Drum

USAF HISTORICAL STUDIES: NO. 155

The German Air Force Versus Russia, 1943

By Generalleutnant Hermann Plocher

Edited by Mr. Harry R. Fletcher
USAF Historical Division

With an Introduction by Telford Taylor

USAF HISTORICAL DIVISION
AEROSPACE STUDIES INSTITUTE
AIR UNIVERSITY • JUNE 1967

ARNO PRESS • NEW YORK

Reprinted with the cooperation of the Department
of Defense and the Historical Division, the Air
University of the United States Air Force.

Library of Congress Catalog Card No.: 68-22549

Manufactured in the U.S.A.
by Arno Press, Inc., New York, 1968

INTRODUCTION TO THE SERIES

The publication of this series of official historical studies is at once a most significant contribution to our knowledge of the Second World War and a landmark in the development of commercial publishing.

So much is published nowadays—far beyond the capacity of any individual even to screen—and so much is printed that ought never to see the light of day, that one tends to forget the considerable amount of writing well worth reading which rarely or never gets published at all. These volumes are an excellent example. Military monographs by foreign officers whose names are unknown to the public are not attractive items to most commercial publishing houses. But sometimes, as in the present case, they are unique sources of information which should be available in public if not in private libraries. Less often, and again as in the case of these volumes, they are surprisingly well written, and in many parts fascinating to the general reader as well as to the historian or military specialist.

The foreword of the Air Force Historical Division describes the inception and purposes of its German Air Force Historical Project and the circumstances under which these studies were written. Together with others to be published or made available for research in the future, the fruits of the Project are an analytic survey, at once comprehensive and intensive, of the Luftwaffe's structure and operations.

Not the least remarkable feature of the series is its authorship. With the single exception of Dr. Richard Suchenwirth—a one-time Austrian Army Officer and more recently a historian and educator in Munich—they are all former Luftwaffe generals, of low to middling seniority, who were intimately and responsibly involved with the events and problems of which they write. All seven were born within the decade 1891–1901, and thus in their forties or early fifties during most of the war years. Lieutenant-colonels or colonels when the war began, they filled a wide variety of staff and administrative assignments. Only two (Deichmann and Drum) attained three-star rank (*General der Flieger*), and only one (Deichmann) was ever given a major field command.

In military parlance, accordingly, they are all "staff" rather than "command" types, and for present purposes that is a good thing. Staff officers are responsible for the smooth functioning of the military machine; they must anticipate and provide for contingencies, and are expected to possess good powers of analysis and imagination. They spend much time drafting orders, which requires the ability to write with clarity and brevity. All these qualities are reflected in their product; our seven generals must have been good staff officers.

Banned by the Treaty of Versailles, the German air arm was condemned to a clandestine and embryonic life until 1933, and the Luftwaffe's existence was not publicly acknowledged until 1935. Hermann Goering and his colleagues in its command thus had only six years prior to the war in which to assemble and organize an officer corps. Its younger members—those who were lieutenants and captains when the war came—were recruited and trained during those years (1933–39), but the upper reaches of the corps had to be manned in other ways.

The need for experienced staff officers was especially acute, and this was met largely by transferring army (and a few navy) officers to the newly established air arm. Thus it is not surprising to find that all but one (Morzik) of our generals were professional soldiers who made their careers in the *Reichsheer* of the Weimar Republic, and received general staff training at the time Adolf Hitler was coming to power. So far as possible, the officers to be transferred were selected from those who had served in the air arm during the First World War, as had Deichmann and Drum.

Morzik alone represents the other principal type of senior Luftwaffe officer. He was not of the "officer class"; he had been a non-commissioned officer in the air arm during the First World War. Between the wars he led an adventurous and varied life as a commercial pilot, a successful competitor in aviation contests, a Junkers test pilot, and a flying instructor. Like his more famous superiors—Udet, Loerzer, von Greim, and Goering himself—Morzik was a free-lance knight of the air, and one of a considerable company commissioned from civil life in the 1933–35 period.

These generals are writing about events of which they were a part, in the course of a war in which Germany was catastrophically, and the Luftwaffe even ignominiously, defeated. What they have written is certainly not objective in the sense that it is detached; they see with the eyes and speak the language of the air arm, and readily find explanations for their own failures in the mistakes of the Army leadership—often with good reason, to be sure. But their work is objective in the sense that it is dispassionate. Their studies bespeak a deep curiosity about their conduct of the war and the causes of their defeat, and they have, on the whole, endeavored to put the record straight by the lines they are able to perceive.

There is, however, a great deal that they did not perceive. Few, if any, are those who can write at length about other men without revealing a great deal about themselves, and our authors are not in this respect exceptional. At least during this century, the German military profession has been rightly celebrated for its technical and tactical competence, but its record in the field of grand strategy has been abysmal. By and large these studies do not often venture into the rarefied atmosphere of the highest levels of command, and when they do, the results are unimpressive. Plocher's account of the reasons for the German attack against the Soviet Union,[1] for example, is superficial and diffuse. Of course he was not party or privy to the decision, but in telling us what he has heard there is little effort to winnow fact from fable, or to assess the considerations and alternatives.

In other respects, these volumes are not to be faulted so much for what is said as for what is left unspoken. Describing the Russian soldier, Uebe tells us that it is his "inherent character" to be "ruthless" and to place "a relatively lower value on human life" than "Western" peoples do.[2] For myself, I am inclined to discount popular stereotypes about national characteristics, and to judge rather upon a record of behavior. Beyond question the Russian soldier was often ruthless and worse, but what of the German soldier in Russia? Neither Uebe nor any of his colleagues carries the story in that direction. To be sure the Luftwaffe, by the nature of its operations, was not much involved in the exterminations, forced labor impressments, and other atrocities in which the Army was extensively implicated. But this hardly justifies Plocher's chest-thumping conclusion that: ". . . the incom-

[1] Plocher, *The German Air Force versus Russia, 1941,* pp. 1–3 (1965).
[2] Uebe, *Russian Reactions to German Airpower in World War II,* p. 1 (1964).

parable performances of the individual German soldier in combat in the East are above criticism. This applies to all ranks, from the lowest private to general officers, on the land, in the air, and on the seas."[3] Unhappily, the German military records tell quite a different story.

Fortunately such departures from the factual dimension are rare, and the authors have given us a unique and invaluable fund of information. Two of these studies concern the high command of the Luftwaffe, and two more cover particular Luftwaffe functions —air lift and ground support. The remaining six all concern the fighting on the eastern front between the German and Russian forces—a ferocious conflict on a scale greater than any other in human history.

Three of the eastern front studies, all by Plocher, constitute a chronological account of Luftwaffe operations on the eastern front in 1941, 1942, and 1943, one year to each volume. It is a mammoth undertaking of nearly 1,200 pages, well organized, and abundantly supported and illustrated with maps, charts, and photographs.

Plocher was chief of staff of an air corps on the southern part of the front, and remained in the east until the middle of 1943. Thus he witnessed at first hand the Luftwaffe's highly successful operations during the first few days of the campaign in July 1941, in the course of which the entire Russian air force was virtually annihilated, as well as the great encirclements at Minsk, Kiev, Bryansk, and elsewhere, which netted over two and a quarter million Russian prisoners and drove the Soviet forces back to the gates of Leningrad and Moscow and the banks of the Don. No doubt the Wehrmacht's failure to achieve decisive success was more the fault of the Army leadership than of the Luftwaffe, but the air generals made serious mistakes of their own, of which Plocher stresses two of major strategic proportions: (1) failure to carry out strategic bombing attacks on Russian armaments industries, and (2) dispersion of the slender air strength at the extreme northern end of the front, so that Murmansk and Archangel remained in Russian hands, as ports through which the western Allies could help the Russians to recover, following their nearly disastrous losses in the opening months of the campaign.

With the Russian air arm largely destroyed and strategic operations neglected, the Luftwaffe became, in practical terms, part of the German army—"flying artillery," supplemental transportation, additional ground forces. There were few Russian aircraft for the German *Flak* to shoot at, so the anti-aircraft units became front-line artillery.

Later on, as the Army got into even deeper trouble, the Luftwaffe was pulled in after it. Bombers were misused on ground-attack and airlift assignments; efforts to supply encircled German armies by air caused the Luftwaffe catastrophic losses. New Russian aircraft began to appear on the scene, and the balance gradually shifted so that by the end of 1943 the Germans no longer enjoyed air superiority, and the Luftwaffe became, as Plocher puts it, a "fire brigade," constantly on emergency call to plug up holes or salvage hard-pressed Army units.

How the Russians responded to the Luftwaffe's operations is the subject of Uebe's report. Except for the first few days, when the Soviet planes were destroyed in close array on their own airfields, like our own aircraft on Clark Field in the Philippines in December 1941, the Russians reacted to the overwhelming German superiority with great adaptability, and skill in the arts of camouflage and deception. Rails laid on ice did not sink with the thaw, for supports had been built under the ice; ships that appeared half-sunk and useless were under repair, with the bow flooded to elevate the stern. "As events show," writes

[3] Plocher, *The German Air Force versus Russia, 1943,* p. 266 (1967).

Uebe, "Russian reaction to German Air Force operations, however primitive and makeshift in character, and however crude they might have first appeared to be to their more enlightened Western opponents, proved throughout the course of the war to be highly efficient, effective, and ultimately an important factor in the defeat of Germany." A lesson for the American military command in Vietnam?

These same qualities were strikingly manifest in the Russian partisan operations behind the German lines, as described in a short but vivid study by General Karl Drum. The partisan units depended on air transportation for reinforcements, leadership, supplies, evacuation of wounded, and other necessary assistance, and all this was accomplished with obsolete aircraft and improvised equipment, utilizing air-drop or well-concealed air strips. Upon occasion, men were "delivered" to the partisans by parachuteless air-drop, wrapped in straw and dropped from low-flying planes into deep snow. The Germans, counting on a blitzkrieg victory, had made no preparations for anti-partisan warfare. No aircraft were earmarked to deal with the Russian air-supply, no single anti-partisan command was established to deal with the problem as a whole. Brutal occupation policies boomeranged by driving the population into the arms of the partisans. The German failure to take effective countermeasures is a striking demonstration that overwhelming superiority in heavy weapons and a sophisticated military tradition are no guarantee of success against surprise and deception.

Perhaps the most interesting and valuable of the eastern front volumes is Schwabedissen's extensive and perceptive study of the Russian air force as it appeared to the Germans. Through interchange of equipment and manufacturing and training facilities during the Weimar period, the antagonists were well known to each other. The Russian air performance in Spain and Finland had not been impressive, and in 1941, just prior to their attack, the Luftwaffe had a pretty accurate picture of the opposing force: it was far larger than the Luftwaffe, but much inferior in equipment, leadership, and training. The Germans expected to smash it to bits, and they succeeded.

What the Germans failed to reckon with was the Russians' recuperative powers. Most of their aircraft were destroyed on the ground rather than in the air, so that personnel losses were not high. The armament industries were rapidly moved eastward, and an early winter hampered Luftwaffe operations and gave the Russians a badly needed respite. By the winter of 1941–42 new Russian air units, better equipped, were beginning to appear at the front.

Still vastly superior in operational capacity, the Luftwaffe remained dominant in 1942, but in 1943 Russian numerical superiority, and techniques improved by experience, began to tell. During the last two years of the war, general air superiority passed to the Russian side of the front. But superior German technique enabled them to operate and achieve local successes right up to the end of the war; the Russians never achieved the total superiority enjoyed by the Allies on the western front.

German military air transport operations were opened by spectacular successes in the West. By parachute, glider, and landed aircraft, German airborne units descended on the major airfields of Norway and Denmark, on the airfields and tactically crucial bridges in Holland, and on the famous fort Eben Emael in Belgium. Morzik's fine account covers these operations in detail, as well as the later successful but costly assault on Crete, and the planned but never executed airborne operations in England, Gibraltar, Malta, and elsewhere.

The transport workhorse of the Luftwaffe was the three-engined Junkers 52, opposite number to our C-47s (otherwise known as DC-3s, Dakotas, "gooney birds," and now in Vietnam as "dragonships"), and well-known to all European travelers of ancient enough vintage to have flown Lufthansa during the thirties. A sturdy and versatile airplane, it was turned out by the thousands, but by the end of the war there were less than two hundred left. Most of the rest lay shattered and scrapped in Russia, near Demyansk and Stalingrad.

Morzik's account of the Demyansk and Stalingrad airlifts is gripping and enlightening. Retreating from the Moscow sector, the German Second Corps (roughly 100,000 men) was encircled at Demyansk in February 1942. Hitler forbade a breakout to the rear, and decided to supply the Corps by air. This was accomplished, but at a cost of 160 railway trains of gasoline, 265 Ju-52s, and consequent loss of trained crews and disruption of the pilot-training program. The psychological cost was even higher, for the apparent success of the operation made spuriously credible Goering's promise, ten months later, to supply Paulus' Sixth Army of over 300,000 men, encircled at Stalingrad. By then the Luftwaffe had only 750 Ju-52s left; half of them, and many bombers pressed into service as transports, were lost in the futile effort.

Airlift operations were the product of special circumstances, and strategic bombing the Luftwaffe neglected from birth to death. Day in and day out, its basic role was direct support of Army operations: attacking enemy troop columns, strong points, and tanks; impeding the flow of enemy reinforcements or cutting off their avenues of retreat; general intelligence reconnaissance. After 1941, Army support comprised over 75% of the Luftwaffe's operational activity—too large a proportion, as General Deichmann points out in his treatise "German Air Force Operations in Support of the Army." Deichmann traces the development of German air theory from its beginnings in the First World War, and explores the manner in which those theories shaped the Luftwaffe and governed its operational potential. The military air specialist will find this an exceptionally informative study.

In "The German Air Force General Staff," Nielsen takes us into the weird world of the Luftwaffe high command, well stocked with colorful characters, many of them adequately unattractive. Hitler was not much interested in air power and left Goering a free hand as long as things went well. After the period of spectacular initial successes, Goering suffered a sharp decline in influence, and the Fuehrer interjected himself into the Luftwaffe's management. He was not helpful; his decisions were the product of ignorance and favoritism and simply completed the process of demoralization.

Nielsen's study is focused on the general staff—i.e. the group of specially trained officers who held staff assignments—but its perspective is much broader, and includes the interplay of personality and rivalry at the top. Until his fall from grace, Goering's domination was complete, with one exception—Erhard Milch, his second-in-command, who had his own contacts and standing with Hitler and the Nazi Party. A former director of Lufthansa and a man of great energy and administrative ability, Milch was ambitious to the point that his attitude on proposed measures was governed less by the merits than by his estimate of their probable effect on his personal situation. Thus he initially opposed the creation of a general staff, and, when overruled, bent his energies to ensuring that the chief of the general staff would not impair his status as the No. 2 man. The consequence was a running battle between Milch and the succession of chiefs—seven during the Luftwaffe's less than twelve years of life—who served, basically, as Goering's advisors in the field of combat operations.

The results of his jerry-built command structure and riven leadership are graphically portrayed in Professor Suchenwirth's "Historical Turning Points in the German War Effort." Since the Luftwaffe ended the war in a state of total disintegration, the title postulates a study of crucial decisions which proved disastrous.

Perhaps the worst mistakes were made before the war began, and were the almost inevitable consequence of the personal shortcomings of the Luftwaffe leaders. Hans Jeschonnek—a career army officer barely old enough to have had a bit of flying experience at the very end of the First World War—was the Luftwaffe chief of staff from early 1939 to his suicide in 1943. Blindly devoted to Hitler and, until near the end, to Goering, he swallowed whole Hitler's assurances that the war would be a short blitzkrieg. Accordingly, he took no interest in training, neglected air transport, opposed the development of a long-range bomber, and focused all of his considerable ability on army support, and especially on the dive bomber. During the first year of the war these weaknesses did not show, but the Luftwaffe's failure over Britain and its inadequacy to the sustained demands of the eastern front were the direct result of such miscalculations, of which Jeschonnek was by no means the only author. Udet, Milch, Goering, and Hitler himself all contributed greatly to the Luftwaffe's misconstruction, misuse, and miserable fate.

In 1936, when Francisco Franco asked Hitler for help in moving his forces from Africa to Spain, Ju-52s were sent to do the job. Nine years later, as the Third Reich crumbled, Ju-52s—what was left of them—were still the standard Luftwaffe transport aircraft, and in this circumstance the Luftwaffe's intrinsic weakness is strikingly reflected. Messerschmitt 109s and 110s, Dornier 17s, Heinkel 111s, Ju-87 "Stukas," and Ju-88s were all on hand before the war began. With the sole exception of the Focke-Wulf 190—somewhat but not significantly superior to the Me 109—not a single new major aircraft type was added to the Luftwaffe until the last year of the war. Then came the first jet aircraft and the V-weapons, but it was too little and too late.

In retrospect, it is apparent that the Luftwaffe reached its peak of effectiveness before the war had even begun. Germany's bloodless conquest at Munich was achieved largely by the fear of Goering's bombers—a threat that was real enough, though exaggerated far beyond its true dimensions. Spectacular as they were, the Luftwaffe's triumphs in Poland, Norway, Holland, and even against the French (whose air force was woefully decrepit) were not scored against major opponents. As early as Dunkirk the veil was torn, and from then on the story is one of decline, gradual until the winter of 1941–42, rapid thereafter.

And so it came about that the story told, and well told, in these volumes can be fairly summarized in just seven words: how not to run an air force.

Telford Taylor

USAF HISTORICAL STUDIES: NO. 155

THE GERMAN AIR FORCE VERSUS RUSSIA, 1943

by

Generalleutnant Hermann Plocher

Edited by Mr. Harry R. Fletcher
USAF Historical Division

USAF HISTORICAL DIVISION
Aerospace Studies Institute
Air University
June 1967

Intermediary thou art between yesterday and tomorrow;
What is past thou bearest into the future!
Thus thou preservest the fleeting today in life and deed.

Karl Knoblauch
Member of the 4th (Strategic)
Flight, 14th (Muenchhausen)
Reconnaissance Squadron,
Sixth Air Fleet

He who would make wise use of history must recognize in the new circumstances the old kernel, and must not, through engrossment in the old elements overlook the new contexts.

Grillparzer
Historical and Political Studies

FOREWORD

The German Air Force versus Russia, 1943, written by Generalleutnant Hermann Plocher, and revised and edited by Mr. Harry Fletcher, is one of a series of historical studies written for the United States Air Force Historical Division by men who had been key officers in the German Air Force during World War II.

The overall purpose of the series is twofold: 1) To provide the United States Air Force with a comprehensive and, insofar as possible, authoritative history of a major air force which suffered defeat in World War II, a history prepared by many of the principal and responsible leaders of that air force; 2) to provide a firsthand account of that air force's unique combat in a major war, especially its fight against the forces of the Soviet Union. This series of studies therefore covers in large part virtually all phases of the Luftwaffe's operations and organization, from its camouflaged origin in the Reichswehr, during the period of secret German rearmament following World War I, through its participation in the Spanish Civil War and its massive operations and final defeat in World War II, with particular attention to the air war on the Eastern Front.

The German Air Force Historical Project (referred to hereinafter by its shorter and current title, "The GAF Monograph Project") has generated this and other especially prepared volumes which comprise, in one form or another, a total of more than 40 separate studies. The project, which was conceived and developed by the USAF Historical Division, was, upon recommendation of Headquarters Air University late in 1952, approved and funded by Headquarters USAF in early 1953. General supervision was assigned to the USAF Historical Division by Headquarters USAF, which continued principal funding of the project through 30 June 1958. Within the Historical Division, Dr. Albert F. Simpson and Mr. Joseph W. Angell, Jr., respectively Chief and Assistant Chief of the Division, exercised overall supervision of the project. The first steps towards its initiation were taken in the fall of 1952 following a staff visit by Mr. Angell to the Historical Division, Headquarters United States Army, Europe, at Karlsruhe, Germany, where the Army was conducting a somewhat similar historical project covering matters and operations almost wholly of interest to that service. Whereas the Army's project had produced or was producing a multiplicity of studies of varying length and significance (more than 2,000 have been prepared to date by the Army project), it was early decided that the Air

Force should request a radically smaller number (around 40) which should be very carefully planned initially and rather closely integrated. Thirteen narrative histories of GAF combat operations, by theater areas, and 27 monographic studies dealing with areas of particular interest to the United States Air Force were recommended to, and approved by, Headquarters USAF in the initial project proposal of late 1952. (A list of histories and studies appears at the end of this volume.)

By early 1953 the actual work of preparing the studies was begun. Col. Wendell A. Hammer, USAF, was assigned as Project Officer, with duty station at the USAREUR Historical Division in Karlsruhe. General der Flieger a. D. Paul Deichmann was appointed and served continuously as Control Officer for the research and writing phases of the project; he also had duty station at the USAREUR Historical Division. Generalleutnant a. D. Hermann Plocher served as Assistant Control Officer until his recall to duty with the new German Air Force in the spring of 1957. These two widely experienced and high-ranking officers of the former Luftwaffe secured as principal authors, or "topic leaders," former officers of the Luftwaffe, each of whom, by virtue of his experience in World War II, was especially qualified to write on one of the topics approved for study. These "topic leaders" were, in turn, assisted by "home workers"--for the most part former general and field-grade officers with either specialized operational or technical experience. The contributions of each of these "home workers," then, form the basic material of most of these studies. In writing his narrative the "topic leader" has put these contributions into their proper perspective.

These studies find their principal authority in the personal knowledge and experience of their authors. In preparing the studies, however, the authors have not depended on their memories alone, for their personal knowledge has been augmented by a collection of Luftwaffe documents which has come to be known as the Karlsruhe Document Collection and which is now housed in the Archives Branch of the USAF Historical Division. This collection consists of directives, situation reports, war diaries, personal diaries, strength reports, minutes of meetings, aerial photographs, and various other materials derived, chiefly, from three sources: the Captured German Documents Section of The Adjutant General in Alexandria, Virginia; the Air Ministry in London; and private German collections made available to the project by its participating authors and contributors. In addition, the collection includes the contributions of the "home workers." The authors have also made use of such materials as the records of the Nuremberg Trials, the manuscripts prepared by the Foreign Military Studies Branch of the USAREUR Historical Division, the official military histories of the United States and the United Kingdom, and the wealth of literature concerning World War II, both in German and English, which has appeared in book form or in military journals since 1945.

With the completion of the research and writing phases in 1958, the operations at Karlsruhe were closed out. At that time the project was moved to the Air University, Maxwell Air Force Base, Alabama, where the process of editing and publishing the studies was begun by the USAF Historical Division.

Basic revising and editing of the monographs has been handled by Mr. Edwin P. Kennedy (1958-61), Dr. Littleton B. Atkinson (1961-62), Mr. Gerard E. Hasselwander (1962-63), and the present Editor, Mr. Harry R. Fletcher. Final review and editing has been the responsibility of Dr. Albert F. Simpson, Chief, USAF Historical Division, with the assistance of Dr. Maurer Maurer, Chief of the Division's Historical Studies Branch.

The complexity of the GAF Monograph Project and the variety of participation which it has required can easily be deduced from the acknowledgements which follow. On the German side: General Deichmann, who, as Chief Control Officer, became the moving force behind the entire project, and his assistant, General Plocher; General Josef Kammhuber, a contributor to, and strong supporter of, the project, who became the first chief of the new German Air Force; Generaloberst a.D. Franz Halder, Chief of the German Army General Staff from 1938 to 1942, whose sympathetic assistance to the project was of the greatest value; the late Generalfeldmarschall Albert Kesselring, who contributed to several of the studies and who also, because of his prestige and popularity in German military circles, was able to encourage many others to contribute to the project; and all of the German "topic leaders" and "home workers" who are too numerous to mention here, but whose names can be found in the prefaces and footnotes to the individual studies.

In Germany, Colonel Hammer served as Project Officer from early in 1953 until June 1957. Colonel Hammer's considerable diplomatic and administrative skills helped greatly towards assuring the project's success. Col. William S. Nye, USA, was Chief of the USAREUR Historical Division at the project's inception; his strong support provided an enviable example of interservice cooperation and set the pattern which his several successors followed. In England, Mr. L. A. Jackets, Head of Air Historical Branch, British Air Ministry, gave invaluable assistance with captured Luftwaffe documents. The USAF Historical Division also wishes to express its thanks to the Houghton Mifflin Company of Boston for permitting quotations and citations from volume 5 of Winston S. Churchill's The Second World War to be used in this study.

The project is indebted to all of those members of the USAREUR Historical Division, the Office of the Chief of Military History, and the USAF Historical Division, whose assistance and advice helped the project to achieve its goals.

At the Air University, a number of people, both military and civilian, have given strong and expert support to the project. The several Commanders of Air University during the life of the project in Karlsruhe (1952-58) without exception were interested in the project and gave it their full backing. Other personnel at Headquarters Air University who contributed time and experience include: the several Directors of the Aerospace Studies Institute since 1952; Dr. James C. Shelburne, Educational Advisor to the Commander; Mr. J. S. Vann, Chief of Special Projects Branch, DCS/Operations; and Mr. Arthur P. Irwin, Chief, Budget Division, DCS/Comptroller.

The project is grateful to Lt. Col. Leonard C. Hoffman, former Assistant Air Attaché to Germany, who gave indispensable aid during the project's last year in Germany, and to Mr. Joseph P. Tustin, Chief Historian of Headquarters, United States Air Forces in Europe during the years when the project was at Karlsruhe, who rendered substantial assistance by solving a variety of logistical and administrative problems.

Mrs. Mary F. Hanlin deserves special thanks for her expert typing of the final draft.

AUTHOR'S FOREWORD

In the course of the crucial battles in the East at the close of 1942, the only important mission assigned to the Luftwaffe was that of providing for the support of the Army, usually direct support on the field of battle. This remained the Luftwaffe's main mission throughout the year 1943, and was almost exclusively dependent upon Army operations. Therefore, in this third volume on the war in Russia, it is again necessary, in fact even more than before, to treat the ground situation in some detail.

In the existing circumstances it is only natural that the many individual missions carried out by German air forces were very similar, with respect to purpose, assignment, execution, and results achieved, to the tactical support operations which had become the order of the day. Because of this, the various individual missions have not been treated in detail except in those instances in which it could be substantiated by documentary evidence that they had a marked impact upon the overall outcome of military operations. In general, an effort has been made to keep unnecessary details in the text to a minimum.

However, whenever the Luftwaffe played a decisive role in an operation, such as was the case in Operation ZITADELLE, in the battle for the Kuban bridgehead, and in the Crimea, air operations have been treated as exhaustively as available sources permitted. In this regard, the written and oral reports of many participants in these actions have been quoted and included, either completely or in part, in the body of the study.

In volumes one and two of The German Air Force versus Russia* the various operations were treated separately within the several major battle areas (army group areas) in the Eastern Theater, namely, the South, Center, North, and Far North. This could not be done in this study, since all too frequently the large-scale operations of 1943 simultaneously involved several army groups, and most of the major actions were closely interrelated between the various combat sectors. Only in Combat Zones North and Far North (First and Fifth Air Fleet areas respectively) could operations be treated in separate sections or chapters.

---

*Editor's Note: Volumes one and two are USAF Historical Division Studies No. 153 and 154.

Insofar as a specific critique of Army operations, their purposes, scope, and execution, are concerned, appropriate appraisals have been quoted from eminently qualified commanders such as Field Marshal Erich von Manstein and General der Infanterie Kurt von Tippelskirch.

As was true in the previous volumes, the individual chapters of this study were submitted whenever possible in preliminary draft form to actual participants in the particular actions described for their comments, criticisms, and additions. However, the author has not hesitated to express his own opinions concerning these operations, and does so in awareness that the discovery of new documents, war journals and diaries, papers, original reports and orders will more completely round out the story of these great events, and may require a modification of this work. Interpretations and judgments must always be derived from a careful study of all available data as seen in the light of historical perspective. The author wishes to express his warmest thanks to his many comrades whose contributions helped to make possible the compilation and writing of this study. May it be of interest and worth to the coming generations.

Karlsruhe, 10 February 1957

Hermann Plocher
Generalleutnant (Ret.)
German Luftwaffe

PREFACE

Contrary to the considered advice of experienced military leaders, Hitler decided in 1940 to launch an attack upon the Soviet Union. Logistically the Wehrmacht was ill prepared for a long and difficult campaign in the East, and German forces were already heavily committed in many other areas. The Fuehrer confidently waved all of these arguments aside with the supremely optimistic assurance that "it would all be over in a few weeks."

The war began on 22 June 1941 and soon a number of those who had serious misgivings about the gigantic venture were overwhelmed with the almost unparalleled series of military victories achieved by German arms in the East. Within a week the Luftwaffe had swept the skies clear of the Soviet air arm and had virtually destroyed it as a fighting force. The Army was also impressive as it drove through eastern Poland, the Baltic States, Bessarabia, and deeply into the Soviet Union. Leningrad was encircled and German armored forces stood near the gates of Moscow. It began to appear that the Fuehrer's prophesies, despite all logic to the contrary, might again come to pass. Actually, Germany had reached the high-water mark of the campaign.

Hitler, always obsessed with his concepts of Lebensraum and other special ideas, especially with respect to the East, was pleased with the results of the massive encirclement battles at Minsk-Bialystok, Smolensk, Bryansk-Vyazma, Gomel, Uman, Kiev, and the area northwest of the Sea of Azov, in which 2,256,000 Russians were taken prisoner. Yet, despite these gains and the conquest of thousands of square miles of Soviet territory, the Red Army had not been destroyed in the field, and sizeable units were able to withdraw to the east, where they helped to establish defenses in depth.

An unusually early and harsh onset of winter exposed the German Army to conditions for which it was unaccustomed and poorly prepared, and as the year drew to a close neither Leningrad nor Moscow had been taken. In the crucial winter fighting, German forces were not only compelled to fall back from the Soviet capital, but were fortunate that their withdrawal did not turn into a rout. Hitler prevented chaos in this situation through his order to "hold out at all costs" and "not to retreat a step," an expedient which he repeated again and again throughout the war, even when it appeared to serve no useful purpose whatever.

The German Army, having suffered grievous losses, emerged seriously weakened from the winter battles of 1941-42, and, as its leaders had foretold, its failure to make adequate logistical preparations began to tell. Adequate airfields were few and far between, and the primitive unsurfaced roads which characterized the East created immense problems for mechanized forces. Severe weather conditions aggravated matters still more.

Aware of these facts, Generaloberst Franz Halder, Chief of Staff of the German Army, insisted that the Wehrmacht be allowed to rest and rehabilitate itself so that the front could be stabilized and the very unsatisfactory logistical situation improved. Plans could then be laid for a promising offensive at a later date. Hitler, whose eyes were upon the industrial complex of the lower Volga and the rich oil fields of the Caucasus, immediately brushed these arguments aside with the comment that a lull in the fighting would not significantly improve the German position in the East, but would simply allow the Russian giant time in which to recover from the staggering blows he had received in 1941. Moreover, if the war could be quickly concluded in the East, there would be no possibility of Anglo-American aid attaining dangerous proportions, and the victory for Germany would morally strengthen its allies, especially Italy and Japan.

The summer offensive of 1942 laid the groundwork for Germany's defeat in the East. In these operations the relationship between the desired objectives and the forces available to secure them was faulty. The intended linkup of German forces with the Finns around Leningrad was feasible, but the southern operations required more than the Wehrmacht could handle. Hitler could not be dissuaded from his plans, and on 23 July 1942 issued his Directive No. 45, committing the depleted and worn-out army to two widely divergent drives, one toward Stalingrad and the Volga industrial complex, and the other toward the Caucasus. This, of course, entailed an immense dissipation of German airpower, since the Luftwaffe was expected to support all of these offensives, as well as minor operations, on a front extending from the arctic area to the central Caucasus.

Logistically, there was no chance for success in the southern operations unless the Russians were foolish enough to commit the bulk of their forces in the bend of the Don River where they could be quickly encircled and destroyed. German field commanders knew this. But the hope upon which victory hung never materialized.

By September, German forces had reached the environs of Stalingrad and had driven deeply into the Caucasus area, but at the end of that month operations ground to a halt. The Red Army had fought successful rear-guard actions near the Don and had withdrawn most of its forces to the east. A bitter fight then ensued for the city of Stalingrad, a city which refused to surrender. On 21 November, while German forces were locked in battle in that area, the Russians opened a large-scale offensive and quickly rolled up the Italian Eighth and Rumanian Third Armies and encircled the German Sixth Army under Paulus at Stalingrad. At the time there was the even graver danger that Soviet forces might reach Rostov on the Don, cutting off an entire army group in the Caucasus.

The Sixth Army held out against tremendous odds until 2 February 1943. In the course of this struggle the Luftwaffe was unable, despite its utmost efforts, to deliver even the required minimum of food and arms to the encircled force. Thus Goering's frivolous promise that he could "supply the Sixth Army by air" proved to be an idle boast which seriously damaged his standing--and with it that of the Luftwaffe--with Hitler.

Unquestionably the resistance by Paulus' men was an outstanding achievement, but the loss of such a large force was bound to have an adverse effect upon the entire German Army and to create a psychological impact of world-wide dimensions. In the West and the Soviet Union the news of the Sixth Army's capitulation was greeted with unbounded jubilation, while in Germany the news was received by a stunned and melancholy populace. Even Germany's closest allies began to question the possibility of a German victory.

This entire defeat is clouded by another problem, that of command. Following the dismissal of Field Marshal von Brauchitsch in 1941, Hitler had assumed the additional office of Commander in Chief of the German Army. Thereafter, his conduct of operations, his continual faith in improvisations, and his habit of interfering with local decisions through a by-passing of normal command channels were to have disastrous consequences for the German war effort. The Luftwaffe, being more and more drawn into a close-support role, thus suffered accordingly. Nor were matters improved by the fact that the Luftwaffe was represented by a Colonel on the staff of the High Command of the Wehrmacht.

Stalingrad was a turning point in the war. Not only was it a grievous loss to the already weakened front, but it pointed up the multifarious shortcomings of the German Wehrmacht and the German military economy, most of which could no longer be set right.

It is in this setting that Generalleutnant Plocher begins his third volume of _The German Air Force versus Russia_. Facing vastly superior forces on the ground and in the air, the German Command found itself increasingly obliged to resort to desperate measures and improvisations to avoid disaster. By 1943 the Wehrmacht was suffering from almost every conceivable sort of command, logistical, and military difficulty, and probably established a unique record in staving off the inevitable. The author discusses the operations of this year, emphasizing particularly the Luftwaffe's effort to again become a decisive weapon which could decide the outcome of the war.

The original of this manuscript has been abridged and several of the longer quotations have been sharply reduced in an effort to improve the narrative for the reader. Extensive editing has been done by the USAF Historical Division, but in the process it has carefully preserved the character of General Plocher's work, the essence of his commentary, and the significance of the remarks and opinions of others.

In conformity to general practices arising from the difficulty of finding precise American equivalents for grades and positions of German general officers, all ranks above Colonel have been left in the German form, with the exception of Field Marshal.

ABOUT THE AUTHOR

Generalleutnant Hermann Plocher was born 5 January 1901. His career in the German military service began in October of 1918 as an officer candidate in the 126th Infantry Regiment. He was commissioned 1 December 1922 in the 13th (Wuerttemberg) Infantry Regiment, a unit whose junior officers included such able men as Erwin Rommel and Dr. Hans Speidel. Three years later Plocher began training as a pilot, and in 1928 went with other German officers to the Soviet Union to take special courses in aerial combat and reconnaissance during the period when such activities were proscribed in the Reich. Following his promotion to Captain on 1 April 1934 he attended the Army War College (Kriegsakademie) in Berlin, receiving special air force training, and a year later was assigned to the Organization Branch of the Luftwaffe General Staff.

In August of 1936 Plocher, then a Major, was sent to Spain as part of the German contingent to assist Generalissimo Franco, and participated actively in the Spanish Civil War. In October of 1937 he was appointed Chief of Staff of "Legion Condor." By virtue of his record, Plocher earned on 1 March 1938 an extraordinary promotion to Lieutenant Colonel.

Prior to the outbreak of World War II he was assigned to the Luftwaffe General Staff as Chief of Plans and Mobilization. He then assumed the post of Chief of Staff of the V Air Corps (redesignated 1 April 1942 as Luftwaffe Command East) on 5 January 1940 and served with this organization during its operations in the West and in the Soviet Union. On 1 February 1943 he took command and directed the formation of the 19th Luftwaffe Field Division, and in April, following his promotion to Generalmajor, went with his unit to Normandy. General Plocher assumed command on 1 July 1943 of the 4th Air Division, and in October became Chief of Staff of the Third Air Fleet (Western Front). Following his promotion on 1 July 1944 to Generalleutnant, he became Commanding General of the 6th Airborne Division (Western Front). On 10 May 1945 he surrendered to Canadian forces in the Netherlands.

From 1953 until the spring of 1957, Generalleutnant Plocher gave generous and valuable assistance to the USAF Historical Division's German Monograph Project in Karlsruhe, Germany, adding his contributions to those of his colleagues to round out the story of German Air Force operations during the war. On 1 March 1957 he returned to active duty as a Generalmajor in the Bundeswehr as Deputy Inspector of the Luftwaffe and Chief of the Luftwaffe Operations Staff. He later served as Commander of a Luftwaffe division and simultaneously as Inspector for Troop Service in the Luftwaffe, and completed his military career as Commanding General of Luftwaffe Group South, from which he retired 31 December 1961.

As a former commander of German air and ground forces and as a General Staff officer of considerable experience and ability, he is ideally suited to document the course of events on the Eastern Front, where he played such a significant role.

CONTENTS

Page

Chapter 1

THE BEGINNING OF 1943: CRISIS BETWEEN THE DON AND DNEPR RIVERS

Developments on the Eastern Front 1941-1942

Hitler began his campaign against Russia (Operation BARBAROSSA) at daybreak on 22 June 1941. He had always viewed the Soviet Union as the principal ideological enemy of the Reich and hoped to settle matters in the East through a "lightning war" so that he could be free to bring military operations against Britain to a conclusion. [1] He also hoped to secure sources of raw materials in the Soviet Union which were needed by Germany's war program and sizeable areas which could be used for German colonization.*

The Fuehrer was not alone in his anxieties concerning Soviet intentions. Many of his top military advisors shared these views, and were genuinely alarmed over the Soviet Union's aggressive and expansionist undertakings in eastern Europe between 1939 and 1941. They believed that Stalin intended to attack Germany as soon as Russia was ready for such an operation and a suitable pretext for war could be found.†

Forces available for the campaign against Russia consisted of 145 German and allied divisions, which were divided among three major commands, Army Groups South, Center, and North, and one minor command, with less critical objectives, Army Group Far North. This field army advanced from its concentration areas in East Prussia, Poland, and Rumania, overwhelming a large number of Red Army units and scoring victory after victory in rapid succession. The German and allied forces

---

*Editor's Note: See Generalleutnant Hermann Plocher, The German Air Force versus Russia, 1941, USAF Historical Studies No. 153, Maxwell AFB, Alabama: USAF Historical Division, ASI, July 1965.

†Editor's Note: While the U.S.S.R. has always alleged that it seized the Baltic States, attacked Finland, and took Bessarabia as necessary defensive measures, these acts alarmed Germans and other Europeans, and reinforced Hitler's conviction that a preventative war against Russia had to be made as soon as possible.

surged steadily eastward through the dust of the summer, deep into the vast expanses of Russia, taking thousands of prisoners and capturing massive amounts of enemy materiel.

At the same time the Luftwaffe demonstrated its power by immediately destroying the bulk of the largely obsolete Soviet Air Force and quickly establishing air supremacy over the entire Eastern Theater of Operations. So devastating was this air blow that it might have been a decisive factor had the Luftwaffe also been able to destroy the sources of Soviet military power and to interdict the flow of materiel through the ports of the Black and Caspian Seas, and through Arkhangelsk and Murmansk. These goals were never attained.

By October 1941 the Wehrmacht was poised for what the German High Command then believed would be the final assaults upon the strategic objectives of Moscow and Leningrad. In November, however, serious logistical difficulties, including shortages of winter clothing and equipment, unexpectedly fanatical enemy resistance, and an unusually early and severe onset of winter, slowed the German attack along the entire front. By 5 December the great offensive had come to a halt and the key cities of Moscow and Leningrad remained in Russian hands.

During these operations, Russian troops, assisted by mass civilian labor forces, exhibited surprising ability to rehabilitate their units, evacuate heavy equipment, and make hasty improvisations in defense lines and field fortifications. Moreover, they were able to withdraw large numbers of troops to the East before the German forces could surround and destroy them.* In these encounters the individual Russian soldier proved to be a cunning and ruthless adversary, skilled in the use of cover and concealment, and able to endure great physical hardships and privations.

Having failed to secure the strategic objectives of the campaign by the end of 1941, the German Army then found itself forced to fight off heavy Soviet counterattacks launched by newly arrived Siberian units, and, being critically short of supplies and manpower, had to withdraw from its advanced positions and go over to the defensive. Only by implementing the most stringent measures, including the Fuehrer's order

---

*Editor's Note: See Generalleutnant a. D. Klaus Uebe, Russian Reactions to German Airpower in World War II, USAF Historical Studies No. 176, Maxwell AFB, Alabama: USAF Historical Division, ASI, July 1964, pp. 1-6, 83-89.

of 16 December 1941 to hold fast "without retreating a step," was the Wehrmacht able to avert a disaster of immense magnitude near Moscow.[2] With considerable intrepidity and great resourcefulness, German and allied forces were able by the end of January 1942 to check the Soviet counteroffensive and to shorten their front lines for more effective defense.

On 12 February 1942 the German High Command issued orders for a resumption of the offensive, to begin as soon as logistical and weather conditions were propitious. Hitler was certain that the 1942 campaign in southern Russia would be a decisive victory if it resulted in the seizure of the Caucasus oil region. Such a plan, however, entailed the assumption that the Russians would be willing to commit the greater part of their forces in the area of the Don River bend, where the Wehrmacht could envelop and destroy them.*

Hitler issued on 5 April his _Directive No. 41_ (Operation _BLAU_), which outlined a four-step plan for the conquest of the Caucasus and, providing all conditions were favorable, for the seizure of Leningrad as well. While Army Group Center was to hold its position, Army Group North in conjunction with its Finnish allies was to seize Leningrad. In Combat Zone South, the offensive was to begin with a breakthrough in the Kursk area by left flank units (Fourth Panzer Army and Hungarian Second Army) of Army Group South, thereby opening the way for a pincers operation against Voronezh. The two armies were then to advance southeastward, linking up with the Sixth Army thrusting eastward along the Valuy River from Kharkov. These combined forces, spearheaded by strong armored and motorized units, were then to make a rapid advance along the Don to the southeast, meeting near Stalingrad the First Panzer Army and Seventeenth Army of Army Group South, which were to make a swift drive toward the Don River from Taganrog. It was assumed that this would envelop the bulk of the Red Army in the Don River bend and clear the path for a general advance into the Caucasus. All movements were to be made from one phase line to another, making the most judicious use possible of available forces by concentrating maximum force at the crucial points of battle.

---

*Editor's Note: See Generalleutnant Hermann Plocher, _The German Air Force versus Russia, 1942_, USAF Historical Studies No. 154, Maxwell AFB, Alabama: USAF Historical Division, ASI, 1966. See also Maps Nos. 1 and 2.

The summer offensive was launched at the end of the muddy season and by July German forces had advanced to the Don River along a front extending from the area north and east of Orel into the bend of the Don, and thence to Rostov in the south. At this juncture, a radical change was made in the overall plan of attack. On 23 July Hitler issued Directive No. 45, setting forth two principal objectives for a continued offensive in the East, the seizure of Stalingrad and the lower Volga industrial complex, and the conquest of the Caucasus oil region.[3*] In his thinking the Fuehrer without doubt was heavily influenced by logistics and by the conviction that the Red Army must be suffering equally as much as the Wehrmacht from the material and personnel losses of previous operations. Therefore, he was tempted to concentrate upon the seizure of the Caucasus oil fields, which seemed to be much more important to Germany's war effort than the conquest of Moscow, which continued to be urged by some of the German High Command.[†]

In order to implement his plan, the right wing (Eleventh Army and Third Rumanian Army in the Crimea, and the Seventeenth Army and First Panzer Army in the northern Caucasus) of Army Group South was, by late July, redesignated Army Group "A." The remaining forces of Army Group South (Second and Sixth Armies, Fourth Panzer Army, and Hungarian Second Army, with the Rumanian Fourth and Italian Eighth Armies in reserve) were placed under the newly organized Army Group "B."

Army Group "B" was to drive down the Don to Stalingrad to secure the lower Volga River area, while Army Group "A" was to seize Rostov and the Caucasus oil region. Since these drives were virtually at right angles to each other, they violated the principle of advance by phase lines which, until then, had been so successful.

By mid-November Army Group "A" had driven to the Kuma River as far as Alagir and to Mt. Elbrus, deep in the Caucasus, and from thence to the area west of Tuapse, to Iskaya, and then to the Black Sea coast near

---

*Editor's Note: See Generalleutnant a. D. Hermann Plocher, The German Air Force versus Russia, 1942, USAF Historical Studies No. 154, Maxwell AFB, Alabama: USAF Historical Division, ASI, 1966, for a more complete discussion of these operations.

†Editor's Note: Generaloberst Franz Halder, Chief of the General Staff of the German Army, 31 August 1938-24 September 1942, thought that the Russians would be willing to trade space in southern Russia for time, while an offensive in the center toward Moscow might well have succeeded.

Novorossiysk. Army Group "B" had advanced to the Don from the area west of Yelets, and its Sixth Army had reached the vicinity of Stalingrad, while motorized units of the group had penetrated as far southward as the Elista area in the northern Caucasus.* Logistical problems began to mount enormously, and the cost of the offensive was taking a heavy toll of men and equipment in both army groups, especially in the Sixth Army of Army Group "B," which continued to exhaust itself in futile attempts to take the city of Stalingrad.

On 19 November the Red Army opened its first massive counter-offensive of the war all along the Don front from Stalingrad to the area west of Serafimovich, breaking through the left side of the Third Rumanian Army front and rolling up the right flank of the Italian Eighth Army immediately to the north. Within two days the Russians had driven as far as Kalach-on-the-Don, where they reached spearhead units of strong Soviet forces driving westward from Krasnoarmeysk, and on 22 November had completely encircled the Sixth Army, together with elements of many other German and allied units, in a large pocket west of Stalingrad.†

Realizing that the Sixth Army was already critically short of supplies and replacements, and exhausted from months of heavy fighting, several senior Army and Luftwaffe commanders attempted to persuade Hitler either to withdraw the forces from the Caucasus or to approve a Sixth Army breakout to the southwest, since the encirclement of the Sixth Army, serious as it was, might also be the prelude for a concerted Russian drive on Rostov. If that city could be reached, an entire German army group would be cut off in the Caucasus. The Fuehrer, however, assured by Reichsmarschall Hermann Goering that the Luftwaffe could supply all of the entrapped army's needs by air, ordered the Sixth Army to hold at "all costs," and directed the Luftwaffe to establish an airlift to give it all necessary logistical support.

Generaloberst Hermann Hoth and his Fourth Panzer Army then tried to extricate the Sixth Army by a relief attack from the southwest. When his relatively weak force had reached its farthest point of advance, a junction with the encircled army might have been possible if Generaloberst Friedrich Paulus, the Sixth Army Commander, had been willing

---

*See Map No. 1. The Eleventh Army (Generaloberst Erich von Manstein) was transferred 18 September 1942 to Army Group North, but returned to become the framework for the new Army Group Don 22 November 1942.

†See Map No. 2.

to defy his Fuehrer's orders and make a southwesterly dash over the remaining few miles between the armies. This, he was unwilling to do.

The airlift operation was equally ill-fated, since the forces on hand for the undertaking were grossly inadequate even at the outset, especially in view of the fact that the Luftwaffe had to help stem the tide of Soviet attacks on an immensely broad front. Robbing school and training installations of their last transport aircraft did not materially alter the situation at Stalingrad, since the attrition rate was always higher than the rate of replacement. This serious condition was further compounded by acute shortages of personnel, tools, replacement parts, combat aircraft, and other types of supplies and equipment, all during a period of extended adverse weather. It is, in fact, surprising that the Luftwaffe's airlift functioned as well as it did. Yet, despite heroic sacrifices, German air units never came close to the minimum objective of maintaining the Sixth Army's supply levels, much less to the creation of reserve stockpiles.

Operations in 1942 were shattering, and every German effort appeared to have been made in vain. One German army and three of its allies' armies had suffered devastating losses, with at least 50 divisions completely destroyed. Other losses amounted to the strength of about 25 divisions. Along with this were lost incalculable quantities of heavy infantry weapons, light and heavy artillery pieces, tanks and assault guns, and other materiel, an aggregate which was definitely heavier than the losses inflicted upon the enemy during this period. But by the far the most significant losses for Germany were in personnel, since the Soviets, despite their heavy losses, still had far greater reserves of manpower at their disposal.

Battles in the Don-Dnepr River Areas, January-Mid-March 1943

At the beginning of January 1943 the Soviet forces held the initiative in every sector of the entire Eastern Theater of Operations. In the southern area (the main zone of combat operations for the German Army and Luftwaffe at the turn of the year), the critically weakened German armies were, generally speaking, back in the positions from which they had commenced their great offensive of July 1942. The Russian hordes had continued to strengthen their attacks along the break-through areas in the sectors held by Rumanian, Italian, and Hungarian armies, and threatened to bring about a collapse of the entire front in Combat Zone South. If the Soviet Command could achieve its objectives, the result could be far more disastrous than the threatened loss of the Sixth Army at Stalingrad, since a catastrophe involving two German army groups could decide the outcome of the war.

Generaloberst Paulus' Sixth Army, acting as a breakwater in advance of the German lines, was still holding out in Stalingrad at the turn of the year, but its fate was already sealed. 4* All efforts to relieve it or to enable it to break out to the south or southwest had failed, and the army's end was fast approaching. It could, at best, do no more than contain sizeable Soviet forces for a short time by expending its last forces. In this way it could render a positive service to German comrades in the Caucasus who also were threatened with encirclement. 5

East of the Don and Donets Rivers, from the area just south of Morozovsk to the Manych River, Generaloberst Hoth's Fourth Panzer Army, together with the remnants of the Fourth Rumanian Army, were withdrawing west of the Don and Donets along a line extending from Voroshilovgrad to the western Manych. The mission of these armies was to protect the rear of the First Panzer Army (General der Kavallerie Eberhard von Mackensen), then withdrawing from the Caucasus, from Soviet attacks from the region of Millerovo and Kamensk-Shakhtinsky. At the same time, the Fourth Panzer Army and its auxiliary units had to prevent a Soviet breakthrough along the lower Don River in the direction of Rostov. If the Russians could reach the Don estuary, they could cut off the Fourth Panzer Army and all of Army Group "A," the latter being made up of the First Panzer Army and the Seventeenth Army. 6≠

In the critical situation the important thing for the Fourth Panzer Army was not to expend its forces by attempting to offer strong resistance along a broadly extended front, but, rather, to keep its forces tightly concentrated. This was the only way it could render tenacious resistance at crucial points, as the situation might require, or exploit opportunities for surprise blows. It was therefore self-evident that the army at times had to strip certain areas completely, and leave other areas with only a thin defensive covering line.

---

*Stalingrad officially surrendered to the Red Army 2 February 1943. See Map No. 2.

≠Editor's Note: Army Group "A" was under the overall command of Generaloberst Ewald von Kleist. Rostov was not only strategically important for German operations in 1942, it was also Army Group "A's" supply center.

Ably supported by his excellent chief of staff, Generalmajor Friedrich Fangohr, Hoth accomplished his difficult mission by a determined, but flexible, conduct of operations.* Employing clever tactics, he succeeded in delaying the Russians in their hot frontal pursuit, without exposing his force to the threat of a defeat by holding out too long in a given position. He also managed to concentrate his forces quickly in brief attacks against Soviet troops on his flanks, thereby repeatedly thwarting their attempts to outflank and surround his army.[7] Hoth's operations were all the more outstanding because of the bitter winter conditions in which his units were forced to fight, often with bare minimums of supplies and equipment.

Meanwhile, Army Force Hollidt† (Generalleutnant Karl Hollidt), holding the left flank of Army Group Don (Field Marshal Erich von Manstein), immediately north of the Fourth Panzer Army, employed its weak forces again and again to prevent attacks from the north, or, what could have been worse, from the northwest against the rear of the Fourth Panzer Army.†† With the "valuable support of flak artillery units under the tried and proven command of Generalmajor [Rainer] Stahel," Hollidt's force was able to hold up the Soviet advance at the Chir River and later at the Donets River.[8]

Army Group "A" found itself in an increasingly difficult situation in the Caucasus. It should really have been clear to the Supreme Command from the outset that this unit could not maintain its forces there unless the envelopment of the Sixth Army could be broken very quickly. In other words, it was essential to reestablish a relatively stable situation in the main bend of the Don River. Once the Russians had breached

---

*Editor's Note: Manstein mentions that Hoth's naturally "impulsive" nature was perfectly offset by the presence of Fangohr. See Generalfeldmarschall Erich von Manstein, Verlorene Siege (Lost Victories), Bonn: Athenaeum Verlag, 1955, p. 534. Cited hereafter as Manstein, Lost Victories.

†Formed in November 1942 and continued to be so designated until 3 February 1943, when it became the nucleus of a reconstituted German Sixth Army.

††Editor's Note: The Fourth Panzer Army's front faced to the north, east, and southeast in the area northwest of Elista. By 1 February 1943 it faced the same directions from the confluence of the Manych and Don Rivers to the confluence of the Donets and Don, and thence to the west as far as the Voroshilovgrad area. See Maps Nos. 1 and 2.

the right flank of Army Group "B" (Army Force Fretter-Pico,* Second Army, Hungarian Second Army, and Italian Eighth Army) northwest of Morozovsk and opened the way for their drive on Rostov, however, it must have been perfectly obvious that the Caucasus front could not be held under any circumstances. [9/]

On 29 December 1942 Hitler had ordered the withdrawal of the First Panzer Army, operating on the eastern flank of Army Group "A," the area which was most seriously threatened by the Soviet offensive. For the time being the army was to withdraw to the Pyatigorsk-Praskoveyskiy segment of the Kuma River line. It was, of course, evident that this was not to be the last move and that the entire Caucasus would eventually have to be evacuated.

Evacuation of the Communications Zone of Army Group "A," involving the movement of hospitals, ammunition and food supply dumps, permanently installed weapons, and other essential items, was an exceedingly difficult and time-consuming operation. [10] One of the major obstacles to be overcome was the lack of high-carrying-capacity rail and road routes, particularly in the mountainous areas. In spite of these difficulties, however, the first Panzer Army succeeded by mid-January 1943 in retiring to positions along a line extending approximately from Cherkassk to Petrovskoye. It was still separated from the Fourth Panzer Army by a wide gap extending all the way from the area north of Cherkassk to the vicinity of Proletarskaya, a part of which area was impassable for large units even in the winter because of the Manych River swamps.

Covered by the Fourth Panzer Army and with constant support from units of the Fourth Air Fleet, the First Panzer Army in a series of seesaw battles, which included numerous defensive counterattacks, finally succeeded in withdrawing the bulk of its forces across the Don River on both sides of Rostov. There, the army was placed under the command of Army Group Don (von Manstein) and took up positions on the left flank of that organization. The divisions of the First Panzer Army retired across the Don River into the area back of the main line of

---

*Editor's Note: Under the command of General der Artillerie Maximilian Fretter-Pico, this unit was formed 25 December 1942 and became a part of the First Panzer Army on 3 February 1943.

/See Maps Nos. 2 and 3.

resistance just in time to support Army Group Hollidt, then hard pressed between the Don and the Mius Rivers; later, the First would play a decisive role in cooperation with the Fourth Panzer Army, withdrawing across the Don, in defense against a Russian breakthrough of the Dnepr River line. [11*]

The Seventeenth Army was deployed on both sides of the Kuban River in the Kuban bridgehead (later to become famous), its front extending in a line from Novorossiysk to Krymskaya, to Kiyevskoye, to Krasnyy Oktyabr, to the area east of Temryuk. [12] The German Command had to maintain strong ground and air forces to hold this position, and these forces were more urgently needed in the Donets Basin area, where they could have been used far more effectively. In the words of Field Marshal von Manstein:

> . . . a force about 400,000 strong remained more or less inactive in the Kuban bridgehead. The bridgehead admittedly tied down Soviet forces of considerable strength, and the Russians made several abortive attempts to eliminate it, but the bridgehead never attained the strategic significance for which Hitler had hoped. After all, the Russians were free to decide just what troops they would leave in the area to contain the German forces in the bridgehead. Another reason advanced by Hitler for the retention of such a large force at the Kuban River was the necessity of denying the Soviets possession of the naval port of Novorossiysk. However, this reason was also invalid. The port had to be abandoned anyway. [13/]

On 2 February 1943 the battle for Stalingrad ended, bringing to a close the Sixth Army's tragic struggle in its forlorn post. [14] This resulted not only in a merciless captivity for thousands of battle-weary German troops and in the capture of enormous quantities of valuable military materiel, but also in the release of strong Soviet forces which had hitherto been required for the envelopment and reduction of the Stalingrad pocket. These forces considerably increased the power of the Red Army

---

*See Map No. 2.

/Units in the Kuban bridgehead area were supplied from the Crimea.

units attacking along the lines in the southern combat areas, where the Russians already enjoyed a vast numerical and logistical superiority. [15]*

Powerful Soviet forces landed near Novorossiysk on 4 February, and all efforts by the Wehrmacht to dislodge and destroy them failed. The only German achievement in the area was the compressing of these enemy forces into a narrow bridgehead. [16]

Early in February the entire army command in Combat Zone South was reorganized. [17] Army Group Don was redesignated Army Group South, and assigned to command all forces in the area extending from Rostov-on-the-Don to the Kharkov-Belgorod region. This included Army Force Hollidt (later to be the core of the reconstituted Sixth Army), in position at the Mius River; farther to the north the Army Force Fretter-Pico/ (later under the command of the First Panzer Army), holding the area around Artemovsk; the Fourth Panzer Army in the area northwest of Stalino; and Army Force Kempf// (formerly under Generalleutnant Hubert Lanz), then in the process of reorganization in the Kharkov area. Army Group "B" headquarters was withdrawn and the Second Army, hitherto under its control, was assigned to Army Group Center.

Before this reorganization Army Force Lanz had been assigned the double mission of attacking in the direction of Losovaya to relieve the left flank of Army Group South and to hold the city of Kharkov at all costs. It was impossible to carry out either of these missions, especially the latter, but Hitler viewed Kharkov, the capital of the Ukraine, as a prestige symbol and refused to consider a withdrawal. Under the pressure of overwhelming enemy forces, the Wehrmacht had to withdraw from the city on 15 February. Fortunately, the withdrawal was made by the SS Panzer Corps, a unit comprising the core of Army Force Lanz (and later Kempf), so that no retaliation was taken against an army commander.

From the end of February to mid-March the tide turned and parts of the Soviet forces which had broken through the German defenses and

---

*Despite reinforcements, the Germans were outnumbered by Red Army troops in the southern sectors by 8 to 1, and in certain parts of the front the ratio was even less favorable for the Wehrmacht. See Manstein, p. 450.

/Editor's Note: See p. 9.

//Editor's Note: Generalleutnant Franz Werner Kempf.

advanced to the vicinity of Zaporozhye and Dnepropetrovsk were enveloped by the Wehrmacht in numerous counterattacks between the Dnepr and Donets Rivers, and the bulk of the Russian forces in this area escaped destruction only by rapid withdrawals across the Donets River.* Operations against Soviet armored and cavalry forces which had cracked the Mius River defenses north of Taganrog and at Debaltsevo, west of Voroshilovgrad, also ended with the destruction of the enemy forces.

By mid-March the front in Combat Zone South was again firmly integrated and all of the divisions in this area were contiguous to each other, forming a line (albeit thinly manned in places) extending from Taganrog to Belgorod. On 15 March the city of Kharkov was again in German hands, and replacements had filled many of the gaps created in Wehrmacht line units during the bitter defensive battles of the previous winter.† From that time on, however, the onset of the muddy season prevented a continuation of operations, even those on a small tactical scale.

In a review of the overall course of the winter campaign of 1942-43 in southern Russia, and of the results achieved in those battles, it becomes undeniably apparent that the Soviet forces achieved a considerable amount of success. Yet, despite these great gains, the Soviet Command had not accomplished its decisive objective in this area, the destruction of the German southern flank, a victory which would probably have been impossible for the Wehrmacht to offset. Instead, at the conclusion of the winter campaign, the initiative along the entire front passed again to the German side. The Russians had suffered defeats in the area west and southwest of Izyum and around Kharkov, which, although not decisive in character, enabled the German command to stabilize the entire front.

At this juncture it seems proper to enumerate the factors which contributed to the victory that strengthened the German position and prevented the envelopment of the Wehrmacht's southern flank. It must be stated here that Army Group South would not have been able to overcome its initial defeat if the German troops and their officers had not demonstrated almost superhuman resistance and performed in an outstanding manner in the course of these battles, if the courageous infantry divisions had not stood their ground again and again although badly outnumbered

---

*See Maps Nos. 2 and 3.
†See Map No. 4.

by the enemy, and if the Wehrmacht, unlike its allies, had not resisted Soviet armored attacks by closing ranks after breakthroughs, thereby making possible the destruction of Russian tank forces.

In like manner, it would have been utterly impossible to have conducted this winter campaign successfully if the panzer divisions, fighting with incomparable flexibility, had not multiplied their effectiveness by striking the enemy in one area on one day and in another area on the next. It was the constant feeling of personal superiority over the enemy which enabled the German troops to withstand the severest crises, and lent the extra impetus to their courage and devotion to duty, which to a great extent offset the numerical superiority of the Russian forces.

Nor must one forget that the courageous Sixth Army, by its resistance to the last, prevented an annihilating Soviet victory in the southern sector of the Eastern Theater of Operations. If that army had not resisted long after its situation became hopeless, the Russians could have thrown strong additional forces into the decisive points of the front, which, in all probability, would have meant the envelopment of the entire German southern flank.

As Field Marshal von Manstein points out:

> Although the sacrifices made by the troops of the Sixth Army may appear to have been futile in view of the final outcome of the war, nothing can detract from the ethical value of those sacrifices.
>
> Therefore it is only right that the Sixth Army should once again be remembered in closing this presentation of the winter campaign. The troops of that army rendered the greatest service which can be asked of soldiers: to support their comrades by resisting to the last round when in a hopeless situation.[18]

Reading this glowing tribute by the responsible army commander to his officers and men, it seems strange that no mention is made of the tireless and costly efforts of the Luftwaffe in trying to support the fighting men at Stalingrad. The losses suffered in airlift operations to the Stalingrad pocket are well known. Those operations were, unfortunately, futile. They failed because of inadequate forces, which were further hampered by the impact of natural forces in the almost limitless spaces of Russia. These conditions also frustrated all of the German Army's efforts to relieve and extricate the encircled Sixth Army.

It is therefore more than unjust that Army circles for reasons unknown to the author tend to ignore and overlook the important, and sometimes decisive, roles played by the Luftwaffe in surmounting serious crises and in reestablishing firm main lines of resistance in Combat Zone South.

Fourth Air Fleet Operations Between the Don and the Dnepr

At the beginning of 1943, the Fourth Air Fleet, commanded by Generaloberst Wolfram Freiherr von Richthofen, had the following missions to perform in Combat Zone South:

(1) To move supplies by air to the mortally stricken Sixth Army enveloped by the Red Army at Stalingrad, and

(2) To provide air support for German and allied ground forces in their difficult, and frequently critical, battles.[19]

For the accomplishment of these tasks the Fourth Air Fleet controlled the VIII Air Corps (Generalleutnant Martin Fiebig), which was engaged in combat and supply missions in support of the Sixth Army;[20] Air Division Donets (Generalleutnant Alfred Mahnke), primarily engaged in operations to support the hard-pressed Army Force Hollidt; the IV Air Corps (General der Flieger Kurt Pflugbeil), then committed in support of the delaying battles of the Fourth Panzer Army and the remnants of the Fourth Rumanian Army withdrawing across the Manych River toward the lower Don; the Royal Rumanian Air Corps, employed in tactical operations between the Don and Manych Rivers; and Luftwaffe Group Caucasus (Staff of the I Air Corps under General der Flieger Otto Dessloch), supporting the First Panzer Army and the Seventeenth Army in their withdrawal from the Caucasus.[21]

The command staff of the Fourth Air Fleet was established on a headquarters railway train and had moved to Taganrog South. Flying units of the Fourth, whose effective fighting strength had been reduced below the level of operational effectiveness, and all usable materiel, especially operational aircraft, were utilized to bring other units up to strength. Insofar as was possible, personnel were sent to the Communications Zone for rest and rehabilitation for their later return to the front.

Weather conditions in the south around the turn of the year were unsettled, days with relatively good visibility or high cloud ceilings being followed by days with heavy fog, low cloud ceilings, snow, rain, and ice storms. German air units operated to the maximum extent possible in these conditions, supporting all areas of the far-flung front from the Caucasus to the Don and Donets River areas to the vicinity of Kharkov.[22]*

The ceaseless Soviet attacks, the deep penetrations, and dangerous breakthroughs in the German front, all threatening the withdrawal routes of Army Groups "A," Don, and "B," and the Wehrmacht retrograde movements, alternating with counterattacks to protect the withdrawals, obliged the Fourth Air Fleet to adopt extremely flexible tactics in the employment of its units, and to constantly shift the emphasis of its support operations.[23]

Owing to the lack of mobile army reserves, especially panzer and motorized divisions, the usually bottomless Russian roads, the irregular pattern of the main lines of resistance, and the immense distances involved, the Luftwaffe was the only highly mobile instrument available to the German Command to stop the Red Army threats, or to slow down enemy advances so that German ground forces could reestablish defensive positions. An example of such action could be seen in the operation of 10 January 1943, when Army Force Hollidt, ably supported by Air Division Donets, succeeded in halting a Soviet armored attack and in cleaning out an area of Russian penetration.

In the course of these operations it frequently became necessary to open the way for isolated or enveloped army units to make their way back to the German lines. The garrison of Chertkovo, which had been surrounded by the Red Army for weeks, fought its way back to the German lines in the night of 15 January and during the following day. Early on 16 January the group became involved in a Soviet tank attack and suffered heavy losses from enemy tank and artillery fire, backed by mortar and multiple rocket launcher (Stalinorgel) fire, but strong support by German air units and the 19th Panzer Division enabled 15,000 German and Italian members of the withdrawing group to arrive in Streltsovka during the next two days.[24]/

---

*See Map No. 3.

/Editor's Note: This was a considerable undertaking, since it involved a withdrawal under adverse conditions, beginning with a breakout, and with rear guard actions all of the way. Chertkovo is situated north of the Don River, about 100 miles east of Rostov, and Streltsovka is located in the vicinity of Voroshilovgrad.

The gap between the left flank of Army Group South and the right (southern) flank of Army Group Center* provided an avenue through which Soviet forces were able to advance toward the west with practically no interference. Occasionally these enemy forces were halted by heavy German air attacks and, in a few instances, some of them were even compelled to withdraw because of timely Luftwaffe intervention.[25] Repeated and concentrated air attacks forced the Russians to withdraw from the gap between the VII and LV Corps, where they had penetrated as far as the Kursk-Orel railroad.[26]/

On 20 January the Russians assaulted the lower Manych River line in Combat Zone South with the intention of driving through to Rostov and Bataysk. If they had achieved a breakthrough there, the First and Fourth Panzer Armies would have been cut off in the course of their withdrawal movements to the west. Therefore, all available units of the Fourth Air Fleet in the area were concentrated to attack and destroy Soviet armored units spearheading the enemy attack, with the result that the Soviet breakthrough toward Rostov was solidly checked. This success was due exclusively to the immediate concentration of German air power at the crucial point of battle.

Strengthened by unusually heavy support from bomber and tactical support units of the IV Air Corps, German forces on 27 January repelled the Red Army units attacking the front of the Seventeenth Army south of Krymsk. The powerful Soviet forces opposing the LVII Panzer Corps of the Fourth Panzer Army were badly decimated in the action.

In the ensuing days strong bomber forces of the IV Air Corps also carried out repeated attacks against Soviet units advancing toward Rostov-on-the-Don and toward the Sea of Azov to the south of Rostov. On 12 January 1943 the Seventeenth Army began its withdrawal from the mountainous area near the famous peak Mt. Elbrus. Its objective was to reach the area which became known as the Kuban bridgehead.// To accommodate to this defensive situation, the Luftwaffe Group Caucasus was redesignated on 27 January as Luftwaffe Group Kuban.

Near the end of January, Soviet air activities increased steadily. Airfields and rail depots in the rear areas were frequently attacked by

---

*Army Group Center was strengthened on 14 February 1943 by the addition of the Second Army.

/See Map No. 2.

//See Map No. 5.

Russian air units, both by day and by night, which necessitated stronger and more effective antiaircraft defenses for all airfields and supply routes in the Communications Zone. Everything available was pressed into service to build up the antiaircraft forces, especially at Zaporozhye and Dnepropetrovsk, in order to protect the Dnepr River bridges. At the same time, flak units employed in ground combat were required to establish a supporting line in the Dnepr sector between Zaporozhye and Dnepropetrovsk. Responsibility for establishing and developing these defenses was placed in the hands of Generalmajor Rainer Stahel, an officer who had proven himself again and again in the most difficult situations.[27]

Early in February powerful Soviet units crossed the Donets River on a broad front northwest and west of Lisichansk. Emphasis in Luftwaffe aerial operations was then immediately shifted to the left flank of Army Group Don. Once again, all available forces of the Fourth Air Fleet were concentrated under the command of Air Division Donets to halt the Soviet advance across the Donets River. While enemy crossings were being made at Lisichansk, Red Army units landed at three points near Novorossiysk. Two of these beachheads were eliminated immediately, but Soviet forces succeeded in maintaining and reinforcing the third.[28] The possibility of Soviet amphibious operations of this type had long been a source of concern to the German Command, and armed aerial reconnaissance missions had been flown regularly over the Black Sea ports, especially Gelendzhik, Tuapse, and Poti. Conspicuously heavy concentrations of shipping had been noted at Gelendzhik, and very frequent heavy bombing and aerial mine-laying operations had been carried out against this port with gratifying results.

The increasing Soviet air activity in the Caucasus and Kuban areas also obliged the Fourth Air Fleet to attack all recognized enemy airfields which appeared to be in operation.

The tragic end of the Sixth Army* had released the units of the VIII Air Corps for a new assignment. This force was accordingly sent into action to provide air supply and combat support for the Seventeenth Army in the Kuban bridgehead.[29] A considerable supply operation was necessary to maintain the Wehrmacht forces in the Taman Peninsula,

---

*Editor's Note: On 31 January 1943 the command staff of the Sixth Army surrendered to Russian forces. A few units still held out, however, until the official capitulation on 2 February.

and the movement of supplies by naval barges could be accomplished only after German air units cleared the way by destroying drift ice barriers in the Straits of Kerch by bombardment.

After 18 February, Headquarters, Fourth Air Fleet, still situated on a railway train, conducted operations from its new location at Chortiza.* The main ground effort, and therefore also the principal focal point for air operations, in mid-February was in the northern part of Army Group South (formerly Army Group Don), which was threatened with envelopment by a wide sweeping Soviet flanking maneuver. In this area strong enemy armored and cavalry forces were advancing with speed toward the bend of the Don River at Dnepropetrovsk, Zaporozhye, and the Sinelnikovo railway depot.

At this time the radio intercept service of the Fourth Air Fleet intercepted Russian radio messages revealing the intentions of General Markian Popov's Soviet armored corps, its critical shortage of fuel, and its location. With such a unit almost immobilized because of a lack of fuel, the time was highly opportune for a concentrated air attack.[30] Mustering all of its available bomber and tactical support aircraft, the IV Air Corps carried out very effective attacks in the Pavlograd-Kramatorsk area against Popov's tanks, halting the enemy advance, and eliminating all of the tanks which had advanced upon Zaporozhye.[31]/

General Popov himself admitted that his rapid advance was brought to a halt by the ceaseless assault by the Luftwaffe. Because of the gratifying results of these air attacks, the German Army which arrived later on the scene was able to drive back the remnants of the enemy armored force. This successful operation by the IV Air Corps is but one example of the action taken by the Luftwaffe before ground forces could be brought to bear in the area, thereby averting the threat of an impending envelopment.

In February a special antitank air unit was organized under the command of Lt. Col. Otto Weiss.[32] This unit was comprised of ground-attack and twin-engine fighter aircraft, which were employed on many occasions with conspicuous success against Soviet tanks which had penetrated into the German rear areas. The effectiveness of the new arm was

---

*Editor's Note: The precise location of this point cannot be determined, but it is presumed to be in the vicinity of Zaporozhye.

/The attacks against Soviet armor near Zaporozhye were carried out by Ju-88 units.

proven by the fact that during the Soviet armored breakthrough in the small bend of the Don River a few small antitank air units set ten Russian tanks afire and scored observed hits on a number of other tanks in the two-day battle. During this time, other dive-bomber and bomber units went into action in the area and achieved practically no successes whatever. In assessing the value of antitank air units one should not consider merely their destructive power in stopping enemy forces, but also the very favorable influence exerted by them upon the morale of friendly troops, a factor which should not be underestimated.

From the beginning of March 1943 the Fourth Air Fleet directed its main effort toward the support of the offensive of Army Group South (First and Fourth Panzer Armies and Army Force Kempf), whose objective was to regain the Donets River line. It was fairly clear that the Russians, having failed to achieve very much in their latest attacks between the Donets and Dnepr Rivers, were no longer as strong as they had been along the front of the First Panzer Army, and it appeared that the Wehrmacht stood a good chance of regaining its Donets position in that area.

The first task, however, was to beat the southern wing of the Soviet forces around Kharkov in order to give the army group a free hand to cross the Donets on a broad front. The only problem which might seriously complicate the advance was an early onset of the muddy period. By 2 March the enemy had taken a severe beating in the first counterattack by the Fourth Panzer Army and the left wing of the First Panzer Army in the area between the Donets and the Dnepr. Army Force Hollidt also performed well in repulsing Soviet attacks along the Mius River line. So badly were the Russians beaten, especially in the area of earlier penetration near Army Force Kempf, that they were no longer fit for effective combat. Three Soviet infantry divisions and the Soviet XXV Armored Corps were destroyed, and many other enemy units badly decimated in the contest. According to the German count, 23,000 Red Army troops had died in the encounter between the Donets and Dnepr Rivers, while 9,000 prisoners, 615 tanks, 354 guns, 69 antiaircraft pieces, and immense quantities of small arms were captured.[33]

By 5 March the Fourth Panzer Army had driven to the Berestovaya River and faced the southern wing of the Russian forces defending Kharkov. Many of the enemy forces in advance of the army were already decimated by earlier battles, yet a German frontal attack was sure to be costly. Enveloping maneuvers were not favorably considered because of the prevailing weather conditions. Since the ice over the Donets was beginning to break up, which was likely to hamper the use of ponton bridges, an attack upon

Kharkov from the rear did not appear to be possible. The only feasible course, therefore, was to roll up the enemy flank from the south.[34]*

The drive on Kharkov began on 6 March and continued to gain ground as the Fourth Panzer Army and the SS Panzer Corps pushed ahead in a northerly direction to the west of the Donets, strongly supported by bomber and ground-attack units of the I and IV Air Corps.[35] Soviet units which were concentrating or moving out of Kharkov and villages farther to the north were heavily bombed and strafed by the Luftwaffe, and, when the Russians began their disorderly retreat on 10 March in the area between Kharkov and Belgorod, Fourth Air Fleet squadrons destroyed many troop and vehicle columns.[36]

It soon became clear that the Russians were beginning to evacuate Kharkov, whereupon the Fourth Panzer Army and Army Force Kempf, supported by Fourth Air Fleet planes, harassed the withdrawing columns. On 11 March I Air Corps units were committed to strike retreating Russian forces in the Volchansk-Belgorod area.[37] Luftwaffe airmen also carried out highly concentrated attacks to interdict Soviet retrograde movements toward the Donets River.[38]

Tactical support air units attacked Belgorod, where the headquarters of the Soviet II Guards Tank Corps was situated, and made a decisive contribution to the defensive successes achieved by the Division Gross Deutschland on 14 March. On that day the forces of the Fourth Panzer Army drove toward Kharkov and the SS Panzer Corps took the city.[39]

The Soviets then threw strong armored forces against the Wehrmacht from the Belgorod area. These units were countered by powerful thrusts from the Division Gross Deutschland and the SS Panzer Corps pushing ahead from the south. In these encounters the support of the I Air Corps was a vital factor in favor of German units, which soon pierced Belgorod's defenses and took possession of the area.[40] With the seizure of this point the first phase of the German offensive came to a close. The arrival of the muddy season precluded any immediate extension of the front.†

---

*See Map No. 3.

†See figures 1 and 2. For a more detailed account of the capture of Kharkov and Belgorod in March 1943, see U.S. Department of the Army, OCMH, German Defense Tactics Against Russian Breakthroughs, DA Pam. No. 20-233, EUCOM, Historical Division, October 1951, pp. 3-8.

Figure 1
Small German submarine, bound for the Black Sea, on the Autobahn between Dresden and Ingolstadt on the Danube, 1943
(Courtesy of the United States Naval Institute and Fregattenkapitaen a. D. Friedrich Popp)

Figure 2
German motor-torpedo boat (S-Boot) operating in the Black Sea

The successful outcome of the foregoing operations, all of which had heavy air support, clearly indicates the decisive character of Luftwaffe assistance to the German ground forces both on the offense and defense. The crowning achievement of the Wehrmacht's counteroffensive was the recapture of Kharkov, an accomplishment which was effected essentially by a well coordinated and highly concentrated assault by both air and ground forces. All available aircraft, including long-range bombers, were thrown into the battle and employed in a tactical role for close support in consonance with the classical German pattern.[41]

The development of areas of main effort through the closest possible concentration of all available forces, a flexible command, and extremely close cooperation between participating air and ground commands were the principal ingredients for success in all Luftwaffe operations.

Von Richthofen's Fourth Air Fleet was thrown into the battle for Kharkov as one integrated whole, with the participating commands supporting each other, thereby insuring the availability of maximum air power at the crucial point. The main factors behind Richthofen's successes were extreme flexibility, good coordination, and concentration, the latter being secured through the creation of *ad hoc* battle groups to give air support to spearhead units of the ground forces (SS Division "Das Reich"*) which led the assault on the city. "Massive concentration," "drastic concentration," "concentration of all forces to the highest degree," were phrases which appeared again and again in Fourth Air Fleet battle orders.

Another factor which played a role in these operations was Richthofen's reservation of the right to switch his area of main effort from one air corps to another as the tactical situation required. Both the I and the IV Air Corps were instructed to make sure that their tactical units could be immediately brought to bear in other operational sectors.[42]

Once the objectives of the winter counteroffensive had been realized with the capture of Kharkov and Belgorod, the ceaseless air operations in support of the Army, which had become the German trump card in so many critical situations in the winter, were no longer required. The Luftwaffe was therefore free to carry out its real mission of operating against hostile air forces and sources of enemy military power, including communications routes and feeder lines.

---

*Editor's Note: 2nd SS Panzer Division.

In addition to a number of successful strikes against industrial targets in Saratov and Kamyshin, and shipping (including mine-laying operations) on the Volga as far as Astrakhan and the Caspian Sea, continuous and increasingly heavy attacks were carried out against Soviet railroad trains, rail installations, bridges, and depots.[43] As early as February 1943 German bomber units had been increasingly employed in attacks against Soviet rail lines and railroad installations in efforts to prevent or seriously hamper the forward movement of Russian supplies and replacements and the regrouping of forces in areas of critical concern.

Once the city of Kharkov had fallen, air operations against Soviet rail systems gained considerably in importance, especially since the early thaw had turned all of the main and secondary roads into quagmires and virtually precluded motor transportation. The few special railroad interdiction squadrons, which were organized within the various air wings in 1942, were committed regularly against Soviet rail traffic, while larger rail installations and junctions were attacked by powerful concentrations of bombers.[44]

Soviet air activities had also increased apace since the beginning of the year, for which reason the Fourth Air Fleet now became more immediately concerned with Russian flying units and attacked their bases whenever possible. These expanded operations of the Fourth Air Fleet against rail and air installations continued until the end of June 1943. Although the attacks achieved considerable local success, their overall effect was felt only gradually. There was no escaping the fact that the forces available to the Luftwaffe in Combat Zone South were too weak to completely destroy or interrupt for any considerable period enemy rail traffic, road traffic, or air activity.[45]

Chapter 2

LUFTWAFFE OPERATIONS IN DEFENSE OF THE KUBAN BRIDGEHEAD

The planned evacuation of the Caucasus began at the turn of the year 1943. It was designed to extricate the First Panzer Army, which had advanced as far as the Groznyy area in its drive along the Terek River, and the Seventeenth Army, which was engaged in heavy fighting on a wide frontage extending from Novorossiysk to Mt. Elbrus. A broad flanking maneuver by the Red Army threatened both of these armies with envelopment.[1*] The withdrawal of the First Panzer Army from phase line to phase line, protected in the north and northeast against close Soviet pursuit, until it was able to cross the Don River above and below Rostov to its new positions on the left flank of Army Group Don, has already been discussed.[2]

The Seventeenth Army synchronized its movements with those of the First Panzer Army and tried to withdraw farther to the south, with Novorossiysk as the pivotal point for its right flank. This army, under the command of Generaloberst Richard Ruoff, continued its deliberate retrograde movements, harassed by pursuing Red Army units. Frequently the Seventeenth Army was forced to establish interim defensive positions from which it fought numerous delaying actions, until it finally reached the area of the lower Kuban River. There it established a bridgehead which was intended as its final defense line.

By about the end of April 1943 the bulk of the Seventeenth Army's forces were situated in their new positions behind a front extending in a line from Novorossiysk-Krimsk-Kiyevskoye-Krasnyy Oktyabr-east of Temryuk.[3] During the army's slow withdrawal and the establishment of its positions on the Kuban, the Fourth Air Fleet directed the VIII Air Corps to give it all possible support.[4] The corps committed its dive-bomber forces immediately in advance of the German front, repeatedly attacking Soviet troop concentrations and assemblies, while its bomber and reconnaissance units harassed Soviet traffic leading to the front.

---

*See Map No. 1.

Weak fighter units available to the VIII Air Corps carried out frequent attacks upon Soviet air forces and air installations, downing a considerable number of enemy planes. Owing to Russian numerical superiority, however, they were unable to prevent many Soviet ground-attack squadrons from inflicting a substantial amount of damage on German installations and losses on German troop units.

Supported by the massed fire of heavy artillery batteries, including naval guns, and strong air forces, the Red Army succeeded on the night of 3 February in crossing the three-mile-wide Bay of Novorossiysk and in securing a foothold at a number of points. These sites were then immediately reinforced by the arrival of additional Soviet units. [5] The German V Air Corps began its counterattacks at once, cleaning out two of the small enemy beachheads and driving the Russians back across the sea. Yet the Wehrmacht's counterattack against the Soviet beachhead south of Novorossiysk, after initial progress, failed, with heavy losses of life. Here the Russians not only were able to maintain their position by fierce fighting but to expand and reinforce it.

The VIII Air Corps repeatedly attacked this beachhead and seaborne traffic leading to it, placing main emphasis upon air strikes in the Novorossiysk area, where this support helped to relieve the pressures on German ground troops.* During this time Soviet fighters began to appear in ever greater numbers, frequently attacking German airfields and ports, especially in and around Kerch, in strong attempts to isolate the German Seventeenth Army from its logistical bases. [6]

Along the rest of the Caucasus front the withdrawal of the Seventeenth Army to the inner perimeter of the Kuban bridgehead, the so-called *Gotenkopf Stellung* (Goth's Head Position), proceeded generally according to plan. VIII Air Corps units gave valuable support to the Seventeenth Army by attacking Soviet spearheads again and again with good results. On the ground, the young soldiers of the 615th Field Training Regiment rendered particularly conspicuous service, especially during the heavy fighting on 12 February, during which time they were effectively supported by weak, but determined, German air units. [7]

Meanwhile, specially assigned railroad interdiction aircraft flew repeated missions against Soviet rail routes, junctions, and bridges in the

---

*Attacks were made by Ju-88 and He-111 units, including (for the first time in this area) the 1st Group, 3rd Dive-Bomber Wing.

Caucasus, achieving good results, thereby delaying and reducing in amount the reinforcements and supplies of all types which were brought up to enemy organizations on the front. [8]

Daily Soviet air attacks increased steadily against Seventeenth Army positions, the few airfields located within the Kuban bridgehead, the important supply port of Taman, and ships crossing the Straits of Kerch. [9] In spite of good results achieved by German fighters stationed in the area, Luftwaffe forces here were numerically too weak to protect the entire Kuban bridgehead against hostile air action. German fighter and interceptor units were also hampered severely by the soggy condition of the airfields. [10] For these reasons it was especially important to provide increased air defense by the greater use of flak artillery batteries with the ground forces as well as with rear installations.

On 7 February 1943 the newly organized 9th Flak Division* (Generalmajor Wolfgang Pickert) was placed in command of all antiaircraft artillery forces in the Seventeenth Army area and assigned the mission of assuming, in collaboration with two weak fighter and one dive-bomber groups, responsibility for the air defense of the field of battle, and especially the supply ports of Kerch, Taman, Anapa, and Temryuk, shipping in the Straits of Kerch, and airfields situated within the bridgehead area and in the Crimea. [11] Initial emphasis was to be on the Straits of Kerch. [12]

Realizing the inadequacy of the flak forces available for the accomplishment of this mission, the Supreme Command initiated on 10 February a special rail movement which, within 10 to 12 days, advanced 23 heavy, 6 light flak, and 8 searchlight batteries to the Crimea. These were immediately assigned to the 9th Flak Division.

At the beginning of March, before reinforcements arrived at the front, the dispositions of flak artillery forces were approximately as follows:

4 heavy (8.8 cm) and 2 light batteries in the vicinity of Novorossiysk

---

*Editor's Note: This was formed around the remnant of the Divisional Staff, the only part of the original 9th Flak Division which did not fall within the Stalingrad pocket. At the time the unit surrendered on 31 January 1943, it had destroyed 460 aircraft and 820 tanks, most of them after being surrounded (22 November 1942).

2 heavy (8.8 cm) and 2 light batteries at the port and airfield of Anapa
2 heavy and 2 light batteries in the area west of Krimsk
3 light batteries in the Kurchanskaya area
3 light batteries at the Kuban bridgehead at Temryuk
4 heavy and 3 light batteries at the port and airfield of Taman
2 heavy batteries, for action against seaborne targets and incidental hostile air action, situated at the southern entrance to the Straits of Kerch

In addition to the units mentioned above, relatively strong antiaircraft forces had to be assigned to airfields and naval bases in the Crimea. At the beginning of March, 47 heavy, 31 light, and 8 searchlight batteries were temporarily available. Of these, 16 heavy batteries were withdrawn after just a few weeks, as soon as the overall situation had settled down a bit, and before these batteries could be transported across the Kuban River to reinforce the antiaircraft defenses in the bridgehead.

Flak units in the southern sector of Combat Zone South were controlled by three regimental headquarters, one situated in the Kuban bridgehead, one at Kerch, and one in the western Crimea.[13] The available flak forces were then initially assigned to the main combat sectors of the bridgehead area, Novorossiysk, Krimsk, and Kurchanskaya, with special concentration around the Straits of Kerch and Taman. Sufficient antiaircraft artillery was also laid around the decisively important Kuban River bridge at Temryuk.*

Since most of the heavy batteries deployed around the Straits had a seaward field of fire, there was a chance to bring under relatively heavy fire Soviet naval units which were expected to attack at any time. Because of the possibility of night attacks by sea, a number of searchlight batteries were stationed in the area of the Straits, and heavy flak batteries there were issued ample quantities of star shells.[14]

In this connection it seems appropriate to discuss briefly the naval situation in the Black Sea. In numerical strength and in types of vessels available, the Soviet Black Sea Fleet was vastly superior to the weak German Navy units, which consisted primarily of S-boats (Schnellboote)

---

*See Map No. 6. This was an important link in the German supply line.

or motor torpedo boats.* The light Rumanian naval forces could scarcely provide any material increase in German naval strength in the area. Yet, with the exception of a few attacks by motor-torpedo boats, the Soviet Black Sea Fleet remained surprisingly inactive. Its units remained in ports between Tuapse and Batum, under the protection of Russian fighter forces.[15] This remarkable passiveness can possibly be explained by an intention of the Soviet Command to save its Black Sea Fleet in case it was needed for decisive action later in the war.+ All Soviet naval units and installations, including ships at sea and in port, were kept under constant surveillance by reconnaissance units of the VIII Air Corps++ and the German Black Sea Naval Air Command.

Besides supporting army operations, the VIII Air Corps also had the concurrent mission of moving large quantities of supplies by air to the Seventeenth Army.[16] Nonessential equipment, troops required for other assignments, and considerable numbers of casualties were daily flown out of the bridgehead area, while large amounts of ammunition, weapons, fuel,

---

*Editor's Note: S-boats and several other types of small naval vessels, including small submarines, were floated up the Elbe River from Hamburg to Dresden, taken thence by road (Autobahn) past Bayreuth and Nuernberg, a distance of 280 miles, to Ingolstadt. They were then floated down the Danube to Linz, where they were completely fitted out, then driven under their own power downstream to the Black Sea. The trip from the North Sea to Linz took eight days and cost 34,000 Reichsmarks. A total of 428 ships, 16 of which were S-boats and 6 of which were submarines, were brought in this way to the Black Sea, a total of 40,000 tons. See Jan Mayen, Alarm-Schnellboote! (Alarm! Motor-Torpedo Boats), Oldenburg/Hamburg: Gerhard Stalling Verlag, 1961, pp. 140-144. See also Friedrich Popp, "Overland Transport of German Ships during World War II," United States Naval Institute Proceedings, Vol. 81, No. 1, January 1955. See also figures 1, 2, and 3.

+Editor's Note: The Soviet Black Sea Fleet included the battleship Sebastopol, 6 cruisers, 21 destroyers and torpedo boats, 30 sea-going submarines, 50 motor-torpedo boats and gunboats, as well as a number of auxiliary craft. See Friedrich Popp, "Overland Transport of German Ships during World War II," United States Naval Institute Proceedings, Vol. 81, No. 1, January 1955.

++Later by the I Air Corps. See figure 4.

Figure 3
German storm boat, armed with quad-20-mm. guns, in the Black Sea

Figure 4
Luftwaffe Hs-126 reconnaissance plane over the Kerch area

and replacements were flown in.[17]* On 9 March 1943 seaplanes were also utilized for the first time in this airlift operation.[18]

Russian units continued to exert heavy pressure against the Seventeenth Army as it withdrew to the Gotenkopf position, and German units frequently had to fight their way through Soviet forces which were already in their rear. By constantly changing the areas of attack, the Russians endeavored to split and breach the well-integrated German front, which was gradually falling back. This retrograde movement was further complicated by the spring mud season which commenced as early as mid-February. With effective support from units of the VIII Air Corps, the Seventeenth Army succeeded, despite the adverse conditions, in halting and repelling all Soviet attacks, sealing off or cleaning out each penetration as it occurred. These problems were especially acute on the army's flanks, since the Russians constantly tried to outflank or envelop Wehrmacht units operating there. Such an attempt was made by the Soviet Fifty-eighth Army in the vicinity of Shedogub, an effort which was frustrated by German forces (4th Mountain Division and 13th Panzer Division) after four days of bitter fighting.[19]

On the right flank the Soviet bridgehead south of Novorossiysk was a constant and particularly critical danger point. Soviet units could only supply and reinforce themselves in this area by transporting men and other required needs across the Bay of Novorossiysk. Since daylight traffic across the bay was exposed to the observation and artillery fire of German forces and to the frequent attacks by units of the VIII Air Corps, the Russians restricted their supply movements to the nights, which were still long in February and March.

Because of problems in transporting supplies caused by the soggy condition of the roads and by drift ice in the Staits of Kerch, German Army artillery units were forced to economize in the use of ammunition. Therefore the bridgehead and supply traffic could not be kept under constant harassing fire. In this situation the Luftwaffe's flak artillery was a welcome and most effective support for the ground forces.

---

*On 28 February 1943 the Commander in Chief of Army Group "A," Field Marshal Ewald von Kleist, extended his thanks to the VIII Air Corps for having transported 50,000 soldiers out of the bridgehead. See _Einsatz der Luftflotte 4 im Kampfraum Sued der Ostfront, 1.1.1943-12.9.1943_ (_Employment of the Fourth Air Fleet in Combat Zone South of the Eastern Front, 1 January - 12 September 1943_), G/VI/4d, Karlsruhe Document Collection. See figures 5 and 6.

Figure 5
The Me-323 "Gigant" brings in supplies

Figure 6
Unloading aviation fuel from
an Me-323 "Gigant"

Individual 8.8-cm guns and a number of searchlights were moved into position in the port of Novorossiysk to prevent the Russians from capturing the port and expanding their beachhead through an amphibious assault. These guns repelled Soviet sorties which were being made by small naval craft.*

Another important requirement in the area was to keep enemy traffic across the bay under observed fire as completely as possible. Illuminating devices necessary for this purpose were lacking in the initial stages, and with parachute flares it was possible to light up the bay for only a short period of time. During most of the night, therefore, an 8.8-cm gun, especially assigned for the purpose, fired hundreds of parachute flares and star shells over the bay at irregular intervals. By the illumination afforded by these flares and star shells Army artillery was able to bring most of the enemy sea traffic under fire.

Parachute flares used in the area were a special supply item issued for coastal defense. Shells could be set to release a parachute flare at any given altitude, and the released flare then lighted up the target area with considerable brightness for several minutes. Flak units were the only organizations that had adequate supplies of these flare shells, with which they were able to offer a signal contribution to Army defensive operations.[20]/

A marked increase in shipping was noted along the Soviet controlled shores of the Black Sea, and it was assumed that this had some bearing upon the enemy beachhead at Novorossiysk. The VIII Air Corps therefore directed its units to attack this shipping in collaboration with German Navy units. Air reconnaissance forces of the corps detected an enemy tanker on the night of 12 March 1943 and directed several German motor-torpedo boats (S-boote)// to the target. On the following morning air reconnaissance located the tanker aflame outside the port of Tuapse.[21]

Luftwaffe units also carried out repeated aerial mining operations against the port of Gelendzhik, from which the Russians were shipping supplies. Other enemy ports were bombarded by individual Luftwaffe aircraft.

---

*See figure 7.
/See figure 8.
//See figure 2.

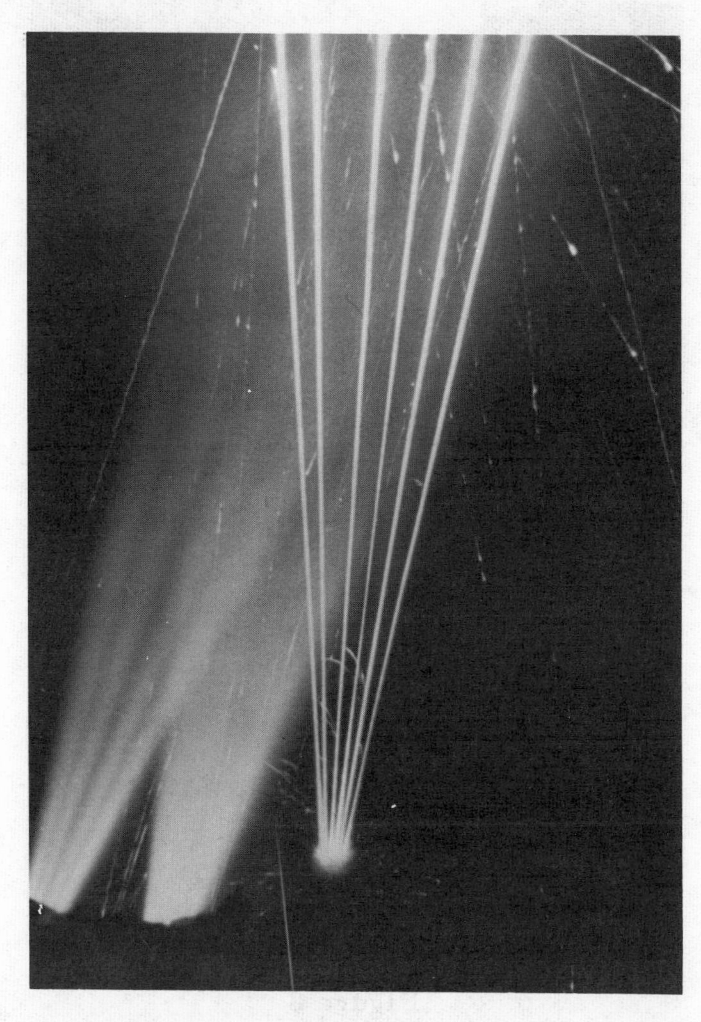

Figure 7
Searchlights and light flak guns
in air defense action near
the Straits of Kerch

Figure 8
Heavy (8. 8-cm.) flak gun firing
at night in the Kuban area

The last airlift of German personnel and equipment into the Kuban bridgehead was flown on 30 March, and on the next day a change was made in the Luftwaffe command in the Kuban-Crimean area. VIII Air Corps Headquarters was withdrawn and transferred to the northern flank of the Fourth Air Fleet to support Army Force Kempf.[22]* I Air Corps assumed command of the German air forces supporting the Kuban bridgehead. This corps, under the command of Generalleutnant Guenther Korten,[23] was established at Simferopol in the Crimea, with an advanced command post at Kerch. The mission of units assigned to this headquarters remained primarily one of direct combat support of German ground forces in action against Soviet troop concentrations, particularly concentrations of armor, against enemy occupied settlements in the vicinity of the front, and against targets such as enemy artillery batteries and troop movements.

Strong air forces were still committed to attack Soviet reinforcement movements, regrouping of enemy forces, and supply traffic moving over road and rail routes to the front opposite the Kuban bridgehead. Owing to lively Soviet air activity, German fighter units had a multitude of targets and achieved good results in shooting down Russian aircraft.

On 14 April 1943 powerful Soviet forces achieved a breakthrough at Krimsk. The I Air Corps then supported the Seventeenth Army in its defensive battles by making repeated concentrated air attacks at the points of penetration.[24] Fighters and ground-attack aircraft shot down 56 Soviet airplanes, while antitank air units destroyed 8 enemy tanks.

On 17 April Operation NEPTUN was launched, an operation by the V Corps (4th Mountain, and 73rd and 125th Infantry Divisions) to eliminate the enemy beachhead south of Novorossiysk, which was such a constant source of anxiety to the German Command. Powerful air forces, comprised of 2 fighter groups (reinforced by Rumanian and Slovakian squadrons), 2 dive-bomber groups, and a bomber wing of 2 groups, concentrated under the I Air Corps, flew repeated missions in support of the ground attack. They rained a merciless hail of bombs on the beachhead area and on the batteries along the eastern shores of the bay, but in spite of concentrated air and artillery fire, the attacking German troops achieved only slight penetrations into the tenaciously defended Soviet positions. The rugged terrain of the Caucasus foothills, covered by numerous small woods,

---

*Editor's Note: Named after its commander, General der Panzertruppe Franz Werner Kempf. This unit was known as Army Force Lanz until its redesignation 22 February 1943 as Army Force Kempf. On 15 August 1943 it was again redesignated, this time as the Eighth Army.

provided excellent cover and protection for the Russian defenders and reduced the effectiveness of German bombing attacks. Even the heaviest concentrations of air power and artillery produced rather poor results, and the infantry again had to bear the brunt of the battle, seizing bunkers one at a time at great cost.[25]

On 17 April, German assault forces attacking the enemy beachhead south of Novorossiysk encountered strong Soviet positions in the rocks, organized in great depth like a fortress. German infantrymen made slow progress against these powerful bastions in spite of heavy support by the Luftwaffe.

Dive-bomber units under the leadership of Col. Dr. Ernst Kupfer were directed to attack and destroy enemy pockets of resistance, observation posts, and troop concentrations, and to make repeated attacks to break Soviet defenses in the line of advance. The first mission flown by this unit was badly hampered by unfavorable weather, yet its bombs were dropped on target, scoring one direct hit on a Soviet battery and hits upon other adjacent infantry and artillery positions. Two light explosions and two heavy explosions--the latter were probably ammunition or fuel dumps going up--were observed somewhat after the main bomb bursts. Kupfer's flyers also destroyed 10 horse-drawn vehicles, and strafed field positions and troop concentrations with good results.

During these operations Soviet antiaircraft fire of all calibers was noticeably heavier in the morning than in the afternoon, and Red fighter-interceptors appeared at irregular intervals over the front. German losses in these engagements consisted of three damaged Ju-87's which crash landed on their airfield, four Ju-87's so badly damaged that they were out of action for a brief period of time, and four Ju-87's which sustained some damage by Soviet antiaircraft fire. A total of 494 Ju-87's took part in the operation.[26]

On the following day, 511 Ju-87's went into action in attack waves of 25 aircraft each, the first units taking off at 0445 and the last unit landing at 1830 hours. Only a few enemy fighters were encountered and the Soviet antiaircraft fire was relatively light, mostly by light and medium guns. These missions were flown in support of Army Force Wetzel,* which was then trying to capture the enemy beachhead. In the first mission, one group of Ju-87's attacked the Soviet-held southern part of the city of

---

*Editor's Note: Named for its commander, Generalleutnant Wilhelm Wetzel, who later commanded the V Infantry Corps.

Novorossiysk, while four other groups attacked alternate targets farther to the south, including the railroad bend, the old fort, and the mud baths.*

The heavy cloud cover broke up only a few times during the day, and then for brief moments only. Nevertheless, hits were scored by the Luftwaffe upon the Jaegerhoehe (Hunter's Summit), Russenriegel (Russian Obstacle), and artillery positions, one gun being definitely destroyed.[27]

A force of 294 Ju-87's, operating in 16 group-size missions, carried out air operations on 19 April in support of the Seventeenth Army's fight for the beachhead. Good results were achieved against infantry and artillery positions and troop concentrations, smothering the Tafelberg and Zuckerhut heights with well-placed bombs. Strong enemy antiaircraft and fighter forces attempted to halt the air attacks.[28]

The German Army launched another attack to seize the Soviet beachhead on 20 April, but made very slow progress. Some small gains were achieved in the direction of the Jaegerhoehe, where the Russians had established their fortress-like positions and offered tenacious resistance. Wehrmacht losses were so heavy that the attack bogged down and, on the following day, had to be called off. During these battles the Russians committed very strong air forces against German ground forces and against Luftwaffe bombers. While the German Air Force employed all available combat aircraft in the area and succeeded in scoring a number of direct hits on infantry and artillery positions, and upon the observation post on the Tafelberg, the advance of the friendly ground troops was almost negligible.[29]

In the afternoon, the 1st Group, 2nd Dive-Bomber Wing and 2nd Group, 77th Dive-Bomber Wing successfully attacked a high-level Soviet headquarters in target area 9 (near the beachhead), and at dusk all of the available bomber forces attacked jetties and other landing sites in the beachhead. During the night, 165 Ju-87's of the 1st and 3rd Groups of the 2nd and 3rd Dive-Bomber Wings attacked landing points in the Novorossiysk beachhead area, diving upon the objectives from an altitude of 10,000 feet. For unknown reasons, one of the Ju-87's crashed in flames west of Kayarovo just before landing.[30]

Because the Russians had begun to use large masses of airpower over the beachhead area, sizeable air battles developed. In the course of

---

*Editor's Note: This area had been a spa of some repute.

these, units of the I Air Corps shot down 91 enemy planes on 20 April, while German fighters operating over the right flank of the Seventeenth Army shot down 56 aircraft.[31]

In the latter part of April the Russians staged a new breakthrough attack against the XXXXIV Corps at Krimsk. Units of the I Air Corps immediately went into action against the Soviet forces which had broken through. Bombers, dive-bombers, and ground-attack aircraft dropped their bombs on enemy-held wooded areas, enemy tanks, artillery batteries, and villages, and effectively strafed every hostile troop concentration and troop movement in the battle area. German fighters found "rich grazing" against the strong Soviet fighter and ground-attack forces, suffering only light losses of their own. The numerically inferior German fighter force shot down 63 Soviet planes on 29 April, 32 on 30 April, 35 on 3 May, and 24 on 7 May.[32]

On 29 April the Red Army again launched a major attack against the eastern sector of the XXXXIV Corps area, with main effort against the 97th Light Infantry Division. Following an artillery and mortar preparation during which 20,000 rounds were fired against the German main line of resistance at Krimsk alone, and using air support on a hitherto unprecedented scale in this area, nine Soviet rifle divisions and three tank brigades hurled themselves at the German positions. The German Army repelled this initial assault with only slight losses of its own, but at a heavy cost to the enemy.

On the next day the Soviet command shifted its main effort to the 9th Division, and later extended these attacks to the 101st Light Infantry Division. Again German forces halted the enemy onslaught, and immediately cleaned out the small areas of hostile penetration. Soviet losses were exceptionally heavy in this battle. Immediately in front of and within the positions of the 57th Infantry Regiment the Wehrmacht counted 1,200 enemy dead after two days of fighting. Losses on the German side were also considerable. The Russians enjoyed air superiority in the area for a number of days, despite Luftwaffe efforts, and, because of this fact, Soviet forces were able to neutralize much of the German artillery.[33]

On 26 May, after a few days of comparative quiet, Red Army units again tried to break through the XXXXIV Corps front. This battle raged on until 7 June. In the course of the fighting, Soviet objectives were the commanding heights known as Hills 121.4, 114.1, and 95.0. Russian forces applied heavy pressures against the badly weakened Wehrmacht forces on the line, especially against the 9th Division, and the 97th and 101st Light Infantry Divisions.

The Soviet infantry attack was preceded by heavy night air attacks and artillery barrages. On the first day the Russians achieved a deep penetration in the 101st Light Infantry Division sector, north of Moldavanskoye.[34] This dangerous situation was alleviated by the 97th and 101st Light Divisions, which launched a determined counterattack, supported by the Luftwaffe, and succeeded in narrowing down the enemy penetration. Again and again Red Army tanks broke through the German lines, but in each case the infantry following the armored drive became separated from the tanks, which were then rapidly destroyed behind the German front. Some tanks were able to withdraw in time to avoid being knocked out, but these were few in number.

In this battle the German air forces successfully contested Soviet air superiority and, by exemplary cooperation with German ground forces, were able to break up numerous enemy attacks in the assembly stage and to force Soviet artillery to move to new positions. The Red Army employed 13 rifle divisions, 3 rifle brigades, and 6 large tank units in this engagement, but was forced to break off the attack after losing 100 tanks and 350 aircraft.[35]

Luftwaffe bombers repeatedly attacked Soviet airfields by day and night, achieving excellent results and materially relieving the pressures on German ground forces. Because of the success of these German air attacks the Soviet air activity slackened off markedly from time to time.

On the southern shore of the Sea of Azov, northeast of Temryuk, the Red Army tried to land troops from specially constructed flat-bottomed boats and landing craft, but these efforts were frustrated almost at once by the outstanding work of newly committed German antitank air units.* Because of German air power these Russian attempts were extremely costly.[36]

Col. Hans-Ulrich Rudel,/ who had been so successful in antitank air operations, assumed command of the experimental antitank air units which were dispatched on their first combat assignment to the Kuban bridgehead area.[37] The Antitank Air Command was equipped with Ju-88 aircraft, some of which were armed with a single 75-mm. gun mounted under the pilot's cockpit, and with Ju-87's (dive-bombers), such as flown by Colonel

---

*During the winter of 1942-43 tests were carried out with Ju-87 antitank aircraft at Rechlin (Mecklenburg) in the Zone of the Interior, and at Bryansk, in the Communications Zone of the Eastern Theater of Operations. A total of 43 tests had been made by the spring of 1943.

/Editor's Note: A veteran of 2,530 combat missions, he was Germany's most highly decorated flyer. See biographical section in the back of this study.

Rudel, outfitted with a 37-mm. antitank gun mounted under each wing. Special ammunition, consisting of regular ammunition with tungsten-hardened cores, was designed for these weapons. These projectiles were reported to have been able to penetrate any thickness of armor plate then in use and to explode after piercing the armor.

The Ju-87 Stuka, a slow-flying aircraft, was highly vulnerable to modern fighter attacks. Because of this it had been used since 1941 chiefly in the East, and in other theaters only when good fighter cover could be provided or under unusual circumstances. The Ju-87 G, a special development of the "D" series, was even more susceptible to enemy air defense forces, since the installation of the two 37-mm. guns lowered its speed substantially. Maneuverability and general flying characteristics were hampered by these innovations and by the removal of the Stuka's dive brakes. Fire power was the quality most needed in the East at this time, and this factor was given priority over considerations of handling and speed.*

The Ju-88 P experiments with the large-caliber (75-mm.)† gun were soon discontinued because the tests showed no real prospects for success. Experiments indicated that operations with the Ju-87 G would also result in heavy losses. Most of Rudel's pilots were therefore quite skeptical about going into combat with these planes, although Rudel was favorably impressed with the new innovations. Test flights flown by him proved that the 37-mm. guns could be fired with accuracy to within 8 to 12 inches of a given target. He thus concluded that tanks could be easily destroyed if the Ju-87 could be flown close enough to the targets.

Rudel's unit memorized the silhouette patterns and characteristics of the various types of Soviet tanks, including the precise location of their most vulnerable parts, the engines, fuel tanks, and ammunition chambers. This had to be done because it was not enough to hit a tank; it had to be struck precisely at a point where the shell would strike inflammable or explosive material, thereby destroying the vehicle. After 14 days of final testing the Air Ministry ordered the unit to proceed immediately to the Crimea, where Soviet forces were exerting heavy pressures, and where opportunities for further experiments were infinitely greater.

---

*Editor's Note: The Ju-87 D had a top speed of about 250 miles per hour, and had rather poor landing characteristics.

†Editor's Note: The 75-mm. gun was the standard PAK 40 (antitank gun).

It was too dangerous to fly low with these planes and to fire at an altitude of only a few feet over areas which had well-established fronts and strong local ground defenses. The Luftwaffe knew that losses in such situations would be greater than the results which could thereby be achieved. If the Ju-87 G could be used at all, it could only be in areas where the fronts were relatively fluid and the ground situation was constantly changing.

Capt. Hans-Karl Stepp, Commander of the Experimental Command in Rechlin, Mecklenburg, remained in Bryansk for a time, while Colonel Rudel took off with all operational aircraft by way of Konotop and Nikolayev to Kerch. Rudel's old wing was then flying bombing missions at Krimsk in the Kuban bridgehead area, where fierce fighting was in progress. From old comrades it was ascertained that Soviet tanks, in case of achieving a breakthrough, never operated more than 1,000 to 1,600 yards from the old main line of resistance. This meant that they would have to be attacked while they were still under the protection of permanently installed, and therefore very strong, antiaircraft batteries.

The defensive fire power of the Red Army was highly concentrated in the small battle area, where it had moved in just about everything that it had from remote areas near the Caspian Sea and the oil centers. These forces came to the scene of combat by way of Mozdok-Pyatigorsk-Armavir and Krasnodar.*

A few days after Rudel, the famous "Panzerknacker" (tank cracker), arrived on the Eastern Front he began operations with his unit south of Krimsk. Soviet tanks had penetrated the outer German defenses in that area and were within 900 yards of the main line of resistance. The anti-tank air unit immediately flew in to see what it could do to counter this attack. Rudel's plane was hit by antiaircraft fire while he was still over his own lines, and other aircraft of the unit fared no better. To make matters worse the Russians also countered with an early model of the Spitfire, which performed well in combat against the Luftwaffe aircraft. This was the first time Rudel had noted these fighters on the Eastern Front.

The results of the first test operations were none too rosy. Wherever members of the antitank unit appeared, other flyers were quick to

---

*See Maps Nos. 1, 6, and 7.

paint gloomy pictures and to prophesy a short life for them. It was clear that bombs would have to be brought along to combat the Soviet ground defenses, but bombs, in addition to antitank guns, would be too heavy for the aircraft. Also, with large-caliber guns mounted on its wings, the Ju-87 could not dive, since the strain on the airfoils would have been too great. Therefore, the most practical solution was to operate under the escort of dive-bombers.

A new offensive operation by the Russians brought the big change for the unit. Northwest of Temryuk Red forces tried to outflank the Kuban River front. Elements of two Soviet divisions began to move through the lagoon region by boat to bring about the collapse of the German Kuban lines. Only a few friendly outposts and small strongpoints were located in this swamp and lagoon area. Their defensive capabilities were naturally limited and by no means adequate to cope with the new Soviet operation.

Reconnaissance uncovered large concentrations of boats in the ports of Yeysk and Akhtarsk, which were immediately attacked. Yet, the targets were so small and the boats so numerous that these attacks alone could not possibly deter the Russians. The boats then commenced moving in masses through the lagoons, traveling approximately 30 miles. As they worked their way through the lagoons and the narrow connecting channels, they came closer and closer to Temryuk, behind the Kuban front, and penetrated far into the German rear. Russian troops usually rested among the tall reeds or on the islands, and when thus hidden were very hard to spot. But, to make any progress, they had to come out into open water, and every day the Luftwaffe was over the area from morning until night searching for boats. As Rudel describes these movements:

> Ivan [the Russians] were coming in the most primitive of boats; seldom did one see a motor boat. They conveyed themselves across in the little boats, 5 to 7 men at a time; up to 20 men were crowded into the larger ones. Of course we didn't make use of our special armor-piercing ammunition here, because a high penetration power was not needed, but rather a good bursting effect for strikes upon wood, which was the surest way to shatter the boats. Normal flak ammunition, with a suitable detonator, proved to be the best. Everything that traveled on top of the water was lost. The boat losses for Ivan must have been very heavy. In a few days I alone destroyed 70 boats with my plane.

> The [Soviet] ground defenses increased slowly but proved to be no obstacle to us. First Lieutenant Ruffer, an excellent gunner in an Hs 129 of one of the other anti-tank squadrons, fell out of his plane and landed like Robinson Crusoe on an island in the midst of the lagoons. He had luck; a German patrol rescued him unharmed.[38]

German forces carried out a successful attack on 3 and 4 July, sealing off the penetrations made by Soviet forces on the northern flank of the Seventeenth Army northeast of Temryuk. This timely attack saved the XXXXIX Mountain Corps from envelopment. Wehrmacht units, operating in exceptionally difficult terrain, defeated Red Army forces in the lagoon area, capturing 428 prisoners, 207 deserters, and 92 boats. Luftwaffe flying units destroyed another 427 boats, while flak batteries gave highly effective support to German ground forces by repelling Soviet troops attempting to outflank their positions in the jungle-like lagoon area.[39]

The Russians became increasingly active in the air and no longer restricted their field of action to the near front areas, but began to attack by day and night targets deep in the German rear. Their main objectives were the bridge at Temryuk, the port and supply installations at Taman and Kerch, traffic across the Straits of Kerch, and the air and naval bases located on the Crimean Peninsula.[40]

In the early months of 1943 the I Air Corps was comprised of the following units:

1 strategic reconnaissance squadron (Ju-88) at Sarabuz
1 tactical reconnaissance squadron (Hs-126 and FW-189) at Kerch
1 fighter group (Me-109) at Anapa
1 night fighter squadron at Bayerovo
1 Rumanian dive-bomber group (Ju-88) at Bayerovo
A number of training planes used for night harassing raids, later incorporated into night ground-attack squadrons

Besides these, the I Air Corps controlled Air Command Black Sea, which had:

2 squadrons (Bv-138) at Konstanza
1 squadron (Bv-138) at Sevastopol
3 Rumanian fighter squadrons at Yevpatoriya and Odessa
1 air-sea rescue squadron at Orta-Eli[41]

A night fighter squadron was moved in to reinforce the night air defense forces and, with the aid of available searchlight batteries, helped to organize an illuminated night fighter defense in the Kerch area.[42] Despite the lack of efficient communications and other facilities which are normally available in the Zone of the Interior, the effectiveness of the night defense system was improved by the addition of night fighter-interceptors and heavy flak batteries.

The heavy batteries opened fire the moment antiaircraft searchlights spotted a plane, and continued firing until the alerted night fighters (guided by radio from their base to the target) signaled that they were ready to attack.* The flak batteries then immediately ceased fire and the fighters attacked. By close cooperation it was possible to sharply reduce the time interval between the batteries' cease fire order and the opening of the night fighter attack to less than a minute. Using these methods, by mid-July of 1943 the Luftwaffe had shot down 59 Soviet aircraft operating at night in the area. Twenty of these planes were destroyed by night fighter forces and the rest by heavy (8.8-cm) flak batteries.≠ Because of the sound air defense operations, Russian airmen began to avoid the Kerch area in the night raids.

Night bombing and strafing attacks in the bridgehead area by Soviet planes proved to be quite unpleasant, especially for German supply traffic, which was particularly heavy at night. These harassing raids were a well-known feature of service in the Eastern Theater of Operations, and were particularly frequent in the Kuban area. Here, too, an improvisation brought about a considerable reduction in the number of enemy nuisance raids. Since the illumination provided by the two searchlight battalions in the Kerch areas was indispensable to air defense operations, the smaller (60-cm) searchlights assigned to certain flak batteries were placed in positions in the Temryuk area, and distributed in such a way that a new night fighter area was established.≠≠ Once these defenses were set up the Soviets also avoided the Temryuk area.

A point deserving special mention is the successful establishment by the 129th Air Signal Battalion of the 9th Flak Division of a broad and

---

*See figure 7.

≠Editor's Note: Part of the aircraft reported here were shot down in the Temryuk area.

≠≠Two Russian aircraft were brought down by the confusion caused by the searchlights. Apparently more inexperienced pilots were being used here than elsewhere.

intricate wire and radio communications network, so necessary for coordinated night operations using searchlight, flak, and night fighter units. This battalion proved itself thoroughly and exemplified the best traditions of the Air Signal Service by setting up the network in surprisingly short time and in maintaining it well, despite a critical shortage of personnel, terrain difficulties, and enemy action.[43]

From 7 February (the date on which the 9th Flak Division assumed command of area air defenses) to 23 July 1943, flak units in the Seventeenth Army area shot down 224 Soviet aircraft during daylight hours and 39 at night. In addition to these obvious and tangible results, flak units must also be accorded high ratings for repelling the enemy and for shielding troop units on the field of battle.[44]

In August a fierce defensive battle again developed in the blood-soaked area west of Krimsk, and on the 7th the storm broke again in the eastern sector of the line held by the V and XXXXIV Corps. After an exceptionally heavy artillery preparation, the Soviet forces, using air support which exceeded anything hitherto experienced in the area, attacked the 9th Infantry and 97th Light Infantry Divisions. Because of the massive air support, German defenders were virtually paralyzed for hours.[45]

Luftwaffe fighters went into action and were able to effectively restrict the activity of Soviet ground-attack planes, enabling the two German divisions to reëstablish an integrated defense line by employing their last available reserves and those at corps level.[46]

Under the impact of their exceptionally heavy losses, the Russians broke off their attack on 12 August 1943. Excellent cooperation and mutual support by all arms of the Army and Luftwaffe had made it possible to hold the line. Although the Red Army launched other attacks along the Seventeenth Army front during the period which followed, Soviet efforts in the first 10 days of August were the last major actions fought in the Kuban bridgehead. Early in September the German High Command decided to abandon the bridgehead and withdrew the Seventeenth Army across the Straits of Kerch to positions on the Crimean Peninsula.[47]*

While this evacuation movement was getting under way, the Russians made another attempt, preceded by a powerful artillery barrage, to seize the city and port of Novorossiysk. German Army troops immediately counterattacked and repulsed them with heavy losses. While

---

*See Map No. 6.

Figure 9
Generaloberst Wolfram Freiherr
von Richthofen, Commander in
Chief, Fourth Air Fleet

Figure 10
General der Flieger Otto Dessloch, Commander, Luftwaffe Group Caucausus

ground forces were engaged in bitter combat, fighter-bomber units of the I Air Corps supported the action by destroying Soviet landing craft and troop concentrations in the Russian beachhead.[48]

The evacuation of the Kuban bridgehead commenced on the night of 14 September, all troop units retiring according to plan by short movements. Because the 9th Flak Division had deployed very strong forces along both shores of the Straits of Kerch, and because fighters of the I Air Corps maintained a continuous cover over these retrograde movements and all crossing points, the initial stages of the withdrawal proceeded without enemy interference.* Luftwaffe airmen carried out their tasks very well, considering that the Russians enjoyed a great numerical advantage on the ground and in the air in this sector. It was thus inevitable that some Soviet ground-attack aircraft would get through to accomplish their missions.[49] These planes repeatedly attacked German rear guard positions, but were invariably turned away by the concentrated fire of light and heavy flak batteries, which had been deployed there between February and April during the battle for the Kuban bridgehead. At that time 21 light and 16 heavy batteries had been posted in the area, doubling the number of flak units within the bridgehead. Of this number, 13 light and 4 heavy batteries were fully mobile, while the remainder had to rely upon flak artillery transport batteries for transportation. The latter had to be evacuated during the early stages of the withdrawal. This naturally necessitated a sizeable increase in flak forces in the Straits area, where it was believed that the Russians would soon step up the number and intensity of their attacks.

To further improve the protection for evacuating units, two light flak batteries were mounted on Siebel Ferries† to escort traffic across the Straits in the last four days of the withdrawal. Furthermore, all batteries received orders in this closing period not to withhold their fire while awaiting the approach of hostile aircraft, but to open fire at extreme range. Light batteries normally waited until the attacking planes were within optimum range, but in this instance what was urgently

---

*See figures 4, 9, and 10.

†Editor's Note: Siebel Ferries were motor-driven firing platforms, invented by Dr. Fritz Siebel in an effort to combat Soviet transport shipping on Lake Ladoga and also in the Black Sea area. They were extremely slow and unmaneuverable, and were not particularly effective when operating by themselves. See figure 11. See also Generalleutnant a. D. Hermann Plocher, _The German Air Force versus Russia, 1942_, USAF Historical Studies No. 154, Maxwell AFB, Alabama: USAF Historical Division, ASI, 1966.

Figure 11
A Luftwaffe expedient, a floating flak platform, the Siebel Ferry

required was early firing to repel enemy aircraft, which were coming in in substantial numbers. This, of course, meant a heavy consumption of ammunition. These means made it possible to ward off decisive enemy air interference during the crossing movement and to reduce greatly the effectiveness of Soviet attacks against the temporary, but unavoidable, accumulations of vehicles and materiel at the crossing points. The virtual absence of trees or bushes on the eastern shore of the Straits made matters particularly difficult for the troops, who had no choice but to disperse as well as they could and to dig in to avoid hostile air action. An increased commitment of fighter forces by the Luftwaffe greatly reduced the danger of Soviet air attacks during the entire operation.

On the night of 9 October 1943 the last flak unit, the 81st Light Flak Battalion, together with the rear guard troops of the Seventeenth Army, crossed the Straits at Ilyich. This ended the evacuation of the Kuban bridgehead after many months of exceedingly heavy fighting.

Flying units under the command of the VIII (and later the I) Air Corps, flak batteries of the Army and the Air Force under the command of the 9th Flak Division, and numerous air signal units played a most decisive role in the successful defense of the bridgehead area.

The unusually heavy losses suffered by the Russians, including 1,045 tanks and 2,280 aircraft, were due in no small measure to action by Luftwaffe units, all of which were badly outnumbered by their Soviet opponents.[50]

Chapter 3

LUFTWAFFE COMMAND EAST IN COMBAT ZONE CENTER OF THE EASTERN THEATER OF OPERATIONS

Operations, January - July 1943, Prior to Operation ZITADELLE

In early January 1943 severe defensive battles raged along the front of the left wing of Army Group Center, in particular along the fronts of the Third Panzer Army and the Ninth Army from the vicinity of Velikiye Luki to Rzhev. Soviet armies pushed the German lines back in the direction of Vitebsk, and again threatened to break through the pocket which had been created in the offensive late in 1942.* Yet, despite these pressures, Army Group Center was able to hold its lines fairly well and to prevent a serious penetration.[1] The Ninth Army stood exposed in a salient projecting to the east of Rzhev, a matter of concern to the German Command. Despite this problem, only one important point was lost in the entire sector during this period, and that was the small fortress of Velikiye Luki, which fell after a heroic defense on 17 January.†

During these operations Luftwaffe Command East had concentrated its forces and provided day and night combat and logistical support (including glider and air-drop missions) for the Velikiye Luki garrison. But, these efforts, which had to be made in the most adverse weather and in the face of heavy small and large arms fire, turned out to be in vain, since the German forces were too weak to hold off the vastly superior Russian forces. A few of the defenders succeeded in breaking out of the envelopment on the night of 15 January and in fighting their way through to the Wehrmacht relief forces.[2]††

After the fall of Velikiye Luki the front in this area remained relatively quiet for some time, although it was obvious that the Russians would try to capitalize on their advantageous position as soon as they had amassed a sufficient predominancy in men and arms and as soon as the concentration movements had been completed. In order to delay the enemy's offensive

---

*See p. 5.

†See figure 12 and Maps Nos. 2, 3, and 7.

††See Maps Nos. 2 and 3. Despite heavy air support, the relief forces were unable to reach the Velikiye Luki fortress.

Figure 12
Generaloberst Robert Ritter von Greim visiting
a flak unit near Velikiye Luki

Figure 13
Pock-marked battlefield on the edge
of the city of Rzhev

plans and to prevent build-ups of men and materiel near the front areas, Luftwaffe units concentrated from mid-January on upon interdicting Soviet road and rail supply traffic. In the course of these actions German flyers caused heavy damage to the rail supply depots at Kalinin, Toropets, and Velikopolye.

In case of a full resumption of the attack by the Red Army, the German Command had no experienced troops available to use as reserves, and the only forces at hand which could strengthen the defenses in any way were some rather weak Luftwaffe units, which were scraped together wherever they could be spared. In the face of this situation, Generaloberst Kurt Zeitzler finally succeeded in wringing from Hitler approval to retire the front line in the area between Yukhnov and Rzhev to a line extending approximately from Spas Demensk to Bely.*

Thorough and systematic preparations were made for the retirement. All Army and Luftwaffe supply depots were evacuated to the rear; all permanent installations, particularly airfields, railroads, and bridges, were completely demolished; and the proposed new main line of resistance was reinforced with strong positions. This movement, known as Operation BUEFFEL (Buffalo), commenced at Rzhev on 26 February. About half of the Fourth and Ninth Armies, their southern flank anchored at Spas Demensk, fell back in good order from phase line to phase line into the new positions.

The withdrawal to a new position meant that German air units in the near front areas also had to move back, this time to Smolensk-North. Ground service installations from advanced bases were evacuated by truck between 25 and 28 February, and on 1 March Luftwaffe demolition teams blasted the billets and shelters, buildings which were so familiar to many German servicemen in the area and had served the Luftwaffe so well.† The last crews flew out of Dugino on 2 March. Reconnaissance units moved back to their old quarters in an abandoned cloister at Smolensk and were soon back in a normal routine.

During this time, despite frequent spells of very bad weather, tactical and strategic reconnaissance units furnished highly valuable information on the activities of the enemy, in many cases discovering assembling and concentration movements. Early in February the 4th Strategic

---

*See figure 13.

†See figures 14 and 15.

Figure 14
The railroad station at Vyazma being systematically leveled by Luftwaffe demolitions men, 19 March 1943

Figure 15
Dugino airfield (south of Rzhev) being demolished by Luftwaffe demolitions teams, March 1943

Reconnaissance Squadron* of the 14th Reconnaissance Wing detected large Soviet troop movements between Kalinin and Ostashkov and kept surveillance over this area, even during the worst weather conditions. On 10 February the weather was so bad and the cloud ceiling so low that reconnaissance could be carried out only at extremely low altitudes, with the result that one aircraft was shot down. On the following day the clouds parted and the 4th Squadron identified Soviet columns, including tank forces, moving toward the northwest at Ostashkov. While this meant an attack against Army Group North rather than Army Group Center, it gave the German Command timely notice of the Red Army's concentration for an offensive against Staraya Russa.

The Russians detected the German retrograde movement around Rzhev at a very late stage and were thereby unable to prevent the successful reestablishment of a new, and much-straightened German front. Rzhev was evacuated on 3 March, Gzhatsk on the seventh, Sychevka on the eighth, Bely on the tenth, and Vyazma on the twelfth. The entire withdrawal movement was completed by 16 March, an operation which released about 10 divisions for other employment and shortened the front by 120 miles.

Throughout the month of January Red Army forces continued to exert pressure along the right wing of Army Group Center, and by early February were able to mount a sizeable offensive against the entire front of the German Second Army (then part of Army Group "B") and the right flank of the adjoining Second Panzer Army to the north. This assault soon assumed gigantic proportions and rolled back everything before it. On 8 February 1943 Soviet forces seized the important city of Kursk and pushed rapidly beyond, chiefly toward Glukhov and Sumy. The penetration pushed back Wehrmacht units from the area east of Orel in the north to the vicinity of Belgorod in the south, and gravely threatened not only the Second Army, but the Second Panzer Army as well, which now stood exposed in a bulbous salient around Orel.

In order to secure uniformity of action against this Soviet offensive, the Second Army was transferred from Army Group "B" to Army Group Center, while all available air forces of Luftwaffe Command East were immediately sent into action, fighting with good effect in checking the enemy inroads. After 9 February, air power had to be concentrated in support of the Second Panzer Army in the broad eastward extending bulge around Orel.

---

*This squadron, known as the Muenchhausen Squadron, was permanently assigned to Luftwaffe Command East (later Sixth Air Fleet).

During this period the Red Army launched simultaneous attacks designed to cut off the Second Panzer Army, one from the Kursk area against the south and even southwestern flanks of the army, while three Soviet armies drove toward the south from the Sukhinichi area.*

The winter battle in the Orel area lasted well into March, compelling Luftwaffe Command East to commit its forces almost exclusively in support of the hard-pressed Panzer Army. It also carried out sizeable operations against enemy rail junctions at Kursk, Yelets, and Livny, which were especially important points in the Soviet logistical network. With heavy air support German forces north of Spas Demensk and those in the Orel area repulsed all enemy attacks in their sectors.

Again and again the air forces of Luftwaffe Command East intervened successfully in support of German ground forces, inflicting heavy losses in men and materiel upon the enemy throughout the entire depth of the Combat Zone. German flyers were especially active in the Orel area, where friendly armored and infantry units were engaged in counterattacks against a determined foe. On 20 February Luftwaffe fighters shot down 38 Soviet aircraft, and on the following day antitank air units destroyed 61 Russian tanks south of Orel, annihilating at the same time several Red Army troop and armor concentrations.[3] During the ensuing week strong German air forces supported ground operations north and south of Orel, helping to break up enemy troop concentrations,[4] and on 27 February these units bombed and strafed a number of hostile troop columns in the immediate vicinity of Orel, inflicting heavy losses.[5]

The Luftwaffe continued its attacks in this sector through the end of February and early March, although flying conditions were far from ideal. On 18 March German airmen destroyed 116 Russian tanks in the southern part of this area, severely disrupting enemy offensive plans and assisting friendly forces to hold their positions. By the latter part of the month Soviet leaders were obliged to concede that their Orel offensive had been a failure.[6] In the meantime, the Red Army had launched a determined attack southwest of Vyazma, which was broken up on 31 March by well directed artillery and dive-bomber bombardment.[7]

Early in April German photo-reconnaissance units received orders to carry out reconnaissance missions over the Soviet bulge at Kursk. In

---

*See Map No. 7.

spite of strong enemy ground and fighter defenses, two Luftwaffe planes executed this operation, obtaining excellent 20 x 30 cm panorama photos (scale 1:25,000) from an altitude of 17,000 feet. The sector covered in this mission was approximately 7,200 square miles,* the largest tract ever taken in a single sweep by the squadron.

On 22 April Soviet bombers attacked the German airfield at Orsha, destroying aircraft of the 4th Strategic Reconnaissance Squadron of the 121st Reconnaissance Wing and the 1st Strategic Reconnaissance Squadron of the 100th Reconnaissance Wing.[8] Because of this raid, the only operational strategic reconnaissance squadron available to Army Group Center was the 4th (the "Muenchhauseners") of the 14th Wing. Since this unit lacked manpower, it could only assist with reserve aircraft.

On the following day, crews from the two destroyed squadrons arrived and thereafter flew their missions from the same airfield. The additional aircraft servicing and the photo-processing work were handled smoothly by technical service personnel and the Photographic Section of the 4th Squadron, 14th Wing.[9] Through the success of its aerial reconnaissance operations, Luftwaffe Command East made a considerable contribution to all of the German ground defenses in Army Group Center, especially in the winter battles around Orel in the Second Panzer Army sector, where fighting lasted for many weeks.

At the end of April the mud season set in and brought all combat on the ground to a standstill. It was then no longer necessary for Luftwaffe Command East to fly continuous support missions for ground forces, especially those involved in cleaning out areas of Soviet penetration. It was therefore only logical to take advantage of the spell of relative quiet to rehabilitate the flying units and to improve their operational status.[10]≠ At long last there was also an opportunity to operate against railroads and rail installations, air bases, and particularly important industrial installations, deep in the Soviet rear.[11]

From the point of view of ranges of available aircraft and that of location of well developed airfields suitable for supply movements, Combat

---

*12,000 sq. kilometers.

≠See Chart No. 6 for the strength and organization of German air fleets in the East in 1943.

Figure 16
Situation conference, Sixth Air Fleet, in Russia, 1943: L. to R.: Maj. Helmut Mahlke (GSC), Op. Off., Maj. Guenther Seekatz (GSC), Asst. Op. Off., Generaloberst v. Greim, Col. Fritz Kless (GSC), Chief of Staff. Rear, L. to R.: Lt. Borski, Capt. Lichtenberg, and Meteorologist Jacobi.

Figure 17
Generaloberst von Greim in conversation with
Generaloberst Hans Jeschonnek, Chief
of the Luftwaffe General Staff

Zone Center, the operational area of the Sixth Air Fleet, was particularly well endowed.[12]* Furthermore, the radio intercept service and air reconnaissance had detected large concentrations of Red Army units along the entire front of this area, with a clearly defined point of main effort in the Yelets-Kastornoye-Kursk sector. Besides these forces, they detected strong concentrations of air forces, including the First, Second, Third, Fifteenth, and Sixteenth Soviet Air Armies, which were placing heavy emphasis upon the southern flank of Army Group Center. The assemblage of such gigantic forces--apparently the movements were not even completed in May--could not be considered simply as an indication of preparations to meet a possible German summer offensive. Quite obviously, the Russians were getting ready for a new major offensive of their own against the German center.

Regardless of the decisions the German Supreme Command might take with respect to the conduct of operations in the East in 1943, it was clear at the end of April that the Sixth Air Fleet had to take decisive action against the assembling and concentrating of Soviet armies, mainly by striking enemy road and rail movements as well as airfields situated within the Red Army's concentration areas.†

On 12 May the Luftwaffe attacked by day and night a number of troop concentrations, enemy rail targets and air bases, and, five days later in both Combat Zones South and Center, destroyed a large number of Soviet transport aircraft and several important rail depots.[13] On 21 May German air units bombed and strafed Soviet troop concentrations, transport trains, and supply dumps in all of the probable areas of enemy main effort. Wherever reconnaissance planes detected important Russian activity German air forces made concentrated surprise attacks and, as a rule, achieved very good results. If key railroad bridges or thoroughfare axes could be destroyed, the resulting jam-ups would force troop and supply trains to come to a stop in the open, where they would be quickly dispatched by German flyers.

By day or night, whenever weather and visibility permitted, special aircraft were sent out to attack railway trains, even those at extreme ranges. These single plane attacks interfered seriously with the Russian concentration and supply operations.

---

*Luftwaffe Command East was redesignated Sixth Air Fleet on 11 May 1943. See figure 16.

†See figure 17.

For the first time in 1943 the Luftwaffe also carried out concurrent attacks against enemy industrial targets, especially factories which were known to be closely connected with deliveries for Soviet concentrations and assemblies. For these missions, the Sixth Air Fleet frequently took temporary control of the bomber forces of the First Air Fleet (Combat Zone North) and of the Fourth Air Fleet (Combat Zone South).

On 2 June the Luftwaffe successfully attacked the rail depot at Kursk, followed by bombardments between 4 and 8 June of the Soviet tank factory at Gorkiy, on the 10th by attacks on the rubber processing works at Yaroslavl, on the 13th by the destructive raid on the marshaling yard at Yelets, and on 4 July by strikes against the supply bases at Yelets and Valuyki. [14*]

Maj. Friedrich Lang, Commander of the 3rd Group, 1st Dive-Bomber Wing, wrote the following description of the highly successful surprise attack upon Kursk:

> The previously mentioned attack against the Kursk railroad depot was flown with sizeable forces prior to the opening of the offensive. Wing headquarters units and our group were the first to make the attack, which opened a few minutes after four o'clock in the morning. Our approach flight was not interrupted, despite the fact that our planes were clearly visible against the closed and even cloud ceiling about 13,000 feet up. Only when the group was flying around the city, within the range of the defensive fire of the heavy [Soviet] antiaircraft guns, in order to get into position for our northward bombing run along the axis of the rail depot did the Soviet fighters take off from their bases east of Kursk. It was remarkable how many red and green Very lights were fired while the fighters were taking off, which gave us the impression that the Russians were in confusion and that we had perhaps taken them by surprise.
>
> A Soviet fighter attacked the group's lead plane just as it was leveling out after the dive, but the group commander shot it down. The rest of the group escaped attack, although there must already have been quite a large number of Russian fighters in the air. Today I

---

*See figures 18 and 19 and Map No. 8.

Figure 18
He-111 bomber above the clouds en route
to bombing mission over Gorkiy

Figure 19
He-111 bomber returned from Gorkiy with tail section
damaged by ramming from Soviet aircraft

can no longer recall if our escort fighters were on hand. Our second group which attacked a few minutes later suffered heavy losses while leaving the target area due to enemy fighter action.[15]

German twin-engine fighter forces also attacked Soviet operational airfields with a great measure of success, thereby making a substantial contribution to the reduction of Soviet combat strength. The main area of activity for German fighters, however, was over the Orel area, where protection was needed for the crowded airfields around Bryansk, Orel, and Sechinskaya. In these operations, fighters of the 51st Fighter Wing (Moelders) shot down 40 Soviet aircraft on 5 June, 67 on the 8th, and 65 on the 10th.

As part of the training program, crews without combat experience or training in blind flying and navigation were used in attacks on villages known to be occupied by partisans, particularly in the difficult terrain around Bryansk and Kletnya, much of which was heavily forested. In this way all units could use their full striking force against targets in Soviet held territory.

The Russians were becoming steadily more active in the air.[16] Most of their missions were daylight or night nuisance raids in the near front sectors, placing particular emphasis upon the Second Army and Third Panzer Army areas. After units of the Sixth Air Fleet had completed their first successful attacks against Soviet industrial targets, Red air forces countered by launching repeated night attacks against German airfields, traffic centers, and supply points. Major Lang, a German group commander, gives an account of one of these Soviet air strikes:

> The only daylight attack against the Orel rail depot by Soviet ground-attack units occurred shortly before the offensive and ended with a resounding defensive success for the German fighters. We were resting on that day and could observe the entire attack well from our positions. There was a cloud cover of about 4/10 at 2,600 feet. A sizeable Soviet fighter force, flying above the clouds, approached the town from the east. German fighters took off; there was a little firing, and the Soviet fighters turned back toward the east. At this moment a large number of IL-2 planes flew in at an altitude between 660 and 1,000 feet. Before they could even reach the rail depot they came under attack by the German fighters which were already in the air, and by others which continued to take

off. One could see as many as four and even more IL-2's crashing to the ground simultaneously.

What struck us was the stubborn way in which the Russians flew. Hardly any of them tried to fly in defensive curves. The final score showed 70 Soviet planes downed. Interrogation of captured Russian pilots revealed the plan of attack: Soviet fighters were to engage the defending [German] fighters at Orel in combat and decoy them eastward. It had been assumed that the IL-2 units could then attack their target undisturbed.

Although some of these Soviet bombing attacks did cause considerable damage, particularly in the case of the Orel and Bryansk rail depots, the results achieved were generally meager and had no decisive effects.[17]

The obvious Soviet intention of using air attacks and increased partisan activities to deprive German forces in the Orel salient of their supplies, thereby reducing the German defensive capacity--this was clearly a strategic objective--could therefore be considered a failure.

Flak artillery forces also participated very effectively in the successful defensive operations. In the Orel area, units of the 12th Flak Division shot down 40 Soviet aircraft (20 of them at night) in the month of June 1943, while during the same period batteries of the 18th Flak Division (a unit deployed primarily in the Smolensk-Roslavl area) successfully engaged 130 Soviet planes during daylight and 617 at night.* In the Second Army sector the 10th Flak Brigade was primarily employed in repelling small-scale night harassing attacks.

In the Orel-Bryansk sector, units of the German night fighter service which were improvised by the Sixth Air Fleet, together with searchlights and radar equipment mounted on railway cars, shot down approximately 30 Soviet aircraft between April and June 1943.

In summary it can be said that the major assemblies and concentrations of very large enemy air, armored, and other ground force organizations in the Kursk-Kasternoye-Sukhinichi sector were detected during May and June by the excellent aerial reconnaissance and combat

---

*See figures 20 and 21.

Figure 20
Command Post of a flak division near the Dugino airfield camouflaged as a farm house

Figure 21
Searchlight unit near Orel scanning the skies for attacking Soviet aircraft

work of the Sixth Air Fleet.* The air fleet correctly assumed these concentrations to be a preparation for a major Soviet offensive, and reported its findings and interpretations at an early stage to the Commander in Chief of the Luftwaffe.

By exploiting various factors such as timing, prevailing weather conditions, and visibility in order to achieve surprise, by frequently changing objectives, and by combining high and low altitude attacks with fighter escort operations, the Sixth Air Fleet succeeded in seriously disturbing the detected Soviet concentration movements in the Kursk-Sukhinichi sector during April, May, and June. In the course of these operations the Luftwaffe inflicted very heavy personnel and materiel losses upon Russian units and even compelled them to move their railheads farther to the east, approximately to the Kastornoye-Livny-Shchigry area. This, in turn, forced the Red Army to make time-consuming overland marches, which proved to be extremely costly because these forces were then exposed to repeated German air attacks.[18]

Because the Sixth Air Fleet lacked sufficient force, particularly suitable special units, and because its operational area was so vast, it was unable to seal off the probable battle area or to annihilate the enemy concentrations.[19] With its units committed in too many theaters of operations, in the West, in the Zone of the Interior, in the Mediterranean, and in the Arctic, the Luftwaffe was numerically too weak to fully accomplish such a mission.

Operation ZITADELLE

The Problem of Continued Operations in the East in 1943

The operations of Army Group South came to a close with the onset of the spring mud period. As has been noted, the German Command and its stubbornly courageous troops were able to reestablish a firm front at the end of March 1943 and hold it against all Soviet attacks. The winter crisis of 1942-43, which had threatened to assume catastrophic proportions grave enough to decide the outcome of the entire war, was past. During the 1941 and 1942 campaigns the German Supreme Command had failed in its efforts to deal an annihilating blow and to conquer the Red Army. Instead, the Wehrmacht had been forced back by costly retrograde movements

*Editor's Note: Its advanced command post was at Kamenets, 9 miles north-northeast of Kromy.

to its old jump-off positions. In the spring of 1943 the German Command was thus faced with the difficult military and political problem of deciding how the war in the East was to be prosecuted or how it could be brought to a favorable conclusion.

Was there any chance of finding a solution? Was it possible at least to end the war without a military decision, provided Hitler as the supreme military commander and supreme political leader was willing to seek such a solution and to create the necessary political conditions therefor?

What in any circumstances was the only feasible way to continue operations in the East in 1943? A full and critical examination of the various possibilities would exceed the scope of this presentation, which is primarily concerned with the operations of the Luftwaffe in the Eastern Theater of Operations in 1943.[20] Yet, this problem which had to be solved will be outlined briefly in order to facilitate an understanding of the aerial operations which were to follow.

In the spring of 1943 the German armies in the East were stretched along a front deep in the interior of the Soviet Union, extending approximately from Leningrad through Novgorod, Smolensk, Sevsk, Rylsk, and Kharkov to Taganrog on the shores of the Sea of Azov.* They had been able to stabilize these lines in most places, and still represented an imposing military power.[21] The Russians had suffered gigantic losses in men and materiel, but their resources seemed literally to be unlimited. Of course Hitler neither believed this nor admitted that it could be true. The Soviet conduct of the war was really typical of the Russo-Asiatic mentality:

> . . . the brutal expenditure of masses in attack. Men and materiel were usually employed mulishly and ruthlessly, but always with greatest effectiveness. Men and equipment were as dust in Stalin's hands. This son of the Ossetian Mountains† was no respecter of human life. He chose the most inhuman and costly methods--the method of oriental sultans and Mongolian khans--and he could afford to do so.

---

*Editor's Note: See Map No. 7. This, of course, does not include the Far Northern Combat Zone, stretching from the Leningrad area through the forests northward to the Barents Sea. See also Chart No. 2.

†Born in 1879 in Gori, Georgia, in the Caucasus.

His manpower reserves were inexhaustible. Adequate numbers of reserve divisions were at his disposal to enable him to pull out shattered divisions and replace them with new ones.[22]

Hitler was unable to divest himself of his habit of wishful thinking, which invariably led him to minimize the power resources of the Soviet enemy.[23] He was fully aware that American newspapers estimated Soviet losses (including civilians who had died of hunger) at 30 million, and reckoned that the Russians had lost between 12 and 14 million men of military age and qualifications. In view of such heavy losses he thought it could definitely be expected that the Soviet Union would collapse at some time or would sink into an endless agony similar to that of China.[24]

One of the major problems in the Russian campaign was how to control the vast spaces of the Soviet Union. It was quite evident that this problem could only be mastered through numerical strength, meaning a sufficient superiority in manpower and arms to defeat the Soviet enemy in his vast special area. But, there was considerably less chance of Germany being able to muster the required forces to seek this combat decision in 1943 than had been the case at the beginning of the campaign in 1941 or even in 1940, when Operation BARBAROSSA was in the planning stages.[25] Because of the increasing pace of Soviet armament activities and the mounting volume of Anglo-American deliveries,* the strength ratio was continually becoming more and more favorable to the Soviet Union. It was therefore obvious to every reasonable person that in 1943 it was no longer possible to completely defeat the Soviet enemy. In fact, by that year, because of its great numerical inferiority alone, the German Wehrmacht in the East was no longer able to stage a major offensive aimed at distant objectives as had been the case in 1941 and even in 1942.

It must also be said that from the standpoint of quality the Wehrmacht in the Eastern Theater of Operations had lost much of its striking

---

*Editor's Note: In 1942 the United States delivered 2, 343 combat aircraft to the Russians, and between January and April of 1943 delivered an additional 1, 383. See Office of Statistical Control, USAAF, Army Air Forces Statistical Digest, "World War II," Washington: December 1945, pp. 129-130. Between 1941 and 1945 the United States also gave enormous quantities of other items to the Red Army, including 281, 606 trucks, 920 combat vehicles, and 7, 172 tanks. Theodore E. Whiting, Carrel I. Tod, and Anne P. Craft, The United States Army in World War II, Statistics: Lend-Lease, Washington: Office of the Chief of Military History, U.S. Army, 15 December 1952, pp. 24-34.

power as a result of losing so many troops, especially commissioned and noncommissioned officers,* men who had been superbly trained in peacetime and hardened by combat experience. Another critical factor was the fact that deficient production, and therewith an insufficient supply, especially of fuel,/ severely reduced the combat power of the Wehrmacht in the East. This was true despite the fact that German forces had been able to overcome the shock of costly withdrawals and the Stalingrad catastrophe, and to reestablish combat morale and good training standards.

Hence, the only possible course of action in the East was defense, and this did not imply a defense which had become torpid and rigidly restricted to repelling attacks dictated by the uncertain caprices of the enemy, but an extremely active and flexible type of defensive operation, always with clear and limited attack objectives designed to weaken the Russians and make them inclined to accept a military and political draw.

Of course, in official or military circles of any size there was no opportunity to discuss the hope for a draw, since anyone who did not profess to believe in final victory (Endsieg), or expressed even the slightest doubt about it, was considered a defeatist and a traitor to the Fatherland.//

---

*Editor's Note: By August 1943 German losses in the East totalled almost 1,500,000 dead, wounded, and missing. This was almost 50 percent of the strength of the German armies on the Eastern Front at the time of the invasion, 22 June 1941. See Walter Goerlitz, Der Zweite Weltkrieg 1939-1945 (The Second World War 1939-1945), Vol. 2, Stuttgart: Steingrueben Verlag, 1952. Cited hereafter as Goerlitz, Vol. II.

/In addition to the regular refining and processing of petroleum, much of Germany's gasoline was being produced synthetically.

//Editor's Note: The closer the relationship between Hitler and his officers, the less able were these officers to undertake either independent action or to express ideas displeasing to the Fuehrer's ears. Generalleutnant Walter Warlimont, Deputy Chief of the Wehrmacht Operations Staff, commented: "Lest anyone should misunderstand him [Hitler], as the fronts began to collapse in all directions he [Hitler] would say over and over again to those around him, . . . 'anyone who speaks to me of peace without victory will lose his head, no matter who he is or what his position.'" Generalleutnant Walter Warlimont, Inside Hitler's Headquarters 1939-1945 (translated from the German by R. H. Barry), New York: Frederick A. Praeger, 1964, p. 462. Cited hereafter as Warlimont, Inside Hitler's Headquarters.

Thus the desire that the war against the Soviet Union would end in a draw remained an objective, albeit an unexpressed and invisible one, in the strategic planning at all higher military command levels, and was a hope concealed in the minds of many.*

The expectation of being able to deal the enemy repeated telling blows from the defensive was frustrated by Hitler, who was unwilling in any circumstances to allow the Red Army to retain the initiative. Therefore the plan Operation ZITADELLE (Citadel) finally evolved. While the victories achieved in the winter campaign between the Donets and Dnepr Rivers, and at Kharkov, had made it possible to reestablish a defensive line from Taganrog along the Mius and Donets as far as Belgorod, enemy forces still held a large salient extending far to the west (north of Belgorod) in the boundary area between Army Groups South and Center. The Soviet main line of resistance in this place described a wide curve from Belgorod through Sumy and Rylsk to the area southeast of Orel, and enclosed the Kursk sector. This bulge which protruded into the German front was far more than a mere beauty blemish. It extended almost 300 miles along the front lines, consequently forcing the Wehrmacht to deploy considerable forces in that area to seal it off in the north, west, and south, and it severed the rail route from Army Group Center to Kharkov, depriving German forces of what had been one of their most important lateral communication routes behind the front. Finally, it gave the Russians a staging area for an attack directed at the northern flank of Army Group South and at the southern flank of Army Group Center.

It would have been particularly dangerous if the German Command at any time should plan a counterattack from Kharkov against some future Soviet offensive in the zone of Army Group South. For this reason, Army Group South had originally intended to exploit its successes achieved at Kharkov to clean out this salient while the Russians were still off balance and before the onset of the mud season. The plan had to be dropped, however, because Army Group Center announced that it was unable to participate in the operation. Although the Red Army had become very much weakened by its defeat at Kharkov, the forces available to Army Group South would still have been too weak to attempt to clean out such a large area.

---

*Editor's Note: Although Walter Goerlitz mentions that there were some inclinations on the Soviet side for a negotiated peace, the central body of the Communist Party remained dedicated to the "war to annihilate fascism." See Goerlitz, Vol. II.

The bulge had now become an objective for an attack in which the German Command would have to make the first move. The tactical importance of the objective has been described. Apart from the fact that removal of the salient would release a considerable number of German units for employment elsewhere, an added incentive for the attack was the possibility that, through synchronized attacks from the north and south, relatively strong Soviet forces could be cut off.

However, from Army Group South's point of view, the planned operation would also serve another purpose, since it assumed with certainty that the Russians would throw in their strategic reserves (then assembled opposite the northern flank of Army Group South and the southern flank of Army Group Center) at an early stage in order to retain possession of the strategically important area. If the Germans could stage their attack soon enough after the close of the mud season, it was likely that the Soviet Command would be compelled to commit its armored and motorized corps and armies before they had completed their rehabilitation. This would have been a distinct advantage for the Wehrmacht, which could then hope to complete an earlier rehabilitation of its own units.

If the Soviet armored reserves could be destroyed in the battle, it would then be possible to strike a new blow, this time at the Donets line, or in some other area. The development of these conditions was just as important an objective in Operation ZITADELLE as the removal of the bulge itself, desirable as the elimination of this threat was.[26]

The restricted scope of the objective in this last German offensive in the East reveals most strikingly how the factors of space and numerical strengths influenced the conduct of operations in Russia in 1943. In 1941, German armies had attacked on a frontage of about 1,200 miles to rout the Red Army in a series of major battles of envelopment.[27*] In 1942, the German drive on Stalingrad and the Caucasus had taken off from a frontage of only 360 miles, but with an immensely far-flung objective. In 1943, the planned offensive was to begin on a frontage of only 120 miles, and the objective was only 90 miles away.

---

*Editor's Note: See Generalleutnant Hermann Plocher (Ret.), The German Air Force versus Russia, 1941, USAF Historical Studies No. 153, Maxwell AFB, Alabama: USAF Historical Division, ASI, July 1965.

The Plan of Attack for Operation ZITADELLE

The relatively straight German main line of resistance from Taganrog to Leningrad was interrupted by a Soviet wedge with a base of approximately 120 miles and a depth of about 90 miles, protruding west of Kursk. Pursuant to directives from the Army High Command, the enemy wedge was to be cut off at its base in a pincer movement, with Army Group Center attacking from the north and Army Group South from the south. Soviet forces in the sector were to be annihilated.[28]*

In the south, the Fourth Panzer Army (Generaloberst Hermann Hoth) was assigned the mission of breaking through to Kursk. Army Force Kemp had the mission of covering the breakthrough operation by "offensive action."[29] From the north, the Ninth Army (Generaloberst Walter Model) was also to break through to Kursk to meet the Fourth Panzer Army. The Fourth Air Fleet was to support the two armies attacking from the south, while the Sixth Air Fleet was to support the drive from the north.

The two army group commanders, Field Marshals von Manstein/ and von Kluge, held the view that Operation ZITADELLE must be staged as soon as possible, therefore immediately after the termination of the spring mud season, probably about the beginning of May. The planned intention was to strike the enemy while he was still off balance.[30] It was, of course, obvious that the Russians would not remain idle during this time, and that they would also take advantage of the period of inactivity brought on by the muddy season to reequip their units and bring them up to strength, to reorganize their command, and to prepare new offensive plans. Therefore, the sooner the German offensive commenced the greater would be the chance that it would stagger the enemy before he had completed his offensive preparations.

Hitler's order of 15 April 1943, which prescribed an attack with limited objectives against the Kursk bulge, commenced as follows:

> I have decided to carry out the offensive "Zitadelle" as soon as weather conditions permit, as the first of this year's attack plans.

---

*See Maps Nos. 7 and 11.

/See figure 22.

Figure 22
Field Marshal Erich von Manstein, Commander in Chief, Army Group South

This attack is therefore of decisive importance. It must succeed quickly and completely. It must put the initiative for this spring and summer in our hands.

All preparations must therefore be made with the greatest care and energy; the best units, the best weapons, the best commanders, and large quantities of ammunition shall be committed in the areas of main effort.

Every commander and every man must be filled with the decisive meaning of this attack. The victory of Kursk must have the effect of a beacon for the entire world. [31]

The Fuehrer, however, postponed the opening of the offensive again and again because he considered it essential to reinforce the available panzer forces with the new "Panther" and "Tiger" tanks, which had just been placed in serial production.* The commanding generals of the two army groups remonstrated repeatedly that time would favor the Russians, but Hitler adhered to his decision to postpone the attack.

The views of the army group commanders were supported by Generaloberst Jeschonnek, Chief of the Luftwaffe General Staff, during a Fuehrer Conference in Munich on 4 May 1943. Jeschonnek declared that, from the Luftwaffe's point of view, a postponement of ZITADELLE offered no advantages whatever, since it was impossible to effect any material increase in the strength of the combat air forces, and since changes in the air situation indicated that the enemy appeared to be planning a decisive offensive in the sector of Army Group South. [32]

On 1 July 1943 Hitler held a conference at his headquarters at Rastenburg in East Prussia† to which he summoned all Army and Luftwaffe commanders from corps level upward who were participating in Operation ZITADELLE. During this meeting he finally announced his decision to

---

*Editor's Note: The "Panther" (Pzkw V), a tank weighing about 40 tons, armed with a 75-mm. gun, appeared in 1942. The "Tiger" (Pzkw VI) was in the 60-ton weight class, and was armed with the very excellent long-barreled 8.8-cm antitank gun. See Generaloberst a. D. Heinz Guderian, Erinnerungen eines Soldaten (Recollections of a Soldier), Heidelberg: Kurt Vowinckel Verlag, 1951, pp. 250-257.

†About 110 miles southeast of Koenigsberg.

begin the operation on 5 July, opening the attack with a bold, tightly concentrated, and speedily executed drive by one army each from the Belgorod area and the area south of Orel, respectively. The plan was to encircle the Soviet forces present in the Kursk area and to annihilate them by a concentric attack. 33*

Preparations for the Strongest Luftwaffe Concentration for ZITADELLE

Reichsmarschall Goering ordered the following measures for the planned offensive. The Fourth Air Fleet, supported by the consolidated units under the command of the VIII Air Corps, was to back the attack by the southern group (Army Force Kempf and Fourth Panzer Army), while the Sixth Air Fleet, with those forces which were consolidated under the command of the 1st Air Division, was to support the attack by the northern group (Ninth Army).

Insofar as was possible, both air fleets were to strip the units within their commands of forces, including flying, flak, and signal troops, so that they would have available the real bulk of their forces for the development of well defined concentrations of power in the two major attack areas. Other air forces were to be moved in from the outside, such as, for example, from the First Air Fleet area (Combat Zone North).

The Fourth Air Fleet, under General der Flieger Otto Dessloch, † with command post at Dnepropetrovsk, directed the VIII Air Corps (Generalmajor Hans Seidemann), which had its headquarters at Mikoyanovka, 18 miles south of Belgorod. Assigned to it were:

---

*See Map No. 7.

†Freiherr von Richthofen was promoted to Field Marshal 16 February 1943, and assumed command of the Second Air Fleet in Italy 12 June 1943. Von Manstein made a plea for his retention in the Russian area for ZITADELLE, and declared, "My efforts to secure the return of von Richthofen to command the Fourth Air Fleet failed, and led only to a sharp controversy with Goering, who was unwilling to admit how decisively important the influence of a personality such as von Richthofen was for the combat forces." Generalfeldmarschall Erich von Manstein, Verlorene Siege (Lost Victories), Bonn: Athenaeum Verlag, 1955, p. 496.

Unit	Stationed At
Reconnaissance:	
2nd Strategic Reconnaissance Squadron, 11th Wing	Kharkov-East
6th Wing (2 Me-109, 5 Fw-189, and 3 night squadrons)	Airfields southwest of Mikoyanovka
Fighters:	
3rd Fighter Wing (3 Me-109 groups)	Kharkov-East
52nd Fighter Wing (3 Me-109 groups)	Airfields southwest of Mikoyanovka
4th Group, 9th Antitank Air Wing (4 HS-129 squadrons)	Airfield near Mikoyan-ovka
Fighter-Bombers:	
1st Ground-Attack Wing (2 Fw-190 and HS-129 groups)	Two airfields south of Belgorod
2nd Dive-Bomber Wing (3 1/3 Ju-87 groups)	Kharkov-East
77th Dive-Bomber Wing (3 Ju-87 groups)	Airfields at Tolokonoye and Bebarovka south of Belgorod
Bombers:	
3rd Bomber Wing (2 Ju-88 groups)	Poltava
27th Bomber Wing (3 He-111 groups)	Dnepropetrovsk and Zaporozhye
55th Bomber Wing (3 He-111 groups)	Kharkov-East
Other Air Units:	
A group of harassing bombers of various types	Kharkov-North
Several liaison squadrons	Kharkov-North
1 Ju-52 air transport squadron	Kharkov-North
2 air signal regiments	Kharkov-North

The VIII Air Corps also had tactical control over the Hungarian Air Division, composed of the following units, all located at Kharkov-Southeast:

1 Ju-88 strategic reconnaissance squadron
1 Fw-189 tactical reconnaissance squadron
1 Me-109 fighter group
1 Ju-87 dive-bomber group
1 Ju-88 bomber squadron

All in all, the VIII Air Corps at the end of June thus had a striking power of 1,100 operational aircraft.[34] The Fourth Air Fleet ordered this corps to secure air superiority over the line of advance of the attacking German ground forces in the south and to support both Army Force Kempf and the Fourth Panzer Army. For these purposes, the available air forces were to be closely concentrated in the areas of attack, especially in advance of the II SS Panzer Corps, in order to facilitate the forward thrust of the spearhead units. All air units were to be used exclusively in tactical support missions, against targets within the battle area, the strongly developed Soviet defense positions, and Soviet artillery emplacements. Rail and road targets were to be attacked only if large transport movements were observed.

The Fourth Air Fleet also controlled the I Flak Corps (Generalleutnant Richard Reimann) and Luftwaffe Administrative Area Command Kiev (General der Flieger Bernard Waber).* The I Flak Corps received instructions to employ three regiments as a strong air defense force for the extremely crowded airfields, placing main emphasis upon the Kharkov sector; to assign one flak regiment as antitank artillery in the Fourth Panzer Army sector; and to deploy its units so as to provide an adequate air defense for the ground troops.

Air Administrative Area Command Kiev had the responsibility of developing the ground service organization within the VIII Air Corps area, for maintaining supplies at the tactical airfields from which assigned flying units would operate, and for transporting and controlling Luftwaffe supplies, both prior to and during the offensive.

---

*Editor's Note: Waber, an Austrian, was tried and executed late in the war for subverting (misuse and misappropriation of materials) the defensive power of the Wehrmacht. See biographical section in the back of this study and Chart No. 4.

Situated in the northern part of the concentration area was the Sixth Air Fleet under Generaloberst Ritter von Greim. This organization commanded the 1st Air Division (Generalmajor Paul Deichmann), which had its command post near the Orel airfield, and which was directly responsible for the conduct of combat air operations. At the end of June the division had a striking force of 730 aircraft, consisting of 3 tactical reconnaissance groups, one each with the Second and Ninth Armies and the Second Panzer Army, and the following units (located at airfields in the Orel-Bryansk-Shatalovka area):

Fighters

51st Fighter Wing (3 1/3 Fw-190 groups)
54th Fighter Wing (Fw-190's)
2 to 3 antitank squadrons (known as the 14th Squadron)

Fighter-Bombers

1st Dive-Bomber Wing (3 Ju-87 groups)
1st Twin-Engine Fighter Wing (1 1/3 Me-110 groups)

Bombers

3rd (Ju-88) Group, 1st Bomber Wing
4th Bomber Wing (2 He-111 groups)
51st Bomber Wing (2 Ju-88 groups)
53rd Bomber Wing (2 He-111 groups)

Other Air Units

1 to 2 squadrons of harassing bombers, liaison squadrons, and Luftwaffe signals regiments

Sixth Air Fleet ordered the 1st Air Division to attack the over-crowded Soviet airfields in the Kursk region, employing at the same time certain of its elements against Soviet artillery positions around Maloarkhangelsk; then to concentrate its forces ahead of the XXXXVII Panzer Corps, which would spearhead the ground attack, silencing enemy artillery; and to attack Russian units in the Second Panzer Army's line of advance. Such actions were to be given prior approval by the air fleet headquarters. Besides these important tasks, the air division was to maintain fighter patrols over the entire assault area.

The 1st Air Division controlled a number of ground units as well, including the 12th Flak Division under Generalleutnant Ernst Buffa (CP located at Orel), and the 10th Flak Brigade, commanded by Generalmajor Paul Pavel (CP located at Konotop).* The 12th Flak Division, through its 5 regimental staffs (which included a railroad flak regiment), controlled about 16 mixed flak battalions (12 motorized and 4 truck-drawn), each with 3 heavy and 2 light batteries; 7 light battalions made up of 5 motorized and 2 truck-drawn units; 3 railroad flak battalions of 3 batteries each; and 2 to 3 searchlight battalions of 3 batteries each.

The mission of the 12th Flak Division was to provide antiaircraft protection for German supply bases, especially around Orel, provide at least minimum necessary antiaircraft defense of the operational airfields, protect the attacking German divisions' main supply routes against Russian air attacks, and, what was unusual, have its forward batteries participate in the artillery preparation fire on the morning of 5 July 1943.

The 10th Flak Brigade had a single regimental staff which controlled 2 motorized and 2 to 3 truck-drawn flak battalions, 1 light flak battalion, 1 improvised railroad flak battery, and 2 searchlight batteries. Its mission was to provide antiaircraft protection in the Second Army sector, with main concentration in the Konotop area, and to prepare for the deployment of its motorized batteries for air defense of German ground troops.

In addition to the above-mentioned organizations, the Sixth Air Fleet assumed command over a number of special units for the impending Operation ZITADELLE. These consisted of 1 night-fighter group, 1 strategic reconnaissance group of 2 to 3 squadrons, and 2 Luftwaffe signals regiments (all in the Orel area), a Luftwaffe operations staff, the 3rd Air Command, an *ad hoc* organization held ready to commit its attached units, if necessary, to action northeast of Bryansk,† and the XXVII Special Air Administrative Area Command (previously designated Air Administrative Area Command Moscow).††

This latter unit, commanded by Generalleutnant Veit Fischer, operated from its headquarters at Minsk and had the mission of developing

*See Chart No. 4.

†As events worked out, this was not deemed necessary.

††See Chart No. 2.

the ground service organization, building up supplies for the coming operation, securing the logistical life lines during the course of the battle, and making preparations for development of a ground service organization in the Kursk area if the tactical objectives should be achieved.

Such a massed concentration and commitment of air forces within small areas involved extraordinary preparations. The development of the ground service organization, and the procurement of additional necessary personnel and materiel for the purpose, particularly the build-up of large stockpiles of supplies, were handled by Air Administrative Area Command Kiev for the VIII Air Corps (attacking in the south), and by the XXVII Air Administrative Area Command (Minsk) for the 1st Air Division (attacking in the north).

Since the existing airfields were inadequate for the many air units which were to be employed, a number of new tactical air bases and forward airfields had to be speedily reconnoitered and developed for operations, making sure that sufficient stocks of fuel and ammunition were on hand. In the Orel sector alone, the number of airfields was increased from 3 to about 15.[35]

Equipment supply points, aircraft recovery detachments, mobile field workshop battalions, workshop platoons, Reichs Labor Service (Reichsarbeitsdienst or RAD) battalions, air base command staffs, airfield operations companies, and supply columns were assembled in the Kursk area and prepared for their coming tasks, giving special attention to the immediate build-up of supplies at the airfields.

Little difficulty was encountered in stockpiling all types of ammunition. Enough ammunition was stored at each airfield in the VIII Air Corps sector for 10 missions, and arrangements were made to assure an adequate supply of bombs for 15 days of major battle at each field in the 1st Air Division area.

The supply of fuel proved to be a serious bottleneck for the Wehrmacht. This situation had been generally difficult to master for some time because of deficient production. As a result, the Sixth Air Fleet in June received only 5,722 tons of B-4 fuel against a total consumption of 8,634 tons, and only 441 tons of C-3 fuel (so necessary for Fw-190 units) against a total consumption of 1, 079 tons.* Efforts were made to surmount these difficulties by a partial redistribution of existing stocks, using the uneconomical means of air and truck transportation.

The already very serious rail transport situation was worsened considerably by the steadily increasing number and scope of partisan sabotage operations against the few available supply routes. It seemed obvious that this increased partisan activity was directed by the Soviet Command for the dual purpose of interrupting and delaying German military preparations and of weakening the Wehrmacht's defensive capabilities against impending Red Army operations. Partisan actions reached a peak in June of 1943 with 841 separate acts of sabotage, including the loss or damage of 298 locomotives, 1, 222 railway cars, and 44 bridges in Combat Zone Center alone. During this time the partisans stopped rail movements at an average of 24 points daily. 36≠ The conduct of air operations was governed largely by fuel supplies, so it became essential to introduce what could only be termed "fuel availability tactics." Power concentrations had to be developed not so much by the assignment of air units as by the quantities of fuel which could be released for the purpose. In order to have air power available for particular crises and major phases of battle, it became necessary to refuse air support in many situations which would normally have been recognized as critical. Every assigned mission had to be carefully examined to determine whether it was really worth the fuel expenditure. In deciding what type of units to employ, it often became necessary to accept certain disadvantageous conditions because of the possibility of saving a few tons of fuel. 37

---

*Editor's Note: B-4 (blue) aviation fuel (rated at 91 octane) was primarily used for bomber and general-purpose aircraft. C-3 (green) aviation fuel was almost exclusively a fighter fuel, and contained high percentages of aromatic naphtha, which gave it an excellent rich-mixture performance. By 1943, this fuel was rated at 97 octane (weak mixture) and from 110 to 130 (rich mixture). DB-601 and BMW-801 engines were supposed to use C-3 fuel, although B-4 and even other types were used in emergencies. The Luftwaffe needed 350, 000 tons of fuel per month in 1943, but, because of deficient production and transportation problems, only 160, 000 tons were delivered each month. See "Die Betriebsstofflage in Deutschland 1939-1944" ("The Power Fuel Situation in Germany 1939-1944"), C/I/5, Karlsruhe Document Collection.

≠Editor's Note: Combat Zone Center was the most active area of partisan warfare. See General der Flieger a. D. Karl Drum, Airpower and Russian Partisan Warfare, USAF Historical Studies No. 177, Maxwell AFB, Alabama: USAF Historical Division, RSI, March 1962.

As is always the case when large air forces are to be committed, an important and, in fact, decisive requirement was the timely establishment and development of a properly functioning communications network, a system so vital for the flexible and speedy control of operational units and, thus, for the establishment of conditions conducive to success. Alternate wire, radio, and radio-beam channels had to be established so that if one medium of communication failed, reports and orders could still be transmitted between the various Luftwaffe and Army command staffs. The radio intercept and aircraft warning services were expanded, since experience had shown that these organizations often furnished the necessary data for the successful and effective commitment of air and flak units. In view of the exceptionally heavy concentration of German flying units in a small area and the crowded condition of each airfield, radio intercept and air reconnaissance units had especially heavy responsibilities to keep Luftwaffe commands apprised of the presence of hostile air forces.

Pursuant to orders, the I Flak Corps assumed responsibility for the antiaircraft defenses in the southern area, particularly the airfields around Kharkov, but also for the defense of forward airfields in the near front areas, where it deployed many light and heavy flak batteries. The 10th Flak Brigade was committed in the Second Army Zone, with main emphasis around Konotop. The German Command was gravely concerned over the increasing frequency of Soviet night air attacks in German rear areas, where so many good targets were to be found, including rail and road supply routes and numerous depots crowded with supplies for the impending operation.[38]

Strong Soviet air units flew repeatedly into the Orel and Kharkov areas. Since the German night fighter service had downed only a few Russian planes of the large number which were able to penetrate the area, the Luftwaffe clearly had to reinforce its night fighter forces for Operation <u>ZITADELLE.</u>

After discussing the matter with the Chief of the Night Fighter Arm (General der Flieger Josef Kammhuber), it was agreed that five of the existing nine night fighter flights should be assigned, two from the Berlin area and three from the Western Theater of Operations. In June 1943, after approval of this recommendation by the Commander in Chief of the Luftwaffe, additional night fighter units were committed in the Orel sector, and periodically in the Kharkov sector as well. These operations were controlled by radar mounted on a railway train.

On the evening of 4 July the last air units earmarked for participation in the attack arrived at their assigned tactical airfields. For reasons of security and deception they had been held at rear area airfields as long as possible, with only the more important ground personnel and several key officers arriving earlier for orientation on their coming missions and for making necessary preparations. That day all unit commanders attended a situation conference at 1st Air Division Headquarters, where they were told that the results achieved in the initial air attacks would decisively influence the Army's attempt to penetrate the Soviet front. Every crew was to be thoroughly imbued with the vital importance of its specific mission. Furthermore, they were told that the relatively weak German ground units had to rely completely upon their air support and that they counted upon Luftwaffe airmen to make a supreme effort.

By nightfall of the 4th, the VIII Air Corps was ready for action with about 1,100 aircraft, as was the 1st Air Division with about 730 aircraft, making a total of 1,830 operational aircraft available for employment in ZITADELLE.

The Last German Offensive in the Eastern Theater of Operations*

According to plan, the forces of the German armies (Army Force Kempf, Fourth Panzer Army, and Ninth Army) jumped off to the attack. Large numbers of Luftwaffe flak units were added to the conventional artillery to participate in opening barrages. About 100 heavy flak guns (8.8-cm) participated with the northern attack forces alone.[39]

Units of the 1st Air Division took off on their first attack missions on 5 July at 0330 hours. While units of the VIII Air Corps were taking off for their respective targets, reports came in from the aircraft warning service and from Freya radar units/ that very powerful Soviet air formations were approaching Kharkov. If this enemy force intended to attack the five overcrowded German airfields and if it should arrive while the

---

*Editor's Note: For additional details on the operations of Army Group Center see Appendix 20, original German draft of this study, Karlsruhe Document Collection, and for details on the air effort see Appendices 21 and 22 of this draft. See also Manstein, Lost Victories, p. 497. See also Map No. 9.

/Editor's Note: The "Freya" radar unit was an aircraft warning and fighter direction device with an altitude searching range of about 5 miles and a horizontal searching range of 75 miles. It could only traverse 36°. See F/X, Karlsruhe Document Collection.

German bombers were still taking off or in the process of assembling in the air, there was a grave danger that the first massed attack of the VIII Air Corps for ZITADELLE would be broken up in its initial stages or, at least, seriously hampered. This would, of course, materially weaken the air support which was planned for the ground forces' opening attack.

Alerted by these reports, all of the German fighters stationed at Kharkov and all of those at airfields near the front southwest of Belgorod took off immediately, not following their own bombers as had been planned, but flying directly to meet the incoming enemy formations. As the Russian squadrons approached the target airfields, Messerschmidt (Bf) 109's, coming at them out of the grayish haze of the early dawn, struck them in alternating waves in a well-directed attack. In these encounters German pilots achieved exceptional results in enemy planes shot down, while the Russians, rigidly employing their usual obstinant and inflexible tactics, continued steadfastly on their set course. In so doing they lost most of their aircraft. The battles, which were taking place at great height, could be seen clear across the skies.* At those altitudes German defense forces had an indisputable advantage. It was a mass aerial engagement such as is seldom seen, with burning and crashing Soviet bombers and their escorts falling to the ground almost everywhere. Generaloberst Jeschonnek, Chief of the Luftwaffe General Staff, happened to be at the advanced command post of the VIII Air Corps at the time, and was able to personally witness this Soviet debacle.

Flak artillery units also took their toll of the incoming Soviet planes. Without regard for their own fighters, light and heavy flak batteries opened fire on the approaching formations, coming in at altitudes ranging from 7,000 to 10,000 feet, and scored a number of direct hits.

Since few of the Russian bombers reached the target areas, few bombs were dropped, and those which were dropped were released in such haste and in such a haphazard manner that few of them even came close to any airfield installations. German bombers were thus able to continue their takeoffs and to continue operations on schedule.

In the course of the air defense action, approximately 120 Soviet aircraft were shot down, while German losses, including those destroyed on the ground, were so slight that the outcome could be described as a complete victory. The timely anticipation of the Soviet air attack and the

---

*10,000 feet and above.

personal initiative exercised by fighter commanders saved the day, and gave the Wehrmacht air superiority over the entire area for the next few weeks, during which time the Russians refrained from any aggressive air activity. The Luftwaffe was therefore able to give almost full support to the ground attack (which began precisely on schedule). The rise in Luftwaffe morale was marked and remained up for a considerable period of time.[40]

Before the general offensive opened, the Fourth Panzer Army was obliged to take by storm a few observation points which, in enemy hands, might have endangered the entire operation. On the next morning, 5 July 1943, this army drove to the north and northeast in the direction of Oboyan, Marino, Belgorod, and Pokhorovka in an effort to link up with forward units of the Ninth Army driving southward from the area just south of Orel. Just ahead of the Fourth Panzer Army the VIII Air Corps' bombers attacked targets immediately behind the Soviet front, while its ground-attack and dive-bomber units bombed and strafed enemy pockets of resistance, batteries, and reserves within the actual battle area. This support greatly expedited the drives of the II SS Panzer and the XXXXVIII Panzer Corps.

The area of main effort of Army Group Center (the left wing of the operation) lay to the west of the Orel-Kursk railroad line and along the general area of the line. From this area the Ninth Army was making its drive toward Kursk. The attack in this sector was supported by bombers of the 1st Air Division, which, in their first mission, attacked crowded Russian airfields around Kursk, while the division's close support units repeatedly struck flanking Soviet artillery concentrations, especially those in the Maloarkhangelsk sector, and those in the forested fringes ahead of the advancing Ninth Army. These attacks shattered the enemy positions.[41] In the first few days of battle the 1st Air Division flew an average of five or six missions daily, attacking all targets which could be found in the line of advance. It destroyed a complete armored train in the course of these operations. As always, German flyers were far more impressed by the enemy's light antiaircraft and small arms fire than by Soviet fighters, which seldom showed themselves when German bombers had a good fighter escort.

The first large numbers of Russian fighters appeared in the 1st Air Division area late in the afternoon of the first day of combat, and in the fierce fighting which ensued 110 of them were destroyed by German fighters. The German units had very slight losses of their own. This successful action helped to assure air superiority over the Ninth Army sector, just as the VIII Air Corps enjoyed over the Fourth Panzer Army area.[42]

Air liaison officers attached to ground divisions at the points of main effort relayed again and again the Army's requests for air support at specific places, and the Luftwaffe responded by quickly bringing such objectives under attack. These operations were enhanced by fine summer weather, which enabled all air units to fly as many as six or eight missions daily. For the next few days both the VIII Air Corps and the 1st Air Division continued to make a maximum support effort. Again and again waves of Luftwaffe planes attacked massed Soviet artillery, troop concentrations (especially tanks), antitank positions, enemy reserves approaching from deep in the Russian rear areas, and enemy logistical movements by rail and road. German air forces also attacked Russian airfields which were reported to be heavily occupied, in order to strike enemy air units before they could launch their attacks. However, the main emphasis in Luftwaffe operations was upon direct support of friendly ground forces on the actual field of battle. Although the German Command was aware of the need for attacks deep in the rear of the operational area in order to interdict the battlefield--this was to have been done largely through cutting off railroads as had been done around Kiev in 1941--the air forces available for such purposes were far too weak.[43]* Because of inadequate forces to carry out such diversified air missions, the heavy losses incurred in close support work, the steady decline in operability of units, and insufficient supplies received, the Luftwaffe had to exercise extremely tight control over all of its forces, even those used for flexible operations, in order to achieve power concentrations for the currently decisive sectors.

What had been feared from the outset became apparent after the first week of the attack: the replacement services could not keep pace with the aircraft attrition rate, and, in the long run, could not measure up to the tremendous replacement capabilities of the Soviet forces.[44]

Red air activities increased steadily, and the Soviet air formations began to penetrate even as far as 15 miles into the German rear area to attack supply routes and airfields.† The general impression in German circles was that the Russians were always able to make up their heavy

---

*Because the number of operational aircraft was less in 1943 than it had been in 1941, the operations of 1943 were almost entirely confined to the front line areas.

†See figures 23, 24, and 25.

losses and maintain their numerical strength through the receipt of replacement aircraft and the assignment of new personnel. Yet, wherever German fighters appeared it was usually a relatively simple matter for the Luftwaffe to achieve local air superiority and even air supremacy over the Russians, even when the odds were very great. Under the pressure of this long period of major combat, however, the technical operability of German units unavoidably began to decline. Consequently, it was impossible to prevent the Russians, with their great numerical superiority, from making periodic air strikes against German ground troops during the absence of Luftwaffe fighters. The effects achieved in these Soviet attacks were always exceedingly small, irritating though they were. The excellent functioning German radio intercept service often succeeded in intercepting take-off reports of Soviet air formations, so that the Luftwaffe could meet approaching enemy forces in time and inflict heavy losses upon them.

In this head-on encounter between the two opposing air forces in a narrow area in which there was no possibility of evasion, the advantageous features stressed in the evaluation of the Soviet air forces became more clearly evident than ever before. The Russians were quantitatively very strong, but were mediocre in quality and inadequate in development. Yet, they had learned a lot in the past years of warfare, and had come a long way from their primitive condition of 1941. The performances of some hostile air units, especially among the ground-attack forces, were quite commendable.[45*]

German preparations for the attack against the Kursk salient had not escaped the Russians' notice. Exceeding their customary practice of immediately and thoroughly developing every individual position, they had built up a defense system, organized in great depth, and protected by wire entanglements and antitank obstacles. Its strongest features were the deep flanks of the bulge[/] and the reinforcements provided by numerous armor-piercing weapons. Strong reserve forces were also held behind all threatened sectors of the front.[46//]

General Walter Bedell Smith, General Eisenhower's Chief of Staff, declared that the Germans would again go over to the offensive on a monstrous scale, but that the Russians were prepared and had erected

---

*See figure 23.

/Editor's Note: During World War II, the Russians invariably established flank defenses in great depth.

//See Maps Nos. 9 and 11.

a defense system in immense depth in the sector which would probably come under attack. He also mentioned that the two Soviet army groups in the Kursk area, Army Groups Voronezh and Steppe, were establishing a complex of antitank positions, extending in places as far as 60 miles behind the main line of resistance, to halt the German tanks with massed antitank and artillery fire.

The "bag" of Kursk, where the Soviet Command (probably supported by reports from partisans and other intelligence agents) awaited the attacking German spearheads, was transformed into one gigantic field of fortifications. Russian engineers were favored in their tasks by the heavily forested terrain, dissected in many places by numerous gorges. Villages became fortified strongpoints, one antitank and artillery obstacle following the other, and the whole system was further strengthened by mine fields, antitank ditches, tank traps, batteries of dug-in flame throwers and dug-in tanks. Behind these positions tactical and strategic reserves were held ready--there were entire divisions of artillery and tank corps in abundance--many of them equipped with American materiel, including General Lee tanks.[47*]

In spite of strong air support for ZITADELLE, German attack forces in both northern and southern sectors of the operation made very slow progress. In the Ninth Army area, German troops in the first two days of the attack effected a breakthrough of Soviet positions about nine to ten miles in depth, and carried their advance forward on a seven-mile front until they encountered the Soviet reserve forces, which had been thrown in on 7 July near the northern part of the Kursk bulge, just ahead of the Orel salient.

In the southern wing of the attack forces, Army Force Kemp ran into a myriad of difficulties. Its XI Corps (Generalleutnant Erhard Rauss)

---

*Editor's Note: Medium tank (M-3) known as the "General Grant" when mounting a British turret or the "General Lee" when it had an American turret (smaller than the British type). The same chassis was used on the Canadian RAM I and II tanks. This tank was powered by a 9-cylinder Wright air-cooled engine, and armed with one 37-mm. gun and two 30-cal. machine guns. See United States, War Department, Basic Field Manual, Military Intelligence: Identification of United States Armored Vehicles, January 9, 1943, Washington: U.S. Government Printing Office, 1943, pp. 20-21. USAAF, Teaching Manual for Ground Vehicle Recognition, Orlando, Florida: AAF School of Applied Tactics, Intelligence Department, 1 October 1943, Appendix I.

Figure 23
Soviet IL-2 "Stormoviks" attacking German airfield at Smolensk-North

Figure 24
Damage caused by Soviet air attacks on the field at Smolensk-North

Figure 25
Damage caused by Russian air attack upon Luftwaffe base at Shatalovka, U.S.S.R., August 1943

Figure 26
Flak (8.8-cm.) in action against ground targets in support of the Army

failed to reach Korodsha as planned, and succeeded only in reaching the Koren sector, where Russian reserve forces from the area west of Volchansk were pitted against it. As a result, the XI Corps' advance devolved into a defensive battle in which German troops had to stave off sizeable Soviet armored attacks. On the left (northern) wing of Army Force Kempf, the III Panzer Corps (General der Panzertruppe Hermann Breith) made its assault across the Donets with great difficulty, and finally became stuck at a Soviet line about 11 miles northeast of the Donets River. It had become obvious that the Russians intended to hold the Kursk salient at all costs.

To the left of Army Force Kempf the SS Panzer and XXXXVIII Panzer Corps of the Fourth Panzer Army made substantial headway in the first week of the battle and, despite heavy odds, helped to break down enemy resistance in the path of the southern attack force. Exceedingly heavy losses in men and materiel were inflicted upon Soviet units by all of the attacking forces, but German units were badly battered in the process and their striking power was markedly reduced after the first four days of combat. Whenever the ground forces had taken one Soviet position they found their way barred by the next. The Wehrmacht thus had to fight its way, by costly and laborious action, through a gigantic system of positions in terrain infested with mines and packed with weapons of all types, a system which seemed to be interminable.

On 7 July the XXXXVIII Panzer Corps (Generalleutnant Otto von Knobelsdorff) broke through the second Soviet position and into the open, seven miles south of Oboyan. Immediately thereafter, however, it had to defend itself against powerful enemy attacks from the northeast, north, and west. Before it, as well as before the SS Panzer Corps (General der Waffen SS Paul Hausser), appeared strong Russian tactical reserves, three armored and one mechanized corps under the Soviet Sixty-ninth Army and the 1st Tank Army, to which were added other mobile units which were rapidly advancing from east of Kharkov. [48]*

The Red Army launched one counterthrust after another in steadily increasing strength, each with exceedingly heavy armored support. Thus, tanks confronted tanks in all sectors of the front. German flak artillery units committed to antitank action on the ground proved to be particularly effective, and throughout the battle these batteries served as the backbone of the Army, providing security for German troops and helping them to

---

*See Maps Nos. 9 and 11.

maintain a high level of morale.[49]* Without question, the remarkable suitability of the 8.8-cm gun for repelling tank attacks and, most important of all, for knocking out tanks which had broken through the German lines, was due to its high rate of fire, high muzzle velocity and flat trajectory, and great penetrating power. The large numbers of destroyed Russian tanks were clear evidence of the repelling and destructive force of these pieces.

German antitank air units also rendered material service to the ground forces. Col. Hans-Ulrich Rudel describes the battle scene near Belgorod on 5 July when German tanks faced oncoming hordes of Soviet armor:

> Large-scale tank battles raged beneath us during these operations. A scene as we had rarely seen since 1941. The tank formations stood opposed to each other in the open terrain, and in the background the opposing antitank forces had taken up positions. Some of the tanks were dug in, particularly those which had become unmaneuverable but still had their fire power. Numerically, the Russians had, as always, a towering superiority, but in point of quality the superiority of our tanks and self-propelled artillery was immediately evident. Here, for the first time, our Tiger tanks were committed in large units.† They are far superior to anything hitherto existing in the tank arm. All of our tank models are materially quicker in firing and shoot more precisely. This was due primarily to the better quality of our weapons, but the decisive factor is the better men who handled those weapons.
>
> More dangerous to our tanks were the Soviet heavy and super-heavy antitank guns, which appeared at every important point of the battle area. Since the Russians are masters of camouflage, their antitank guns are very difficult to detect and combat.

---

*See figure 26.

†Editor's Note: Some attention was given to the idea of reproducing the very durable Soviet T-34 tank for use against the Red Army, but its aluminum Diesel engine involved certain production problems. Instead, the "Tiger" (Pzkw VI), a heavy 60-ton tank was developed, outfitted with the long 8.8-cm gun. Heavier caliber guns were rejected in favor of the fine-performing, high-velocity 88.

> Catching sight of these numbers of tanks I remembered my plane with its cannon from the Experimental Antitank Command, which I had brought along from the Crimea.* With these gigantic target offerings of enemy tanks, an attempt on them would be possible.[50]

The Soviet armor was heavily defended by antiaircraft artillery, but Rudel noted that since German panzer forces were only about 1,500 to 2,000 yards from the Russian tanks, he could probably crash land in friendly territory if his plane should receive a serious hit. On his first sortie Rudel destroyed four enemy tanks, and by the end of the day he had bagged a total of twelve. His fellow airmen were elated over these victories and the realization that they could play a leading role in stopping the Red Army and in saving the lives of their Army comrades.

Dive-bombers and other aircraft flying close-support missions always have a rather limited life span, since they must fly through considerable amounts of ground fire, and sometimes fires and explosions caused by their own attacks. But the main thing was that Luftwaffe leaders up through corps level now knew that they had an aerial weapon available with which they could quickly and effectively counter Soviet armored attacks.

To insure the delivery of replacement aircraft, all elements of the Experimental Antitank Squadron were instructed to immediately fly all operational aircraft, together with their crews, into the area. This was the real beginning of the operational Antitank Air Squadron, which was placed under the tactical control of Colonel Rudel. Within a few days further successes were scored by this unit. The aircraft with mounted cannons attacked enemy tanks while bombers attacked Soviet ground defenses, with some aircraft circling overhead "like a broody hen circling her chicks" to protect the antitank planes against Soviet fighter attacks.[51] These air operations were always dangerous, however, as Rudel points out:

> Gradually I learned all of the details. One often learns through misfortune. We lost planes in areas with sparse ground defenses because we were circling in an area over which German and Soviet artillery were fighting a duel. Areas through which the trajectories of artillery shells passed had to be avoided; otherwise there was the chance of being shot down by accident.

---

*See pp. 39-41.

After some time the Russians succeeded in adapting themselves quite well to antitank attacks from the air. Whenever it was possible to do so, Soviet tanks towed their antiaircraft guns right up to the front. These tanks were also issued smoke cartridges with which to protect themselves by smoke screens or with which to simulate fires, so that the attacking plane would cease its attack on the assumption that the tank was on fire. Experienced air crews soon recognized these maneuvers and could no longer be deceived. A tank which is really burning will soon show the brightest flames, and to simulate such a fire would be a far too dangerous business. In many cases they would explode because the fire reached the ammunition, which is normally present in every tank. It is very unpleasant when a tank explodes immediately after being hit, and when your plane is flying over it at an altitude of only 15 to 30 feet. This happened to me twice within the first few days, when I suddenly found myself flying through a wall of flame and thought, "This is the end for you." However, I got through entirely unscathed, even though the green camouflage paint was scorched off my plane and although fragments from the exploding tank put holes through my bird.

At times we dived to attack from the rear, at other times from the side against the steel colossi. We could not dive at too steep an angle so as to be able to descend almost to the ground without the danger of grounding. If the plane comes down too low, it is hardly possible to prevent scraping the ground, with all of its dangerous consequences. 52*

Antitank air units always try to strike armored vehicles in their weakest points. Since the front side is the most heavily armored part of all tanks, tank drivers always try to offer this side to the enemy if at all possible. The flanks are most vulnerable, but the best point to attack is in the rear, for this is where the engines are located, and, because of the cooling requirements, only a thin sheet of armor plate covers this part. In fact, to increase the cooling action, these thin plates are perforated with large holes, making the target even more inviting. The rear is well

---

*Editor's Note: For a more detailed discussion of Soviet reactions to German air power see Generalleutnant a. D. Klaus Uebe, *Russian Reactions to German Air Power in World War II*, USAF Historical Studies No. 176, Maxwell AFB, Alabama: USAF Historical Division, ASI, July 1964.

worth attacking also because there is the possibility of knocking out the engines or striking the fuel supply. Bluish exhaust vapors can easily be seen from the air while a tank is in operation.*

Other targets of opportunity presented themselves to the antitank flyers. These were Russian soldiers who rode along atop the tanks. In Rudel's words:

> . . . In sectors where they know us, these armored infantrymen invariably jump from the tanks the moment they sight us, even when [the tanks are] traveling at top speed. Each of them thinks he is the next one to be attacked, and Ivan prefers to face attack with firm ground under his feet. 53/

In many instances air units were the only forces at hand which could deliver really destructive fire to repel Soviet armored attacks. This was the case a few days after the opening of the offensive in Army Group South's (Fourth Panzer Army) sector. During that part of ZITADELLE the SS Panzer Corps in extremely heavy fighting had advanced by 8 July approximately 24 miles to a position north of Belgorod. The corps' extended right flank was exposed at this point, which was close to an extensive forested area. The advancing 6th Panzer Division coming from the area east of Belgorod was to envelop and clean out this woods, but, before the encirclement could be accomplished, air and ground reconnaissance detected Soviet troop movements in the sector, principally in the forest. Although it was impossible to ascertain the strength of the forces involved, the area was an ideal site for the launching of an attack deep into the right flank of the Fourth Panzer Army. // If this happened, it would then be impossible for the Wehrmacht to continue its northward drive, at least until the situation in this highly vulnerable sector could be restored in its favor.

---

*Fuel and ammunition are normally stored along the sides of tanks, but the armor plating is also thicker there than in the rear.

/Editor's Note: A further discussion of this topic is to be found in the document: OKL, Luftwaffenfuerhrungsstab Ia, Nr. 03300/43, gKdos. (Op), "Planung fuer die Panzerbekaempfung an der Ostfront im Winter 1943-44" (High Command of the Air Force, Air Force Command Staff for Operations, Top Secret, "Planning for the Combating of Armored Forces on the Eastern Front in the Winter of 1943-44"), F/V/1c, Karlsruhe Document Collection.

//See Maps Nos. 9 and 11.

The German Army was alive to the threat which these Soviet troop movements presented, but it was so fully occupied with its direct combat missions--it had already committed its last reserves in this effort--that no troops could be available in the sector for counteraction if fighting should break out.

On the afternoon of 8 July 1943 the Russians opened their expected attack from the vast forested sector.[54] VIII Air Corps Headquarters had ordered a constant air surveillance of the area and was informed of this event very soon after the enemy armored, motorized, and infantry units got under way. It had prepared for such a contingency by making certain that it could send all available dive-bomber and antitank air units into action there on short notice.

Before the SS Panzer Corps or Fourth Panzer Army Headquarters even knew what was happening, and before the weak German holding force in the area could deploy for the defense, VIII Air Corps units were already on their way to battle the oncoming Soviet forces. The 4th Antitank Air Group of the 9th Dive-Bomber Wing was dispatched with its four squadrons of 16 antitank aircraft each, Henschel (Hs) 129's, twin-engine aircraft armed with a 30-mm. cannon. The group attacked the westward moving Soviet forces* which had already crossed the Donets River and the Belgorod-Kursk railroad line on a broad front.

Squadron after squadron attacked, returned to base (about 20 minutes away by air), reloaded and refueled, and then went back to the attack. This uninterrupted aerial assault lasted about an hour, and not only delayed, but, some places, completely stopped the Russian advance. It also compelled Soviet armored units to face about and hasten back to their jump-off positions in the forests. The Russian forces lost large numbers of tanks and motor vehicles, and suffered heavy casualties. Most of the enemy tanks and vehicles were left burning on the battlefield. It was clear that the new anti-tank cannons aboard the Luftwaffe's planes had great penetrating power and that they very effectively put all of the vehicles struck out of action.

Meanwhile, the noise of battle had drawn the SS Panzer Corps'/ attention to the threatened flank position. Before the need arose for the corps command to take action, however, the matter had been settled by the Luftwaffe. Some time later, when the VIII Air Corps received a

---

*Estimated at the strength of a tank brigade with mounted infantry.

/Editor's Note: This unit is also known as the II SS Panzer Corps.

request from Fourth Panzer Army Headquarters for action against this Soviet offensive force, the corps was able to reply that appropriate action had already been taken. If the air corps had not made aerial reconnaissance and thereby detected the dangerous menace, and if the antitank air units had not been held ready for action, the Soviet armored drive would undoubtedly have had such a grave effect upon German ground operations that the offensive must have been broken off, perhaps for some time to come. This was a case in which the situation was restored by antitank air forces alone, without ground assistance.[55] Once again Luftwaffe units, flexibly directed, had eliminated a threat to the ground forces and thereby settled a crisis which influenced the entire operation.

On 9 July, while the battle in the Army Group South sector was still hotly contested, the Ninth Army's offensive in the northern attack sector bogged down. Faced with numerous, fresh Soviet reserves, the Ninth Army chose to consolidate its positions and to regroup, moving in new units so that it might resume the attack for the final breakthrough on the 12th.

The lead units of the two assault wedges, the Fourth Panzer Army in the south and the Ninth Army in the north, were still about 60 miles apart when the Russians opened their decisive offensive on the 11th from the east and northeast against the projecting German Orel bulge. With vastly superior forces, the Soviet units attacked the Second Panzer Army (left wing of Army Group Center) west of Novosil, east of Bolkhov, and north of Ulyanovo, where they achieved a broad penetration, 1 mile deep, in a sector of the German lines which was held by a weak force of 1 panzer and 14 infantry divisions.[56] This was the turning point of the battle.

Chapter 4

THE AFTERMATH OF ZITADELLE

The Air Battle Over the Orel Salient

On 11 July 1943 vastly superior Soviet forces attacked German positions in the Orel salient from the north, northwest, and east. These Soviet armies had cracked through the thinly manned defenses of the Second Panzer Army east of Zhizdra, Bolkhov, and on either side of Novosil, and, heavily supported by tanks and ground-attack aircraft, were rapidly gaining ground, especially in the southward push in the forested tracts east of Zhizdra. The Soviet Command's obvious goal was to achieve a breakthrough to the south in the direction of Karachev in order to cut off the entire Orel salient and thereby envelop the Ninth Army and the Second Panzer Army in the general vicinity of Orel.[1*]

Meanwhile to the south the Wehrmacht's fortunes appeared brighter. The II SS Panzer Corps (Hausser) of the Fourth Panzer Army and Army Force Kempf had by this time broken through the last enemy positions into the open terrain, and were combining against the Soviet Sixty-Ninth Army. The SS Panzer Corps stood before Porokhorovka, while Army Force Kemp continued its advance toward Korodsha.

Yet, despite the propitious gains in the area of Army Group South, the threat of a repetition of Stalingrad loomed ominously in the Orel sector. To counter this grave menace, Army Group Center was compelled to employ Ninth Army troops which were regrouping for a renewed attack upon Kursk, and to send them forward as fast as possible against the Russian forces which had broken through to the north. Within a matter of hours the area of main effort had shifted from the Ninth Army's offensive sector to the defensive positions of the Second Panzer Army.

The Sixth Air Fleet went immediately into action and committed all of its available forces in support of the currently endangered sector, the area east of Zhizdra, in hope of halting or at least slowing down the enemy advance, thereby gaining time for the arrival of German ground reserves.[2] Air support for German troops in this area was not very effective and could not be effective as long as enemy units were able to

---

*See Map No. 10.

find such excellent cover in local forested tracts. The only thing that could be done was to halt the daylight movement of enemy units, especially the movement of armored forces, on the few roads and paths which cut through the area. It was practically impossible, however, to detect and interdict Russian troop units moving through the woods. Repeatedly the Luftwaffe struck Soviet railheads around Sukhinichi and attacked rail installations and trains along the Kozelsk and Kaluga areas in order to interrupt the forward flow of supplies and reinforcements. Nevertheless, no noticeable results were achieved owing to the paucity of available attack forces and to the adverse weather conditions which temporarily halted all flying operations. [3]

The crisis on the ground snowballed to gigantic proportions. The Ninth Army was forced to call off its attack. In an effort to improve the situation, command over the two armies in the Orel salient, the Ninth Army and the Second Panzer Army, was vested in Generaloberst Walter Model (known as The Defensive Lion of the East).* Reinforcements were hurried into the area by rail and road at top speed.

Units of the 1st Air Division, reinforced by fighter, dive-bomber, and antitank air squadrons which had hitherto been committed under the VIII Air Corps, went into action in front of the southern prong of the German attack against Kursk. This force ceaselessly attacked with bombs and small arms fire all visible Soviet forces and the forested sectors and villages in which enemy forces were suspected of hiding. [4]≠ When a powerful Russian tank force emerged from the forests into open terrain and attempted to cut the Bryansk-Orel railroad, the lifeline of German divisions fighting in the Orel salient at Khotynets, Luftwaffe units attacked and stopped its advance. [5] No German ground forces were then in the immediate area of Khotynets to halt the Soviet tank drive and protect the Bryansk-Orel rail and road routes.

All available antitank air units and fast ground-attack units made repeated low level attacks from morning until nightfall against advancing enemy forces, especially Russian tank formations. Hundreds of Soviet tanks were destroyed by aerial gunfire and the bulk of the oncoming tank

---

*According to Manstein, "He [Model] became increasingly the man whom Hitler assigned to restore a critical situation or to bolster a wavering line, and his performances in the execution of these missions were extraordinary." See Verlorene Siege (Lost Victories) (German edition), p. 489.

≠1st Air Division Commander at this time was Generalmajor Paul Deichmann.

corps was smashed. By the time the Soviet Command was able to launch a raid under cover of darkness, a German flak battalion had already moved into Khotynets from Karachev. For two whole days Luftwaffe forces alone denied Soviet armored units access to the Bryansk-Orel railroad, making it possible to keep the route under German control until the first Wehrmacht ground forces arrived, an achievement which was of decisive importance.[6] By its dashing and annihilating antitank attacks, the Luftwaffe destroyed most of the enemy tanks which had broken through the German lines and were directly threatening the Orel-Karachev rail and road routes (a Soviet armored brigade reached the railroad line but was eliminated before it could consolidate its position).[7*] A teletype message from Generaloberst Model, then in command of the two German armies in the area, read:

> For the first time in military history the Luftwaffe has succeeded, without support by ground forces, in annihilating a tank brigade which had broken through [the defenses].[8]

The steady commitment of 1st Air Division forces along the entire front of the Orel bulge sector, with its innumerable critical points, subjected the flying units to an increasingly excessive strain, resulting in a serious diminution of operational units. Supply difficulties, particularly with respect to fuel, increased at an alarming rate. At the same time, Army requests for air support multiplied because of the heavy losses sustained in antitank guns and other types of artillery. In order to avert any dissipation or dispersal of effort, and to insure that the available airpower would be properly employed in the real areas of main effort, it was unavoidable that in many instances during the frequent and widespread ground crises, the air commander sometimes had to refuse support to the hard-pressed Army forces, even when the requests were fully justified.

Because of heavy losses in antitank artillery, precisely at the time when the Russians were using more and more tanks, emphasis in the employment of German flak units shifted steadily from air defense missions to direct-fire action against incoming Soviet armor. Motorized 8.8-cm. batteries, as well as the light batteries of the 12th Flak Division, were committed in special antitank switch positions with rear buffer positions, and often formed the inflexible, hard core of defenses around which still battle-worthy infantry elements crystallized during the fluctuating tank battles. Few similar cases can be found in the history of the

---

*See figure 27.

Figure 27
Luftwaffe "Destroyers" (Me-110) on an attack mission in the Orel sector

war on the Eastern Front in which a flak division, outside of its real mission of air defense, so often became the decisive bulwark of the ground defense.[9]

The commitment of the bulk of the flak artillery in antitank missions left almost no units available to provide air defense for the ground forces, the natural and original mission of the 12th Flak Division. This left the field clear for Soviet fighters and ground-attack units to operate virtually unhindered against German ground troops, which in turn naturally increased the volume of requests for fighter protection. The entire problem was a vicious circle resulting from the compulsory but illogical use of airpower and a general inadequacy of available air forces.

On 13 July, at a time when the battle for Kursk was approaching its climax and Army Group South was possibly on the brink of a successful conclusion of its operations, Hitler ordered von Kluge and von Manstein to his headquarters for a top-level conference.* There the army commanders were told that the Fuehrer was vexed over the Allied invasion of Sicily on 10 July, and by the mediocre fighting which had been done by the Italians. Furthermore, he feared that landings might be imminent in the Balkans or on the Italian mainland. Because of this, Hitler desired that forces from the Eastern Front be redeployed as soon as practicable to the Mediterranean Theater of Operations. ZITADELLE was to be discontinued.[10/]

In the meantime Soviet armies continued to exert pressure against Army Groups Center, South, and "A." On 17 July enemy forces attacked along the Mius-Donets Front against the Sixth Army and the First Panzer Army as had been expected. Although only local successes were achieved, the threat was clear, which allowed the army group commander to retain for a somewhat longer period the SS Panzer Corps and the 24th Panzer Corps, both of which had been earmarked for redeployment to the Mediterranean Theater.

---

*Editor's Note: Hitler was reluctant to go to the Eastern Theater of Operations and more frequently ordered his commanders to leave their posts and to fly back to his headquarters in East Prussia. Because of this, he was seldom seen in the East, and fell more and more out of touch with conditions there.

/Since the Russians had already committed all of their available strategic reserves in the Kursk sector, victory was almost within Manstein's grasp at this time. See Map No. 9.

In the Orel bulge, in the Ninth Army and Second Panzer Army sectors, the Soviet forces were gaining more and more ground, and by 25 July had reached a point immediately to the east of the city of Orel. In repeated attacks strong German air forces held up the Soviet breakthrough long enough to permit the arrival of adequate ground forces to bring the enemy advance to a halt. However, the line in the Orel bend had been broken in numerous places and had become almost untenable. Crushingly outnumbered by the attacking Red armies, which had increased in the course of the battle to 82 infantry divisions, 14 tank corps, and 12 artillery divisions, besides numerous independent tank units, the German Ninth Army and Second Panzer Army were withdrawn from the Orel salient to a line called the Hagenstellung (Hagen Position) which lay across the base of the salient immediately to the east of Bryansk. [11*]

On 26 July 1943 the two armies received orders to prepare to withdraw from phase line to phase line to the defensive Hagen Position, and on the evening of 31 July (pursuant to Hitler's orders) the movement began, albeit under exceedingly difficult circumstances. Days of continuous rain had turned practically all roads and paths in the Orel sector into quagmires similar to the conditions found during the mud season. [12] Nevertheless, the evacuation movement was carried out in an exemplary manner without any trace of panic.

Anticipating the withdrawal--it was the only possible solution to the situation in view of Hitler's plans and the Soviet strength--the Sixth Air Fleet as early as 18 July had commenced the removal from the sector of all nonessential materiel and other stores to more secure positions west of the Desna River. One great advantage that now became fully evident was the fact that during the preparations for ZITADELLE every effort had been made to commit only motorized combat, technical, and supply units in the Orel area. Therefore, it was possible with a supreme exertion to move out all supplies and equipment of military value in spite of the pressures of time. [13] The only supplies which were not evacuated were bombs, but these were put to practical use in the demolition of airfields, and large quantities of them were turned over to ground force units for the destruction of railroads and bridges. Nothing

*Editor's Note: The Hagen Position ran from the old main line of resistance just east of Kirov, south to just west of Zhizdra, thence to a point west of Karachev, and south to a point a few miles southwest of Dmitrov, where it again joined the old main line of resistance. The withdrawal to this line meant relinquishing an area 63 miles in depth.

which was deemed to be of use to the Russians was left behind.* The large airfield at Orel was demolished with especial thoroughness.[14]

During the evacuation to the Hagen Position, units of the 1st Air Division helped to delay the Soviet frontal pursuit by preventing enemy armored units from overtaking the withdrawing German armies. They also attacked Russian flying units in the air as well as at Soviet advance bases in order to stop or to limit the scope of Soviet air activity in the salient area. Most of the battles against attacking Russian squadrons took place over the main Orel-Bryansk evacuation route.

A few days after the Hagen movement began, the Luftwaffe shifted its area of main effort from the Second Panzer Army sector to that of the Ninth Army in the southern part of the salient (particularly the sector between Chern and the Orel-Kursk road) where Soviet forces were increasing their pressures against the German XXXXVI Corps. The southern perimeter of the front, the Kroma River sector, had to be held as long as possible to prevent attacking Soviet armies from pushing far enough to the north to link up with Red forces advancing from the north toward Khotynets, an obvious attempt to cut off the two withdrawing German armies.[15] Luftwaffe units went into action to fend off the attacks in this sector, and on 1 and 2 August destroyed approximately 150 Soviet tanks.† Because of excellent air support, the hard-fighting 7th, 258th, and 31st Infantry Divisions, although badly outnumbered, were able to hold the lines and to prevent an enemy breakthrough. There were, of course, a number of local crises.

The decisive role played by the 1st Air Division of the Sixth Air Fleet in Operation ZITADELLE, in the bitter defensive battles in and around the city of Orel, and during the dangerous evacuation of the Orel salient, can be best judged by the following figures furnished by the Ninth Army and the Second Panzer Army:

> . . . the 1st Air Division tirelessly switched back and forth between the Ninth Army and the Second Panzer Army to participate in both air and ground battles, an effort which was particularly impressive. In many hours

---

*Prior to departure from each sector Ju-52 units had already completed the air evacuation of as many wounded personnel as possible to the rear areas. The remainder were transported by vehicles.

†General der Panzertruppe Hans von Zorn, Commander of the XXXXVI Corps, was killed by a Soviet air attack on 2 August 1943 in the course of these defensive battles.

of the most major crisis it was this division which turned the scales. In the battle of the Orel bulge its units averaged 5 to 6 missions per day and flew a total of 37,421 missions, achieving 1,733 aerial victories, of which 1,671 were accomplished by fighters alone, with a loss of only 64 German aircraft. In addition to this, Luftwaffe units put out of action more than 1,100 tanks, 1,300 trucks and tracked vehicles, and numerous artillery batteries. The division delivered more than 20,000 tons of bombs on Soviet targets, thereby inflicting heavy casualties and heavy losses in railway rolling stock and supplies.[16]

Complementing the flying units of the 1st Air Division were the batteries of the 12th Flak Division, which brought down 383 Soviet aircraft and two anchored balloons, destroyed 229 Soviet tanks, a large number of fortified positions, heavy weapons, and vehicles, and inflicted heavy personnel losses on Russian units while repelling numerous attacks.[17]

German operations were hampered by additional factors besides the normal military activities of the enemy. At the most crucial moment, while the battle was being bitterly fought all along the front of the two withdrawing armies and while badly weakened German divisions were clinging desperately to their ground in order to carry out an orderly evacuation of the salient, Russian partisan groups hiding in the deep forests in the rear of Army Group Center went into action.

In army and army group Communication Zones, primarily in the general area of Mogilev and the rear area of the Third Panzer Army, partisans set off during the night of 2 August about 5,000 demolition charges, destroying 30 miles of rails and interrupting rail traffic in the demolished sections for periods ranging from 24 to 48 hours. The several German commands were seriously concerned and wondered whether this was only the beginning of partisan operations on a much larger scale. According to Karlheinrich Rieker, the German aviation writer, it was well known that the partisan bands were large enough and well enough equipped to carry out such operations, which could have made it practically impossible for the withdrawing German armies to have mastered their difficulties in the Orel salient. However, after setting off a smaller number of charges (1,763) on the following night, at a moment when the entire supply system was seriously endangered, the increased partisan activities ceased as suddenly as they had begun. This was just another of the many unsolved riddles of the Eastern Theater of Operations.[18]

The Russians opened their expected major assault against the XXXXVI Corps front on 5 August, using more than 200 tanks and powerful infantry units. The immediate objective seemed to be Kromy, where Ninth Army troops had performed so well in evacuating a large ammunition dump, the loss of which would have been a severe blow to the Wehrmacht.* For two days the heaviest sort of fighting raged in the Kromy sector, especially along the front of the 258th Infantry Division, which withstood 15 major attacks. Yet the line held and the Soviet plan to encircle the two armies was frustrated. Much of the success was due to the outstanding support given by the 1st Air Division.

Meanwhile the city of Orel was evacuated on 5 August, after the Second Panzer Army had moved out 53,000 tons of materiel and 20,000 wounded men, and after it had demolished all bridges and military installations of importance in its sector. While this was being accomplished, however, the Soviet Command regrouped its armored forces for another assault, and on the following day caused another severe crisis, this time west of Uzskoye, where they tried to break through that portion of the front (northern) held by Panzer Force Harpe.† Within two days the problem was mastered through stubborn fighting, a shortening of the lines, and by shifting personnel quickly to the endangered area.

Sixth Air Fleet units had been successfully redeployed to airfields back of the new main line of resistance. The evacuation of these squadrons had gone smoothly and with little enemy air interference. Soviet air forces made unexpected attacks upon withdrawing German troops and the important traffic center of Bryansk, through which so many of the evacuating units had to move. These hostile air strikes, particularly those against Bryansk, had little effect upon the overall operation, and Russian flyers made no attacks west of the Desna River. The failure of the Soviet Air Command to strike withdrawing German air units and to make a concentrated effort against Bryansk was a serious shortcoming, and one which had much to do with the success of the German withdrawal. For the Russians it was a rare opportunity lost.[19]

By 9 August the German front had been safely pulled back to a line running roughly north and south of Khotynets. At the southern end of this

---

*See Map No. 11.

†Commanded by General der Panzertruppe Josef Harpe, who later commanded the Ninth Army.

line Soviet forces were still engaged in an attempt to turn the German flank or effect a breakthrough in the Dmitrovsk area, which was held by the 72nd Infantry Division backed by a combat reserve of the 31st Infantry Division.* The attack had begun in this sector on 8 August, and although the Russians employed all of their available forces in the area, the 72nd Division stood as "solid as iron." Red Army units made their last attack on 10 August, an assault which was repulsed with heavy losses. Thereafter the German evacuation movement proceeded smoothly according to plan.

The last phase of the Hagen operation began on 13 August and was virtually completed within three days. Pursuing Soviet armies still tried to break through, and were especially active in frontal engagements on both sides of Karachev. As the German lines became shorter and straighter, however, the defensive power also increased, and for a time the Russians seemed to be unaware that the two armies had reached the final evacuation position, the Hagen Position. All enemy attacks were repulsed as the positions were strengthened and consolidated. By 26 August German units were ready for the expected new large-scale Soviet offensive.[20] The Sixth Air Fleet then gave its units a brief respite for rest and rehabilitation, and by September had its units at their bases ready for new combat missions.

The Battles of Army Group Center in the Autumn and Winter of 1943-44/

The next Russian assaults followed the stereotyped pattern adopted by the Soviet Command in the winter of 1942-43; that is, as soon as they had achieved the collapse of one sector of the front or compelled German forces to withdraw in that area, they would shift their point of main effort to the neighboring sector, thus endeavoring to break up one part of the front after another along the entire line.[21] In accordance with this pattern, once the Germans had abandoned the Orel Salient, the Russians immediately shifted their attack to the next German army to the north, the Fourth Army

*See Maps Nos. 11 and 12.

/Editor's Note: For the sake of continuity, this section has been deliberately inserted here rather than as a separate, subsequent chapter. The withdrawal from the Orel area is, of course, related to the later German retirement behind the Dnepr River. For this cause-and-effect relationship see the section entitled "Air Support During the Withdrawal Behind the Dnepr River," p. 119.

(Generaloberst Gotthard Heinrici), situated in the area west and southwest of Vyazma. Other strong enemy forces attacked in the Third Panzer Army sector in the Belyy sector. Although local withdrawals became necessary, Wehrmacht forces succeeded in preventing breakthroughs in the direction of Smolensk (Minsk-Orsha-Smolensk main highway [Rollbhan]) and Roslavl (the southern main highway artery), which were assumed to be the strategic objectives of the Soviet Command.

The Sixth Air Fleet operated continuously in support of the hard-pressed ground forces in these areas. In the northern sector of Combat Zone Center the newly established 4th Air Division was instructed to support the defensive action of the Fourth Army and the Third Panzer Army east and north of Smolensk.* In the southern sector the 1st Air Division (Generalmajor Paul Deichmann), / which had given such a good account of itself in the Orel salient, was ordered to support the Second and Ninth Armies in the Mosyr-Gomel-Bobruysk area. 22

The Sixth Air Fleet concentrated the various units according to the situation in the current area of main effort, and assigned them to one or the other of the two air divisions. The most critical area was in the Second Army sector, on the southern flank of Army Group Center. With its lines breached at a number of points, the Second Army was compelled in late August and early September to withdraw behind the Desna River and later behind the Dnepr and Sozh Rivers under exceedingly heavy enemy pressure. For a time the army maintained a bridgehead at Gomel, but there was a wide gap separating it from the northern wing of Army Group South (Fourth Panzer Army) which the army was unable to close with the forces at its disposal.

Immediately to the north of the Second Army, the Ninth Army (and with it the Second Panzer Army) was also compelled to withdraw its right (southern) flank across the Desna River to maintain contact with the Second

---

*The 4th Air Division was established in Smolensk at the end of July 1943. Its headquarters were initially in Smolensk, later at Kamari, southwest of Vitebsk, and, after the Soviet breakthrough, at Orsha. It was under the command of Generalmajor Hermann Plocher and later of Generalmajor Franz Reuss. See figures 28 and 29.

/From December 1943 this unit was under the command of Generalmajor Robert Fuchs. See figure 30. For General Deichmann's role in the USAF Historical Division's German Air Force Monograph Project, see the Foreword of this study.

Figure 28
Generaloberst Jeschonnek, General der Flieger Guenther Korten, and Generalmajor Hermann Plocher (the author), being photographed by General-oberst Robert Ritter von Greim

Figure 29
Generalmajor Franz Reuss (left) of the Luftwaffe conferring about an air logistical operation with General der Artillerie Robert Martinek

Army. The Ninth Army still held Bryansk, however, and its northern flank was still to the east of Roslavl. *

To maintain a cohesive front and to release reserves for use in critical areas, Army Group Center ordered a large-scale withdrawal along the entire front to positions extending generally from 30 miles west of Chernigov along the Sozh River, through Lenino to Rudnya, east of Vitebsk, to approximately 15 miles southeast of Nevel. This withdrawal was to be carried out in a series of retrograde movements taking about five weeks to complete, but Soviet pressures forced the army group to complete its withdrawals more quickly than planned.

As was always the case, the Sixth Air Fleet assisted the withdrawing ground forces by supporting the delaying actions by day and by making systematic harassing night raids against Soviet rail and road movements of supplies and replacements bound for the front areas. Bryansk was evacuated on 17 September and Smolensk and Roslavl on the 24th. Despite heavy Soviet pressure all along the front, the armies of Army Group Center were able by 1 October to reach their objectives and reestablish themselves in their new positions.

The Russians achieved a breakthrough at only one point, Lenino, where one of their cavalry corps drove into the German rear before it was halted and almost completely annihilated by German security forces and local reserves, with support from air units. The general area, however, remained a sector of concern to the army group. The German side, with its hopelessly inadequate screening forces, barely managed to hold back the enemy advance, while Soviet units steadily increased the pace of their buildup in the penetration area.

On 6 October enemy forces broke through in the boundary area between Army Groups Center and North, east of Nevel, and advanced beyond Gorodok and Dretun. Only very weak German forces, consisting of security and police units, could be sent into action against the rapidly advancing Russians, who were extending the front northward against the Sixteenth Army of Army Group North, and west and south against the Third Panzer Army. This advance was brought to a halt, by a great effort on the part of the German troops, along a wide arc running from north of Velikiye Luki west and southwest to the area west of Nevel and Dretun, southward nearly to the Dvina River southwest of Gorodok, thence eastward to the old line just north of Vitebsk. †

---

*See Maps Nos. 11 and 12.

†See Chapter 3, pp. 51-53.

Figure 30
General der Flieger Paul Deichmann visiting the Eastern Front, 1943. L. to R.: Capt. Walter v. Kruska, 3rd Gp, 4th Bomber Wg; General Deichmann; Capt. N. Just, 4th Bomber Wg; 1st Lt. Dr. Herbert Klein Ordnance Off.; Capt. Ernst Goepel, Cdr., 1st Gp, 4th Bomber Wg

Figure 31
Capt. Walter Nowotny, German ace with over 200 aerial victories, being congratulated on his achievement, Eastern Front, 1943

Red Army forces did not achieve a strategic breakthrough, although this should have been possible in view of the meager forces the defenders then had available. Heavily engaged in battle with Army Group South, the Soviet Command apparently did not have sufficient forces available for more extensive breakthrough operations against Army Group Center.

In the first half of October German Air Force units in the area concentrated mainly upon the Nevel sector, particularly in providing direct support for the II Luftwaffe Field Corps, which was under attack by greatly superior Soviet forces in the area between Vitebsk and Nevel.* In this crucial period even the He-111 bomber units flew close-support missions, bombing targets on the actual battlefield just ahead of the German lines. This was possible because of the presence of conspicuous and easily memorized terrain features, which practically excluded the possibility of false orientation and, therefore, faulty bombing.

From time to time it became necessary to shift the emphasis in air operations to the northern flank of the Fourth Army because of repeated Soviet attacks. The Russians, in four unsuccessful major breakthrough attacks on either side of the Smolensk-Orsha Rollbahn, tried to fight their way through the north flank of the Fourth Army to Orsha. In each of these attacks, some of which lasted as long as seven days, they committed a tremendously superior number of divisions and massed artillery units. With a gallant effort the Fourth Army beat off these attacks (which occurred late in October, in the first and the last part of November, and in early December) with only slight losses of ground, while it inflicted very heavy casualties upon the attacking enemy force.[23]

Air Operations in Combat Zone Center, Autumn-Winter 1943-44

The Intelligence Branch, Office of the Commander in Chief of the Luftwaffe, reported that on 10 October 1943, 960 aircraft were concentrated in support of the Third Panzer Army. Of this number, 496 bombers, dive-bombers, and ground-attack aircraft attacked Soviet troop concentrations, tanks, and artillery positions in the Nevel area, destroying a number of tanks and artillery pieces, and striking ammunition and fuel depots, while 218 bombers and harassing aircraft attacked partisan groups southeast of Daugavpils, north of Borisov, north of Minsk, and southeast

*See figure 31. See Map No. 11.

of Bialystok. That night, 88 aircraft concentrated for support missions in front of the Third Panzer Army. A total of 52 bombers were dispatched in this effort, 38 of which attacked the rail depot at Velikiye Luki, damaging 7 railway trains and causing a number of fires. Twelve other aircraft attacked road traffic in the Velikiye Luki-Nevel area, while a thirteenth struck the airfields at Smolensk and Yukhnov, setting one sizeable fire at the latter field.[24]

On the following day, 747 aircraft were prepared for operations in support of the Third Panzer Army. A force of 552 bombers, dive-bombers, ground-attack, and fighter-bomber aircraft attacked Soviet concentrations northwest of Chernigov, in the Nevel penetration area, and partisan bands in the Minsk area and southeast of Brest-Litovsk. After dark 114 aircraft concentrated for night missions in the Third Panzer Army area. Eighty of these (bombers and harassing aircraft) were committed against the partisans north of Minsk, against the Smolensk airfield, where a number of fires were observed, against the Velikiye Luki-Toropets and Velikiye Luki-Rzhev railroad lines, where they destroyed a number of trains and locomotives, and against Soviet forces concentrating in the Nevel penetration area.[25]

A force of 908 aircraft was concentrated for action on 12 October and assigned to missions in the boundary area between the Fourth Army and the Third Panzer Army. Of this number, 488 bombers, dive-bombers, ground-attack, and antitank aircraft were dispatched against enemy targets in the Lyubavichi, Propoysk, Orsha, and Nevel areas, where they destroyed a large number of tanks, guns, motor and animal-drawn vehicles, and equipment. More than a hundred bomber and harassing aircraft attacked designated targets in the Baranovichi area, the area southwest of Mogilev, the Okulovo area, and the area west of Nevel. During the night, 81 aircraft were sent out in support of the Third Panzer Army (61 of them attacking targets along the Rzhev-Velikiye Luki and Toropets-Velikiye Luki railroad lines) and against Soviet forces in the Nevel area. Other attacks were carried out in the Smolensk-Serpukhov area and against partisan groups in the areas south of Mogilev and north of Minsk.[26]

On the 13th of October, 829 aircraft were designated for action in front of the left flank of the Fourth Army, 519 of them being committed northeast of Gomel, east of Orsha, and in the Nevel penetration area. One bridge, 36 tanks, and several gun positions were destroyed. On that day 58 bomber, harassing, and reconnaissance aircraft carried out attacks against partisan bands in the areas west of Pinsk, north of Minsk, around

Barany, and south of Polotsk.* After dark 47 aircraft were committed in the general area of Combat Zone Center, without any specific sector of main concentration. About half of them attacked tactical targets west of Smolensk, troop concentrations in the Nevel area, and the Rzhev-Velikiye Luki and Toropets-Velikiye Luki rail lines, while the remainder attacked targets of opportunity.[27]

Reports by the Intelligence Branch of the Luftwaffe showed a commitment of 722 aircraft on 14 October 1943 in support of the northern flank of the Fourth Army. Of this total, 441 bomber, dive-bomber, ground-attack, antitank, and fighter aircraft attacked troop concentrations and positions, and occupied enemy villages in the areas southwest of Chernigov, east of Mogilev, and east of Orsha, damaging or destroying numerous motor vehicles in the process. Nearly a hundred aircraft went into action that night, attacking targets in the area southwest of Smolensk, rail traffic on the Ostashkov-Velikiye Luki-Rzhev line and in Velikiye Luki, airfields at Serpukhov and Kaluga, and various partisan groups in the areas north of Borisov, north of Bobruysk, and north of Minsk.[28]

Reports from 15 October indicated a force of 752 planes for commitment in advance of the northern wing of the Fourth Army. More than half of this force (379 aircraft) was committed against Soviet troop concentrations in the areas north of Chernobyl and Lyubich, south of Chaussy, east of Orsha, and around Nevel, while another 94 bombers and harassing aircraft attacked partisans in the areas northeast of Polotsk, south of Polotsk, south of Vitebsk, north of Bobruysk, and west of Nevel. On the night of 15 October 85 aircraft were committed to action without any

---

*Editor's Note: Since conditions in the north and the south were not particularly favorable for partisan activities, Combat Zone Center remained the principal center of partisan warfare in the East. Some partisan "bands" numbered 500 men in strength, and special units had to be detached to deal with them. As Raymond L. Garthoff points out, "It is often not realized that the partisans usually lived in permanent or semi-permanent camps and in most instances did not melt back to their homes after an engagement." Soviet Military Doctrine, Glencoe, Illinois: The Free Press, 1953, p. 399. See also General der Flieger a.D. Karl Drum, Airpower and Russian Partisan Warfare, USAF Historical Studies No. 177, Maxwell AFB, Alabama: USAF Historical Division, RSI, March 1962, pp. 6-11, and U.S. Department of the Army, Rear Area Security in Russia: The Soviet Second Front Behind the German Lines, DA Pam. No. 20-240, Washington: OCMH, EUCOM Historical Division, July 1951.

specific main area of concentration. This force attacked tactical targets northeast of Orsha, at Serpukhov, Kaluga, and Yukhnov, the Rzhev-Velikiye Luki and Velikiye Luki-Toropets railroad lines, and partisan "bands" in the forested tracts southeast of Minsk and northwest of Borisov. Seven Soviet railway trains were also damaged in the course of these attacks.[29]

These few reports reveal the extent to which available air units were utilized in Combat Zone Center in extremely close cooperation with Army Group Center and the Sixth Air Fleet, which involved constantly changing areas of main effort and almost exclusive assignment to direct support roles.[30]

The majority of the flak batteries assigned to the Sixth Air Fleet during the retrograde movements in the central sector in late 1943 were also committed in direct-support missions, in this case to provide fire for German ground forces. In costly battles these batteries made a considerable contribution to the overall defensive success which was finally achieved.

Worthy of special mention are the operations of the 12th Flak Division in the Gomel area and the operations of the 18th Flak Division in the battles fought on both sides of the Orsha-Smolensk highway (Rollbahn), as well as those in the Vitebsk area along the Luchessa River and on either side of the Rudnya-Vitebsk road. In this latter action, motorized battalions, including some from the 10th Flak Brigade, made decisively important contributions to the defeat of Soviet breakthrough attempts.

At the end of October, after the Luftwaffe field divisions had been transferred to Army control, III Luftwaffe Field Corps Headquarters was dissolved and the staff elements were used to reestablish the II Flak Corps Headquarters.[31]* The II Flak Corps was assigned on 3 November 1943 to the Sixth Air Fleet with orders to support Army Group Center. Generalleutnant Job Oldebrecht assumed command of the corps at its headquarters in Bobruysk.[32]

The II Flak Corps was comprised of the 12th Flak Division (command post at Bobruysk), which had the responsibility of supporting the Second and Ninth Armies; the 18th Flak Division (command post at Orsha),

---

*The original II Flak Corps had been dissolved in April 1942.

which was to provide support for the Fourth Army; the 10th Flak Brigade (command post at Vitebsk), which had the mission of supporting the Third Panzer Army; and the 27th Flak Division (command post at Minsk), which was responsible for the protection of the airfields, main supply areas, and similar objectives of the enemy in the German rear areas.

At the end of October deteriorating weather conditions considerably restricted air operations, and in November and December only a few days were suitable for operations in support of fighting German infantrymen. During this period Luftwaffe units carried out attacks mainly in the Nevel penetration area (Third Panzer Army sector), and around Rechitan (Second Army sector). [33*]

The Luftwaffe was able to continue its successful antipartisan operations during the closing months of 1943, since the partisans had only the most meager antiaircraft defenses, and German air units could thus take advantage of periods of bad weather for low level attacks. The frequent interruption of rail traffic by partisans and the increasing impassibility of roads due to adverse weather necessitated an increase in logistical support by air. This was especially true in the case of shipments of ammunition and special weapons urgently needed by combat units. As in the past, aircraft returning from their supply missions were used for the speedy evacuation of the wounded.

In Combat Zone Center the last three months of the year 1943 were characterized by the almost ceaseless attacks launched first at one place and then another by the First and Third White Russian Army Groups. The enemy's objective was to outflank Army Group Center while simultaneously disintegrating its front by means of frontal breakthrough attacks. The flank attacks were intended to force the German army group to overextend its lines, while the attacks directed at Mogilev and Orsha were designed to cut the major lateral communications forming the backbone of the German logistical network. A further, and quite obvious, intention of the Soviet Command was to contain the German forces by continuous attacks and to wear them down, while preventing any transfers to Combat Zone South, the area of main effort in the overall Soviet offensive plan. [34]

---

*On 9 December the Luftwaffe carried out day and night attacks against Soviet troop movements in the Nevel area, and destroyed 33 enemy aircraft in the course of these operations. See Von Rohden Reports, Karlsruhe Document Collection.

An extraordinarily large share of the credit for the individual defensive successes achieved in Combat Zone Center was due to the operations of the Sixth Air Fleet. This force, commanded by Generaloberst Ritter von Greim, supported the operations of Army Group Center, even under difficult situations. When the Sixth Air Fleet was at its maximum strength for the year (1943), it had only 3 fighter, 3 dive-bomber, and 5 bomber groups. At full strength--these units never actually reached this level--the air fleet would have represented a force of more than 300 aircraft.[35] The badly understrength but extremely active units by their tireless operations, many of which involved combat missions in widely separated areas of crisis on the same day, provided the desperate ground forces with the vital support needed to withstand the enemy attacks. This air support, indeed, helped them to master many a seemingly hopeless situation.[36]

<u>Air Support During the Withdrawal Behind the Dnepr River</u>*

On 10 July 1943, before Operation <u>ZITADELLE</u> was called off and the Orel salient became critically endangered, the 27th and 53rd Bomber Wings and one group of the 52nd Fighter Wing had been transferred from the VIII Air Corps to the IV Air Corps behind the Mius River line.† The Fourth Air Fleet, which was unable to support Operation <u>ZITADELLE</u> during those days because of weather conditions, was requested to take action in the Mius-Donets River area in order to break up detected Soviet concentrations preparing for an attack.[37]

After a massive heavy artillery preparation, the Russians, supported by strong air forces, launched on 17 July their expected offensive along the Mius-Donets line. In the first onslaught they achieved a deep penetration into the sectors of the Sixth Army†† (General der Infanterie Karl Hollidt), along the Mius River, and the First Panzer Army (Generaloberst Eberhard von Mackensen),** holding the Donets River line to the north. Once again the Luftwaffe was the first effective means available to the German Command to halt the Soviet penetration. With the support

---

*<u>Editor's Note</u>: In the original German manuscript this section followed the Orel salient action (see footnote, p. 107).

†See Maps Nos. 11 and 12.

††The Sixth Army was reconstituted after the original unit bearing this number was destroyed at Stalingrad in early 1943.

**Son of Field Marshal August von Mackensen (officer of the "Death's Head" Hussars) who served as Adjutant-General to Kaiser Wilhelm during World War I.

of IV Air Corps (Fourth Air Fleet) units under the command of General der Flieger Kurt Pflugbeil, the two German armies managed by the end of July to temporarily seal off the dangerous enemy inroad. The numerous aircraft shot down were evidence of the enemy's strong reliance upon airpower, particularly fighter and ground-attack aircraft, in support of the ground operations.[38]

Records of the Fourth Air Fleet describe the defensive battle along the Sixth Army front, a contest which was waged with unabated fury. After prisoner of war statements indicated that Soviet attacks were imminent in the Taganrog sector, the IV Air Corps committed strong air units to support the Army forces in the area. When the attack began on 18 July it was countered by immediate German thrusts to clean out the enemy gains along the Mius and Donets Rivers. Air units supporting the counterattacks destroyed three and damaged several more Soviet tanks, and brought down 18 enemy aircraft. Fighters of the Royal Rumanian Air Corps shot down 17 Russian planes in advance of the Mius, and on 19 July the IV Air Corps destroyed an additional 17 enemy aircraft in the air.[39]

Soviet ground forces continued their assault on 20 July, placing main emphasis in the Donets area along the front of the First Panzer Army. On that day the IV Air Corps relieved the pressures on German Army troops by sweeping the skies clear of enemy aircraft, shooting down 15 in the process. Flyers of the IV Air Corps continued their successful operations throughout the month of July, during which time they were able to substantially increase the number of rail interdiction missions. The bulk of the IV Air Corps was committed throughout the month at the point of enemy penetration northwest of Kuybyshevo, flying more than 1,000 support sorties.

On 30 July the Sixth Army counterattacked and restored the situation in the Kuybyshevo area, reestablishing the old main line of resistance. Although this action was met by tenacious Soviet resistance, including strong tank forces, the operation was a decided success. The 16th Panzer Division, in conjunction with left flank units of the XXXIX Corps, drove ahead and captured Malopetrovskiy and Grigoryevka, while the 23rd Panzer cleaned out the Soviet forces enveloped south of Mogilskiy. These undertakings were carried out despite torrential thundershowers which hampered all ground and even air operations. Whenever possible, however, IV Air

Corps units flew air defense and close support missions. 40 In the course of these attacks numerous Soviet tanks and aircraft were destroyed.*

With the reestablishment of the old main line of resistance in the Kuybyshevo sector the battle along the Mius River ended for the time. Nevertheless, the Second Panzer Army front on the Donets remained a source of serious concern to the German Command.† On 2 August reconnaissance units detected sizeable Russian forces massing in the Balakleya-Andreyevka area, probably assembling for a renewed assault upon the left wing of Army Group South. Luftwaffe units were immediately called in--some had preceded the request--and attacked these large enemy units, inflicting heavy personnel and materiel losses upon them and destroying a number of Soviet aircraft. 41 But, despite these local successes, the initiative had passed over to the Red Army along the front of Army Group South, where a most modest assessment indicated that Russian forces outnumbered the Germans by a ratio of seven to one.

After the termination of ZITADELLE operations near Belgorod on 17 July, fighting continued in that sector. Since there was no way to conceal the withdrawal of sizeable panzer and Luftwaffe units, it was little wonder that the Russians endeavored to exploit the situation by launching a major attack of their own to the east of Kharkov in the Don River bend. Under this tremendous pressure, the forces of Army Force Kempf and the Fourth Panzer Army barely managed to hold their positions.

At this time the VIII Air Corps had under its command only the Hungarian flying division and a few German units. Yet, with what was available, it supported the defenses of the Sixth Army and the Second Panzer Army as well as it could, and rendered outstanding service in attacking Soviet crossing points along the Donets River. These bridge sites could be seen from afar by the piles of material and by the approach roads which had been cut through the swampy forest. VIII Air Corps units attacked these points every day, usually in the morning, to destroy all of the landing ramps and bridge sections which had been constructed during

---

*Because of their great strength, Soviet forces could attack in many places at once, and they appeared to be able to replace personnel, tank, and aircraft losses almost at once.

†While the I Air Corps was committed in the Kuban area, the IV Air Corps and the Rumanian Air Corps were employed along the Mius River line.

the night.* Throughout the remainder of the day VIII Air Corps squadrons were so fully occupied that they were not able to fulfill the urgent requests for air support in all of the hotly contested sectors. Sometimes no air forces were available at all for days at a time except the corps' tactical reconnaissance squadron and the Hungarian air division, since the Fourth Air Fleet had concentrated in the Mius River sector all units not fighting in the Orel area.

Units were continually shuffled back and forth. Scarcely had the situation farther to the south been stabilized than the Soviet forces would break through in some other sector of the front, which required immediate air support to restore the lines. The 77th Dive-Bomber Wing, the only really permanent component of the VIII Air Corps, was transferred to the IV Air Corps area at Kramatorsk on 16 July 1943, to Stalino on 22 July, back to Kramatorsk on 25 July, to Makeyevka on 27 July, and on 3 August was returned to the VIII Air Corps at Tolokonoye because air support was most urgently needed east of Kharkov and at Belgorod.[42]

On 3 August Russian forces, supported by 50 to 60 tanks and strong air forces, launched a powerful attack from the vicinity of Bogorodichnoye against the First Panzer Army and, at the same time, against the front of Army Group South west of Belgorod, held by the right wing of the Fourth Panzer Army.† In the latter area, Red Army troops, supported by 200 tanks, breached the German main line of resistance on a broad front between the western reaches of the Donets River and Butovo, and, by repeated heavy blows, drove a deep wedge between the Fourth Panzer Army and Army Force Kempf to its south. This advance against the right wing of the Fourth Panzer Army was brought to a stop in a few days at a line extending approximately from Shopini, north of Belgorod, to Rakovo. In this action the VIII Air Corps played a leading role, destroying 25 tanks and 56 aircraft on the opening day of battle†† and achieving excellent results on the next day against Soviet forces which had penetrated into the area south and southwest of Tomarovka.[43] During the latter encounter VIII Air Corps units destroyed

---

*Luftwaffe attacks at Zmiyev were a complete success. They churned up the muddy roads with bombs, making the bridge approaches impassable for Soviet troops and allowing German reserves to be transferred to the Kharkov sector.

†At this time Army Group South consisted of the Fourth Panzer Army and Army Group Kempf, the latter of which was redesignated on 15 August 1943 as the Eighth Army.

††Seven of these planes were shot down by Hungarian pilots.

114 enemy tanks and 67 aircraft (seven aircraft being shot down by flak artillery).[44]

In the ensuing days Army Force Kempf came under heavy attack as the Russians captured the sector to the east and southeast of Belgorod. In these attacks, enemy casualties and materiel losses were enormous, but the Soviet Command never hesitated for a moment to throw new unit after new unit into the engagements, regardless of the cost in human life.

On 5 August the VIII Air Corps destroyed 26 tanks in the area between Belgorod and Tomarovka in the course of the initial Soviet assault, and by the end of the day accounted for 60 tanks and 32 aircraft. Two days later Luftwaffe flyers added another 44 Soviet tanks to the list of destroyed equipment. Yet, bright as these achievements were, the situation for Army Group South remained highly tense and critical, since months of heavy fighting and the recent subjection to the most determined enemy attacks had seriously weakened both the Fourth Panzer Army and Army Force Kempf. Moreover, there was a great danger that Red forces would be able to capture the main communication route in the area, the Belgorod-Kharkov Rollbahn, thereby enabling Soviet armored and motorized units to plunge on to Kharkov itself. It was therefore obvious that Soviet forces could not be held back for any considerable period unless the German main line of resistance drew back behind the Dnepr River. The immediate, and only logical, recourse in the sector was to pull back toward Kharkov by fighting a series of delaying actions.*

To the south, in the Donets-Mius sector, Russian forces had also attacked the front of the Sixth Army. On 4 August, after a heavy artillery preparation, strong Soviet assault units struck the Mius position and, supported by 60 tanks and numerous ground-attack aircraft, advanced on a seven-mile front from the area east of Dmitriyevka. Although this attack was pursued with great determination for about two days, the Sixth Army managed to hold its line intact, inflicting heavy casualties upon the enemy, and destroying more than 50 tanks. During these operations Rumanian air units bombed and strafed Soviet villages across the Mius River and shot down seven enemy aircraft, thus adding to the equally impressive results achieved by flak units.[45]

---

*Editor's Note: During the delaying actions south of Belgorod, German forces of the XI Corps withdrew in eight successive stages, each about five miles in depth, to the Kharkov area, a masterful feat. All other units north and west of Kharkov withdrew carefully to prepared positions, losing remarkably few troops in the process.

By 6 August the situation had worsened around Belgorod. Soviet forces had reached Bogodukhov and advanced rapidly beyond it with sizeable armored units. To avoid immediate annihilation the XI Corps of Army Force Kempf was obliged to withdraw from its position near Belgorod in the direction of Kharkov. Within two days Soviet forces had widened the breach between Fourth Panzer Army and Army Force Kempf units to 34 miles. The way to Poltava seemed to be open. It appeared that the Russians intended to push to the Dnepr River and thence to the south, thereby cutting off all German units situated just north of the Sea of Azov. The III Panzer Corps (II SS Panzer Division and 3rd Panzer Division) was ordered to the Kharkov area to prepare for a defensive stand.

While Army Force Kempf was still engaged in its desperate withdrawal operation, Soviet advance units on 9 August broke through the thin line of the XI Corps along the Rollbahn and threatened to roll up the entire corps. The corps commander then hastily organized several defense points, studded with antitank units, and took personal control at the point of main effort. In a short time the attack was brought to a halt. Crucial to the defense were fighter sweeps made by the VIII Air Corps which very soon eradicated the Soviet air support and enabled German ground forces to concentrate upon their primary defense mission. Luftwaffe flak units also rendered an invaluable service by knocking out numerous Russian tanks.

During the desperate action the 6th Panzer Division, situated on the left flank of the XI Corps, was obliged to defend a front which had shortly before been held by two divisions. Only the accurate strikes by antitank air forces of the Luftwaffe enabled it to hold its position and to turn back the approaching Soviet units.*

On 12 August an extremely tense situation developed for Army Force Kempf as the Red Army opened a heavy attack to the east and southeast of Kharkov. With the German forces in and around Kharkov threatened with encirclement, General Kempf was anxious to withdraw. Hitler, however, ordered the city to be held at all costs, presumably

---

*Editor's Note: Heavy personnel losses and 60 tanks destroyed were a part of the price paid by the Soviets for this attack, which was stopped cold at the Lopan River. On the following evening (10 August 1943) the division withdrew to prepared positions about six miles to the rear.

because of international policy considerations.* While fighting continued around Kharkov the Red Army opened a new assault on 16 August on both sides of Izyum and Kuybyshevo. Both the First Panzer Army and the Sixth Army of Army Group "A" had great difficulty in holding their positions. Strong forces of the IV Air Corps and ground-attack units of the Rumanian Air Corps supported them in their bitter defensive battles, shooting down 29 enemy planes.[46]

The Kharkov area came under attack from two directions. A strong westward assault was launched from the Chuguyev area to the east, while another powerful Soviet force moved southward toward the area east of Bogodukhov from the sector between Volchansk and Belgorod. These attacks compressed the Eighth Army‡ ever more closely around the city of Kharkov. Meanwhile, fighters of the VIII Air Corps supported the defenses by destroying 14 Soviet aircraft, while flak units downed another 8 planes.[47]

By 20 August the situation around Kharkov had deteriorated considerably as a result of a strong Soviet drive between Akhtyrka and Bogodukhov in the direction of Poltava. The Soviet Command had had little success in frontal assaults on the city and hoped to cut off the salient by a pincers movement across the narrowest point of the bulge, the so-called bottleneck. Fortunately for the defenders, the attack toward Poltava was blunted by a counterattack to the northeast by the XXIV Panzer Corps of the Fourth Panzer Army. Air support by the bulk of the VIII Air Corps' available forces resulted in the destruction of 32 enemy tanks, 2 armored cars, and 34 aircraft.

On this same day Red Army units attacked the Sixth Army front west of the Mius River, an operation which turned out to be costly for Soviet forces, and yielded very little in gains. IV Air Corps flying and flak forces strengthened the defense and destroyed 2 tanks and 38 aircraft.[48]

---

*Editor's Note: According to Manstein, Hitler feared that the loss of Kharkov might possibly have an adverse effect upon the official positions of Turkey and Bulgaria toward Germany. See Manstein, Lost Victories, p. 518. General der Panzertruppe Franz Werner Kempf was removed from his post on 15 August 1943 for expressing a desire to evacuate Kharkov. He was replaced immediately by General der Panzertruppe Erhard Raus, and shortly thereafter by General der Infanterie Otto Woehler. Manstein agreed with this change.

‡As of 15 August 1943 the newly designated name of Army Force Kempf.

Unfortunately for the Wehrmacht, all of these defensive achievements were quite temporary in character, since the Russians quickly sent in fresh units and renewed their onslaughts, losing heavily in men and materiel, but giving the German forces little respite.

Units of the Fourth Air Fleet sent their forces again and again into action in support of the Army. Emphasis in these operations had to be constantly shifted in accordance with the various crises which developed, so that individual units often had to be transferred back and forth from one sector to another on very short notice. On a given day they might be operating under the IV Air Corps at the Mius River, on the next under the VIII Air Corps in the Kharkov-Poltava area in support of the Eighth Army, and on the following day in some other sector where a new and more dangerous crisis had developed.

Although seriously weakened by long and arduous weeks of combat, the remaining units of the VIII Air Corps contributed more than their share in the defensive battles of Army Group South, a contribution which required the highest degree of devotion to duty and outstanding improvisation in every aspect of military aviation.

Frequently air units which were dispatched to relieve pressures on the ground forces arrived at the latest possible moment. Actually, this made their attacks particularly effective, for the entire disposition of enemy forces could thus be clearly seen and concentrated attacks carried out. Soviet units usually assembled during the afternoon under cover of hollows, ravines, or other protective terrain features. The masses of men and equipment assembled offered excellent targets for dive-bombing attacks, which usually broke up the formation so that the enemy ground attack had to be postponed. German ground forces thus enjoyed a brief respite from fighting.

An example of this sort of Luftwaffe operation occurred when the 27th Bomber Group, based on airfields at Uman, after returning from a bombing mission in a southern sector of the front, was dispatched late in the afternoon to strike a Soviet assembly area. Despite the strain imposed upon the aircrews by additional combat missions, it was essential to strike the target, for it was a threatening group of armored vehicles which seemed "ripe" for an attack. This large Soviet tank force had been observed just to the west of Kharkov at Olshany by General der Panzertruppe Erhard Raus,* and from all indications it seemed to be concentrating

---

*Briefly in command of the Eighth Army (15 August 1943) after Kempf was relieved and before General Woehler assumed command.

for an attack. German ground forces in the area were far too weak to repel the expected assault, and there was a great danger that if the coming attack succeeded the line at Kharkov would be breached from the west, thereby isolating German units to the east.

All of the VIII Air Corps' units were still out on missions and could not arrive in time for the necessary action. Corps headquarters therefore contacted the commander of the bomber group by telephone and requested support, even though it had no actual command authority over this particular unit. The group commander grasped the special significance of the situation and undertook the combat mission. Having no suitable bombs at his base, he ordered his planes to load up with aerial mines. Attacking with these, the group swept the Soviet tank force, which was caught just as it was moving forward to attack, completely annihilating it. According to General Raus, the blast effect of the aerial mines was "terrific," the Soviet tanks being "blown over and their infantrymen annihilated."[49]

Again and again during these anxious weeks of crisis the weakened Luftwaffe units were the only available means by which effective support could be given to the ground forces. It is therefore only natural that these ceaseless operations, many of which involved excessively frequent transfers, would result in a marked decrease in operability of both ground service and flying units, and this at a time when the ground forces' needs and requests for air support were increasing at an immense pace. Both the newly designated Eighth Army and the Fourth Panzer Army frequently made impossible requests of the VIII Air Corps; yet, all things being considered, they could often do little else since they really had no other recourse.

Although reconnaissance units were tireless in carrying out their missions to provide the necessary data for Army and Luftwaffe forces, the few available fighter units of the 52nd Fighter Wing had a formidable task in combating the rapidly increasing number of enemy fighter and ground-attack forces, Yet, although the Soviet forces had great numerical superiority, they were never qualitatively superior in combat, a fact which could be attributed either to low training standards for Soviet flying schools, or to a healthy respect, bordering at times on outright fear, of German airmen. In any case, it was known that the Soviet Eighth Air Army, which was committed against the German Eighth Air Corps, had not yet recovered from the beating it had taken in the air battle at Kharkov on 7 July 1943.[50] At least it had failed, despite its numerical superiority and the pronounced weakness of German units, to develop into an opponent worthy of respect.

On the ground the Soviet Command continued to commit great numbers of troops and armored equipment in combat, often losing and replacing entire units in a relatively short time. Corresponding German losses were much lighter, yet the overall effect was more serious for the Wehrmacht, since the German Command had no large pool of replacements with which it could offset the steadily rising attrition rate. This was a problem which beset every German commander on the front, and played an important role in considerations with respect to Kharkov.

Although during the course of the war the possession of the city of Kharkov had been so often and so hotly contested, Army Group South was not prepared to lose an entire army in its defense, especially in 1943. Consequently, German forces were withdrawn from the area on 22 August, a move which allowed the Eighth Army to avoid encirclement and to redeploy its forces for the reinforcement of its threatened flanks.* On this same day the southern sector of the Eastern Front was subjected to a strong enemy assault. In this crisis the First Panzer Army and Sixth Army had been able to prevent a serious breakthrough on the Donets River front, but, in withstanding these heavy attacks, the fighting power of their units had been sapped.† So serious was this situation that the army group commanders requested a meeting with Hitler to discuss the possibility of some radical changes in the defensive arrangements.

On 27 August Hitler finally left his headquarters in East Prussia and came to Vinnitsa in the southwestern Ukraine to discuss matters with von Kluge and von Manstein. After carefully explaining the situation, Manstein told the Fuehrer that only two alternatives were open: (1) an immediate reinforcement of the southern front with at least 12 fresh, combat-ready divisions, or (2) to abandon the Donets River area in order to shorten the lines and permit a better utilization of manpower for the defense. At first Hitler attempted to pacify the commanders by promising to move "all available" units not urgently required by Army Groups North and Center to the southern sector. But, before such a possibility could be explored, Red Army units opened a heavy attack upon Army Group Center, tying down all of the forces in that area. Hitler then suggested that everyone take a "wait and see" attitude for the time being.

---

*Editor's Note: A new, but purely provisional, front was established on 27 August for units of Army Group South, extending approximately from Kharkov to Sumy.

†The Sixth Army, consisting of 1 panzer and 10 infantry divisions, was pitted against an enemy force of 31 infantry divisions, 2 mechanized corps, 7 tank brigades, 7 additional tank regiments with 400 tanks, and some independent battalions.

The Soviet Command, however, gave the Wehrmacht no rest, and continued to attack in great strength, especially on the Donets-Mius front. While the Fourth Panzer Army and the Eighth Army had been able by brilliant defensive action and daring counterattacks, and with constant support by the VIII Air Corps, to maintain a reasonably cohesive front in the Poltava-Kharkov sector, the situation was more immediately threatening in the south. Here, the overwhelming pressures exerted against the Sixth Army front had led to the loss of the Mius River line, and this despite all possible support by the IV Air Corps. Consequently, the XXIX Corps, holding the right flank along the coast, was threatened with encirclement.

The Red Army's capture of Taganrog on 29 August made it clear to the German Command that the Mius position could not be regained and that the present line could not be held.* Therefore, the army group ordered the Sixth Army on 31 August to withdraw to the west behind the line known as the Tortoise Position (Schildkroetenstellung). This became the first step in the evacuation of the entire Donets area, an industrial region much desired by the Soviet Union.

On 3 September Hitler again attempted to dispel the fears and anxieties of Manstein and Kluge with respect to the ominous threats of the Red Army along their fronts by promising to reinforce the southern area with units to be withdrawn from quieter sectors, such as the area of Army Group North. These proposals were not greeted with much enthusiasm by the two army group commanders, since they regarded them as impossible to fulfill. They did, however, hope that some sort of unified command might be established to coordinate matters in the Eastern Theater of Operations. All discussions concerning the creation of a Commander in Chief East (Oberbefehlshaber Ost), comparable to the arrangement in the Mediterranean Theater, were quickly and sharply rejected by the Fuehrer.

As Manstein expected, the situation along the southern front continued to deteriorate, forcing the German Command to make a decision about a withdrawal. A meeting was arranged for the 8th to discuss the grave issues involved. Hitler summoned not only von Kluge and Manstein, but also Field Marshal von Kleist, Commander in Chief of Army Group "A,"

---

*Since the Fourth Air Fleet was required to commit its forces simultaneously in the Mius River area, at Taganrog, and in the First Panzer Army sector along the Donets River, units had to be constantly shuffled from one area to another. This weakened the larger units by dissipating their power, and made control over them difficult. However, many a command crisis was mastered by excellent communication lines, which Luftwaffe signal units always managed to reestablish.

and Generaloberst Ruoff, Commander of the Seventeenth Army. The army leaders quickly agreed that all Wehrmacht forces should be immediately withdrawn in the southern area to positions behind the Dnepr River.

Hitler issued the order on 15 September for the withdrawal of Army Group "A" (Sixth and Seventeenth Armies and Rumanian Third Army) and Army Group South (Eighth Army and First and Fourth Panzer Armies) to a line extending from Melitopol to the Dnepr River bend at Zaporozhye, and thence along the Dnepr to a point just north of Kiev. During the previous night the Seventeenth Army had already begun its evacuation of the Kuban Bridgehead.[51]*

This retrograde movement became a continuous battle of withdrawal, with frequent delaying actions and moments of extreme crisis. The speed of the operation depended largely upon the fighting power of individual units and on favorable terrain features which could be used for defensive purposes. The Russian civil populace was evacuated during the withdrawal from an area extending eastward from the Dnepr River to a depth of about 18 miles in order to deny Soviet forces fresh sources of replacements and laborers.ƒ These civilians were not driven out, but were allowed to take their cattle, horses, and all moveable goods with them as long as it could be transported. These long columns moved westward in convoy with German combat and transport units, leaving nothing of human or material value behind for the pursuing Red Army.[52]

The movement promised to be relatively simple in the Sixth Army sector, but the withdrawal of the Eighth Army and the First and Fourth

---

*See pp. 24-25.

ƒEditor's Note: It was standard Soviet practice to round up all available men in combat areas (including older men) for use in military or labor forces. Grain, cattle, and other commodities were also confiscated from the civil populace for the use of the Red Army. Because of this, some Russians began their westward treks before the Germans ordered a general withdrawal. See Manstein, Lost Victories, pp. 539-540. A cardinal fault of German policy in the East was the failure to understand and to properly exploit the native population's disaffection for the Soviet regime. Excesses committed by German police and political units--these were the principal offenders--then turned the Russians away from the Wehrmacht, which they had once greeted as "liberators," and into the arms of the Soviet government, which, although brutish and oppressive, was at least a native oppressor.

Panzer Armies was much more complicated. The latter three armies held a front more than 450 miles in length, behind which were only five adequate crossing points over the Dnepr. To make matters worse, because of the disposition of forces and the natural terrain features, the Eighth Army and the First Panzer Army did not dare withdraw to the west in a vertical line running north and south, but had to effect their withdrawal along a slanting line running from the northwest to the southeast. The entire operation was completed by 30 September 1943, and with more modest losses to the Wehrmacht than had been anticipated by the German Command.*

Once across the Dnepr River, German forces turned their energies to strengthening and improving the defenses by establishing field fortifications in depth. As long as mild weather prevailed, however, the river presented the greatest natural obstacle to an enemy attack. 53/ Just as the major Russian rivers, the Don, the Volga, the Kuban, and the Terek, had influenced the conduct of operations during the German advance in 1942, so during the Wehrmacht's withdrawal in 1943 a determining factor was again the principal rivers along which defensive lines could be established, such as the Don, Mius, Seym, Donets, and Dnepr.

In the final stages of the withdrawal behind the Dnepr, rapidly pursuing Red Army units had been able at a few points to cross the river with the retreating German ground forces and to establish small bridgeheads west of the river, halfway between Dnepropetrovsk and Kremenchug, and north of Kanev to the west of Pereyslav. Owing to the lack of combat reserves, German forces in the area were unable to eliminate these small centers of enemy penetration. Although initially of minor significance, these bridgeheads were to become decisively important as staging areas for coming enemy offensives.

---

*200,000 wounded men were also evacuated during this operation.

/Editor's Note: The strength and concentration of German forces behind the Dnepr River was insufficient to make the water body more than an obstacle to enemy assault forces. Hitler's reluctance to allow an earlier build-up along this line was to have dire consequences. During the winter most of the Dnepr freezes to a sufficient depth to support tanks. For a more detailed discussion of Soviet terrain see U.S. Department of the Army, Terrain Factors in the Russian Campaign, DA Pam. No. 20-290, Washington: OCMH, EUCOM Historical Division, July 1951, and Generalleutnant a.D. Hermann Plocher, The German Air Force versus Russia, 1941, USAF Historical Studies No. 153, Maxwell AFB, Alabama: USAF Historical Division, ASI, July 1965.

During all of the withdrawal battles the Fourth Air Fleet closely supported Army Groups "A" and South, especially the latter, sending its squadrons again and again into action against targets on the battlefield, particularly tanks. Operations of this sort became known as fire-fighting tactics and air units which carried them out were called fire brigades.* Air units of the First Air Fleet were transferred back and forth between its air corps as the ground situation and air support requirements demanded.[54] The active role played by Luftwaffe organizations in halting and delaying the pursuit of the Red Army at the Dnepr is described in the following account by Colonel Rudel:

> By now it was high time to evacuate our field and we took off after setting fire to all inoperable aircraft which had to be left behind. . . . We flew west-northwest by compass. After a while we flew low over a road and met heavy antiaircraft fire from a large motorized column traveling beneath us under tank escort. We dispersed and circled the vehicles. There were Soviet tanks and trucks, most of them American models, so they were obviously Russian. . . . We climbed higher and I gave the order to attack the antiaircraft guns, which had to be put out of action first so that we could have time for our low level attacks.
>
> After silencing most of the antiaircraft guns we spread along the column and destroyed all vehicles without exception. It was darkening, and the entire road presented the appearance of a flaming serpent. . . . Hardly one of them escaped and once again the Russians must have lost a considerable quantity of material. But what was that? I flew to the head of the column, to the first three or four trucks. Each of them had our flag painted on its hood. These trucks were German models, and 200 yards up the road someone was firing white signal flares, the identification signal for our own troops. It was a long time since I had felt as badly as I did at that moment. . . . Had it been a German column after all? Everything was in flames. But why were we fired upon so heavily from the vehicles? How was it that the trucks had been American models? And, I had definitely seen men in brownish-green uniforms running. . . .

---

*Shortages of heavy weapons, especially field artillery, made Luftwaffe ground-attack forces the only available means for stopping large-scale armored attacks.

> It was already fairly dark by the time we reached base at Pavlovgrad. Not one of us said a word. We were all troubled by the same thought; had it really been a German column after all? . . .
>
> Toward midnight an Army soldier arrived and my staff officer shook me out of my exceptionally restless sleep, telling me it was important. Our Army comrades wanted to express their gratitude because they had been able to escape that day because of our help. They told us how a Soviet column had caught up with their vehicles. All they could do was to run a few hundred yards up the road and take cover in a ditch from the Soviet shells. At this moment we arrived and shot up the Russians. They had taken advantage of the situation and run another 200 yards or so up the road. This took a load off my mind and my comrades and I were very happy. [55]

In the course of the retrograde movements it was not long before air units were assigned individual targets, which they had to seek out and strike within a general target area. This entailed entirely different modes of operation for the air command staffs. Unit leaders at lower levels were given greater freedom of action, and no longer had to be given detailed orders. Conversely, they then required continuous and detailed orientation on the situation, including all current changes, a most essential prerequisite for successful attacks.

Each unit commander then became more or less the chief of a small tactical support command and, within certain limitations, could issue his own orders and employ his own force independently. The control of specifically combat operations was shifted to lower command levels. For the command staffs at air fleet, air corps, and air division level, the most important function during these circumstances, apart from the distribution of forces, was to insure continuous aerial surveillance of the entire area in order to obtain as precise a picture as possible of both the air and ground situation. Other important missions (in order of priority) were: (1) to arrange for the timely preparation and supply of new tactical bases; (2) to secure timely and sufficient amounts of supplies for the tactical bases already in use; (3) to arrange for the prompt establishment of command posts in the probable areas of main effort (in the light of a clear interpretation of probable developments) and, concurrently, for the rapid development of a command signal communications network to secure the control of all operations and supply movements.

To these missions must be added that of evacuation, a particularly difficult undertaking. Owing to the general shortage of supplies, the evacuation of all equipment and supplies was especially important, and often decisive, for the operability of the units and even for the execution of missions themselves.

The evacuation of airfields was particularly difficult because of the dual requirement that airfields were to be destroyed as thoroughly as possible but would be kept in operational use up to the last possible moment. For this reason, sheds, billets, shelters, signal communication and command post installations, and similar structures were demolished first. The airfields were plowed up and mined, and only one take-off and landing runway was maintained until the moment when the planes took off to transfer to another field. Frequently this last runway was not blasted until after the last aircraft had taken off and the first shells from Soviet tanks or artillery had begun to fall in the area.

Often these last-minute demolition tasks were only possible because of defensive action by flak units which were committed to protect the airfields. After the flying units had evacuated the field, these flak units assumed a ground-defense (direct-fire) role, and maintained effective fire to halt the Russians until all demolitions were completed.

By the end of September 1943 the armies of the southern front in Russia had been safely withdrawn and established in their new main line of resistance behind the Dnepr River, and their materiel had been evacuated without serious interference over the few existing bridges. Strong flak and fighter forces then were assigned to protect the new positions, while ground force units reorganized and reestablished their forces.

Luftwaffe Support in Defense of the Dnepr River Line

German leaders correctly assumed that the Russians would allow the Wehrmacht no opportunity to rest and rehabilitate itself or to improve its defenses behind the Dnepr River. They also expected that the enemy would soon launch new major offensives, particularly in the southern areas, once he had regrouped his assault forces and brought his armies up to the desired strength through the addition of new replacements.

As was noted previously,* during the German withdrawal across the Dnepr River a Soviet force had also managed to make a crossing

*See p. 131.

north of Kanev and southwest of Pereyslav and to establish a small bridge-head, which was soon reinforced by eight infantry divisions and a tank corps.[56] Taking advantage of islands in the river, the Russians also crossed the river between Dnepropetrovsk and Kremenchug, where they set up a second bridgehead.

Troops in the Soviet bridgehead in the Pereyslav sector received support from strong partisan groups which had organized some time before in the area west of the Dnepr. It was during the operations connected with this bridgehead that the Red Army for the first time in the campaign (25 September 1943) committed substantial paratroop and other airborne forces with the intention of taking a tactical objective.[57*] The purpose of the airborne operation was to breach the new German line along the Dnepr by an attack from the rear.

On the night of 24 September reports came in to VIII Air Corps Headquarters that a Soviet airborne operation was underway. Armed with this information, reconnaissance units took off in the first light of dawn on the 25th to view the area. Numerous white parachutes left lying about in open territory by the Russian forces immediately revealed not only the drop zone, but also the approximate strength of the enemy force.[58/] German reserves on their way to the front, who happened to be in the area where the first landings were made, went into action at once and very soon annihilated nearly the entire Russian airborne force. Only small remnants made good their escape into partisan-held territory.

Other large-scale airborne operations were also carried out by hostile forces during the month of September 1943. The Soviet Command launched such undertakings in the Ukraine in the strength of two brigades each at Kanev, Kiev, and Cherkassy. All of these attempts, however, ended in failure.[59]

While Soviet airborne units could be quickly located and eradicated, German ground forces were manifestly too weak to breach and eliminate

---

*Editor's Note: The German word operativ, which is used here in the original text, can mean either strategic or tactical, and sometimes operational. While "tactical" is implied in this instance, the objective was one that had definite strategic possibilities.

/Statements concerning the strength of this force are not in agreement, but it seems clear that the unit was between two and five brigades strong. For additional details see Appendix 26, original German draft of this study.

the two Soviet bridgeheads by counterattack, thereby clearing the entire western bank of the Dnepr of enemy troops. These points therefore remained as open abscesses along the front.

On the northern flank of the Fourth Panzer Army, along the boundary with Army Group Center, Soviet forces had also crossed the Desna River and, in early October, proceeded to establish two new bridgeheads west of the Dnepr River, one on either side of Kiev.[60] The Soviet Command then regrouped its forces, with main concentration in the sector just north of Kiev. About 10 October a night reconnaissance unit of the VIII Air Corps detected a large Soviet force east of Kiev moving from south to north. Since these vehicles were traveling with headlights on, it was easy for German observers to ascertain the size and direction of the movement. News of this regrouping movement was naturally of decisive importance to the Fourth Panzer Army, which was thus able to withdraw forces from its main defensive concentration south of Kiev for commitment elsewhere.[61]

The VIII Air Corps placed main emphasis during the defensive battles raging from Kremenchug to Chernigov in the Kiev area. It supported the XXXXVIII Panzer Corps' action against Russian units advancing from the enemy bridgehead at Pereyslav, and bombarded the bridgehead just north of Kiev. Although good results were achieved again and again, the Soviet troops always repaired their damaged bridges and approaches within a surprisingly short time.*

A bomber group based at Shitomir went into action periodically and, with the help of a Freya radar device at the base, was able to plot the precise route to the Soviet bridgehead north of Kiev. Using another Freya instrument, which was situated west of Kiev parallel to the approach route, German aircrews were able to control the time of release of their bombs and to carry out very effective harassing raids against the bridge sites. Approaching by night or above the clouds, Luftwaffe bomber units surprised the enemy with the accuracy of their attacks.[62]

According to Generalmajor Hans Seidemann, commanding the VIII Air Corps, the Dnepr River was at a low stage, so that it was possible to

---

*Editor's Note: See Generalleutnant a. D. Klaus Uebe, Russian Reactions to German Airpower in World War II, USAF Historical Studies No. 176, Maxwell AFB, Alabama: USAF Historical Division, ASI, July 1964, pp. 83-85.

cross at some points on foot. Apparently the Russians failed to notice this fact, since they neglected to exploit these favorable conditions. However, enemy forces later proved to be extremely clever in all of their efforts to gain a foothold on the western bank. Footbridges and even larger bridges were so constructed that the tops were about a foot or two below the surface of the water.* Consequently, they were not endangered by artillery fire since they were not detected until a careful study of aerial photographs raised suspicions concerning tracks which ran to the water's edge. The Russians later built even a large railway ponton bridge, across which they moved railroad cars, either singly or in groups. There was no doubt about it, in matters involving the use and exploitation of terrain the Russians were masters.[63]

German fighters gave an excellent account of themselves in every operation. Fighters of the VIII Air Corps, based on the Kiev-West airfield close behind the front lines, were extremely successful against the enemy air forces, and in the course of these frequent attacks one officer shot down 18 aircraft in a single day.‡

A night harassing group, newly assigned to the VIII Air Corps during this period, also achieved very good results in its operations. The Soviet practice of moving its columns at night with headlights on enabled German flyers to locate and to successfully attack these valuable targets. Orientation from the air was also facilitated by the readily recognizable landmark, the broad Dnepr River.

Meanwhile, farther south, the Fourth Air Fleet on 10 October committed 867 aircraft in a concentrated support effort in behalf of the Sixth Army. Bombers, dive-bombers, and ground-attack aircraft attacked Soviet troops, concentrations, and all enemy installations which were detected in the Bolshoy Tokmark-Melitopol, Zaporozhye, and Kremenchug sectors. Certain elements struck the Dnepr bridges at Cherkassy and other enemy targets near Chernigov and Pereyslav.[64] That night, 158 aircraft, mostly bombers and harassing planes, continued the support operations along the Sixth Army front, attacking the Brovari-Bakhmach-Lgov and Preluki-Bakhmach railroads, tactical targets at Pereyslav, the Poltava-Kharkov-Valuyki railroads, and ground targets in the Melitopol

---

*Editor's Note: See USAF Historical Studies No. 176, pp. 44-45. See also U. S. Department of the Army, Small Unit Actions During the German Campaign in Russia, DA Pam. 20-269, Washington: OCMH, EUCOM Historical Division, July 1953, pp. 220-228.

‡Lt. Friedrich Lang.

area. At least five sizeable trains were destroyed in these attacks and eight others damaged.

Luftwaffe units continued their support operations through the month of October along the entire southern front, defended by the First and Fourth Panzer Armies and the Sixth and Eighth Armies. Although understrength, the Luftwaffe carried out its support missions with great determination and destroyed a number of bridges, large amounts of enemy materiel, and many Russian troops.[65*]

On the right flank of Army Group South at the bend of the Dnepr, German forces managed to maintain a bridgehead east of the river near Zaporozhye, despite several heavy Soviet attacks. The Luftwaffe supported this defense with over 300 aircraft. Nevertheless, by 14 October enemy pressures had become irresistible and the position had to be abandoned. Just prior to the withdrawal, the railway bridge and river dam, both of which had only recently been repaired and put back into operation, were destroyed by Wehrmacht demolition teams.

The German Sixth Army held its positions between Melitopol and the knee of the Dnepr River at Zaporozhye against heavy Russian attacks until 23 October 1943. On that day Soviet forces breached the defenses at Melitopol and advanced toward the lower reaches of the Dnepr, while some elements of the assault force wheeled about to drive in the direction of Perekop at the neck of the Crimean Peninsula.

The flat plains of the Nogaya Steppe offered no natural lines behind which the Sixth Army might have been able to reestablish itself. Because of this, it was compelled to withdraw its forces rapidly behind the Dnepr River. However, in the course of this retrograde movement, it was able to maintain a strong bridgehead around Nikopol, where its forces halted the Soviet drive and thus protected the rear of the First Panzer Army.

---

*Within the Fourth Air Fleet area, the I Air Corps (operating in the southern sector) transferred its headquarters on 14 October 1943 from the Crimean Peninsula to Nikolayev. In the central part of the air fleet operational area, the IV Air Corps carried out its tasks from its headquarters at Kirovograd and later at Novo Ukrainka, while in the northern part of the air fleet's area the VIII Air Corps command post was located at Belaya Tserkov.

Southeast of Kremenchug Soviet forces had crossed the Dnepr on 17 October, and by the 24th other units followed on both sides of Dnepropetrovsk. The Red Army then quickly threw fresh units into the attack, which began to assume grave proportions.

Meanwhile, weather conditions began to deteriorate rapidly all along the southern part of the Eastern Front, with lowering temperatures and some snow. This had an immediate impact upon all military operations in the area. Around Kiev, the heavy concentrations of enemy tanks and artillery, which had been reported in the southern bridgehead area by air and ground reconnaissance, was found to have been a bit of clever enemy deception. After the first snowfall no tracks could be seen on any of the aerial photos indicating entrance into or exit from the bridgehead. This was further confirmed when dive-bombers carried out a small attack on these positions and splintered the timbers from which they had been constructed.[66]

By 10 November the Russians had breached the German defenses on a 90-mile front between Dnepropetrovsk and Kremenchug. Forces consisting of 61 infantry divisions, 37 tank brigades, and 14 motorized brigades drove a deep wedge between the First Panzer Army and the Eighth Army, advancing on a broad front far across the Ingulets River north of Krivoy Rog.[67]

The Fourth Air Fleet committed all of its available units in continuous combat operations in support of the hard-pressed ground troops, adopting whatever expedients it could to accomplish its mission. A case in point was the airfield situated in the northern outskirts of the village of Bolshaya Kostromka, on the road to Apostolovo, southeast of Krivoy Rog. The road was usually impassable for motor vehicles. For this reason the Fourth Air Fleet immediately trained its personnel to use horses and even oxen, in order to keep the field operational in any circumstances. Quite often crews rode on horseback to their aircraft, dismounting directly from their horses to the planes because the field was in as bad a condition as the road leading to it. In rainy weather the field resembled a muddy lake, with the surface broken here and there by small islands of terra firma. The aircraft could take off only because they were equipped with wide-track tires, such as those used by Ju-87's.

There were certain advantages in the close proximity of German air units to the Dnepr, since the forces could quickly deploy all along the line, depending upon the local situation. Combat missions therefore varied from north to south to east, and changed on very short notice. In the east and southeast Soviet forces brought their weight to bear against the Nikopol bridgehead. German air units then struck all Soviet troops and equipment moving in that direction from the Melitopol area, and provided direct support at the focal points of the fighting.

In some of the most crucial areas the map carried numerous German place names such as Heidelberg, Gruental, Gustavfeld, and the like. These were areas inhabited by Germans, whose ancestors had settled there centuries ago.* Farther to the north the main line of resistance ran along the far side of the Dnepr River, to east of Zaporozhye, where it crossed the Dnepr and extended into the Kremenchug area. Dnepropetrovsk lay in the Soviet rear area.

As had happened so often before, the Russians exerted pressure at several points, and were able to achieve penetrations in more than one place. These were then cleaned out by German counterattacks, usually carried out by panzer divisions. During these actions the Fourth Air Fleet flew numerous close-support missions. Air activity might have been more effective if the Luftwaffe could have used the air base at Krivoy Rog, which was equipped with concrete runways, but, unfortunately for the Wehrmacht, one of the Soviet thrusts reached the airfield and brought it under fire. Red Army units continued to pour in from the area north of this point, in the direction of Pyatikhatki. The situation was restored in the area after a local counterattack, and the front was pushed back a few miles toward the north.

These Soviet forces were receiving their supplies in an uninterrupted flow, for which reason the Luftwaffe attacked the significant Dnepr River bridges. Every third or fourth day the IV Air Corps ordered new attack missions against these structures, usually in the area between Kremenchug and Dnepropetrovsk.[68] Emphasis in these operations changed daily, just as one would expect in a regular fire company, which would be called upon to extinguish one conflagration after another.

On 3 November 1943 the Russians renewed their attack with tremendous force in the Kiev area. This new assault struck the completely

---

*Editor's Note: In Kiev and in the area to the south of Kiev traces of German influence, such as tiled roofs which dated from the 15th century, could be seen. The author is probably referring, however, to the descendants of Germans who migrated to this area and to the Volga during the reign of Catherine the Great (1762-1796).

exhausted troops of the Fourth Panzer Army and the Second Army (Army Group Center). It did not seem to be immediately clear whether the Soviet Command had some long range strategic plan in mind or whether it merely sought to obtain as much room as possible for staging further attacks. Within two days it was clear that Kiev would have to be abandoned. Since it was impossible to shift reinforcements to this area to brace up the reeling German front, Red Army units were able to breach the defenses in places, and on 6 November took the city.

After cracking the Dnepr defenses, Red armies drove rapidly through Fastov and Radomyshl in the direction of Berdichev, Zhitomir, and Korosten. The German Command viewed these developments with foreboding, and saw the threat of an enormously deep and wide penetration between Army Groups South and Center, the results of which might be unpredictable. The left wing of Army Group South appeared to be especially endangered.[69] By 13 November Soviet forces had captured the important rail junction of Fastov and had advanced 96 miles to the west of Kiev into the Zhitomir area, enveloping the LIX Corps at Korosten. At the same time pressures of the heaviest sort were exerted against the German Second Army south of Gomel.

The attack by the main body of Red Army forces at the beginning of these operations between Kiev and Smolensk apparently had produced the results desired by the Soviet Command. It was probably by design that the main attack had been directed at the center of the German line in the Pripyat Marsh area between Zhitomir and Bobruysk, where the lack of roads seriously hampered the movement of Wehrmacht reserves.

For several days in succession Soviet tank divisions and motorized infantry units carried their attack forward on an average of 15 miles a day, and by 15 November 1943 a crisis had developed in the Eastern Theater of Operations on a scale which was then unprecedented in the war. On the following day the advancing Soviet armored forces encountered German panzer divisions (under the command of Generaloberst Hoth and the Fourth Panzer Army) which struck them in the flank and brought their offensive to a halt west of Zhitomir.* All available German air units assisted in stopping this advance.

Counterattacking German ground forces even succeeded by 19 November in driving the Russians back across the Teterev River to a

---

*Elite units such as the Motorized Division "Grossdeutschland" and the 7th "Ghost" Panzer Division played a role in these actions.

position east of Zhitomir. Yet, despite the recapture of this area, Korosten remained under siege, Fastov was still in Soviet hands, and the north flank of the Fourth Panzer Army remained open.*

While these operations were still in progress west of Kiev, the Russians again attacked the Sixth Army, the First Panzer Army, and the Eighth Army, but German forces varied their actions from defense to counterattack as the situation required and succeeded time after time in preventing enemy breakthroughs on a large scale.

The VIII Air Corps and its units contributed materially to the successful outcome of the counterattacks, especially that of the 7th Panzer Division in the recapture of Zhitomir and the airfields in that area. Frequent spells of bad weather and poor visibility because of autumn fogs, as well as the nearly unserviceable condition of the airfields, did not prevent the Luftwaffe from attacking every Soviet target sighted. It was then that the old Hs-123 proved its value. The Henschel 123 was an obsolete biplane with a top speed of about 225 miles per hour, but which was very maneuverable and robust enough to operate even under the worst of weather conditions when other aircraft would be grounded. These planes worked out very well, especially since bad weather had also greatly reduced Soviet air activity.

Apart from the issue of the open north flank of the Fourth Panzer Army, the situation on the ground remained unchanged for some time. In the north, however, the gap in the swampy region around Korosten, which separated the army from Army Group Center, grew gradually wider. The grave danger of a flank threat was fully realized, but no substantial forces were available to stop the slow but steady westward advance of the Soviet forces. The landscape in this area is dismal, the major features being swamps and trackless forests in a region known as the Pokitno swamp. Here the Soviet forces were able to exploit with great adroitness the difficult terrain and to continue their westward progress.. The German Command assumed that they would soon outflank the German lines in the Korosten area in the direction of Sarny and that a new Soviet assault would soon take shape in that area.

---

*The High Command of the Wehrmacht report covering the period 9-15 November 1943 listed Soviet losses at 20,000 dead, 4,800 prisoners, and 603 tanks and 1,505 guns captured or destroyed.

The VIII Air Corps did its utmost to insure that the Fourth Panzer Army would have reliable air reconnaissance information. Strategic reconnaissance missions were carried out by the 2nd Squadron of the 11th Strategic Reconnaissance Group from Berdichev, and by tactical reconnaissance units operating out of Kalinovka. The airfield at the latter location had been used as a transhipping center during the time when the German front was still far east of the Volga River and later had been developed as a good air base.

German air units were heavily crowded on the few serviceable airfields available. Fortunately for them, the Soviet Eighth Air Army (opposing the German VIII Air Corps) gave little evidence of aggressiveness. Nevertheless, it was a question how long some of these bases could be held. The field at Kalinovka provided good shelter, signal communications, and runways which were useable even during muddy periods, but its facilities came to be used almost exclusively for the bomber units of the VIII Air Corps rather than for general supply and repair services.

One after another, the airfields around Belozerka* and Usin had been abandoned, as the German lines withdrew to the west. Even before the Soviet offensive the retention of the Belozerka field had been in serious doubt because of increasing attacks from large bands of partisans operating from the wooded areas to the east. This greatly facilitated the Red Army's footing in the area. German troops found themselves in exceedingly difficult circumstances in the rough terrain, and the wonder is that they were able to hold out as long as they did.

Farther to the south at Kremenchug, the Eighth Army had also been compelled to withdraw its troops, and after November there could be no further talk of a Dnepr River defense line in that sector.

In the latter half of November, rains created a muddy condition, a gummy morass, which brought all military operations to a halt until freezing weather set in early in December. Mud, slush, fog, and low ceilings restricted air and ground operations so severely that, for all practical purposes, everything had come to a standstill. The Fourth Panzer Army, which had not had time to consolidate its positions properly, was thus able to regroup and make further preparations. More important than this, however, was that the threat of a strategic breakthrough and

---

*Editor's Note: The author does not make clear whether this was Bolshaya Belozerka or Malaya Belozerka, each close to the other in this sector.

the splitting of the entire Eastern Front had been forestalled, allowing German combat units all along the front a temporary breathing spell before the arrival of winter.[70]

By this time it appeared that the exaggerated hopes of the Western Allies, which they had built up after hearing of the Russian advance at Kiev, had turned to pessimism. For example, on 18 November a report of the British Broadcasting Corporation admitted quite frankly that the hopes which London had placed in the Soviet offensive in the Kiev area had not materialized, and that the only possible result could be a shortening of the German lines, which would increase rather than weaken the Wehrmacht's capability to resist.

Considering this operation against the German center from a tactical point of view, it must be said that the Soviet Command should have proceeded with the aim of effecting an enveloping maneuver, since it has been generally recognized as a time-honored rule that any breakthrough in the center can be halted by moving reserves into the area. In this instance the German counterattack not only stopped the enemy advance, but succeeded in enveloping and destroying a Soviet task force at Zhitomir, and this despite otherwise unfavorable conditions. German air units gave excellent support during these battles, even in poor flying weather.[71]

Although the Red Army had suffered a temporary setback far west of Kiev, and although there was momentary comfort in the uneasy stalemate caused by the muddy terrain, Army Group South's position was far from good. Large numbers of Russian troops were regrouping and concentrating for a coming offensive blow, and Wehrmacht leaders realized that far graver events would be in store if the Soviet armies had time to prepare for their next attack.

Hoping to take advantage of the general inertia of the period, the XXXXVIII Panzer Corps* late in November assembled its forces back of the center of the front of Army Group South in preparation for the execution of a spoiling attack against the menacing Soviet concentration. By the beginning of December freezing weather and some snow had arrived, making the ground hard enough for operations by armored and motorized

---

*The corps comprised the 1st Panzer Division, an outstanding unit, commanded by Generalleutnant Walter Krueger; the 7th ("Ghost") Panzer Division, Rommel's old division, commanded by Generalmajor Hasso von Manteuffel; the 1st SS Panzer Division "Leibstandarte Adolph Hitler," commanded by SS General Josef "Sepp" Dietrich; and some auxiliary units.

units. The XXXXVIII Panzer Corps thereupon moved northwestward through Zhitomir to a position behind the left wing of Army Group South. Under cover of darkness these armored forces moved out into the open flank area to the north along the road from Zhitomir to Korosten. All arms and services cooperated in assisting to mask the movements of this corps until the moment for the attack, which was to be the great hour for several outstanding armored force commanders whose names were to find a place in the annals of military history, Generalmajor Hasso von Manteuffel and Colonels Adalbert Schulz and Hyazinth Count Strachwitz von Gross-Zauche und Camminetz.*

On 4 December 1943 the German XIII Corps (defending the left wing of Army Group South just below the exposed flank area), strengthened by the addition of rocket and artillery units, opened the attack toward the north and northeast, an attack which the Russians immediately interpreted as an indication that the Wehrmacht was again going to try to force a decision along that part of the front. The Soviet Command then launched a strong counterattack, sending as many units as possible up to the front area. Here they were met and stopped, despite their numerical superiority, by the surprisingly heavy firepower of the XIII Corps and its supporting units. At this moment, the XXXXVIII Panzer Corps struck the right flank of the attacking Soviet force and drove deeply into its rear area. Maneuvering with great speed over the frozen terrain, the corps soon enveloped and annihilated all Russian units at or near the front lines. The LIX Corps, which had been encircled at Korosten, was also able to execute a successful breakout and establish contact with the XXXXVIII Panzer Corps.

The surprise assault had succeeded, and by 9 December the objectives of the attack had been achieved. Not only was an entire Soviet Army wiped out, but three others suffered such heavy casualties that they were unable to remain on the line. Moreover, the imminent danger of a large-scale enemy offensive had been removed and the German lines were closed from the area east of Korosten southward to a point east of Radomyshl and thence to the road to Fastov, southeast of Radomyshl.

South of the VIII Air Corps area the IV Air Corps was fully occupied in repulsing Soviet attacks along the Dnepr River. In the constantly critical

---

*Editor's Note: All of these officers were subsequently recipients of the Knight's Cross of the Iron Cross with oak leaves, swords, and diamonds.

battles, particularly in the Krivoy Rog-Nikopol-Kremenchug-Kirovograd areas, units of the IV Air Corps supported the defensive battles and counterattacks of the Eighth and Sixth Armies and the First Panzer Army. Main emphasis was placed upon the First Panzer Army sector. There recurring crises frequently necessitated daily transfers of supporting air units in order to carry out missions in the main battle sectors. Thanks to an excellent communications system, IV Air Corps units were highly successful in their direct support missions, even though their numerical weaknesses prevented them from achieving really decisive results. Luftwaffe-Army cooperation was particularly close and smooth in this sector, a fact which did much to insure the success of air operations. *

Owing to a lack of appropriate forces, IV Air Corps was unable to accomplish any strategic missions, except for those performed by a night railroad interdiction squadron of the 55th Bomber Wing (equipped with He-111 aircraft), which was dispatched against Soviet supply movements in the rear areas. Although this squadron achieved local successes, it was unable to stop or seriously hamper the flow of Soviet supplies. This was not surprising in view of the fact that the aircraft available for this type of mission were too few in number to effectively attack and destroy all of the numerous targets which were to be found in the enormous area.

The IV Air Corps also flew some attack missions against the bridges at Dnepropetrovsk and Zaporozhye, making solid strikes on the latter bridge, but achieving negative results against the Dnepropetrovsk structure.[72]

In December the headquarters staff of the IV Air Corps was withdrawn from the front line area for employment in planning and executing strategic air missions.[73]

In the extreme southern part of the Eastern Front the IV Air Corps was obliged to shift its units from one sector to another in support of the Sixth Army, and occasionally to send forces to the Crimean area in support of the Seventeenth Army which was defending there, isolated from other German forces.[74]

---

*Generalleutnant Rudolf Meister assumed command of the IV Air Corps on 13 October 1943, replacing General der Flieger Kurt Pflugbeil, who then became Commander in Chief, First Air Fleet. See figure 32.

Figure 32
General der Flieger Kurt Pflugbeil leaving IV Air Corps Command Post, 13 October 1943, after turning over his command to Generalleutnant Rudolf Meister (walking behind him). Emerging from CP is Col. Anselm Brasser (GSC), Chief of Staff, IV Air Corps

In their almost continuous combat commitment the command and troops of the I and IV Air Corps achieved nearly impossible performances, and provided most effective support for the ground forces in their grim battles. Although both corps were too weak to exercise more than a local effect upon operations, their help was undeniably important to the ground fighting in a particular area, even if it could never result in any strategic change in the situation.*

By mid-December frost and snow had produced the characteristic Russian winter landscape in the Army Group South sector, making the seemingly endless tracts even more barren and desolate. Bitter cold, snow, and driving winds worked a tremendous hardship upon all personnel. On German airfields Luftwaffe personnel worked against the elements, preparing aircraft for take-offs, thawing out and defrosting aircraft and equipment, repairing and maintaining aircraft, and shoveling snow from the runways and hardstands. Under these grueling conditions air support of the ground fighting continued. Being wounded meant freezing to death if help was not immediately at hand, and food was usually frozen solid. Pilots who were forced to make emergency landings in the deep snow usually lost their aircraft and its supplies since salvage operations were so difficult to carry out. Yet, in comparison with the ground forces the Luftwaffe had much to be thankful for. German flyers usually had habitable quarters, and decent, or passable, rations were always assured.

Just prior to the Christmas season there was a deceptive spell of quiet along the front. Numerous signs indicated that the Russians would soon launch an offensive. The VIII Air Corps and the IV Air Corps were ready for it if it came, but Army Group "A" was in a difficult position. Its Seventeenth Army remained isolated in the Crimea, fearful that it might at any time be brought under heavy amphibious attacks, while the Sixth Army clung to its line along the lower reaches of the Dnepr River. Adjacent to it on the north was Army Group South's First Panzer Army, and north of that the Eighth Army and Fourth Panzer Army in positions extending from Nikopol to Zaporozhye to the Krivoy Rog area to Kremenchug, along the western bank of the Dnepr River to the Kanev area, and thence in a wide arc to the Zhitomir area farther west.[75]

---

*Editor's Note: During this period of weakness and decline in the Wehrmacht the Soviet Union had greatly increased its war production. (T-34 tank chassis were being made at a rate of 2,000 a month.) This, added to the Lend-Lease assistance, gave the Russians an overpowering advantage. See Kenneth R. Whiting, The Development of the Soviet Armed Forces, 1917-1966, AU-10, Maxwell AFB, Alabama: Documentary Research Division, ASI, 1966, p. 52.

In the south the German line presented an almost impossible appearance. While it was bent far back to the west in the area east of Zhitomir, the Eighth Army was still in position along the Dnepr River in the Cherkassy area. South of this the line again bent westward to Kirovograd, where panzer divisions carried on a see-saw battle, endeavoring to halt the Russians, while the Sixth Army held its lines. Shortly before Christmas the Kherson bridgehead had to be evacuated because of drift ice in the Dnepr River, and because there was a serious threat that large Soviet forces would cross the river as soon as it had frozen over.[76]

All along the line in the sectors of Army Group South and Army Group "A" the armies were fully engaged in a flexible mobile defense, being constantly supported by the I and VIII Air Corps of the Fourth Air Fleet. The battle was still in full swing in all areas as the Soviet Command continued to commit new masses of troops. The almost continuous battle was beginning to tell on the German forces, which by this time were nearly exhausted.

The end of 1943 was near, the year in which the tide of fate in the East had turned against Germany. A new giant offensive was to be expected shortly in which the Russians would commit even greater masses of men and materiel than ever before, especially against the left wing of Army Group South in the area west of Kiev, at the most seriously threatened sector. The monstrous storm that was brewing broke on 24 December.[77]

Chapter 5

AIR AND FLAK FORCES IN THE BATTLE FOR THE CRIMEA

On the night of 9 October 1943 the last elements of the Seventeenth Army (General der Pioniere* Erwin Jaenicke) withdrew from the Kuban bridgehead area and crossed over the Straits at Kerch to the Crimean Peninsula. The 9th Flak Division (Generalleutnant Wolfgang Pickert) also withdrew with its 13 flak and 2 searchlight battalions/ along with the Seventeenth Army forces. The Division's mission was to provide air defense over the field of battle, to protect all airfields, naval bases, and the ports of Feodosiya, Sevastopol, Yevpatoriya, Chernomorskoye, temporarily also of Genichesk at the western end of the Sea of Azov, and to provide defenses for the rail junction of Dzhankoy.[1//]

On 14 October the Fourth Air Fleet transferred the staff of the I Air Corps (Generalleutnant Karl Angerstein) from the Crimean Peninsula to Nikolayev. This corps had supported the Seventeenth Army most effectively during the defense of the Kuban bridgehead and was to continue to do so when necessary, although its new primary mission was to support the Sixth Army, which, after mid-October, came under heavy assaults by the Red Army.**

At this time the Seventeenth Army controlled five divisions, two assault gun brigades, and seven Rumanian divisions, two of which were partially motorized cavalry divisions. The only flying units in the area were those assigned to Air Command Crimea (Col. GSC Joachim Albrecht Bauer), whose command post was situated at Seventeenth Army Headquarters at Simferopol. These air forces consisted of a dive-bomber group, a few tactical reconnaissance aircraft, and the naval air units which

---

*Editor's Note: General der Pioniere, like General der Infanterie, General der Flieger, etc., is a German Wehrmacht rank, corresponding roughly to that of a U.S. Lieutenant General. Pioniere (Pioneers) refers to the basic arm of service of the above-mentioned officer, in this case the Combat Engineers.

/These were comprised of 28 heavy and 27 light flak batteries and 8 searchlight batteries, with attached units.

//See Maps Nos. 12 and 13.

**See p. 138.

were stationed in the Crimean Peninsula.[2*] General Jaenicke had joint command authority over all units of the Army, Navy, and Luftwaffe in the Crimea, which therefore included tactical control of Air Command Crimea.

The dive-bomber group represented the only highly mobile reserve force available in the Crimea which could be immediately employed against all land and seaborne targets. Among its successful achievements was the destruction of three modern type Soviet destroyers, which on 7 October 1943 had shelled the coast of Yalta. The dive-bomber group was then just about to take off on a mission against a land objective when it received word from air reconnaissance that destroyers were approaching the coast. Changing bomb loads at once, the dive-bombers quickly got into the air and established contact with the reporting reconnaissance aircraft, which led them to the site. The group carried out repeated attacks upon the three enemy warships, sinking them all.[3]

As early as mid-October the Seventeenth Army, in anticipation of later developments, had prepared what was called Plan MICHAEL, a plan for the systematic evacuation of the Crimean Peninsula. At the time, the situation was becoming increasingly critical along the extreme southern wing of the Eastern Front, especially in the Sixth Army sector, and it appeared more and more likely that the Sixth Army would soon have to retire behind the lower reaches of the Dnepr River.[4] Plan MICHAEL called for a great amount of self-sacrifice and outstanding march performances on the part of all of the involved troop units, and it was understood that much of the heavy equipment might have to be abandoned in the process.

Under the provisions of this plan, Kerch was to be evacuated and all units withdrawn to the Parpach position[†] during the night of 29 October. On the following night the southern coast of the Crimea, with the exception of Sevastopol, was to be evacuated as far as the heights of the Yayla Mountains, and by 2 November the main line of resistance in the Crimea was to run approximately from Simferopol to Karassubasar to the railroad station at Gramatikovo. The final designated line (Yevpatoriya-Oktyabrskoye-Yayla Mountain ridge) was to be reached by 4 November, from which time

---

*When the staff of the I Air Corps was transferred to Nikolayev (Army Group "A" sector), Air Command Black Sea (responsible for reconnaissance and air defense in the Black Sea area in cooperation with Admiral Black Sea) was redesignated Air Command Crimea.

†A fortified line built in 1941 by the Russians across the neck of land from Kamenskoye on the Sea of Azov to the Black Sea northeast of Feodosiya. This line of bunkers changed hands several times in the course of the war.

the further withdrawal was to be accomplished as circumstances permitted. A single-track railroad from Kerch was available for the withdrawal of the 50th Infantry Division. [5]

Because of the gravity of the overall situation General Jaenicke, commanding the Seventeenth Army, acting upon his own initiative, ordered preparations to begin for the implementation of the first phase of Plan MICHAEL. [6] According to Generalleutnant Angerstein, this order was issued contrary to the explicit directions of Army Group "A." Under the evacuation plan, Air Command Crimea was placed under the command of Generalleutnant Pickert, Commanding General of the 9th Flak Division, who, in turn, was subordinate to General Jaenicke. Both of these officers had been caught in the Stalingrad pocket and had been flown out at the "eleventh hour," so that they were naturally sensitive to envelopments.*

All units in the Crimea worked with feverish haste, and the concrete runways at Baggerovo were already demolished when the I Air Corps heard what was happening and took appropriate steps to prevent the destruction of the ground installations which were required for the conduct of operations. At about 2100 hours on this same day (28 October 1943) the highest command interceded and ordered the immediate discontinuance of the evacuation plan and the return of all involved units to their former stations. Some forces moving in the northern Crimea, however, had to continue on their way in order to reinforce points threatened by enemy forces. Because the Seventeenth Army had implemented Plan MICHAEL (I) contrary to orders, and because of the resultant overlapping chain of command, confusion reigned in the Luftwaffe ground organization for two or three days. [7]

Although General Jaenicke had flown personally to the Fuehrer's Headquarters, he had been unable to secure any change in the order forbidding the execution of Plan MICHAEL. In fact, he had been ordered

---

*Editor's Note: Jaenicke was, in some respects, a controversial character. Paulus in December of 1942 called him an ideal army commander, "absolutely firm in crises." On 31 January 1944 Field Marshal von Kleist noted in his efficiency report, "Personally very active and impulsive, so that he requires a steady and sober chief of staff. . . . On 28 October 1943 he ordered the evacuation of the Crimea against the directives of the Fuehrer and the Army Group. Now he presents the matter as if it had not been an act of disobedience, but simply a pressure device to secure additional forces." See personnel data on file, Karlsruhe Document Collection.

to hold the Crimea at all costs. This area was of military importance chiefly because it served as a massive aircraft carrier. There were a number of good airfields there which had been recently equipped for full air operations and which provided favorable bases for Luftwaffe attacks upon industrial targets in southern Russia, the Caucasus oil region, the highly important Anglo-American supply routes from Iran and the Caspian Sea, and against the remarkably passive Soviet Black Sea Fleet.

The significance of the Crimean Peninsula as a base of operations against the Trans-Iran supply route is strikingly revealed in the October 1943 issue of the American periodical Impact:

> . . . in many ways the 9,000-mile air route to the Persian Gulf represents the most spectacular development. Touching four continents, it hops from Miami to Natal to Ascension to Accra to Cairo to the mud flats of Abadan. The route goes on to India and China. But at Abadan supplies are picked up by the Russians and transported by plane and truck through Baku to South Russia.[8]

Early in 1942 work commenced under the supervision of the U.S. Army to develop Abadan, Iran into an important air base for the delivery of warplanes to Russia. This was part of the War Department's plan for creating a supply route to the Soviet Union through the Persian corridor. Preparing this system entailed the construction of assembly plants, roads and bridges, the improvement and expansion of port facilities, and the transfer of railway rolling stock. In order to implement this plan, 1,398 American officers and 26,539 enlisted men were transferred into the area.[9]

By 1 September 1943 the United States had flown 1,702 aircraft (1,000 of them light and medium bombers) via Africa to Abadan, while 602 planes had arrived by sea. Fighter aircraft were transported to the Persian Gulf by ship, then uncrated and assembled at the Allied installation in Abadan, where Russian pilots picked them up. The Air Transport Command took charge of all airborne traffic, and, while many aircraft were delivered to the Soviet Union over the Alaska-Siberia route, this avenue was soon outstripped by the Persian Gulf shipments. The Russians usually determined the desired reception area on the basis of the situation on the fighting front. Those victories in the southern areas during 1943 appeared to be related to the very substantial delivery of American aircraft through the Persian corridor at Abadan.[10*]

Air bases in a Soviet-controlled Crimea would have presented an exceedingly grave threat, particularly to the Rumanian oil fields which were of such decisive importance to the German military effort. Furthermore, the use of the Crimean seaports, especially Sevastopol, would have given the Soviet Black Sea Fleet good additional naval bases and would thereby have considerably improved its operational possibilities. But there were other reasons why the Crimea was important. The uncertain neutrality of Turkey and the equally uncertain behavior of Germany's ally, Rumania, made the possession of the Crimea of primary political significance.

The German flag flying over the ports of Yevpatoriya, Sevastopol, Feodosiya, and Kerch, the drone of German aircraft engines on the airfields at Kerch, Sarabuz and Karankut (the latter two north of Simferopol), and on the large airfield at Khersones near Sevastopol could not fail to impress Turkey, which would thus have assurance that the Straits of the Bosporus were doubly secured. Turkey was therefore prepared to allow the passage of merchant ships belonging to countries bordering upon the Black Sea in accordance with the Montreux Straits Agreement,[†] providing that they were connected with the Axis powers.[11]

In the conflicts of opinion concerning the question of evacuating the Crimea, Hitler insisted upon unconditional retention of the peninsula, just as he had done in the Kuban situation. The entreaties of Generaloberst Zeitzler to withdraw Wehrmacht forces from the Crimea were therefore utterly useless.[12] During a conference on the subject held early in November, the Fuehrer strongly reaffirmed his position to von Manstein,

---

*Editor's Note: For an interesting treatise on the establishment of the Persian corridor Lend-Lease route see Richard C. Lukas, "The Middle East - Corridor to Russia: Lend-Lease Aircraft to the Russians, 1941-1942," _The Airpower Historian_, Vol. XII, No. 3, Montgomery, Alabama: The Air Force Historical Foundation, July 1965. See also Theodore E. Whiting, Carrel I. Tod, and Anne P. Craft, _The United States Army in World War II: Statistics, Lend-Lease_, Washington: Department of the Army, OCMH, 15 December 1952. See also figures 33, 34, and 35.

†Editor's Note: An agreement enacted 20 July 1936 between Turkey and the signatories of the Lausanne Treaty (Italy abstaining) which returned control of the Straits and the right to refortify them to Turkey. Turkey's requests were met because of its support of the League of Nations' position during the Ethiopian crisis.

Figure 33
Anglo-American supplies went overland to U. S. S. R.
from Bandar Shahpur on the Persian Gulf

Figure 34
Trucks moving along dusty route from
Persian Gulf to Russia

Figure 35
American A-20 aircraft lined up on the Abadan airfield for delivery to the Soviet Union

pointing out that the loss of the Crimea would naturally lead to the immediate occupation of the area by Soviet forces and, inevitably, in a change of attitude on the part of Turkey, Bulgaria, and Rumania.[13*]

On 28 October the Soviet Fourth Ukrainian Army Group broke through the Sixth Army front at Melitopol and drove into the Nogayan plains. The Sixth Army, whose southern wing had held the line from the bend of the Dnepr River to the Sea of Azov, was then in danger of being enveloped, and, under crushing enemy pressure, withdrew its right (southern) wing toward the lower reaches of the Dnepr and the crossing point of Berislav. This evacuation included the forces stationed around Genichesk at the western tip of the Sea of Azov. During the withdrawal movement the IV and XXIX Corps of the Sixth Army formed a broad bridgehead south of the bend of the Dnepr River. After this army had retired behind the Dnepr, those areas of its former sector which were not immediately overrun by enemy forces were occupied by the right (southern) wing of Army Group South (Manstein), leaving Army Group "A" with only one serious worry, the plight of the Seventeenth Army in the Crimea. There was, of course, the danger that Red units might drive toward the north to cut off the First Panzer Army near Nikopol.†

Sizeable elements of the Soviet breakthrough forces wheeled across the Nogayan plains southward toward Perekop, the northern approach to the Crimean Peninsula, where they threatened to deprive the Seventeenth Army of its last land communication with the rest of the German front.[14] Because of the serious situation, the Commanding General of the I Air Corps (Angerstein) transferred his headquarters from Nikolayev back to Simferopol.†† He then established an excellent wireless teletype communication network with Army Group "A," the Fourth Air Fleet, and the 2nd Squadron (so-called Supply Squadron) of the I Air Corps.[15] From his new headquarters Angerstein directed the operations of all Luftwaffe units stationed in the Crimea and in the Nikolayev and Kherson areas.

Units of the 9th Flak Division stationed in Genichesk were also withdrawn on 28 October to reinforce the weak Rumanian holding forces on the

---

*The Rumanians entered the war with great zeal, almost with a crusading spirit, but soon became disenchanted when it became clear how great their sacrifices would be in a war of such scope. Moreover, once they regained northern Bucovina and Bessarabia (wrested from them by the Soviet Union in the summer of 1940), they had little interest in the war.

†See Maps Nos. 12 and 13.

††See p. 138.

Chongar Peninsula to the south. Generally speaking, the situation in the northern Crimea was such that the flak batteries were the only available artillery for the weak security forces in that sector. However, the rapid movement of these batteries was hampered by a shortage of transportation, forcing each battery commander to improvise as best he could. This problem notwithstanding, two heavy (8.8-cm.) batteries succeeded in reaching the northern perimeter of the Tatars' wall* at Perekop early on the morning of 30 October, and were able to prepare for action at once against the expected assaults of Soviet armored spearheads. These defenses were also strengthened by the improvised armored flak train which moved through Dzhankoy in the direction of Armyansk. 16

The arrival of these forces was none too soon, for on that day Russian units reached the Perekop isthmus and severed the Seventeenth Army's last land connection with the remainder of the German ground forces in the East, leaving only sea and air transportation for the movement of vital replacements and supplies. 17≠ It was only by the stoutest defensive fighting, supported by the dive-bomber group and the 9th Flak Division, that the Seventeenth Army was able to prevent an immediate Soviet follow-up and breakthrough in the Perekop narrows.

The first Russian tanks (obviously units which had outrun the general enemy advance) actually appeared before Perekop on the 30th, and were immediately brought under effective artillery fire by German batteries. For the next two days 8.8-cm. flak batteries held off these armored forces, destroying large numbers of tanks in the open, flat terrain, where they were visible at great distances and offered such excellent targets for the fast and precision fire of German crews. The armored flak train also achieved particularly good results in its bold forays on the rail line

---

*Editor's Note: A centuries old, 50-foot-deep ditch with parapet across the narrows just south of Perekop, running from the Bay of Perekop to the Sivash Sea, which was an obstacle of some consequence in the German conquest of the Crimea in the autumn of 1941. See Generalleutnant a.D. Hermann Plocher, The German Air Force versus Russia, 1941, Maxwell AFB, Alabama: USAF Historical Division, ASI, 1964, p. 211, and footnote, p. 203.

≠During the initial stages of isolation one squadron of "Gigant" (Me-323) aircraft, called by the troops adhesive-tape bombers, was available as a supplement to sea transports for the rapid movement of vital supplies and equipment.

northwest of the Tatars' wall. In these few critical days the flak train destroyed 24 Soviet tanks.*

On 2 November some small Soviet units crossed the Sivash Sea from the north and reached the Dzhankoy-Perekop rail line west of Voinka. By the following day a large enemy force began to assault the Tatars' wall, defended by elements of the XXXXIX Mountain Corps (General der Gebirgstruppe Rudolph Konrad) of the Seventeenth Army, a badly understrength unit which was weary from months of heavy fighting. It could not expect much assistance from the forces in this area, which included a German battalion, a Ukrainian battalion, a Rumanian battalion, and one battalion of the supply column of the 4th Mountain Division which got left behind in the withdrawal of the Sixth Army. It was also unlikely that help would be forthcoming from the 50th Infantry Division (then in march) for at least two days.

Soviet armor, accompanied with armored infantry forces, broke through the Tatars' wall on 3 November and drove southward as far as Armyansk, where they were stopped by the determined defensive forces, prominent among which was an outstanding battery of the 9th Flak Division.† The dive-bomber group stationed at Karankut and bombers and ground-attack aircraft from Nikolayev and Kherson then participated in the severe actions which followed. The bombers attacked the rear Soviet airfields at Kalanchak and Chaplinka, while the ground-attack planes, escorted by fighters, attacked enemy forces advancing in the northern approaches to the Crimea.

The dive-bomber group was committed in the breakthrough area and performed extremely well under the conditions. On 5 and 6 November, when the fighting around Armyansk was especially heavy, visibility was about 1,000 yards and the cloud ceiling was below 800 feet. The dive-bombers were not properly equipped for instrument navigation, which, of course, ruled out any hopes for accurate air strikes. However, this excellent group still carried out several attacks each day against Soviet forces in the area in an effort to relieve the pressures on the German infantrymen.[18]

---

*An improvised train, mounting two 8.8-cm. and several 20-mm. flak guns on each rail car, the sides of each car being protected by double concrete plates. This train rendered outstanding service and its young commander received the Knight's Cross for his ingenious operations. See figures 36 and 37.

†Of the 86th Light Flak Bn.

Figure 36
Flak crew (8. 8-cm.) preparing for action
aboard an armored flak train

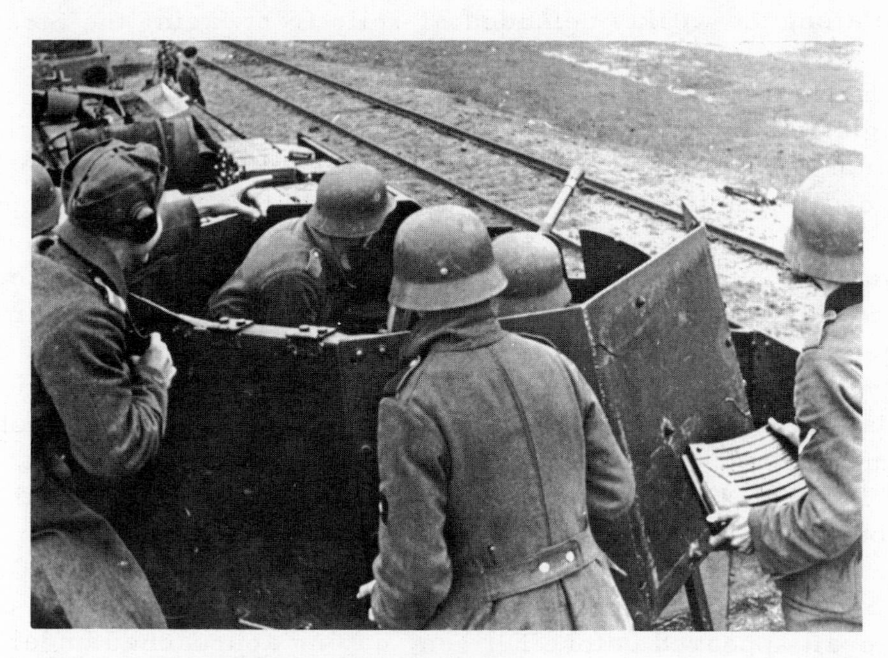

Figure 37
Flak gun (2-cm.) going into action
aboard an armored train

At the end of October, almost simultaneous with the opening of battle around Perekop, a new crisis developed in the eastern part of the Crimea. Soviet forces had landed along the rugged coast at the northern outlet of the Straits of Kerch and were fighting desperately to expand their initially small beachheads. However, before countermeasures could be taken to eliminate these footholds, or before the infiltrations--at which the Russians were so adept--could be halted, a new surprise materialized along the weakly defended 21-mile front facing the Straits.

Early on 1 November 1943 some small Soviet units succeeded in securing a footing along the coast about 18 miles south of Kerch. Rumanian holding forces along the line in this area destroyed one Russian landing craft by antitank fire, and it appeared that the entire operation was just another small-scale attack similar to those of the preceding days to the north of Kerch. Actually it was merely a diversionary movement to cover a large-scale landing which took place after dark near the village of Eltigen, eight miles south of Kerch. At 0230 hours Russian long-range artillery suddenly opened a heavy barrage upon this area, which lay only about nine miles across the Straits. Simultaneously, a force of 20 to 30 harassing aircraft commenced bombing Eltigen and the area farther to the south. The 89th Light Flak Battalion, which was deployed in that sector, could not take defensive action because it had no searchlights.

Soon after the Soviet guns opened fire, a large number of enemy landing craft appeared before Eltigen, having approached under cover of heavy fog. Red Army forces landed, drove out the Rumanian holding group, and in a short time established a beachhead 3,000 yards long and from 400 to 800 yards in depth. The 89th Light Flak Battalion on the western outskirts of Eltigen sank 10 landing craft and halted a further expansion of the beachhead, but was unable to prevent the landing because the Rumanian holding force had withdrawn. During the forenoon German reserves were rushed into the area to prevent any additional enemy advance.[19]

The Russians had been able to make preparations for this amphibious operation without German notice because of the poor visibility and because the few remaining tactical reconnaissance aircraft still in the Crimea had no fighter escorts and were thus unable to carry out adequate reconnaissance missions. V Corps Headquarters, lacking sufficient information on the local situation, rejected the I Air Corps' offer to immediately order out the dive-bomber group stationed at Karankut* on

---

*With its concrete runways, this airfield remained operational despite autumn rains which turned most of the earth into a morass.

an attack mission with small fragmentation bombs. Had this force been dispatched it would undoubtedly have been highly effective.[20]

Pursuant to Seventeenth Army instructions, the I Air Corps ordered all of its available forces from the Nikolayev and Kherson airfields to attack the Soviet vessels crossing the Straits. During these repeated attacks, the Russians suffered heavy losses.

The situation of the Seventeenth Army was truly critical in the early part of November 1943, with enemy footholds north and south of Kerch, without local reserves to throw these forces back into the sea. Inroads in the north were serious with many local breakthroughs along the Sivash Sea area; always there was the threat of a major breakthrough. The problem of defense was aggravated by the poor communication routes in the Crimea. The front along the Kerch area was about 129 miles from the front along the Sivash Sea sector, and the one single-track railroad did not permit rapid transfers of units along interior lines. As if these problems were not enough, long nights and periods of heavy fog caused additional difficulties.

While some German forces were tied down by the new Soviet beachhead at Eltigen, the Russians moved in sizeable reinforcements northeast of Kerch. On 11 November enemy forces attacked from this beachhead, using for the first time armored support, which enabled them to rapidly expand their beachhead to a width of 8,000 and a depth of 5,000 yards. A few of the tanks were destroyed by weapons fire, three of them by flak batteries, but they had achieved their purpose and given the Soviet Command a staging area for a large-scale attack and for the assembly of artillery. Because of this, the German V Corps (General der Infanterie Karl Almendinger), which was responsible for the defense of the sector, had to commit strong forces to hold the line.

The Seventeenth Army's situation was obviously difficult, especially in the Kerch area and on the northern front of the Crimea along the Sivash-Tatars' wall sector, areas which had fallen under Soviet control and from which the Russians could launch a decisive attack for the recapture of the peninsula whenever they desired. In these circumstances it was of primary importance for the Seventeenth Army to conceal its weaknesses, to eliminate Soviet positions through local counterattacks, and to husband its strength by attacking only when and where the chances for success were propitious. The first of these local attacks was in the sector along the

Sivash Sea north of Voinka. Here Rumanian and German units* on 27 November gradually compelled the Red Army forces to withdraw from this foothold toward the north. However, in spite of weeks of hard fighting, the Axis units were unable to throw the Russians back across the Sivash Sea.[21] The Russians held tenaciously to their bridgehead on the Chigary Peninsula, 12 miles north of Voinka, where they succeeded after weeks of night labor in building a causeway for vehicular traffic across the Sivash Sea, which at that point was about 2,000 yards wide. This work was accomplished in spite of repeated aerial bombardments and harassing artillery fire, and must be considered as a remarkable achievement. Unfortunately for German forces in the area, the long nights, frequent spells of heavy fog, and general observation difficulties prevented friendly forces from taking more effective action.[22]

Fighting was less severe during the latter half of November and the first part of December, by which time the Seventeenth Army was able to proceed with plans to regain some of its lost territory by counterattack. There were several choices open: to fight in the northern Crimea with the intention of winning back the Tatars' wall, to seize the Chigary Peninsula, to force back the enemy bridgeheads north of Kerch, or to destroy the enemy bridgehead at Eltigen. The latter course was deemed the most favorable for the Seventeenth Army's weak forces.

After careful preparation, and with powerful support from the I Air Corps and the 9th Flak Division, German and Rumanian units launched on 14 December 1943 a counterattack to eliminate the Soviet bridgehead at Eltigen. The Soviet Command had made desperate efforts to maintain and even enlarge this position, and had resorted to the use of air-drops for the logistical support of forces at that point. Most of the aircraft involved in these operations, however, were shot down by German flak units.

The counterattack was successful and resulted in the recapture of the Eltigen area with a loss to the Russians of 80 boats, 15 aircraft, a large number of weapons, and many casualties. On the night of the 14th, however, a force of several hundred enemy troops broke out through the Rumanian positions without being detected. This force then proceeded northward toward Kerch, overrunning several small German units enroute, and arrived at the heights of Mitridat west and southwest of the city of Kerch. This enemy group was finally eliminated by Wehrmacht forces,

---

*Elements of the German 336th Infantry Division and Rumanian units, supported by the 86th Light Flak Battalion. On 27 November alone, 100 Soviet dead were counted in the 3rd battery area, and on 2 December another 60 dead, according to after-action reports of the 86th Light Flak Battalion.

but not before it had caused a considerable amount of trouble for Seventeenth Army units.

On 16 December a futile attempt was made by Soviet forces, using a few S-boats* and five ground-attack IL-2 aircraft, to assault the German positions at Eltigen. The exact purpose of this attack was uncertain, since the forces employed were by no means commensurate to the requirements of the situation. German flak forces destroyed one boat, drove off the others, and shot down one "Stormovik."

It seemed that the Russians were temporarily satisfied with their gains in the north on the Perekop isthmus and farther to the east along the shores of the Sivash Sea. The Seventeenth Army made a careful study to determine whether further counterattacks such as that at Eltigen could be made in the northern Crimea, but concluded that any such efforts would only result in a weakening of the army's defensive power and in the Chigary Peninsula in the possible loss of considerable heavy equipment, including self-propelled guns.

Fears that the Sivash Sea, despite the salt content of its water, might freeze over and permit mass enemy crossings did not materialize because of the mild weather. Therefore the German defenses were temporarily adequate along this front and the combat activities along the Tatars' wall and Sivash Sea areas remained relatively minor in character. During this time the Wehrmacht improved its positions and laid plans for the eventual evacuation of the peninsula.

One remarkable feature during the winter of 1943-1944 was the large number of propaganda leaflets which were dropped by Soviet aircraft. In these efforts the Soviet Command endeavored to direct its propaganda attack at individual German divisions, giving the names of unit commanders and any derogatory information about them. These leaflets also specified by name persons whom the Red Army had allegedly captured unharmed while on patrol missions. From the information given it was obvious that the paybooks of these men had come into Soviet possession.† The 9th Flak Division was favored with one of these direct

---

*Editor's Note: Similar to the U. S. PT motor-torpedo boat. The term "S-boat" is a German appellation from Schnellboot (fast boat).

†Editor's Note: All members of the German military services were required to carry with them a Soldbuch (paybook), which also served as a personal identification record. This could be demanded at any time by commissioned and non-commissioned officers, police officials, or other proper authorities. Early in the war the designation of the unit to which the bearer belonged was shown in the book, but this practice was later abandoned for security reasons.

addresses, which contained a crude mixture of threats and blandishments.[23]

Frequently repeated enemy air attacks against various parts of the main line of resistance and airfields on the Crimean Peninsula resulted in heavy Russian losses due to German fighter and flak defenses. Russian air units made repeated attacks upon the small supply and naval base at Ak-Mechet in the northwestern corner of the peninsula, and German flak batteries regularly shot down a number of IL-2 aircraft in this area.

The port of Ak-Mechet was also the scene of an interesting incident which occurred during this period. A Russian motor-torpedo boat entered the harbor in broad daylight and was recognized as a hostile craft only after it was already within the port. Without attacking, the boat immediately turned about and attempted to escape. At this very late juncture German light flak guns opened fire and sank the vessel. Members of the crew of this Soviet boat who were rescued by the German Navy stated that they had lost contact with their parent organization and all sense of orientation, and assumed (incorrectly as it turned out) that they were on the opposite shore, which was already occupied by their own forces. Their navigation was off by 180°.[24]

During this time, in spite of Hitler's orders to hold fast in the Crimea, the Seventeenth Army continued its plans for the evacuation of the peninsula, either as a tactical withdrawal or as a last moment retirement in the face of enemy pressure. Plans provided for a rapid retrograde movement to the fortified Sevastopol area, from whence all forces were to be evacuated by sea and air. Seventeenth Army then ordered the preparation of phase lines with antitank defenses to delay the enemy follow-up or a possible enveloping pursuit by Red Army tank and motorized forces in the broad, open terrain of the Crimea.

In the words of Generalleutnant Pickert:

> The fundamental idea was, in a foreseeable time, to prepare the obviously coming evacuation of the Crimea by the construction of positions which would ease and make possible through phase lines the retreat to Sevastopol and the related evacuation. The only possibility for an evacuation seemed to be through this fortified and port area.[25]

Since the evacuations of the Caucasus and Kuban areas, the Seventeenth Army had come to appreciate the capabilities and, therefore, the special significance of air transportation. Great importance was thus attached to the expansion of existing airfields and to the development of additional airfields within the fortified area of Sevastopol. The use of the latter for operational purposes was expressly prohibited in order not to reveal the presence of these fields to the enemy prior to the beginning of the evacuation movement.

Work was commenced in June of 1943 on the repair and expansion of the Khersones airfield, which was used by the Russians in their evacuation of the Crimea during Manstein's operations in 1942. The tremendous blows rained upon the field at that time by von Richthofen's VIII Air Corps had completely demolished the base and rendered it unfit for operations. By the end of September, however, the runways had been completely reconstructed.

Luftwaffe Activity in the Crimea in the Winter of 1943-1944

Generalmajor Paul Deichmann, who assumed command over the I Air Corps early in November 1943, describes the situation in the Crimea as he undertook his new duties:

> On the Crimean Peninsula the corps [I Air Corps] had a few dive-bomber units and a few fighter and reconnaissance squadrons. It also controlled a few Rumanian air units, including a dive-bomber group. Air Command Black Sea, under Lieutenant Colonel Schalke, had only a few naval and air-sea rescue squadrons.
>
> Airfields were available for bombers as well as supplies, the latter being at Sarabuz airfield. In addition, an air base area command (Lieutenant Colonel Wolfien) was at the disposal of the corps in the Crimea.
>
> The corps headquarters staff was then at Nikolayev on the mainland. Initially it was under an acting chief of staff, Lieutenant Colonel Schult (GSC), who was later replaced by a permanent chief of staff, Lt. Col. Krafft von Delmensingen (GSC). This staff was responsible for the conduct of operations in support of the Sixth Army on the southern flank of the Eastern Front, insofar as this support was necessary and available bomber forces were not required in the Crimea.

The bomber units assigned to the corps from time to time were stationed at the Nikolayev airfield. There was also a fighter command headquarters in Nikolayev under Col. Dietrich Hrabask, which controlled the German fighter group operating out of Bagarovo in the Crimea (under Maj. Gerhard Barkhorn*), and a fighter force stationed at Nikolayev-West. Besides this, there were a few reconnaissance squadrons assigned to the corps on the mainland which supported Army Group "A" or the Sixth Army.

Upon examining the situation on the mainland, I discovered that no preparations had been made for air operations in the southern area of the theater if the German lines were retired and Nikolayev lost. I therefore immediately requested Fourth Air Fleet Headquarters to develop airfields in specified areas for light air units and to build up the necessary logistical stocks. The designated areas were in the rear.

I then assumed command in the Crimea. The situation there was very disturbing. German and Soviet forces were face to face at three narrow entrances to the peninsula, and the Russians had succeeded some time before in establishing a bridgehead on the Kerch Peninsula. Other German forces were in positions along the shores of the Sivash Sea in the northern Crimea, with only a narrow and shallow channel between them and the Soviet forces on the opposite shore. The Russians were constructing underwater causeways, with the intention of moving tanks across the water if necessary. In the October Revolution of 1917 the Communists under Stalin captured the Crimea from the White Russian forces in an attack across the Sivash Sea, and it was therefore assumed that preparations were being made here under Stalin.[26]

Besides the Sivash front, German forces clung to the narrow front across the Perekop Peninsula and the Kerch Peninsula. Because the

---

*Editor's Note: Germany's second highest fighter ace, with 301 victories. He flew 1,104 combat missions during the war, on both Eastern and Western Fronts.

Crimea was virtually cut off from the mainland and all logistical connections, supplies and replacements had to be routed through Odessa or Nikolayev for shipment by sea or air to the Seventeenth Army area. There were no substantial numbers of replacements or stocks of supplies available on the peninsula.

If the Russians breached any one of the three main defense lines, they could pour into the plains on the peninsula where it would be impossible to halt them because of a lack of reserves, and the other fronts would then automatically collapse. With this possibility in mind the Seventeenth Army planned for a very speedy withdrawal of its forces from the north and northwest toward the south and southeast through Simferopol to Sevastopol. Antitank defense lines were to be established to halt Soviet tanks which might outrun the general enemy advance. Actually, the only place in which such a line could be well established was along the eastern boundary of the Sevastopol fortress.

In view of these circumstances, General Deichmann ordered the air base area command to use everything available to develop a number of small airfields in the Sevastopol area for light air units and a few landing strips for liaison and transport planes. The larger field at Khersones was to be prepared for use by bombers, and all Luftwaffe stores, such as fuel, ammunition, and the like, were to be moved back within the Sevastopol defense perimeter.

In a study, copies of which were handed to the various unit commanders, Deichmann set up the withdrawal schedules to be followed in case any of the three army fronts should be breached. The study provided for a retirement by phase lines or an all-out withdrawal in a single movement according to the situation. The I Air Corps' mission in the Crimea was to: (1) interdict the movement of supplies across the Straits of Kerch to Soviet forces in position on the western shore; (2) attack Soviet shelters, billets, and artillery concentrations in the Kerch beachhead; (3) interfere with the construction of causeways across the Sivash Sea, insofar as it was possible to interfere with underwater structures; (4) protect the German front at the Kerch beachhead against Soviet air attacks, this being the area of main emphasis for enemy air action; (5) maintain day and night air reconnaissance in the areas around the Crimea, keep under observation the Soviet Black Sea Fleet in the ports of Sukhumi, Poti, and Batum, and conduct strategic reconnaissance in the Soviet rear areas north of the Crimea; and (6) protect German convoy traffic from Konstanza, Odessa, and Nikolayev to the Crimea against Soviet air attacks.

In order to execute the first three parts of the above mission, one or two groups at a time of the bomber wing at Nikolayev were transferred in rotation to Sarabuz to support the German and Rumanian dive-bomber group there. Since the number of trichloroethylene bombs stored at Sarabuz was far in excess of local requirements, and because it was difficult to evacuate them, General Deichmann obtained approval to use them in these missions. They had a tremendous blast effect and were used primarily in attacks against shelters and artillery positions in the city of Kerch.

Attacks with light fragmentation-type bombs were made upon Soviet loading and landing points in order to interrupt enemy traffic (mostly night traffic) across the Straits of Kerch. German aircraft also strafed Soviet shipping, most of which consisted of small craft of one type or another. Owing to the murky character of the water in the Sivash Sea (known also as the Putrid Sea), nothing could be determined concerning the effectiveness of attacks against the causeways being constructed by Soviet forces. Since the top surfaces of these causeways were below the water's level, the Luftwaffe concentrated upon attempting to prevent the construction of these crossings by making night attacks with light fragmentation bombs upon the working parties.

Pursuant to orders from the Commander in Chief of the Luftwaffe, the IV Air Corps (on the mainland behind the Eighth Army) was withdrawn in December for training as a strategic bombing corps.[27] The I Air Corps then had to extend its operational area from the Crimea to the mainland, for which tasks it was to receive a number of light units from the IV Air Corps. General Deichmann recalls the critical nature of the Eighth Army front at this time:

> Since fierce fighting had developed in the Eighth Army sector east of Kirovograd, where Soviet tanks had achieved a breakthrough, and since no combat activity of any appreciable size was in progress at the time in the Crimean Peninsula, I decided to take personal charge of air operations in the threatened area. Placing Colonel Bauer in charge on the peninsula as Commanding Officer, Air Command Crimea, I proceeded by air to the IV Air Corps command post (General Meister) at Kirovograd, where I landed during a heavy snowstorm.
>
> At the Kirovograd airfield I found more than 100 aircraft, including a large number of twin-engine bombers, which had been unable to take off because of bad weather.

Soviet tanks had meanwhile approached to within a few miles of the field and had then unexpectedly come to a halt, probably because of fuel shortages.

A brief spell of better weather then followed which made it possible to evacuate the airfield, leaving behind only a few unserviceable aircraft which were destroyed. While the evacuation was in progress, a formation of Soviet IL-2 planes attacked the airfield, setting one of the large hangars on fire with bombs. I thereupon gave the order to demolish the airfield.

I moved, together with the headquarters staff of the IV Air Corps, to Novo Ukrainka, where my own staff had in the meantime arrived to facilitate the transfer of command.[28]

Because of a lack of space, certain headquarters elements could not transfer to Deichmann's new command post. These included the supply, administration, and medical sections of his staff. Therefore, from that time on the command staff remained separated into first and second echelons.

The few bomber units remaining to the I Air Corps were based on an airfield to the west of Kirovograd, while the light units operated from airfields north of Novo Ukrainka, on which the snow had been rolled flat. Units of the 2nd Dive-Bomber Wing (probably the 2nd and 3rd groups) were at Zlynka, while fighter and ground-attack aircraft were based at Malaya Viska, 6 miles farther to the north.[29]

On the Crimean Peninsula, completely isolated from German forces on the mainland, stood the Seventeenth Army, and with it the 9th Flak Division and the weak forces of Air Command Crimea. As the year 1943 drew to a close they awaited the Soviet offensive which was sure to come, an offensive aiming at the recapture of the entire peninsula.

Chapter 6

OPERATIONS IN THE NORTHERN AND FAR NORTHERN AREAS IN 1943

The Defensive Battles of Army Group North

At the turn of the year 1943, Army Group North, under Field Marshal Georg von Kuechler, held a line extending from the area east of Nevel to Demyansk to Lake Ilmen to Petrokrepost (Schluesselburg), with the Sixteenth Army (Field Marshal Ernst Busch) on the right wing, and the Eighteenth Army (Generaloberst Georg Lindemann) on the left. These positions had changed very little in the past year, and since the opening of the winter battles of 1942-43 Army Group North had held its lines against all attacks.

The First Air Fleet (Generaloberst Alfred Keller) had been highly successful in supporting the Sixteenth and Eighteenth Armies in their defensive battles, in spite of the weak air forces available for these operations.[1] In January 1943 the initial main emphasis in air operations centered upon aiding the northern (left) flank of the Eighteenth Army, anchored on the southern tip of Lake Ladoga.* Here, the Russians, after a heavy artillery preparation, had launched on 12 January two simultaneous attacks against the XXVI Corps, one by units driving from the west across the Neva River, the other by massed forces on a narrow front coming from the east along the shore of Lake Ladoga.

The weak defending ground forces were unable to resist such a powerful and determined pincers attack and were forced to fall back from the lake. On 18 January the Red Army captured Petrokrepost and succeeded in establishing and holding a corridor of 4 to 6 miles in width between its lines and the German forces enveloping Leningrad.† Until

---

*See Maps Nos. 1 and 14.

†Editor's Note: The reestablishment of land contact with Leningrad had a tremendous effect upon the Finns, who had begun to lose confidence in their German ally after Stalingrad, the outcome of which was no longer subject to speculation. In February the Finnish Parliament was told that Germany could no longer win the war, and a month later the U. S. State Department offered to establish contact between Finland and the U. S. S. R. The Wehrmacht then tried to hang on to its very effective Finnish units, but was soon forced to give many of them up, including the Finnish SS Division.

that time the Soviet Union's only contact between the city of Leningrad and the rest of the Red Army front had been by way of the ice road across Lake Ladoga.* Nevertheless, despite all of the terrible privations the populace of the city kept up its resistance with fanaticism. Death and disease had become commonplace to the people of Leningrad, yet, under the iron discipline of Party leaders (who controlled the city), they continued to work in the factories and to turn out war materials even under the harshest of living conditions.†

During operations in the Petrokrepost area it became necessary for the First Air Fleet to airlift supplies to a temporarily enveloped German force until that unit was able to fight its way out toward the south. Weak air forces were also continuously committed in interdiction operations against the traffic on the ice road across Lake Ladoga. In actual fact, the road itself was attacked, since most of the Soviet columns moved at night and the available means to effectively counter this were insufficient. German bombers tried to temporarily sever the routes across the frozen lake by using large-caliber demolition bombs or by attempting to melt the ice with oil bombs.[2] The German Command realized, of course, that the effects of such action were questionable.

Later, attempts were made to interrupt traffic by dropping small-caliber bombs (painted white) fitted with stabilizing vanes and highly sensitive point-detonating fuzes. The writer cannot state with certainty whether it was ever possible to estimate the success of these operations. Perhaps they were merely shots in the dark.[3] The holes melted by the oil bombs usually froze over very quickly, but the small caliber bombs armed with their super-quick detonators were practically invisible in the snow and therefore produced some good results. Scattered repeatedly in large numbers, they had the effect of a minefield.[4]

---

*Editor's Note: See Generalleutnant Hermann Plocher, The German Air Force versus Russia, 1941, USAF Historical Studies No. 153, Maxwell AFB, Alabama: USAF Historical Division, ASI, July 1965, pp. 146-150. See also Generalleutnant Hermann Plocher, The German Air Force versus Russia, 1942, USAF Historical Studies No. 154, Maxwell AFB, Alabama: USAF Historical Division, ASI, June 1966, pp. 90-92.

†Editor's Note: For an excellent account of conditions within the besieged city of Leningrad see Leon Gouré, The Siege of Leningrad, Stanford, California: Stanford University Press, 1962.

In February, under the 3rd Air Division (Generalmajor Herbert J. Rieckhoff),* units of the First Air Fleet were again employed almost exclusively in direct support operations, concentrating mainly against the Russian troops attacking south of Lake Ladoga and south of Lake Ilmen.†

In order to straighten the front and thereby allow a more economical use of manpower, Hitler approved in mid-February the evacuation of the Demyansk bridgehead, a salient which jutted far out in front of the general main line of resistance. The tactical withdrawal from this bridgehead commenced on 21 February 1943 and proved to be an extremely difficult operation, since all of the divisions in the sector had to pass one after the other through the narrow corridor east of the Lovat River in full view of the Russians and under constant enemy pressure. Nevertheless, the movement was accomplished smoothly, and in early March the Sixteenth Army had its forces firmly reestablished in a line extending from Kholm to Staraya Russa. From this new line the Sixteenth Army then repelled massive Soviet breakthrough attempts on both sides of Staraya Russa, inflicting heavy casualties upon enemy forces.[5]

In connection with this operation special mention must be made of the 21st Luftwaffe Field Division, which held a sector of the line south of Demyansk, a frontage of 62 to 66 miles in breadth. With its back to a virtually impassable area, this division held its lines with meager forces which could not have resisted a serious enemy attack. The German Command feared that as soon as the Russians noticed the evacuation of the Demyansk pocket they might launch an attack in the direction of Dno-Pskov to outflank this division. Fortunately for the Wehrmacht, the Soviet Command failed to exploit its opportunity, as a result of which the 21st Luftwaffe Field Division, in spite of its overextended lines, was able to repel all attacks until forces released from the Demyansk sector arrived in the area.[6]

Tactical support units of the First Air Fleet provided effective assistance to German ground forces during this withdrawal, so that the Red Army could make only a slow follow-up. Luftwaffe units concentrated primarily upon operations in support of the Army all along the front in Combat Zone North until well into April, when more or less

---

*Organized in January 1943 from the air command staff which was established in August of 1942 for the attack upon Leningrad. Generalmajor Rieckhoff was, until 15 March 1943, also the Chief of the General Staff of the First Air Fleet.

†See figure 38.

Figure 38
Soviet ground-attack planes are repelled by an 8. 8-cm. Luftwaffe flak section on the Lake Ladoga front, 3 February 1943

continuous bad weather hampered, and sometimes altogether stopped, air operations. Whenever conditions permitted, however, they flew support missions, especially for the LIV Corps south of Leningrad, which was then struggling to hold back Soviet forces trying to break out of the city area.

On 13 March 1943 Hitler ordered Army Group North to make preparations to recapture the positions surrounding Leningrad and to take the city itself. There was a serious danger that the Russians would soon take steps to push the Germans far back from the city or would strike south of Lake Ilmen between Army Groups North and Center, thereby splitting the two and forcing Army Group North to retire toward the Baltic coast. In the ensuing weeks Field Marshal von Kuechler formulated a plan to take Leningrad, which was named Operation PARKPLATZ. In accordance with this plan the siege artillery on hand would have been adequate, but 8 or 9 additional divisions were required, divisions which could not be made available until after the Kursk offensive.*

Between January and April 1943, whenever the situation seemed to be promising, the Luftwaffe attacked Soviet rail traffic and installations, airfields, and even a few industrial targets. In January, for example, strong air forces concentrated primarily against the Shum-Tikhvin rail line, and in the following month against the Ostashkov and Toropets rail depots. In March, German squadrons struck the Bologoye, Tikhvin, and Volkhov railroad depots, as well as two airfields which served the Soviet flying units that operated against the Sixteenth Army. German units destroyed 40 Soviet aircraft on the ground in these attacks and caused large fires in the shelters and billets. They also attacked an aircraft engine factory in Rybinsk, two electric power stations in Leningrad, and an oil refinery.† April air activities included a number of attacks upon the Shum-Tikhvin railroad line, a concentrated strike upon two airfields on which large numbers of enemy aircraft were standing, and aerial mining missions by a number of bombers over the coastal waters around Kronstadt.

Soviet ground attacks in the northern area slackened considerably in May, for which reason the Luftwaffe gave more attention to Soviet supply

---

*See p. 72. These forces were never to be available for such an undertaking, since crises in the Orel-Kursk areas prevented any weakening of the German positions there.

†Probably a refinery located near Novaya Ladoga.

movements. Elements of the 53rd Bomber Wing attacked with good effects the Tikhvin and Volkhov railroad depots, supply traffic moving across Lake Ladoga for Leningrad (including the landing stages), an aircraft engine factory in Rybinsk, a cellulose processing factory in Seyastroye, and a number of supply dumps and fuel depots.

In June main emphasis remained on railroad interdiction missions. In Combat Zone Center a few units of the bomber forces controlled by the Sixth Air Fleet carried out successful attacks against the rubber processing combine in Yaroslavl, causing serious destruction to industrial installations and fires of long duration. [7] In addition, some squadrons attacked the locks at Novaya Ladoga and a large oil depot at that place, while other units repeatedly attacked partisan camps which were reported southwest of Wilna and in the rear of the German Volkhov River front.

Early in July most of the First Air Fleet units were transferred to the Sixth Air Fleet in Combat Zone Center, where they were committed in support of Operation ZITADELLE.[8*] The only air forces remaining in the First Air Fleet sector were a bomber squadron and a fighter-bomber squadron, and the harassing units. For the time being these weak forces were concentrated primarily for direct support missions in the XXVI Corps sector, south of Lake Ladoga. In the meantime, von Kuechler became more pessimistic about the prospects of launching an operation for the seizure of Leningrad, and, with the opening of the Soviet offensive on 22 July, which aimed to throw German forces even farther back from the city, the entire idea of PARKPLATZ was jettisoned.

On 28 July General der Flieger Guenther Korten replaced Generaloberst Alfred Keller as Commander of the First Air Fleet. Korten remained in command of this organization for only a short while, however (until 23 August 1943), since on 19 August he was appointed Chief of the General Staff of the Luftwaffe to replace Generaloberst Hans Jeschonnek, who had suddenly committed suicide. [/] The Commander of the IV Air Corps (General der Flieger Kurt Pflugbeil) assumed command on 24 August over the First Air Fleet. [9]

The position of Chief of Staff, First Air Fleet, also changed hands repeatedly during the spring of 1943. The arrangement whereby the Chief of Staff, First Air Fleet, simultaneously commanded the 3rd Air Division often resulted in considerable friction. For this reason, Col. Hans-Detlef Herhudt von Rohden (GSC) was appointed on 15 March to the post of

---

*See Chapters 3 and 4.

/See biographical section at the back of this volume.

Chief of Staff, while General Rieckhoff remained in command of the 3rd Air Division.*

In mid-August emphasis in air operations had to be shifted to the area south of Lake Ilmen, the Sixteenth Army sector, where the Red Army on 18 August had again commenced a heavy attack against the powerfully fortified stronghold of Staraya Russa. This attack also was repelled with effective support from units of the First Air Fleet. Until well into September units were also sent out to attack Soviet supply depots, airfields, and railroads, as well as shipping in the Gulf of Finland and Lake Ladoga. Since the normal combat aircraft available were far too few to accomplish all these missions, First Air Fleet Headquarters instructed all air reconnaissance units to combine their reconnaissance activities with harassing raids upon rail installations, airfields, and Soviet-occupied settlements, a measure which produced highly satisfactory results.

From the beginning of spring the Russians had again and again attacked the lines held by the Sixteenth and Eighteenth Armies and, in some cases, had achieved penetrations, most of which, however, were cleaned out by immediate counterattacks. The front of Army Group North, which was supported by the First Air Fleet, had remained relatively unaffected by the large-scale enemy offensives, which were waged against Army Groups South and Center, yet it had its own local problems. All during August it fended off a number of Soviet attacks, as it worked to build the so-called Panther Position (Pantherstellung), the Narva River to Lake Peipus line.

There had been considerable discussion concerning the possible withdrawal of the entire Army Group, but this was immediately ruled out. Not only did the Eastern Front require that these positions be held, but it was essential to consider the attitude of the Finnish ally, whose assistance in the areas farther to the north was essential. Thus, no substantial withdrawal was made, and at the end of September the Sixteenth and Eighteenth Armies were approximately in their old positions, defending a line running generally from east of Vitebsk to west of Velikiye Luki to Kholm to Staraya Russa to the front held by the forces investing Leningrad. Because of the relative quiet along this front, while severe pressures were being exerted against the other two army groups to the south, 13 German divisions were withdrawn from Army Group North for employment in these more critical areas.[10]

---

*In August Col. Klaus Uebe (GSC) relieved Colonel von Rohden as Chief of Staff.

On 6 October 1943 an exceedingly heavy Soviet attack on both sides of Nevel struck the thus weakened northern front in the most vulnerable sector, the boundary between the Third Panzer Army (Generaloberst Hans Reinhardt), on the north flank of Army Group Center, and the Sixteenth Army, holding the southern flank of Army Group North.* East of Nevel the Russians broke through the understrength German divisions and proceeded to expand their breakthrough in all directions. An extremely grave danger threatened. What made the threat particularly acute was that the Soviets here were only 72 miles from Daugavpils ,(Latvia) and that a strategic breakthrough in that direction would have placed the entire front of the army group in serious jeopardy.[11]

In the last few days of September, immediately prior to the Soviet offensive, a large-scale police operation had been initiated to clean out the Russian partisans in the boundary area between Army Groups Center and North. The northern group of these police forces had been assigned an air unit which was organized in the field for the purpose. This air force, commanded by Maj. Rudolf Jenett (GSC), was composed of night bomber units containing training aircraft of various types and small Fieseler (Fi) 156 "Storch" planes, and was intended for daylight action against the partisans. However, unusually bad weather, with cloud ceilings from 250 to 3,000 feet, had prevented air operations. Several reconnaissance planes operating at ground altitudes observed the police forces combing through the area in closely integrated lines, but saw no signs of the Russians.

It was into this relatively empty space that the Soviet attack through Nevel was launched. Possibly the Soviet Command was surprised by the speed and scope of its initial successes. Whatever the reasons may have been, the Russians were not adequately prepared for the tactical exploitation of this successful attack and at first restricted themselves to reinforcing the extended flanks of their deep penetration.[12]

No reserves were available to the German Command, so that the only force which could be initially committed to hold the Soviet breakthrough force consisted of the police troops (mentioned previously) who were engaged in antipartisan operations, elements of security forces, and a few similar units which were scraped together wherever they could be found.

---

*General der Artillerie Christian Hansen had assumed command over the Sixteenth Army on 12 October 1943.

In this situation the Luftwaffe was once again the last hope, and was called upon to halt and break up the attacking Soviet forces and thereby to prevent a strategic breakthrough. Most of the air units committed for this task were from the Sixth Air Fleet, operating in Combat Zone Center. At the time, the First Air Fleet, which was responsible for air support in Combat Zone North, had very inconsiderable air units under its command, and these were employed almost exclusively in night harassing raids. 13

With very effective air support the Third Panzer Army (Army Group Center) and the Sixteenth Army succeeded in halting and sealing off the Soviet breakthrough, but they were unable to clean out the Nevel penetration area because of a lack of reserves. A dangerous Soviet wedge thus remained in the thinly manned German defensive line.

Up to the end of 1943 the First Air Fleet took every opportunity permitted by the existing weather conditions to employ its weak remaining units in continuous air support missions for the defending ground troops. Concurrently, units were dispatched against partisan groups, particularly in the areas around Pskov and Luga. Reconnaissance units continued their harassing raids against occupied settlements and rail targets, particularly along the Ostashkov-Toropets-Velikiye Luki route and against the Ostashkov, Vishera, and Toropets rail depots, until the end of the year.

General der Infanterie Kurt von Tippelskirch (Ret.) describes the development of events along this front, a front whose boundaries had not changed appreciably from 1941 to 1943:

> . . . In January 1943 the Eighteenth Army had been compelled to abandon the close investment of the southeastern front at Leningrad as it lost Petrokrepost [Schluesselburg]. In February 1943 the Sixteenth Army had voluntarily evacuated the salient around Demyansk and stood in strong positions forward of Staraya Russa.
>
> Yet the front which appeared so firm in Army Group North had its various weak points. The German forces had never sufficed to eliminate the disturbing Soviet bridgehead at Lomonosov [Oranienbaum], which was supported by the fortresses of Kronstadt and by the Russian naval units which had been transformed into floating batteries. After the loss of Petrokrepost, a Russian salient existed east of Tosno and Lyuban, which caused a constant threat to the eastern flank of the German

front before Leningrad. This corresponded to a German salient north of Chudovo, which could not be withdrawn, although it required four divisions to hold this alone. After the fluctuating battles of the past years, the Russians were able to maintain an 18-mile-wide bridgehead on the Volkhov. In the Lomonosov bridgehead, their salient southeast of Leningrad, and their Volkhov River bridgehead they held three favorable areas for staging an offensive against the Eighteenth Army.

The Sixteenth Army had four seasoned divisions in position south of Lake Ilmen on both sides of Staraya Russa, which had repeatedly come under Soviet break-through attacks since the evacuation of Demyansk. In contrast, the gigantic trackless and swampy forest areas extending from north of Kholm to Velikiye Luki, in which there were no railroads, had not been the scene of any serious combat action with the exception of the fighting for Kholm in the winter of 1941-42. For this reason it was held by only weak forces.

The relative quiet on the front of Army Group North and the severe enemy pressure in the other two army group sectors had resulted in the withdrawal of 13 divisions from the quiet northern area. When the [Soviet] First Baltic Front at the end of December launched its breakthrough offensive against the Third Panzer Army at Vitebsk, the Sixteenth Army was compelled to release two divisions from its front to support the Third Panzer Army, thus further weakening Army Group North, which no longer had any panzer or armored infantry [Panzer-Grenadier] divisions and had not had any for the past two years.[14]

In concluding this section on the activities in Combat Zone North it should be pointed out that during 1943 the First Air Fleet, with its 3rd Air and 2nd and 6th Flak Divisions, committed the bulk of its air, flak, and signal forces in direct-support operations on the various battlefields. Here the air signal units proved to be fully satisfactory as the command instrument of the Luftwaffe; flak batteries in this northern sector, as elsewhere, became the backbone of the ground defenses, thus eclipsing their air defense role, while air units in this sector of the front, as was true in other parts of the Eastern Theater of Operations, became the only immediately available and effective force which could be employed to bring about a favorable change in the course of the ground battle. Missions against supply installations, road and rail supply traffic, and airfields deep in the Soviet rear could be carried out only if the targets involved had a specific operational bearing upon action to repel Soviet offensives and were flown then only if sufficient aircraft were available for the purpose.

The few really strategic attacks flown against Soviet armament factories achieved local successes, but, since they were isolated actions, they actually produced no strategic results. Furthermore, the inadequacy of available forces made it impossible to carry out the attacks in sufficient force and with the required frequency to cause really destructive effects.

That the German ground forces were able to hold their lines in the northern part of the Eastern Front was due largely, and often in a decisive measure, to the support given by the Luftwaffe through the First Air Fleet, the conduct of whose flyers was exemplary.[15] However, this meant that in Combat Zone North, just as in all other parts of the Eastern Front, the Luftwaffe was unable throughout 1943 to perform its real mission, that of conducting aerial warfare and was, instead, restricted as in the previous year to effective support operations for the fighting ground forces.

The Luftwaffe in the Far North: Norwegian and Barents Seas and the Murmansk Front

Finnish Front

The Finnish Front was the northern cornerstone of the German European defense system, the extreme northern flank position of the Eastern Theater of Operations, which at the same time protected the rear of the Norwegian Front. The total frontage of approximately 840 miles was about two-thirds as long as the entire Eastern Front (Leningrad to the Crimea), and large sectors of it were defended by systems of strongpoints.

In the southeastern sectors of this zone the terrain was heavily wooded and quite swampy, while in the northeast it was devoid of trees and in many places consisted of rocky tundra.* Weather conditions varied greatly. On 1 November 1943, for example, temperatures ranged from 0° to 46° Fahrenheit. In the northern areas there were the characteristically long arctic nights in the summer. Mud seasons were inconsiderable.

In the field of military economy the nickel works of Kolosjoko near Petsamo were important, and accounted for 32 percent of the European nickel production.†

The population of Finland totalled 3,800,000 persons, but military operations on a large scale were impossible because of a great lack of communications. With only a single railroad extending from north to south as far as Rovaniemi, and an eastward branch line running to Kandalaksha still under construction, plus a single good north-south road from Helsinki to Petsamo, the area was completely lacking in routes capable of carrying enough traffic to support an offensive. In contrast, the Russians had the highly satisfactory Murmansk railroad route. Operations were therefore conducted primarily in the form of patrol and raiding party activities, with flank battles and some more active fighting for particularly important roads.

Because of its broad extent, the front in this area nevertheless tied down strong German forces. The Twentieth Mountain Army had a strength of 176,800 men, all especially selected for their ability to withstand the harsh rigors of the local natural conditions. Its divisions were at full strength, fully equipped, trained under peacetime conditions, and ably led.[16]

Conditions for air operations were generally unfavorable, and the terrain offered few possibilities for the construction of airfields.[17]

---

*Editor's Note: Tundra areas are covered with primitive vegetation, lichens on the drier sites, mosses and sedge on the poorer areas, while birches and willows grow in the more favorable places. The soils there are mostly bogs of partially decomposing vegetable matter. What is most adverse here are the enormous swarms of flies and mosquitoes, making the area intolerable for most domesticated animals. Germans, like the Finns and Lapps, used reindeer for transport purposes. See George A. Hoffman, A Geography of Europe Including Asiatic U.S.S.R., New York: The Ronald Press Co., 1961, pp. 66-71.

†This was just becoming economically important to Finland when in 1940 it was seized by the Soviet Union.

After the defensive battles in this area in the spring of 1942, the war on the Karelian Front dragged slowly onward. It was characterized by positional warfare, carried out on a small scale. In an estimate of the situation by Generaloberst Alfred Jodl, Chief of the Wehrmacht Operations Staff, which was received at Finnish General Headquarters on 2 January 1943:

> . . . the Wehrmacht High Command considered it possible that the Russians toward the end of winter might seek a decision in an attack against the front held by the Twentieth Mountain Army, probably in the XIX Mountain Corps sector (Murmansk sector) and possibly in combination with an amphibious operation by the Western Allies on the Arctic coast. . . .
>
> Information had been received again and again in Finland concerning an impending large-scale Soviet offensive against the Finno-German front. The Commanding General, Twentieth Mountain Army,* believed these reports and ordered the highest state of alert for his army and issued instructions that close attention was to be given to the presumed Soviet preparations for attack, which was expected to come early in February against the front in the Far North.[18]

Nothing happened, however. On the contrary, the impression grew in the Wehrmacht Command that the Soviet Command was withdrawing forces along the German front in the Far North. All reports that large-scale Russian attacks would soon be launched in this area or that a landing by the Western Allies was impending proved to be false. Probably these reports were intentionally spread by the Western Allies in order to further undermine the confidence of the Finns in their German ally. This confidence was, of course, already badly shaken by the Soviet successes south of Leningrad and by the Stalingrad tragedy. Probably the reports were intended to soften up the Finns politically to prepare them for peace overtures.[19]

The reconnaissance responsibilities of the Fifth Air Fleet included routine long-range reconnaissance over the water, including Soviet ports, and tactical reconnaissance over the Murmansk front areas. The results obtained indicated no sign of any Soviet plans for a major offensive or of the withdrawal of enemy troops from the area. It would also have been

---

*Generaloberst Eduard Dietl.

almost impossible to detect withdrawal movements owing to the almost continuous darkness during the winter months and the general weather conditions, with fog and snowstorms, which made constant surveillance of the area by means of aerial photography practically impossible. Added to these difficulties was the well-known ability of the Russians to take full advantage of current weather conditions to cover their movements.

Even after the spring thaw the situation along the line held by the Twentieth Mountain Army and the Finns remained quiet. Only partisan activities increased, and these groups of partisans even occasionally caused serious interference with traffic on the Eismeerstrasse (arctic sea road).[20]* For this reason, units of Air Command North (East) were also employed periodically against partisans, especially against partisan camps in the Ukhta or Uhtua region.

Soviet agents had also become increasingly active. For this purpose the Russians attempted to induce German prisoners of war to work for them, and tried to employ any such persons who seemed to be suitable and willing. During the summer of 1943 it frequently happened that German soldiers reported to the nearest German military authorities stating that they had just recently been dropped in the vicinity of the arctic coast by the Russians. Such drops were made at night by Soviet harassing aircraft or other suitable type planes operating from nearby enemy airfields. One such incident was reported by Generalmajor Ernst-August Roth, ≠ Commander of Air Command Lofoten Islands:

> A Luftwaffe noncommissioned officer had been shot down over the Soviet lines. After a few days he had been removed to Murmansk, where he was initially imprisoned and interrogated. After questioning him on all manner of military matters the Russians offered to employ him in intelligence work in German-occupied territories after a lengthy period of training in Murmansk. He was promised better living quarters and rations and more liberty, insofar as he would be allowed to see Murmansk, if he so desired. This would naturally have to take place with an appropriate escort and in civilian clothing, which would be provided. After a few days to consider, the noncommissioned officer accepted the offer, hoping that he would thus find a possibility to

---

*Running from Rovaniemi northward to Ivalo, thence northeast to Petsamo and northwestward to Lakselv.

≠From time to time also Chief, Air Command North.

escape. He was sent to a special school (I assume that this was the same school in which Norwegian agents received training). Here he received training in radio transmission, including encoding and the operation of special transmitters, in matters such as behavior in "enemy" territory and behavior towards German military personnel. One day, or rather one evening, he was taken to an airfield, where he was blindfolded and placed in a plane, outfitted with a parachute, radio transmitter, and code material. He was put in the bomb bay, with the static line of his parachute attached to the plane. After a flight of about 30 minutes' duration he was dropped close to the main road along the arctic coastline. His instructions had been to report on the volume and type of traffic observed moving in both directions along the route and on the forces stationed at the Kirkenes air base. Immediately after reaching the arctic sea road, however, he "thumbed" a ride to the nearest military installation, where he surrendered, together with his transmitter and code material. The man (a sergeant) made a completely trustworthy impression, and was described by his unit as "above suspicion." He had been absent from his base for about three weeks.[21]

Neither the Finno-German nor the Soviet side did much of anything to disturb the calm in the Murmansk railroad area. Conditions in the area were those of positional warfare, and both sides busied themselves in improving their fortifications, shelters, and the like, and in developing the roads for supply traffic. It really seems inexplicable that the Finno-German Command did nothing to plan and execute a new offensive, such as, for example, the seizure of Murmansk or the severing of the Murmansk rail line. The importance of the northern Anglo-American logistical route was obvious. Equally obvious was the withdrawal of Soviet forces, which greatly enhanced the strength ratio in favor of the Finns and the Germans, and which had a direct impact upon the hard-pressed German front between Leningrad and the Black Sea. The seizure of Murmansk, which would have considerably reduced Anglo-American Lend-Lease deliveries, would necessarily have lessened the effects of Soviet attacks and thereby relieved the strain upon the German defenses. This was most important, and it is therefore necessary to ask what the German-Russian strength ratio was at this time.

It is impossible in retrospect to overlook the fact that a noticeable disparity existed in the autumn of 1943 with respect to the overall distribution of forces along the entire front in the Eastern Theater of Operations from the Black Sea to the arctic coast west of Murmansk. Whereas conditions of perpetual crisis for the Wehrmacht had developed in Russia proper (between the Black Sea and the Gulf of Finland) because neither German command measures nor the assignment of new forces could offset the great superiority of the Red Army all along the line, an exactly opposite ratio of forces existed along the Finno-German front. The Soviet withdrawal of forces from this area, which had begun in the spring of 1943 and continued throughout the summer, had resulted in a considerable weakening of the Russian position in the north in comparison with the situation which existed in the summer of 1942. In an evaluation made by the Finnish General Headquarters on 15 September 1943, the overall strength of the Soviet forces opposing the Finno-German front was estimated at only 270,000 men, of which 180,000 were opposite the Finnish sector. Finland at the time had 350,000 men in the field, and the German troops within the command area of the Twentieth Mountain Army totalled about 200,000. In the autumn of 1943 the ratio of strength in the entire area was thus two to one against the Russians (550,000 Finns and Germans against 270,000 Russians). Such a favorable ratio had never existed before at any part of the German front in the East, and this large German superiority was not only a superiority in numbers, but also from a standpoint of quality.

The Finnish and German troops on the line between the Gulf of Finland and the arctic coast were rested and in the best condition. Physically and psychologically they were perfectly fit; further, the Finnish comrades in the field quite generally rejected the disquieting maneuvers of the political opposition in the Finnish Parliament.[22] Of the Twentieth Mountain Army it can be said without exaggeration that it was the strongest and best army available to Germany in 1943. The Army in Lapland had been brought up to full strength, and the troops had accustomed themselves to the special conditions of the area and lacked nothing in the way of weapons and other equipment. Simple calculation proves that a joint Finno-German offensive at that time would have held out the best prospects for a quick and decisive success. The 550,000 Finnish and German troops

---

*Editor's Note: Earl F. Ziemke cites the arguments given here for an offensive in the summer of 1943, but points out that, "In reality, there was no way an offensive out of Finland could have permanently influenced the course of events. The Murmansk railroad could possibly have been cut, but by then it was no longer vital to the Russian war effort; Soviet production had increased and supplies from the West were moving through the Persian Gulf." See _The German Northern Theater of Operations 1940-1945_, DA Pam. 20-271, Washington: Department of the Army, OCMH, 1959, p. 249.

would undoubtedly have been able to deal quickly and thoroughly with the 270,000 Red Army troops opposing them.[23] What were the reasons for the inexplicable failure to launch such an offensive?

In a conference held on 4 March 1943, in which the possibility of a Finno-German offensive in 1943 was discussed, Field Marshal Carl Gustaf Freiherr Mannerheim, the Finnish Commander in Chief, brought the talks to an end with a flat statement to the German Generals present, "I shall not attack again. I have already lost too many men."[24] Impressed by the German retrograde movements in the East and by the successes of the Western Allies in the Mediterranean Theater, Mannerheim had lost faith in the possibility of a German victory. Furthermore, Finnish opposition circles were pressing with increasing urgency for negotiations with the Soviet Union before it was too late, which meant immediately. These circles believed that they could still conclude a relatively favorable armistice and even a peace treaty.

Since the disaster of Stalingrad the Finnish efforts to get out of the war had increased at a great pace. After Britain's declaration of war on Finland on 5 December 1941 Finnish politicians had turned toward Washington. They wanted no war with the great powers of the West, and by 1943 they hoped that President Roosevelt would be able to throw the weight of his influence into the scales in Moscow to the advantage of the Finnish nation, which had enjoyed such widespread sympathy in the United States, especially during the tragic winter war of 1939-40.[25] To the responsible governmental and military leaders in Finland it was perfectly clear at the time that a resumption of the offensive would lead to an immediate declaration of war against Finland by the United States, which was clearly contrary to the wishes and intentions of the great political majority in Finland. Thus, the Finnish General Headquarters exercised extreme caution in order to avoid creating any conditions which might lead to the burdening of the national parliament with responsibility for a state of war with America. This naturally ruled out any plans for a new Finnish offensive.

While in Finland political considerations increasingly overshadowed military decisions, the High Command of the Wehrmacht failed to launch an offensive with German forces alone, a military action it could have taken by stripping other sectors of the front in order to build up a powerful concentration under the XIX Mountain Corps.[26] The XIXth could then have advanced along the coast and, with periodically increased air and naval support, seized Murmansk. After the war General der Infanterie Waldemar Erfurth (Ret.), who had held the post of German General attached to the Finnish General Headquarters, commented upon the possibility of a purely German offensive in the Far North in 1943:

A resumption of the offensive by German troops in the XIX Mountain Corps sector, which for some time was desired by the High Command of the Wehrmacht, was emphatically rejected by Dietl,* and in my opinion rightly rejected, because it would not have been possible to supply a sizeable German force in the tundra region.

> . . . I do not believe that the . . . operation with a strong force (without Finns) along the arctic coast would have been successful because of maneuvering and logistical difficulties. The Murmansk rail route could only have been opened from the south (Soroka, Doukhi).[27]

Generalleutnant Andreas Nielsen, who served as Chief of Staff, Fifth Air Fleet, believed that the German operation would have succeeded:

> With a proper disposition of forces and timely preparation, a German offensive, even without Finnish participation, would have been possible and most probably would have succeeded. It is obvious that such an operation would have been much easier with Finnish support and, in view of the existing numerical and general military superiority, would certainly have been successful. Following the withdrawals of Soviet troops, however, there would have been no necessity to assume any less favorable strength ratio than 1:1. With the seasoned, rested, and well-equipped German troops available, and given such a strength ratio, success surely could have been considered secure, particularly if the attack had been launched with a very clearly defined point of main effort.
>
> In an offensive with German troops alone, certain reinforcements in special weapons and units admittedly would have been essential. This applied particularly to the Luftwaffe, which was considerably outnumbered by the Soviet air forces in the area, in contrast to the opening phases of the campaign and earlier in 1943. These reinforcements would have been needed only temporarily, but it would have been absolutely essential to move in for

---

*Commanding Twentieth Mountain Army. See biographical section.

> a time at least another bomb group, two dive-bomber groups, and a fighter wing. In view of the decisive importance which the collapse of the Soviet arctic front would have had for the movement of supplies from the Western Powers to Russia, and its impact upon the overall situation in the Eastern Theater of Operations, including the political influence upon the future attitude of Finland, the assignment of reinforcements would certainly have been worth while.[28]

But, as Nielsen points out, neither the Wehrmacht High Command nor the locally responsible Twentieth Mountain Army took any such courageous action. At Fifth Air Fleet Headquarters, which as far back as the end of 1941 had submitted a memorandum recommending an offensive solution for the situation along the Barents Sea front, the impression existed that the decisive importance of this northern flank of the front, with its outlet to the oceans, was not fully realized or appreciated by the Army and Wehrmacht High Commands. After much time had been lost through the very late realization that the Russians had weakened their defenses, and after endless conferences with the Finns concerning the continuation of operations, the remaining time was wasted instead of being utilized for timely planning and preparation of an operation such as was heretofore described. As events unfolded in the East, the chances of success became less and less and the year passed without the German Command seizing this singular opportunity for a large-scale and perhaps decisive success. Thus, as far as the arctic sea front is concerned, the year 1943 must be considered one of the lost opportunities of the war.[29]

This opinion is shared by the author, who believes that, in view of the existing strength ratio, an offensive with German forces alone would have met with success. The German Twentieth Mountain Army possessed the finest prerequisites for success with respect to its strength, its equipment, and the physical and psychological condition of its troops, and its supply situation was secure.* All that was lacking was the single most important requirement, the will for courageous action and decision. To

---

*According to Generalleutnant Nielsen, adequate supplies for an entire year were available in the command area of the Norwegian-Barents Sea front. See also General der Infanterie Kurt von Tippelskirch, Geschichte des Zweiten Weltkriegs (History of the Second World War), Bonn: Athenaeum Verlag, 1951, p. 445; "Back of the Murmansk sector were supplies enough to last for nine months."

have taken such a decision certainly would have involved a risk, but the decisively significant impact which the possible success would have had should have been a compelling reason to have accepted the risk. As it was, the positional warfare continued.

There was, to be sure, the danger that Finland would at some future time succumb to suggestions by neutral nations, to American political pressures, and to its own desire to save what could be saved, and would thus separate from its German ally. In the late summer of 1943 the High Command of the Wehrmacht and the Twentieth Mountain Army Headquarters exchanged ideas on the possible consequences for the Twentieth Mountain Army of a Finnish defection.[30] The Wehrmacht High Command then instructed the Twentieth Mountain Army to prepare for a withdrawal of its forces into a wide arc (with a radius of 240 miles) around North Cape against the eventuality of Finland's capitulation.[31] All planning, preparation, and the possible execution of the retrograde movement were to be carried out under the code name Operation BIRKE (Birch).

In September 1943, Generaloberst Dietl and his chief of staff, Generalleutnant Ferdinand Jodl, explored for the first time the possibility of carrying out a movement of this kind, in which tens of thousands of persons would have to travel with bag and baggage northward over a distance of hundreds of miles. The troops could undertake such a risky enterprise only if they received a logistical base consisting of all types of supplies sufficient for several months, including everything needed for subsistence in the barren tundra regions, materials for the construction of field fortifications, shelters, medical installations, and the necessary sanitary and medical equipment, and if the supporting air forces found adequate ground service installations readily available. The roads in this area were totally inadequate for troop movements on such a scale. Hitherto, apart from the Eismeerstrasse (arctic sea road) and the roads in the vicinity of the coast in Norwegian territory, the road network had been required to carry only the small volume of traffic necessary for the sparse Lapland population, which moved about by carts or reindeer sleds, or possibly for sportsman tourists.

The important thing therefore--this was more or less a precautionary measure--was to move in supplies through the main ports along the Norwegian fjord coast and to construct the necessary roads for the operation and improve those already in existence. These activities commenced in the winter of 1943-44, but were limited in scope by the bitter, arctic winter and by the limited available labor. The necessary directives were issued by the Twentieth Mountain Army and by the

Fifth Air Fleet from Oslo. The execution of this plan in Norwegian territory was the responsibility of the German Army of Norway (Generaloberst Nikolaus von Falkenhorst) and the Chief Supply and Administrative Officer for Norway. In Finnish territory the work was supervised by Dietl's mountain army. The projected march routes and supply arteries were as follows: the road following the Tornio and Muoniojoki valleys along the Finno-Swedish border (which was merely a wagon trail from Muonio to the three-nation boundary corner) and the road from Ivalo to Lakselv, which required considerable improvement. The third major route was Reichsstrasse (State Highway) No. 50, extending 600 miles from Narvik to Kirkenes,* a road which was cut by the Lyngen Fjord.ƒ Wherever possible it followed the coastline of the fjords, but at many points it had to cross the fjells, the treeless, high plateaus on the tops of the mountains separating the individual fjords. In most places it was a single track road with innumerable curves, a road having the characteristics of an alpine road, with grades which could barely be negotiated by horse-drawn military vehicles, especially during icy and snowy conditions. Wherever the road crossed the fjells it was covered by wooden structures for protection against snow, or followed raised embankments which were secured against drift snow by an intricate system of snow fences. Reichsstrasse No. 50, which was constructed by German engineer troops and units of Organisation Todt, or OT,ƒƒ was the shore lifeline connecting the Narvik area with the front in the extreme north. The time was later to come when the fate of the bulk of an army, and of the land-bound elements of the German Navy and Luftwaffe which were incorporated into units of that army, was to rely upon the soundness of this artery. Any serious interruption of this road concurrent with a naval blockade could have spelled doom for tens of thousands of these troops.

The hope may still have been entertained that the necessity for this army movement to the north, and for the hazardous battle by the Twentieth Mountain Army in the most exposed and least habitable part of Europe, might never materialize. Nevertheless, developments on the Eastern Front on the other side of the Baltic Sea made it imperative to

---

*See Map No. 15.

ƒEditor's Note: Situated about 80 miles northeast of Narvik. The Lyngen Fjord cuts into the northern coastline of Norway between Tromsø and Nordreisa.

ƒƒA para-military labor organization, which served as an auxiliary to the German Wehrmacht and which derived its name from the former Reichsminister for Arms and Munitions, Dr. Fritz Todt, who was killed in the year 1942.

act in accordance with the Wehrmacht High Command's directive.[32]* The most important task therefore was to make preparations for the retreat of the Army in Lapland to the tundra region, which appeared to be more and more necessary. It was, in fact, high time to make such preparations. What had remained undone because of the arctic winter conditions now had to be accomplished in addition to the urgent new requirements: serviceable roads, including temporary bridges to replace the inadequate ferry facilities, had to be built for the movement of large bodies of troops, phase line positions had to be set up in which the retiring troops could temporarily halt, and permanent fortifications had to be established from which they were to fight their battles in defense of the most northerly part of Scandinavia and the valuable nickel-bearing area of Petsamo. Arrangements had to be carried out in a similar manner at corps level within the communication zone of the Twentieth Mountain Army. The entire operation had to be carefully thought out and executed in every detail. Success hinged decisively upon the carrying capacities of the main and secondary roads, and upon smoothly functioning logistical services. In these virtually uninhabited regions large bodies of troops must subsist exclusively on supplies stored in advance.

The great unpredictable factor still remained the enemy. What would the Russians do if Finland defected? Would they restrict their activities to annihilating blows aimed against the three corps sectors of the German mountain army in order to liquidate the German forces in Lapland, or would they use railroads and their motorized forces for a drive across the former Finnish lines directly through the heartland of Finland to strike at the flank, rear, and very center of the Twentieth Mountain Army? This heart, or nerve center, was in the area around Rovaniemi, and, in the truest sense of the word, the entire XVII Mountain Corps had no choice in a northward withdrawal but to move through Rovaniemi.[33]

---

*Editor's Note: Germany also pressured Sweden to allow a withdrawal across Sweden to Norway, and, for a time, it appeared that this would be permitted. But, as it became more and more obvious that the Soviet Union would win the war rather than Germany (by mid-1943), the Swedes broke off their trade agreement with the Reich and began to favor the Allied cause.

Luftwaffe Anti-Convoy Operations in the Far North, 1943

Owing to the fact that Dvina Bay, and thus the port of Arkhangelsk, was ice-bound in the winter of 1942-43,* the eastward-bound Anglo-American convoys (PQ)/ again directed their course toward Murmansk. Because of the continually unfavorable weather and the brief periods of daylight in these arctic regions, Air Command North (East)// had to leave the operations against convoy PQ 20 in early January 1943 to the German naval forces in the area.

Since they had incurred such heavy losses in convoy shipping, the Western Allies adopted the system of dispatching their cargo vessels singly, without escorts, during long periods of foggy weather, a fact which greatly complicated German reconnaissance. For this reason, Air Command North (East) organized what was called armed reconnaissance, flown by pairs of aircraft which were capable of long-distance flights and were armed for immediate action against any single ships found traveling in the North Cape-Bear Island-Spitzbergen areas.

Another factor which greatly complicated German anti-convoy operations was the fact that Anglo-American convoys and single ships changed their course west and east of the Bear Island narrows toward the north. Initially, they had traveled south of Bear Island, or about midway between that island and Spitzbergen, but later they followed a more northerly course, which sometimes took them very close to Spitzbergen. This considerably lengthened the distances which German air forces had to cover on their approach and return flights, a fact which made a heavy impact upon their fuel consumption.

Air Command Lofoten Islands (from Bardufoss) successfully attacked two eastward bound convoys, PQ 21 and PQ 22, while they were entering the Kola Bay area between 11 and 15 January and during the night of 25 January 1943. Air Command North (East) then took over

---

*Editor's Note: The Gulf of Arkhangelsk usually freezes over at the end of October and remains frozen for 130 to 140 days annually, while the port of Arkhangelsk is normally closed about 190 days each year.

/Convoys returning from northern Russia were given code designations beginning with QP.

//Under the command of Generalmajor Alexander Holle until June of 1943, then temporarily under Generalmajor Ernst-August Roth, and from September 1943 under Col. Dr. Ernst Kuehl (Res.).

further operations against the remnants of these convoys in the coastal areas of the Kola Peninsula. A period of snow flurries and darkness, however, enabled these vessels to evade the Luftwaffe's surveillance and attacks.[34]

Early in March, air units sank two merchant ships out of a westward bound convoy from Murmansk, while numerous ships which had remained behind in port were severely damaged by Luftwaffe attacks.* Both in tactical and in the strategic sense, anti-convoy actions in the Norwegian and Barents Seas were a combined Navy and Luftwaffe undertaking. The naval operations were conducted by Naval Command Norwegian Sea (Admiral Nordmeer)/ from its headquarters in Narvik, while the air operations were carried out by the air commands at Trondheim, Bardufoss, and Kirkenes in conformity with directives from the Fifth Air Fleet in Oslo or Kemi.

One of the major conditions for these operations was the closest exchange of information between the Navy and the Luftwaffe. For this reason the naval command had a radio receiver constantly tuned to intercept Luftwaffe messages, while the air commands made use of naval radio stations. Although the general route for convoys was from Iceland via Bear Island to the Kola Peninsula, scarcely a single convoy followed precisely the same course as the preceding one. Furthermore, the detection of convoys and the task of maintaining contact once they were sighted was complicated by factors such as tactical maneuvers, including zig-zagging along the main course, varying the cruising speeds, changing course to avoid assumed or actually encountered German submarine blockades, or detouring north of Jan Mayen and east of Bear Island, and by weather conditions, which changed so frequently in those high latitudes where summers were so brief. Besides this it must be borne in mind that the area to be kept under surveillance corresponded in size approximately to that of continental Europe (exclusive of Spain and Italy) as far to the east as the boundaries of Poland and Yugoslavia.

---

*According to Generalmajor Ernst-August Roth, "On 5 March 1943 the Luftwaffe sank a 6,000-ton ship by using three 500-pound bombs and one 10,000-ton vessel was set afire."

/Editor's Note: The post of Commander of Naval Command Norwegian Sea (or Polar Sea as it was sometimes called) was held from mid-1941 until August 1942 by Admiral Hubert Schmundt, and thereafter until March 1944 by Konteradmiral Otto Klueber. This staff operated under the directions of the Naval Group Command North (Marine Gruppenkommando Nord), which was commanded until 1 March 1943 by Generaladmiral Rolf Carls, and from 2 March 1943 until 30 May 1944 by Generaladmiral Otto Schniewind.

In most instances the fact that an eastward-bound convoy was converging upon Iceland would be betrayed by the lively operations of a British radio station which was ordinarily silent. A few days later the German air weather units, operating from Stavanger in the direction of the Faroe Islands, usually sighted the enemy. These planes would first sight either widely spaced and eastward traveling naval escort units spread out toward the Norwegian coast, or they would sight the convoy itself, traveling on a corresponding course in the vicinity of Iceland.

These first reports would alert the Luftwaffe and naval commands. From then on the most important thing would be to establish and maintain constant contact with the convoy. In this effort the Luftwaffe and the German Navy attempted to outdo each other. Drawing upon past experiences, the air commands plotted the conjectured course of the ship formation, making their estimations on a basis of a cruising speed ranging from 8 to 12 knots per hour. A number of Fw-200 "Condor" aircraft* were then dispatched to the calculated area, and made broad reconnaissance sweeps, operating on a frontage which was largely determined by local weather conditions. In most cases these planes would detect the convoy, and one or more of them would then report its location, speed, course, and composition, and details on the escort units and weather. It might appear at first glance that the entire process of locating, identifying, reporting, and maintaining contact with enemy ship formations was a relatively simple matter. However, these operations included innumerable details and adverse technical factors, accompanied by disappointments and frustrations, all of which had to be taken into account at once in order to avoid endangering the success of the attack missions. Just the problem of regular and timely relief of the aircraft maintaining contact with the convoys was in itself an immense task. The distances involved were usually about 600 miles, and there was a constant shortage of personnel and materiel required for the purpose. But, despite these great difficulties, air and ground teams of the reconnaissance units mastered the problems with almost sportlike enthusiasm. Air

---

*Editor's Note: The Focke-Wulf 200 "Condor" was a four-engine transport of the German Lufthansa airline, which was modified as a military aircraft and widely used in the Far North as a long-distance reconnaissance plane. Carrying a crew of eight, it cruised at about 218 miles per hour and had a top speed of more than 260 miles per hour. Between 1940 and 1944 only 262 of these aircraft were produced. See Karlheinz Kens u. Heinz J. Nowarra, Die Deutschen Flugzeuge 1933-1945 (The German Airplanes 1933-1945), Muenchen: J. F. Lehmann Verlag, 1961. Cited hereafter as Kens and Nowarra. See also figure 39.

Figure 39
Focke-Wulf (FW) 200 "Condor," called Charlie by British and American airmen, gives positions of distant Allied convoys in the arctic area

Figure 40
Ju-88's ready to attack an Anglo-American convoy bound for northern Russian ports

Figure 41
Allied convoy en route to Russia. A near miss by a stick of bombs dropped from a German Ju-88, 1943
(Courtesy of the Imperial War Museum, London)

reconnaissance and submarine units supplemented each other almost to perfection in the difficult task of locating and keeping under surveillance Allied convoys, and it was rare indeed when contact, once established, was lost for more than six or seven hours.

The reports received from the contact aircraft provided the data for the most appropriate use of the available attack forces. The Navy usually posted its submarines in successive lines across the convoy's expected route, while the air units had to wait until the convoy was within their striking range, which was approximately 480 miles. The air forces available for the attack included He-111, and later Ju-88 torpedo and Ju-88 bomber, units.* There were just enough airfields available from which these units could operate.

The ideal form of air attack against a convoy was a combined bomber and aerial torpedo attack, in which the torpedo units attacked one minute after the bomber strike. In practice, however, this form of attack was subject to almost insurmountable difficulties, including the great distances separating the several airfields and the varying weather conditions in the individual areas, the time taken by the several units to get airborne when only a single runway was in operation or available, the time required for assembly in the air, the different cruising speeds of the various types of aircraft, and the slight navigational deviations of unit leaders heading for targets 480 miles away. There were other complicating factors as well, so that the ideal tactics for a strike could rarely be employed. When such conditions were achieved, however, the successes were remarkable.

The form of attack least subject to weather conditions was the aerial torpedo strike, for which reason these units were employed most frequently. However, the effectiveness of aerial torpedoes was limited by the release altitudes employed, the strength of side winds, and by heavy seas. The cloud ceiling was rarely high enough in the target area in these latitudes for horizontal bombing or dive-bombing attacks. Although air torpedo attacks always varied in execution, the following example of such an attack comes fairly close to approximately the usual conditions:

> Strength of attacking unit: 25 aircraft. Time required for loading and readying the aircraft for take-off in summer: 2 to 3 hours, individual aircraft taking off at 30-second

---

*See figures 40 and 41.

intervals. Unit assembled in flight in the vicinity of a predetermined prominent shore landmark and began approach flight to target. The air command on the ground reported the anticipated time of arrival over target area to the appropriate naval command for the information of submarines in the area. Contact planes in target area were also notified so that they could commence transmitting position signals approximately 20 minutes before the attack unit was due to arrive. Air command instructed contact aircraft to take up positions as far ahead of the convoy as possible pointing in the direction the convoy was traveling. As soon as the attack force was sighted, the contact plane turned about and headed for the point of the convoy. The leader of the air torpedo units followed, and ordered his pilots and crews to take up combat positions. For the bombing run the aircraft formed into an arc or pincers, with the open end toward the target. Each plane attacked the nearest ship, releasing its aerial torpedoes from an altitude of 100 to 130 feet, and at a range of about 6,600 feet. When out of gun range of the escort ships defending the convoy, the unit reassembled and proceeded on its return flight. The usual time required for the approach to target, the attack, and the return flight was eight hours.[35]

Although the basic features of these tactics were always pretty much the same, just the defensive measures of the enemy were sufficient to prevent them from becoming stereotyped in execution. The increased number of aircraft carriers assigned to escort convoys was the principal factor which finally made it necessary to resort to "armed reconaissance" tactics, since contact planes in such circumstances could only remain close to the convoy if adequately protected by clouds. Even with "armed reconnaissance" attacks, efforts were made to retain the tried and true pincers formation in the bombing run. The losses of Luftwaffe attack aircraft were within tolerable limits, but losses in reconnaissance and contact aircraft were at times excessively heavy.[36]

Air attacks against convoys and single ships received effective support in the form of continuous operations by the few remaining bomber, dive-bomber, and fighter squadrons still under Air Command North (East) against the ports which were not icebound along the Murmansk coast and against targets in the coastal areas around the Rybachiy Peninsula, particularly Murmansk, Motovskiy Bay, and Port Vladimir, but also against ships in smaller ports such as Polarnoye (a Soviet submarine base), and a port for motor torpedo boats in Pumankiy Bay. Good, and sometimes very good, results were secured in all of these attacks, considering the amount of damage done to ships, piers, dock installations, electric power stations, and supply and trans-shipping depots. In the summer and well into autumn of 1943 these operations were extended to include attacks along the ports of the White Sea, especially Arkhangelsk, and highly effective attacks against coastal shipping in the entire area.

Meanwhile, the German Navy carried out as many operations as possible, although hampered by a shortage of surface vessels and bad weather conditions which made identification of targets and accurate firing difficult if not impossible. Surface units of the Navy were directed by the Naval High Command to operate against Anglo-American convoys and to cooperate closely with the air forces. The Fifth Air Fleet and Naval Group Command North (Marine Gruppenkommando Nord)* were thus closely linked in all of these undertakings. According to the diary of Naval Command Norwegian Sea (Admiral Nordmeer), "Success in operations against hostile convoys by our task force was predicated upon cooperation with the air forces, which, under the circumstances of modern naval warfare, must first create the essential conditions for naval operations." 37/

Sir Winston Churchill recognized the threat to Allied shipping in these northern waters and was gravely concerned about it:

> . . . Between January and March [1943], in the remaining months of almost perpetual darkness, two more convoys, of forty-two ships and six ships sailing independently, set out on this hazardous voyage. Forty arrived. During the same period thirty-six ships were safely brought back from Russian ports and five were lost. The return of daylight made it easier for the enemy to attack the convoys. What was left of the German Fleet, including the Tirpitz, was now concentrated in Norwegian waters, and presented a

---

*See footnote, p. 195.

/Editor's Note: These naval operations suffered mainly because of inadequate available forces, but achieved very good results when this factor is taken into consideration. The only large vessels in the entire northern area were the battleships Tirpitz and Scharnhorst (35,000 and 26,000 ton classes respectively) and the heavy cruiser Admiral Hipper (over 10,000 tons). Hitler opposed the concept of large surface fleet operations with capital ships, which he believed to be obsolete. Because of his attitude, and because of the great inferiority of Germany's surface fleet, the Naval High Command exercised great care not to lose any of its large ships unnecessarily.

formidable and continuing threat along a large part of the route. Furthermore, the Atlantic, as always, remained the decisive theater in the war at sea, and in March 1943 the battle with the U-boats was moving to a violent crisis. The strain on our destroyers was more than we could bear. The March convoy had to be postponed, and in April the Admiralty proposed, and I agreed, that supplies to Russia by this route should be suspended till the autumn darkness.[38*]

The Russians were greatly upset over the momentous curtailment of urgently needed Anglo-American Lend-Lease goods, and, in a sharp exchange of notes with Britain's Prime Minister Churchill, they demanded an immediate resumption of convoy movements to the U.S.S.R. regardless of the losses which would thereby be incurred by the Western Allies. This exchange of notes clearly and unmistakably reveals the significance of the northern supply route:

> It was natural that the Soviet Government should look reproachfully at the suspension of the convoys for which their armies hungered. On the evening of September 21, M. Molotov sent for our Ambassador in Moscow and asked for the sailings to be resumed. He pointed out that the Italian Fleet had been eliminated and that the U-boats had abandoned the North Atlantic for the southern route. The Persian railway could not carry enough. For three months the Soviet Union had been undertaking a wide and most strenuous offensive, yet in 1943 they had received less than a third of the previous year's supplies. The Soviet Government therefore "insisted" upon the urgent resumption of the convoys, and expected His Majesty's Government to take all necessary measures within the next few days.[39]

On 1 October 1943 Churchill announced to Stalin that a series of four convoys would be sent to northern Russia, one in November, one in December, and the other two during January and February 1944. Each convoy was to consist of about 35 British and American ships.[40] The first convoy was scheduled to leave the United Kingdom about 12 November and to arrive in northern Russia ten days later, with the others following at intervals of about 48 days. The Allies also intended to pick up as

---

*See figures 41, 42, and 43.

Figure 42
A British convoy being attacked by the
Luftwaffe in arctic waters
(Courtesy of the Imperial War Museum, London)

Figure 43
Cdr. A. G. West, R.N. (4th from left) with his officers on the bridge watching German aircraft diving out of the sun to attack his convoy (Courtesy of the Imperial War Museum, London)

many Anglo-American vessels as possible from northern Russian ports about the end of October and to bring them back with the returning convoys.[41]

One could not disregard the fact that the northern route was the shortest way for the movement of materiel from the Western Allies to the Soviet Union. Persian supply routes were open to be sure, but they could not compensate for the entire amount of shipping which had been going through the northern Russian ports.[42] Because of this fact, and because of the urgency of Soviet demands, the convoys were resumed in late autumn 1943. The first formation left in mid-November and the second in December, a total contingent of 72 ships, all of which arrived safely in the Soviet Union. All of the homeward bound (QP) convoys were brought safely through the northern waters during this period.[43*]

The Luftwaffe's toll of Allied shipping by the end of the year had nevertheless reached a significant level. A total of 420,000 gross register tons of shipping (92 merchant vessels) were sunk, as well as 1 heavy cruiser, 5 submarines, 30 coastal vessels, and 11 escort craft. The German Air Force damaged 125 ships, totalling 710,000 gross register tons of merchant shipping, 3 destroyers, 3 submarines, 1 aircraft carrier, 1 tanker, and 1 outpost patrol boat.[44/]

Enemy air activities had increased considerably since 1942. In efforts to halt the constant German air attacks against the Murmansk rail line (which was such a vital transportation link during the winter months), and to neutralize the German air forces while convoys were approaching the Soviet ports, the Russians as early as the beginning of winter 1942-43 had greatly reinforced their bomber and fighter forces stationed in the vicinity of the Murmansk railroad route and in the Kola Peninsula. They doubled, and sometimes tripled, the strength of these flying forces, and went from the defensive over to the offensive.

---

*The convoys were favored by the seasonal bad weather and long nights, which seriously reduced or altogether prevented anti-convoy action by the Luftwaffe.

/Editor's Note: The Vorposten boats, or outpost patrol boats, were armed trawlers which had the duty of escorting coastal convoys and acting as outposts against motor torpedo boats, small naval units, and submarines. They also reported any aircraft sighted. This was hazardous duty, and especially so for German ships of this sort, which were almost invariably operating in a situation of naval inferiority.

Soviet attacks were directed primarily against the German airfields at Kirkenes, Petsamo, and Banak, and also against those found in the areas around Alakurti and Kemijärvi. Some of these attacks caused considerable damage, especially at Kirkenes. It is inexplicable why the Russians during the period of their increased air activity did not also attack the highly important nickel works and the electric power plants upon which these works depended. The Commanding General of the Fifth Air Fleet (Generaloberst Hans-Juergen Stumpff) wondered why the Russians had never attacked the nickel works at Kolosioki, which were:

> . . . of decisive importance for the German conduct of warfare and which were then being expanded and becoming of increasing importance because of the construction of an ore treating plant for the production of pure nickel on the spot. The more than 300-foot-high chimney of the plant would have shown the way to the target for any attacking air unit.
>
> Another equally endangered target was the Jaeneskowski electric power station in the Nautsi area, which was part of the nickel producing complex and connected with the nickel works by a makeshift cable above the ground about 48 miles in length. The destruction of the reservoir dam would have paralyzed the nickel works and in addition would have flooded the Nautsi air base and sections of the Eismeerstrasse [arctic sea road].[45]

Owing to the increased Soviet air activities the flak forces in the northern Norwegian and Finnish areas had also been reinforced, although only on a small scale because of the general shortage of forces.* The main concentrations of flak artillery were at the nickel works in the Petsamo region, at important supply ports, and at the airfields. Apart from the actual number of planes shot down, the particular value of flak artillery in this area of operations was its repelling effect. Wherever local conditions permitted, the batteries were emplaced so that they could also participate in coastal defense actions.

German shipping in these arctic regions proceeded along the coastline either singly or in convoys of up to eight or ten ships. When the Russians began systematic attacks (mostly by IL-2 "Stormovik" aircraft) with bombs, aerial torpedoes and mines, the Fifth Air Fleet established

---

*See Chart No. 6.

a number of new airfields from which fighters could operate to protect this important logistical lifeline. Increased enemy air operations, which in the Hammerfest-Kirkenes area were expected to commence with the beginning of longer days, had already taken the form of stepped-up systematic reconnaissance against all seaborne traffic, including also bombing and aerial torpedo attacks against convoys. Hitherto, only pairs of enemy aircraft had attacked, but by the summer of 1943 (for the first time) entire Soviet air units launched attacks.[46]

Offensive operations by Soviet fighter-bombers and light bombers, usually the Potez type,* had a noticeable effect from 1943 on. These operations were similar to the German fighter-bomber attacks against single ships traveling close to the shore, and were usually preceded by reconnaissance flights. Earlier, German convoys had been protected only by antisubmarine seaplane patrols, but by mid-1943 direct fighter protection became the more important requirement. This necessitated the construction of fighter airfields in the immediate vicinity of the northern Norwegian coast.† Therefore, one such airfield was built at Alta, one at the northern exit of the Porsanger Fjord, and one at Swartnes, on the eastern tip of the Vardø Peninsula, opposite Vardø Island. By constructing these three airfields, the Wehrmacht made it possible to lessen the general congestion at the few available airfields in the vicinity of the coast.

The new German defensive dispositions proved to be fully satisfactory. On 26 August units of the 5th Fighter Wing shot down 25 Soviet aircraft in the Vardø-Kirkenes area and 10 at Petsamo. On 13 October aircraft escorting a German convoy shot down 25 or 26 out of a force of 65 to 70 attacking Soviet planes,[47] and on 3 November units again

---

*_Editor's Note_: Although the author is not specific, he is probably referring here to the French-made Potez 630 or 631 twin-engine fighter and fighter-bomber. See William Green, _War Planes of the Second World War: Fighters_, Vol. I, Garden City, N.Y.: Hanover House, 1960, pp. 62-64.

†The volume of German convoy shipping is revealed in a summary in the War Diary of Naval Command Norwegian Sea (_Admiral Nordmeer_): "Escorts were provided for 6,332,964 gross register tons of shipping in convoys in the coastal waters between Narvik and Petsamo." Records of the Naval Project, EUCOM Historical Division, Karlsruhe.

employed in escort missions for convoys dispersed an attacking Soviet formation, shooting down 15 Soviet aircraft.*

Concerning the matter of German convoy escort operations between North Cape and Kirkenes or Linehamari, Generalleutnant Ernst-August Roth noted that the greater part of all supplies from Germany for the Twentieth Mountain Army (at least as far as bulk commodities were concerned) was shipped in by sea through the ports of Kirkenes and Linehamari (Petsamo area). The vulnerable sections of this supply route in 1943 were the areas between North Cape and Vardø Island, and the entrance of Linehamari, which were within view of Soviet coastal batteries situated along the southwestern edge of the Rybachiy Peninsula.

In the spring of 1943 the Russian operations against German convoys--there were usually eight to ten ships escorted by outpost patrol boats†--assumed such proportions that not a single convoy escaped attack by submarine or air units. This was a most serious situation so far as the maintenance of the striking power of the forces within the Army's zone of operations was concerned.

Enemy submarines usually attacked between Honningsvag (the northern exit from Porsanger Fjord) and Berlevåg, later almost exclusively between Berlevåg and Makkaur, on the northern coast of the Varanger Peninsula. Air attacks, which were increasing steadily, took place between Harmningsberg and Vardø. It was no wonder that the German Navy pressed with ever greater urgency for air protection for the convoys.

The main forces available to Air Command North (East) at Kirkenes were the 30th Bomber Wing at Banak, the 5th Fighter Wing at Petsamo, and a twin-engine fighter group at Kirkenes. In addition, there was the 56th Air Signal Regiment with its excellent facilities. Although only an indirect instrument of defense, the air signal regiment later proved to be the most effective.

---

*"Of the 20 bombers, twin-engine fighters, and fighter-bombers available, 10 were committed in antisubmarine patrols and 10 in convoy escort missions. Twenty-five hostile aircraft were shot down in aerial combat." See Appendix 58, original German draft of this study, Karlsruhe Document Collection. This action took place on 13 October 1943.

†See footnote p. 207.

Until about March of 1943 it sufficed for the Luftwaffe to drop bombs of up to 110 pounds each at irregular intervals around the convoy to simulate depth charges while the ships were passing through areas in which submarine attacks were likely.* This kept the submarine in the vicinity from getting into an attack position. From April on, the danger of submarine attacks in the Berlevåg area increased steadily and threatened to become a critical menace.

Almost every morning and evening the only Wuerzburg radar instrument still available (situated at Vardø) tracked a Soviet aircraft approaching from the north. Invariably the plane disappeared from the radar screen for about five to ten minutes in the region of Kongs Fjord. After he had convinced himself that there were no fixed points visible on the radar screen along the route over which the Soviet reconnaissance plane was tracked, the chief of the air command assumed that it had either landed or flown so low in the vicinity of Kongs Fjord that it could not be picked up on the radar screen. He drew a further conclusion that the Russians had a secret base for submarines somewhere along the completely isolated coastline, and thus ordered a complete photo reconnaissance over the coastal sector from Pers Fjord to west of Berlevåg.

The aerial photos revealed an almost ideal hiding place for a submarine in a tiny fjord at the entrance to Kongs Fjord. The air command thereupon informed the Navy people at Tromsø of these suspicions and recommended a combined Army-Navy surprise attack operation (without air support) to eliminate the assumed Soviet submarine base. The action which followed was a complete success. It not only confirmed the air commander's suspicions about a Soviet base at the Kongs Fjord,† but also led to the discovery of a reporting agency in the pay of the Soviet Union. This organization consisted of more than 40 Norwegian men and women who had been trained at Murmansk and then landed and supplied by a Soviet submarine at the Varanger coast. It could be assumed with certainty that this organization was responsible for the escape of a Soviet submarine which was anchored in the Kongs Fjord by giving it timely warning of the approach of German naval craft participating in the clean-up operation.

German forces not only captured a number of radio stations, but also the extremely complicated Soviet code which was then in use, making it possible for some time to mislead the Russian submarine headquarters

---

*See figure 41.

†The site of the submarine lair was precisely where the Luftwaffe Command had pointed it out on aerial photos.

base by the transmission of false reports. Submarine attacks thereupon ceased temporarily but were later resumed, although not with the former degree of precision.

An increasing and far more serious threat was the growing menace of air attacks in the Vardø area. Because of the great distances from Petsamo and Kirkenes* and the fact that German fighters could stay in the air for only 60 to 70 minutes because of fuel capacities, there was little chance to intercept Soviet air units in time and this opportunity was limited to just a few seconds. Nevertheless, the German air defense organization functioned so well (because of the excellent cooperation by all concerned) that not a single German ship was sunk or damaged in this area between 5 June and 20 October 1943. In contrast, more than 700/ Soviet airplanes were shot down in the Fifth Air Fleet area during this time, against relatively light German aircraft losses. The teamwork required in such operations generally proceeded in accordance with the following pattern, although, of course, no two interceptor operations were precisely the same because of the obvious reaction of the enemy command after each defeat.

Eastward moving German convoys would be reported to the air command as soon as they left the shelter of the steep cliffs near Honningsvag. The Luftwaffe would then furnish seaplanes and Ju-88 bombers for anti-submarine escorts. After the ships passed Berlevåg they would be given a close escort, sometimes including destroyers, while the alerted 5th Fighter Wing transferred its squadrons from Petsamo to Kirkenes. When the convoy was about even with Hamningsberg, the fighter pilots got aboard their aircraft and remained on ready-alert (monitoring stations had by this time found out that the Russians were making preparations at their airfields for attack). //

---

*These distances could be as great as 150 miles or more over the sea or rugged, mountainous terrain.

/Editor's Note: It is not certain how the author arrived at this figure. Available Fifth Air Fleet figures show 471 aircraft shot down during this period.

//The monitoring of radio traffic between Soviet aircraft crews while still on the ground was carried out by three Wehrmacht radio operators with a perfect knowledge of Russian, who immediately transmitted their observations to the 5th Fighter Wing and the local air commander. In the beginning of German anti-submarine and air defense actions in the Far North this monitoring service was the key to success.

German forces were as well informed about the take-offs of Soviet aircraft as though they were actually visible to the Wehrmacht. The important thing to do then was to track these enemy aircraft with the Wuerzburg radar instrument (located at Vardø) from the Kola Bay area. Thanks to the intensive training given radar personnel and their tireless efforts, everything went off very well. German fighters were thus able to reach the convoy in time to intercept and decimate the Russian force before it could attack. The Russians were courageous and determined opponents in their efforts to execute their mission, and escort fighters attempted, although unsuccessfully, to protect them. In some instances air battles were fought at altitudes of less than 300 feet, immediately above solid cloud banks, and it was by no means rare for the battle to end in the clouds. In such cases the fighters had to be guided back to their bases by the Wuerzburg radar installation. Often they arrived in Kirkenes with their last gallon of fuel.

Red forces usually attacked with bombs, occasionally also with parachute torpedoes which were set to circle in the water. The Russians were, however, quick to realize that their radio traffic was the Wehrmacht's best ally, and the German forces soon had to devise other means of making timely detections of their presence. The Wuerzburg radar device was the answer to this problem. It was portable and was originally used in the foremost lines of the XIX Mountain Corps around Murmansk. Later it was moved to the neck of the Rybachiy Peninsula, after the Russians discovered that it was this instrument which detected their aircraft assembling for actions at sea. When the Russians found out that the radar in its new location detected them leaving Kola Bay at very low altitudes, their only chance was to approach in a wide detour over the sea far to the north of Rybachiy Peninsula in an effort to achieve surprise in their attacks. Coming from that direction, however, they were detected by the radio station at Vardø.

Meanwhile, thanks to the well coordinated efforts of the Army, Navy, and Luftwaffe, the Swartnes airfield was prepared in a surprisingly short time for fighter operations. The almost sportsmanlike enthusiasum over the seemingly impossible achievements of the fighters was what spurred all of these forces on, and accounted for this excellent performance. Everyone knew what was at stake. The new field made it possible to maintain at least one fighter squadron over each convoy from Berlevåg to the destination, and thereby protect it against surprise attacks.[48]

While part of each German convoy remained in Kirkenes, some of the ships left port by themselves after a short stay. These ships again assembled in a fjord near Linehamari in order to proceed (under escort) in convoy to the port of Linehamari. The most dangerous part of this route was the entrance to the narrow fjord, which, as was mentioned previously, was within easy range of the Soviet coastal batteries on the Rybachiy Peninsula. In order to blind these batteries, aircraft laid a smoke screen along the entire route, which was several nautical miles in length, a procedure which was frequently practiced in combined operations with naval units in peacetime. The smoke screen was approximately 150 feet high and 60 feet across and was made even more effective by screening smoke released by escorting naval vessels. Protected by this smoke screen, the German convoy proceeded on an irregular course, covered against Soviet air reconnaissance by German fighter units. During these operations the Soviet artillery batteries on the Rybachiy Peninsula continued to fire upon the entrance area of the fjord, but this was only harassing fire rather than observed fire. Because of this, with some luck, and because the Russian batteries did not have an inexhaustible supply of ammunition, there were good chances of making a safe entrance. Only on very rare occasions were ships damaged by this enemy fire, and then they usually suffered only slight damage from shell fragments.

Air cover was of the essence in helping to get friendly convoys through to their destinations, just as airpower was essential in the combating of enemy convoys. This fact was well appreciated by the Allies, who began to include carriers as a regular part of Allied shipping formations. Yet, despite this opposition, excellent teamwork between the Fifth Air Fleet and the German naval units operating in the arctic waters often enabled the Wehrmacht to hamper or delay the movement of Allied supplies, and at times to scatter or sink elements of Anglo-American convoys. Besides the operations carried out against enemy convoy formations and individual ships--these operations were carried out in cooperation with surface units of Naval Group Command North--the following missions of the Fifth Air Fleet deserve special mention: continuous operations against the Murmansk railroad line, especially the Salla section, by units stationed at Alakurti; long-range reconnaissance missions over the White Sea and Arkhangelsk to ascertain whether and what elements of the Anglo-American convoys reached ports in the Murmansk-Arkhangelsk area; and continuous patrols flown by Fw-200 "Condor" units (transferred from Oslo to Nautsi for the purpose) to protect German convoys against enemy submarine attacks. These patrols went out even during the long arctic nights.

Although the Russians attempted to disperse their aircraft widely at their airfields, Fifth Air Fleet units succeeded time and again in attacking these bases with good results. Apart from the valuable aircraft and installations which were destroyed on the ground at Soviet airfields, German units in the Far North in 1943 shot down approximately 1,400 Russian aircraft in aerial combat.

Because of the uninterrupted quiet all along the Murmansk line, air units operated on only a small scale in support of the ground forces, carrying out artillery fire direction, combat reconnaissance, and photo reconnaissance missions, actions against occasional targets, such as the coastal batteries on the Rybachiy Peninsula, Soviet troop concentrations and shelters, and supply routes located near the front. German air units also dropped large numbers of propaganda leaflets over enemy positions and installations.

Prior to the onset of the long arctic nights, elements of the 5th Fighter Wing were transferred to the southernmost sector of the Twentieth Mountain Army for action against Soviet ski brigades, which more or less continuously infiltrated the front in the corps boundary areas. The Red opponent was a hardy and resilient foe, inured to the rigors of the climate and stubborn in defense. Generalleutnant Andreas Nielsen, Chief of Staff of the Fifth Air Fleet, describes the Red Army as a body of well-trained troops, who were fighting, so to speak, at the very gates of their garrisons. They were frugal, excellent at the art of camouflage, and incredibly patient, but displayed little imagination in the conduct of operations.

It was more difficult to evaluate the Soviet Navy since it was so seldom seen, and when it was seen on rare occasions, it was in the coastal waters in support of the Red Army. It suffered heavily under German bombing attacks at Murmansk and Polarnoye.

Generalleutnant Nielsen characterized the Soviet air forces as lacking in dash, a force of poor aviators in general, poorly equipped in technical respects, especially navigation instruments, and with a command that lacked imagination and flexibility. He pointed out that the Russians did a poor job of aiming during bombing runs, and were not to be taken seriously as an aerial opponent in the Far North.[49]

Service Forces of the Luftwaffe

Generally speaking, the Luftwaffe forces which were committed in the Far North received adequate supplies, although fuel shortages did make it necessary to curtail operations by air units. However, these shortages were not due to any lack of foresight in stockpiling supplies, or to the inordinately long and difficult supply routes, but to the inadequacy of German production, particularly with respect to fuel. A contributing cause was the transportation bottleneck, the shortage of tankers. Generaloberst Stumpff, Commander of the Fifth Air Fleet, was well aware of this problem:

> As was the case on the Norwegian front, grave difficulties were also encountered on the Finnish front in the area of logistics. Quite apart from the wearisome sea route to Kirkenes, where only small unloading and storage facilities were available, the only route for the movement of supplies in Lapland from the Rovaniemi rail junction to Kirkenes, a distance of almost 480 miles, was the arctic sea road. Furthermore, in winter this road was too narrow for two-way traffic. The recommendation to construct a narrow-gauge railroad along the arctic sea road was rejected on the basis of reconnaissance because of the acute lack of materials and time.
>
> A more active air opponent could have caused gravely threatening interruptions in traffic on the only two supply routes in existence. It was only at a late stage that the Russians attempted to interrupt traffic on the sea route to Kirkenes. [50]

Before the winter of 1942-43 a start had been made in expanding the Luftwaffe ground service organization. A special effort was made in the area from Kemi to Petsamo. Work on this project, which included not only the improvement of existing facilities but the construction of new bases, was not interrupted by Soviet action to any appreciable extent. The Finns were most helpful by recommending the construction of natural runways with a mixture of sand, gravel, and clay, rather than concrete. These could withstand considerable heaving, thawing, and freezing.

The unexpected commencement of winter, with temperatures ranging as low as -58° Fahrenheit, caused considerable difficulties, and this situation was relieved only after the procurement of makeshift aids, such as engine hoods and heating wagons. [51]

A particularly important branch of the ground service organization in the Far North was the Weather Reporting Service, especially for operations against convoys. It could be assumed as a general rule that out of every nine bad weather spells reaching Europe, seven of them went across the Norwegian area. This always resulted in frequent weather changes, which often came unexpectedly because of the incompleteness of weather data from western areas. Furthermore, only a small number of tactical airfields were available in the Far North, and at all of them the terrain conditions complicated landings. These conditions were rendered still worse by bad weather. Taking these factors into consideration, one can understand the difficult decisions air commands had to make with respect to the possibilities, timing, and execution of missions.[52]

In connection with the weather service, and with operations against hostile convoys and those in defense of friendly convoys, the various islands in northern waters, from Greenland and Iceland to Jan Mayen, Spitzbergen, Bear Island, and Novaya Zemlya, gained significant importance. The collection of meteorological data was a mission of the special weather reconnaissance aircraft of the weather service squadrons, a very costly undertaking. Some data was, of course, obtained by intercepting enemy weather reports.

Efforts to establish meteorological stations on Spitzbergen and Bear Island succeeded in the early stages, although grave difficulties were encountered.* The meteorological teams at these stations were highly successful at times, but these outposts finally had to be abandoned or were captured by the enemy.† An attempt to establish a weather station on Novaya Zemlya had to be abandoned in the spring of 1943 because the Russians were already there.[53]

Another valuable service in counter-convoy operations was the air-sea rescue service, an organization which was carefully trained to help reduce personnel losses in these arctic areas by picking up men who were shot down at sea. On 1 July 1943 an excellent air-sea rescue organization was established in the command area of the Fifth Air Fleet. The 5th Air-Sea Rescue Service Command (North) was responsible for rescue missions in the ice and snow as well as at sea, and was tactically assigned to the Fifth Air Fleet. For administration and supply it was assigned to the Luftwaffe Administrative Area Command Norway (Luftgaukommando Norwegen). The 5th Air-Sea Rescue Service Command (North) controlled the following units:

---

*According to Col. Dr. Ernst Kuehl, the weather station on Bear Island "functioned well in the winter of 1943-44."

†Editor's Note: The Wehrmacht operated a weather reporting station on Spitzbergen. This small outpost was captured in June 1943 by a raiding party of Norwegians and British troops. In early September this was retaken by the German Navy.

VIII Air-Sea Rescue Service Area Command, Stavanger

Air Signals Operations Platoon A
5th Air-Sea Rescue Squadron, Stavanger
22nd Air-Sea Rescue Service Command, Bergen (with Air Signals Operations Platoon B)
21st Air-Sea Rescue Service Command, Trondheim

IX Air-Sea Rescue Service Area Command, Kirkenes

Air Signals Operations Platoon A
12th Air-Sea Rescue Service Command, Tromsø (with Air Signals Operation Platoon B)
13th Air-Sea Rescue Service Command, Kirkenes (with Air Signals Operations Platoon A)
20th Air-Sea Rescue Service Command, Billefjord (with Air Signals Operations Platoon B)
10th Air-Sea Rescue Squadron, Tromsø
Air-Sea Rescue Service Command, Finland, at Pori (with Air Signals Operations Platoon B)[54]

Between 21 February and 10 November 1943 the Air-Sea Rescue Service Command dispatched 106 aircraft and 68 ships on 121 sea rescue missions. Only 62 of these were successfully accomplished, which was, however, very good considering the conditions. An entry in the war diary of this service describes an air-sea rescue mission in April of 1943:

> On 26 April 1943 an English radio message led to the rescue of a German crew. It was understood from the English message (transmitted in the clear) that the British aircraft had orders to remain in contact with the German pneumatic boat. This measure facilitated the rescue, and both British and Germans desisted from attacking each other during the rescue operation.[55]

In another instance on 29 April 1943 a rescue mission had to be broken off because no fighter escort could be made available. Thus the downed flyers could not always be picked up because the reactions of enemy aircraft could not be trusted in all cases.

On 16 July an air-sea rescue plane had to be recalled from a mission because of the approach of enemy aircraft, and on 16 August an Ar-199 sea rescue plane was shot down by the British while enroute to rescue personnel in a swamp.[56]

Between 1940 and 1943 the forces employed in rescue operations were so increased that there were about 12 Do-24 aircraft (He-59's had been withdrawn from service), 1 Fi-156 "Storch" liaison aircraft at Stavanger, the salvage vessel Karl Meyer of 1,000 tons, 2 whalers, 12 crash boats, about 20 aircraft operations boats, and 25 boats from the Norwegian Lifeboat Society in the contingent.

During the first three years, cooperation with the Norwegian Lifeboat Society was excellent, since help was given without reservation in all cases of distress, including illness on the islands, or in instances in which the patients had to be removed to the hospital. During these years (1940-1943) the air-sea rescue service in Norway rescued about 2,000 Germans and Norwegians, and about 200 enemy personnel, a performance which reflects credit upon this service. In these icy waters the air-sea rescue units more than proved their worth.

From the autumn of 1943 on, the Fifth Air Fleet also commenced making preparations for the evacuation and destruction of Luftwaffe installations for the planned withdrawal operation, Operation BIRKE. Responsibility for these preparations, which in 1943 remained restricted to investigations and conferences, was assigned to Luftwaffe headquarters in Finland (Fifth Air Fleet).

In logistical planning, however, the Fifth Air Fleet provided against a possible later evacuation by refraining from building up large supply reserves in the central Finnish area. Larger stocks, on the other hand, were accumulated at the more northerly air bases.

A signal communications network was operated and developed by the Luftwaffe Command in Finland. In 1943, multiple lines were available throughout the entire area of operations and extended into the Zone of the Interior. These facilities were always adequate and fully operational. Communications between Kirkenes and Bardufoss were rarely interrupted for more than 24 hours, although the overhead cable crossed a particularly difficult region. In the winter, during heavy snowfalls and frosty weather, disturbances in the communications lines were naturally more frequent, and the maintenance of these lines then placed an especially heavy burden upon signal troops.

In 1943 one aircraft spotting company was committed in the XIX Mountain Corps sector, and one was later placed in the XXXVI Mountain sector. Kemi and Kirkenes were simultaneously aircraft spotting and reporting and air traffic control centers. During the year fighter control posts were also established at all airfields, which permitted a centralized

Figure 44
Field Marshal Carl Gustaf Freiherr Mannerheim of Finland greeting Generaloberst Hans-Juergen Stumpff, Commander in Chief, German Fifth Air Fleet

registration of all enemy air penetrations and of operations to intercept hostile aircraft. Operations of fighter forces could then be controlled from each of these outposts.

Every airfield of any size was equipped with a radio and a DF station. The airfields at Kemi and Nautsi, where the air fleet command posts were located, had ultra-short wave radio landing beacons. The airfield at Banak had an ultra-short wave radio beam for aircraft approaching from the north through the 60-mile-long fjord. The entrance to the fjord itself was marked by a small radio beacon. Most airfields, of course, had a small radio beacon in the vicinity.

The radio sending stations at Bodø, Tromsø, and Vadsø (near Kirkenes) were used as navigational aids. In addition, the Fifth Air Fleet established a heavy type radio marker beacon about 30 miles to the south of Kirkenes. This station was used simultaneously for the relay of communications to Fifth Air Fleet Headquarters in Oslo. Signal communications in the Far North functioned on the whole very well.

Command Changes in Luftwaffe Forces in the Far North

Early in November a change took place in the command of Luftwaffe forces in the arctic area. On 5 November 1943 General der Flieger Josef Kammhuber* assumed command over the Fifth Air Fleet, the incumbent commander, Generaloberst Stumpff, being put in command of the Air Defense Command (Luftflotte Reich) at home. 57 Under the Fifth Air Fleet, the Chief of Luftwaffe District Command Finland was placed in charge of all air forces committed in the Finnish area.

With the exception of the exchange of liaison officers, practically no contact existed between the German Luftwaffe and the Finnish Air Force. In the few cases where it was necessary, however, cooperation was always smooth and relationships were excellent. Thus, the two forces remained cordial and comradely despite the great distances between their stations. No details were known on the specific strength and the entire operations

---

*Later Inspector of the new German Luftwaffe.

On 5 February 1944 Luftwaffenbefehlshaber Mitte (Air Force Commander Center) was redesignated Luftflotte Reich (Air Fleet Reich, or Home Air Defense Command). See figure 44.

General Harmjansk, who was preceded by General Schulz, assisted by Chief of Staff, Colonel von Cramon (GSC).

of the Finnish air forces, but it was known that Finnish flyers were able and very courageous, evoking great respect from German airmen.[58]

In the opinion of the author the relationships were not close enough, considering that a war was being waged on a common front and that all details of operations had to be discussed in order to effect a proper interplay of forces. It remains to be said that the Finnish air forces received constant support through the delivery of aircraft, spare parts, and equipment of all kinds. While on a visit to Germany, the Commander in Chief of the Finnish Air Force, General Lundquist, was assured on 17 January 1943 by Reichsmarschall Goering that the request placed for radar equipment by General Talvela* would be met. Besides this, the Commander in Chief of the Luftwaffe offered the Finns a number of Ju-88 aircraft.[59]

Summary of Far Northern Operations

In reviewing the overall course of military operations in the Far North, it becomes obvious again and again that a joint armed forces command in this remote area would certainly have proved to be particularly advantageous. In the changing course of operations, with spells of quiet on the land fronts coinciding with spells of urgent necessity for action against the Anglo-American logistical movements, which were so vital to the Russians, it would have been possible to achieve a much more smoothly functioning and more rational application of all available combat forces of the three Wehrmacht branches. The result would have been a far greater measure of success.

---

*Generalmajor Talvela was the Finnish general assigned to the German Headquarters in the Far North.

Chapter 7

CRITIQUE OF LUFTWAFFE OPERATIONS IN THE EASTERN THEATER IN 1943

Attempts To Conduct Strategic Air Warfare in the Eastern Theater in 1943

In the German manual on aerial warfare Luftkriegfuehrung (Aerial Warfare Leadership), LDv 16, operations against the enemy's sources of power were considered to be of decisive importance:

> By combat action against the enemy's sources of military power and by interrupting the flow of power from those sources to the front, it [the air force] endeavors to paralyze the enemy's military forces.
>
> Warfare in enemy territory is not directed exclusively against the operational forces and their bases. It is also directed against the logistical services and the production centers of the hostile air force, and thus becomes a battle for the sources of military power. [1]

The manual thus gives the impression that a war can be decided only by air operations which would destroy the enemy's sources of power and thereby bring the flow of power to the front to a halt.* However, to bring about the decision of a war in this manner, an air force would have to possess power in numbers and quality fully commensurate with the scope and diversity of all its missions. Over and above what has been said, an air force might be the only means by which the depletion of friendly ground forces could be prevented and a final decision forced in a war in which the fronts have become static. The main condition for success in such a case is a complete shift of emphasis to aerial warfare at the cost of all other methods of conducting the war. A complete change of this sort in the

---

*Editor's Note: As Stefan Possony points out in his book Strategic Air Power, The Pattern of Dynamic Security, World War II was decided by triphibious power rather than by airpower alone, yet airpower enabled the Allies to fight and win some of the most decisive battles in history. Without it the war could not have been won. See pp. 1-14.

mode of conducting a war requires time, and appropriate preparations must be made beforehand as a precautionary measure.[2]

The most important measure which the Supreme Command would have had to take in preparing against the eventuality of such a transition in the type of warfare was that of awarding the Luftwaffe the highest priority in all allocations of personnel and materiel at a very early juncture. This was necessary in order to insure that the German Air Force could attain the required high standards in both amount and quality of personnel and materiel. The Luftwaffe should have had priority over the Army, and especially over the Navy, and this should have extended to all fields of activity, such as the allocation of raw materials, overall production of the German military industry, manufacturing installations, and labor. In the failure to recognize airpower as a factor which would not only decide campaigns, but even an entire war--or at least become such a factor during a protracted war--lay the first serious error and one of the fateful mistakes of the German Supreme Command and its planning.

The concept of blitz warfare had raised the compelling demand to commit the entire Luftwaffe in action on the battlefields of the Army. The successes achieved through blitz warfare tactics had accustomed the Army to the powerful and frequently even decisive effects of air support in all military operations, and, in the long years of combat in the Eastern Theater, continuous air support for the Army in attack and defense operations soon became a permanent requirement. The Army ground forces made a particularly strong and perpetual demand for air support after the winter operations of 1942-43 because it had suffered such heavy losses of heavy infantry weapons, artillery, tanks, and antitank guns, and the Luftwaffe appeared to be the only available source which could compensate for these deficiencies. The Army's ability to resist was also weakened by this time because of the steadily decreasing flow of replacements.

When the constantly recurring crises in operations on the ground developed into a perpetual crisis in 1943, operations in direct support of the Army became the exclusive pattern for air operations. According to Hitler's Directive No. 21 (Operation BARBAROSSA) of 18 December 1940, strategic warfare was to have been precluded only temporarily.* In the

---

*"In order to be able to concentrate all forces against the enemy air force and for the unqualified support of the Army, the armament industry is not to be attacked during the main phase of operations. Not until the close of mobile operations will such attacks be considered, and then primarily against the Ural areas." See Fuehrer Directive No. 21, Operation BARBAROSSA.

critical situation of the German armies in the East in 1942-43, however, the very concept of strategic warfare, in the sense of operations against strategic targets to further the overall conduct of the war, was almost completely lost.

This constant commitment of all air forces to support the Army (usually in direct, and only rarely in indirect support missions) had the result that the Luftwaffe was worn down and bled white while participating in ground operations on the Eastern Front and was compelled to neglect its mission of operating against the enemy's sources of power. It has been repeatedly mentioned that the occasional attacks directed against strategic targets in 1942-43 were due solely to the initiative of the individual air fleets, the only exception being the order from the Commander in Chief of the Luftwaffe to attack Moscow. [3]

Up to the summer of 1943 nothing was done by Reichsmarschall Goering to implement the necessary preparations and planning for strategic air warfare in the Eastern Theater of Operations. It was particularly commendable on the part of the Sixth Air Fleet (formerly Air Command East) that it again and again took up and recommended the idea of operating with specially trained long-range strategic air units against key Soviet industries. [4] From the summer of 1942 on, the Sixth Air Fleet repeatedly sent urgent studies and letters, supported by authentic data, in an effort to convince the Commander in Chief of the Luftwaffe how significant air operations against the Soviet military economy would be for the endangered German fronts. It was summer, however (18 June 1943 before Operation ZITADELLE), before the Commander in Chief of the Luftwaffe finally responded to a renewed letter by the Sixth Air Fleet referring to the successful attacks made against the Gorkiy tank factory. [5] This letter was accompanied by the highly urgent request to "badly damage and, if possible, paralyze the most important branches of the Soviet military industry, which in some fields are highly developed."[6] The Reichsmarschall acknowledged this requirement, commenting that he shared these opinions concerning the significance of attacks against the Russian armament industry. [7]

In like manner there were signs, although they appeared very late, that the Army at last recognized the importance of air attacks against the enemy's sources of power. The Army General Staff noted that one reason for the successes of the Red Army was the increased fire power and mobility made possible by equipping its units with large numbers of automatic weapons, artillery pieces, tanks, and motor vehicles. This was a direct result of the great capacity of the armament industry. German Army leaders therefore concluded that a systematic and intensive campaign against the Soviet armament industry could produce a marked reduction in the materiel pressures by the Soviet armies in the coming battles.[8]

In the above-mentioned letter to the Sixth Air Fleet, Goering also acknowledged the wisdom of specifically organizing an air corps command staff or designating an existing one to control the long-range bombing forces and to conduct strategic air warfare.[9] Initially (in the summer of 1943), no clear concepts existed concerning what the organization of a strategic bomber force might be or whether the Strategic Air Command should be placed directly under the Commander in Chief of the Luftwaffe, under one of the air fleets, or even under a special Commander in Chief of the Luftwaffe in the East. Neither Goering nor his chief of staff could bring themselves to make the decision to bring about a clear-cut division between tactical and strategic air forces, and, with the possible exception of the VIII Air Corps, all corps and divisions which had been in existence since early 1943 were composite units containing fighter, bomber, twin-engine fighter, and, at times, dive-bomber and ground-attack forces.[10*]

Since 1942, however, all of these types of forces had for the greater part been committed exclusively in army support missions. As was mentioned before, the author believes that there was then an absolute necessity for a reorganization of the Luftwaffe entailing: (1) a clear-cut division between strategic and tactical support units, (2) direct control of the strategic forces by the Commander in Chief of the Luftwaffe or possibly by a Commander in Chief, Strategic Air Forces, and (3) a consolidation of the tactical air support units in tactical air corps or air divisions controlled by field commands of the Luftwaffe.[†]

The tactical support air units would have composed the greater part of all Luftwaffe forces, and could have been varied in size and composition as the situation required. They could have been shifted from command to command to meet tactical requirements. Strategic units, on the other hand, would have been rigidly organized and consolidated under an air corps or under a number of air divisions, at all times under the control of the Commander in Chief of the Luftwaffe or under a Commander

---

*The VIII Air Corps was formed and organized in accordance with the tactical principles and requirements of the "Legion Condor" in the Spanish Civil War, and developed through an agency of the Special Purposes Air Command (Polish campaign) as a tactical support air corps. In the course of the year 1943, however, the VIII Air Corps was also gradually transformed into a composite air corps.

†See Chart No. 5.

in Chief of Strategic Air Forces, and committed only for missions of a strategic nature. As an exception, they could have been committed as additional air support for the Army or Navy in campaigns or battles which would exert a decisive effect upon the outcome of an entire campaign or the war.[11] Such employment, however, would have been possible only by order of the Supreme Commander of the Wehrmacht.

Immediately after assuming office, Jeschonnek's successor, General der Flieger Guenther Korten, took up the idea of a clear-cut division of air forces. Korten and his newly appointed Chief of the Luftwaffe Operations Staff, Generalleutnant Karl Koller, realized the need to be able to commit strategic air forces in the form of purely bomber corps both in the East and in the defensive operations against the expected invasion in the West, and that this use of airpower would provide more effective support for the Army than attacks against enemy ground forces on the field of battle. General Korten also believed that the Army could and would have to carry the temporary extra burden which would result if the ground-attack units were simultaneously equipped with Fw-190 aircraft and appropriately consolidated in specifically tactical air support corps.[12]

If these concepts had been implemented sooner, preceded by the necessary preparations in the fields of armament and supplies, and if the attack missions against the Soviet sources of power had not been postponed, the Luftwaffe at the beginning of the Russian campaign would have been able, by vertical development, to strike telling blows upon the Soviet armament industry. This was largely within the range of German bombers at the time, and attacks upon these centers would, at the same time, have afforded the Army adequate air support in its operational areas and upon the battlefield. The failure to take these measures constituted a grave error of omission on the part of the highest levels of the High Command of the Luftwaffe.*

Although Jeschonnek in 1943 was forced by circumstances in the military situation to recognize and acknowledge the need for strategic

---

*It is beyond the scope of this study to examine the problem of whether the conduct of strategic air warfare was within the capability of the German armament industry. From personal experience gained in an earlier assignment in the Reichs Air Ministry (Organization Division of the Luftwaffe General Staff), the author firmly believes that this question could have been answered in the affirmative.

airpower and the parallel necessity for a reorganization of the Luftwaffe, he made very little headway in his efforts to carry out the necessary planning. Possibly he lacked the real will to devote himself wholeheartedly to the cause, particularly since Hitler, with his concepts of restricted areas of operation, always insisted upon the exclusive use of airpower in every sector for the support of the offensive and defensive operations of the Army on the battlefield.

General Korten, who was more gifted in diplomacy than Jeschonnek, succeeded much sooner in gaining acceptance for his views concerning the use of airpower. In the late summer of 1943 the High Command of the Luftwaffe began to realize that a policy restricted to air support of the Army--four-fifths of the entire bomber force in the Eastern Theater of Operations were committed in these operations--could not decide the outcome of the war against the Soviet Union. The Luftwaffe High Command would have preferred a return to the concept of strategic air warfare, in which the bomber forces could have been withdrawn from tactical support missions in order to bomb Soviet industrial targets, thereby preventing the steady and continuous growth of Soviet air and ground strength. Apart from an interval in June 1943, when a lull in the ground fighting made it possible for a short while to bomb Soviet industrial targets, it was only after the German reverses in August at Kursk that a firm decision was finally taken to build up the bomber forces and to employ them as an instrument of strategic air warfare.

Korten was convinced of the importance of strategic bombing, and was on the side of the so-called Defensive Clique which had been gradually gaining ground in the inner military circles since the previous year. It was therefore only natural for him to endeavor to reverse Jeschonnek's policy of giving top priority to the fighting front on the ground and of continuing the offensive under any circumstances.

He intended to reduce air support operations for the Army to a minimum, to improve the general situation by placing Germany on a footing which would make a solid defense possible, and to make the utmost use of his offensive forces in strategic bombing missions. This reversal of policy required changes in the organization of the Luftwaffe General Staff as well as in the composition of command staffs in the field.

The withdrawal of bomber units from tactical support missions in the East was begun, so that retraining and reequipping could take place. A special pathfinder unit was established, the 2nd Group of the 4th Bomber Wing ("General Wever"). Headquarters, IV Air Corps was assigned the responsibility for executing these measures and, early in December, ceased to function as a ground-attack command staff. Commencement of the new strategic operations was planned for February of 1944.

A comprehensive program for operations against the Soviet industries and materiel reserves was worked out in collaboration with the Office of the Minister for Armament and Ammunition and with the Counter-intelligence Office. By means of a careful selection of key targets it was considered possible to eliminate as much as 50 to 80 percent of the Soviet Union's manufacturing capacity. According to German estimates at the time, this would have meant a difference of 3,500 tanks and 3,000 aircraft in the monthly shipments to the front.[13]

From the standpoint of personnel and training, the Luftwaffe would have been quite capable of activating the necessary units for both major missions at the beginning of the war. Initially, the bombers which were available in 1941 would have sufficed, insofar as their ranges and armament factories still were on the near side of the Ural Mountains, and since the Soviet air defenses were clearly inadequate in quality and in strength.

Furthermore, a staff in command of a large strategic bomber force would undoubtedly have pressed for the further development and improvement of its aircraft in consonance with its growing mission. It would have pressed primarily for longer operating ranges, improved payload capabilities, better weapons, and replacements.

In contrast with the Soviet air forces, the Luftwaffe possessed the requisite quality in personnel to conduct strategic air warfare. But, the operations against traffic centers, key industries, and railroad marshaling areas were halted in the initial stages because the overall mission specified that all available forces were to be committed in support of the Army's effort to reach the desired eastern demarkation line between Lake Onega and the Volga River.[14] Hitler, the Supreme Commander of the Wehrmacht, was to blame for this faulty assignment. Although he considered himself to be a military commander and gave orders as though he were one, he failed to grasp the meaning of global strategy in a three-dimensional war and was unable to understand the objective, and, above all, the effects of strategic warfare within the framework of such a war.

It took until 9 November 1943 before the Commander in Chief of the Luftwaffe acknowledged the necessity for a change in policy. In a study entitled "Kurzen Studie: Kampf gegen die russische Ruestungs-industrie" ("A Short Study: The Battle Against the Russian Armament Industry") he declared: (1) that the Luftwaffe could make a greater contribution to victory in the Eastern Theater of Operations if it would do everything possible to attack the "roots of Soviet offensive power, the Soviet armament industry," instead of serving as artillery by dropping bombs in advance of the infantry; (2) that the destruction of as much as possible of the Soviet armament capacity would have a far greater impact upon the fighting front in the East and even upon the course of the entire war than continuous operations in direct support of the ground forces; and (3) that the Luftwaffe therefore should be relieved, at least temporarily, of its direct support mission in the Eastern Theater and of any other missions in that area as well.

Reviewing the tide of events since the opening of the campaign in the East, Goering admitted that the Luftwaffe had been used in 1941 primarily in support of the Army, that after the beginning of the summer offensive of 1942 it had become almost an adjunct of the Army, and that this situation had continued into 1943. He also acknowledged that he had neglected to attack and destroy the enemy's sources of strength, which would have halted the flow of power to the Soviet forces in the field, and that he had allowed the most favorable time for strategic operations to pass by, since which time difficulties had mounted considerably.[15]

On 26 November 1943 the Reichsmarschall issued an order in which he stated his intention to consolidate the bulk of the bomber forces stationed in the Eastern Theater under the IV Air Corps* in Combat Zone Center, and to reinforce them by special units with precision-bombing facilities. The heavy bomber forces which were intended to be consolidated under the terms of this were:

3rd Bomber Wing headquarters with the 1st and 2nd Groups
4th Bomber Wing Headquarters with the 2nd and 3rd Groups
55th Bomber Wing Headquarters with the 1st and 3rd Groups
3rd Group, 100th Bomber Wing

In December 1943 all of these forces (under the command of Rehabilitation Headquarters East)/ were withdrawn from their regular combat

---

*Since 4 September 1943 the IV Air Corps had been commanded by Generalleutnant Rudolf Meister, and was operating in the Fourth Air Fleet area in support of the First Panzer Army and the Eighth Army, both in a defensive situation.

/<u>Wiederauffrischungsstab Ost</u> (Rehabilitation Staff East). This became the code designation for the IV Air Corps. Originally the designation <u>Fliegerschul-Division 6</u> (Flying School Division 6) had been suggested by the Sixth Air Fleet.

missions and transferred to the Brest-Litovsk-Deblin Irena-Baranovichi-Bialystok area, where they were to be prepared and trained for their new mission.

Generalleutnant Meister was ordered on 10 December to Goering's headquarters for orientation on his future mission. Thus, at long last, a start was made to bring about strategic air warfare in the East with the clearly defined objective of paralyzing the Soviet armament industry.

At the turn of the year 1943-44 the German air forces left in the field in the Eastern Theater of Operations were therefore seriously weakened at a time when the steadily increasing power of the Red Army placed before them a far more difficult task than ever before. The great question remained whether the strategic objective could still be fulfilled or whether it was already too late.

German Air Operations in the East, 1943

The Mission

The beginning of 1943 brought the turn of the tide in military operations in the East, and after the winter operations of that year the initiative had passed clearly to the Soviet Union in the entire theater. It is true that the German armies, thanks to a clever conduct of operations and great tenacity and courage on the part of the soldiers in the area, had, by heavy fighting in extremely difficult situations, managed to maintain an integrated front. They had halted the Soviet forces which had broken through their lines and had even succeeded in cleaning out some of the enemy penetrations. In the process, however, they suffered very heavy casualties and lost enormous quantities of materiel, particularly heavy items, such as artillery, tanks, and antitank weapons. Personnel and materiel reserves, which might have alleviated the situation, were completely or almost completely lacking.

In support operations for the Army, the Luftwaffe also suffered almost irreplaceable losses in men and materiel, and it must be pointed out that losses through attrition and enemy ground fire were infinitely heavier than the total losses incurred through Soviet air attacks or anti-aircraft fire. In critical situations, the Luftwaffe was usually the only medium available to the German Supreme Command and other high level commands to compensate for the Army's heavy weapons losses and its lack of reserves. Air forces were highly flexible and could be quickly moved from one place to another.

While airpower had frequently been employed in 1942 to provide indirect support for the Army in missions within the operational zones of armies and army groups, during the entire year of 1943, a year of perpetual crisis throughout the Eastern Theater of Operations, airpower was constantly employed in every combat sector, and almost exclusively in direct support of ground operations. 16* Perpetual crises in these operations restricted the Luftwaffe's activities to missions over the far-flung battlefields in the East. The whole course of military events was determined by such factors as the great expanses of Russia, across which ran a front of 1,800 miles, by the lateral logistical life lines which were just as long, and by the numerical strength ratio, which continued to mount on the Soviet side while it declined on the German. This unavoidably laid the foundation for the deterioration and ultimate defeat of the German Air Force.

Geographical factors and comparative strengths of Soviet and German Armies also had a determining effect upon Luftwaffe operations, and, in the final essence, it was these factors that caused the heavy personnel and materiel attrition in the Luftwaffe and thus depleted its striking power. The only possible course open to the German Supreme Command to counter these factors was a radical withdrawal to a strongly developed line of positions, constructed in good time and in favorable terrain. This withdrawal would have resulted simultaneously in a shortening of the front and the rear supply lines. This would thereby have reduced the area to be held, making it possible to release greater numbers of troops from the front lines. In addition, the defensive capability of the line would have been markedly improved by the presence of prepared positions.

If this course had been adopted, the Luftwaffe would not have been worn down in the continuous crises which developed in those massive areas. On the contrary, it could have been employed in more concentrated form in the smaller operational area. If appropriately organized, it might even have been possible to release units for the real mission of airpower, namely the establishment of air superiority and the destruction of, or at least the reduction in the capability of, hostile sources of military power. ≠

---

*In 1943 combat operations of the flying forces were determined "at least to the extent of 80 percent by tactical cooperation with the Army." See "Ueberblick ueber die deutsche Luftkriegfuehrung" ("Overview Concerning the German Conduct of Aerial Warfare"), a study prepared by the 8th (Military Science) Branch of the Luftwaffe General Staff, Karlsruhe Document Collection.

≠See pp. 224-226.

Furthermore, the missions assigned to a Luftwaffe thus appropriately organized would have made it essential to have established a systematic program for aircraft production and for the logical development of new types of aircraft. The kind of mission, the operations involved, organization, and production would have influenced the entire conduct of operations by the Luftwaffe.

The first and foremost requirement was for fighters, which were needed first of all to repel hostile air forces while on the defensive and to secure air superiority over the front areas or at least in the decisively important sectors. Ground-attack and fighter-bomber forces* should have been increased and consolidated in tactical support divisions with the mission of supporting the Army.

Work should have been intensified to develop existing four-engine models, and the existing multi-engine bombers should have been consolidated in strategic bomber units and employed in accordance with a preplanned pattern against the enemy's military economy. We thus hear once again the same old song and find the same old errors of omission.[17]

From all experience gained in the past years, the Supreme Command and the Commander in Chief of the Luftwaffe had by mid-1943 derived no lessons whatever. It was only from the summer of 1943 on that the realization began to form, and then only very slowly, that a new type of aerial warfare was essential.⸸ Why was it that a regeneration of the Luftwaffe, both with respect to its internal structure and its physical properties, did not materialize sooner? Why was such a regeneration impossible even if the Commander in Chief of the Luftwaffe had been willing?

Hitler, as the Supreme Commander, determined both the scope and the form of the conduct of the war. Bound by his own ideas of obstinate resistance, of unconditionally holding ground, he could not bring himself to the decision to sacrifice ground and space. In the Eastern Theater he stubbornly forbade any timely retrograde movement which was devised to economize forces, and, with his deep and increasing distrust of his field marshals and generals, he interfered more and more frequently in every detail, even in the tactical control of individual units

---

*Including all sub-types, such as antitank aircraft.

⸸See figure 45.

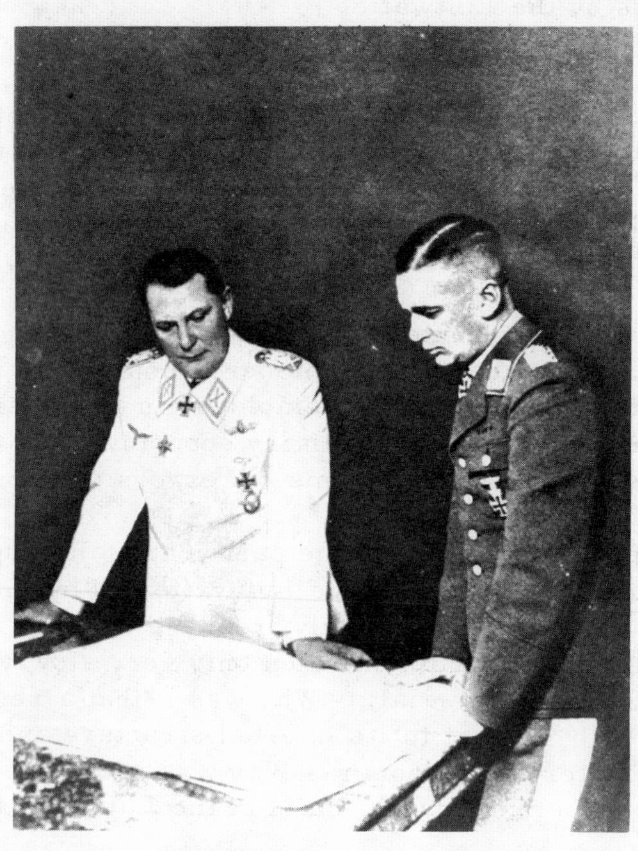

Figure 45
Reichsmarschall Hermann Goering, Commander in Chief of the Luftwaffe, at the planning table with Generaloberst Jeschonnek, Luftwaffe Chief of Staff

in all branches of the Wehrmacht.* He created the concept of strongholds (festen Plaetze) and fortresses (Festungen) for points and areas which were nothing of the sort, but which nevertheless had to be defended to the last man and the last round of ammunition.[18]† In Generalleutnant Kurt Dittmar's words:

> Every town in the Western Ukraine and in Western Ruthenia was declared a "stronghold" when the Russians approached. The only strong thing about these points, which had no permanent defense installations of any kind, was the obstinate decision not to evacuate them under any circumstances, even at the right moment, but to hold them until the Red floods engulfed them. In this way every sizeable town in the western Soviet Union and in what had been Poland became the grave of a German unit from regimental to divisional size. Isolated from the rest of the German line, each such town resisted under the most unfavorable conditions conceivable and was overcome by the superior Soviet forces with relative ease. Hitler committed the mortal sin in strategy of failing to consider the defeat of the opposing forces as the primary objective in military operations, instead of the retention of space.[19]††

Strategic greatness consists of a harmonious blending of certain characteristics which, taken separately, are diametrically opposed to each other: the power of vivid imagination must go hand in hand with sober realism; dash must be matched with circumspection; and persistence must be tempered with versatility in the forming of decisions.

---

*Editor's Note: Hitler was long suspicious of the old professional officer corps, which he generally (and sometimes rightly) associated with the aristocracy. This brooding fear may have stemmed in part from a belief that this group secretly wished to restore the monarchy. This became evident from his initial comments after the 20 July 1944 bomb plot.

†Goerlitz notes that the weaker the German forces became the more rigid and fanatical was the Fuehrer's conduct of operations, "as though his command alone could have made the impossible possible." Goerlitz, Vol. II, p. 223.

††Editor's Note: Hitler's preoccupation with spacial theories such as MacKinder's "Heartland" concept and the geopolitical work of the Haushofers may have influenced his thinking in strategic matters.

A process of balancing will always be necessary in the mind of the responsible person, and only the "refined measure of judgment" (in the words of Clausewitz) can point the sure way along the infinitely narrow dividing line between "too much" or "too little" of one or the other of these characteristics.

Measured by these classical standards, Hitler can be considered anything but a real military leader. He undoubtedly possessed a surplus of one or the other of the necessary qualifications, but what he did possess was discounted by the absence of the counterbalancing character which was essential at the time. Because of his fantasies, his imagination was completely unchecked by sober reasoning, his actions were dictated by wishful thinking, and steadfast persistence became in him simply obstinacy.

One of the most tragic features in the German conduct of operations in the Eastern Theater is the manner in which that conduct, in a steadily increasing measure, was guided by principles which were diametrically opposed to everything that had formerly been considered as sacrosanct law, and which had brought victory after victory to the German colors, while on the Soviet side, exactly the opposite principles gained steadily in predominance. It was along this route that Hitler led the German Army from defeat to defeat, most of which could have been averted.

Through the one-sided system of command in the conduct of operations, a bizarre front had evolved in the East, a front interrupted by dents and bulges, with some areas actually behind the Soviet lines and enveloped by the Red Army. The threats of the Soviet enemy became ever greater while the increasingly weakened German Army found great difficulty in holding the line.[20]

The Luftwaffe was required to give continuous close support in all of the critical areas along the entire front in order for the Army to maintain its positions, but, because of its numerical weakness, it could not possibly accomplish this gigantic mission. To anyone with a reasonable mind the entire problem was a matter of simple arithmetic. First of all, it was not only on the ground that the Soviet Union was gaining in superiority. Germany could commit only 2, 500 aircraft in the Eastern Theater at this time, while the Russians could send out double that number. Moreover, the quality of Soviet aircraft was steadily improving. During this phase of the war the Luftwaffe had reached its peak strength, and had a grand total of about 6, 000 combat aircraft. The fact that not even half of them could be spared to support this decisively important campaign is adequate proof of the importance to the Soviet Union of operations in the Mediterranean Theater and the Anglo-American heavy bombing attacks.

What was felt most severely on the German side was the lack of fighters. Outnumbered in this type of aircraft in the Eastern Theater anyway, the German Command had to reduce the numbers still further in order to reinforce the defenses in the West, where nearly two-thirds of the total German fighter strength was committed late in 1943.

The rapid sequence of the integrated Soviet offensives allowed the German side no respite in which to make the most effective use of airpower. Thus, air units frequently had to be shifted on short notice from one battlefield to another in order to help relieve some newly developed crisis. From whatever sector they were withdrawn, German forces immediately and keenly felt their absence, and when the air units arrived in their new operational areas they again found themselves crushingly outnumbered by the Soviet air forces which were there.[21]

Even the improvised measures which were so frequently requested and ordered, such as the use of training aircraft and obsolete models as harassing units--these were later given the euphemious designation of night ground-attack aircraft--against Soviet forces, could do little to alleviate the situation in the East, far less to bring about a favorable reversal.

Practically the entire Luftwaffe, including all types of aircraft, whether they were suitable for ground-attack missions or not, was engulfed by the Moloch of the East.

In the autumn of 1943, when General Korten, supported by Generaloberst Zeitzler, Chief of the Army General Staff, finally succeeded in convincing Hitler of the need for strategic airpower against the Soviet military economy and Soviet communications networks, and when, at the end of the year, preparations for such operations commenced, the other eminently important factor in the conduct of military operations, time, became a cause for the utmost anxiety on the part of those concerned with the preparations.

What was then required was not only the good will of those concerned to carry out their new mission, but also to give the appropriate units and individual aircrews training in navigation and bombing. Another necessity was the development of the ground services organization. Of course, a further requirement was the continuous development and improvement of the various types of aircraft.

The objective stipulated in the study by Reichsmarschall Goering entitled "Kampf gegen die russische Ruestungsindustrie" ("Battle Against the Russian Armament Industry") was to achieve strength, planned operations, a knowledge of the individual targets, a description of the targets, and to systematize bombing.[22] The most essential requirement for the planned air operations was the stabilization of the front on the ground to allay the danger of German forces being pushed farther to the west. The base areas envisioned for the operations were Bobruysk, Orsha, and Baranovichi (all in Combat Zone Center), because there was a possibility in that area of maintaining operational runways even during the mud season.

Gravely concerned about the development of the general situation in the East in late 1943, the Sixth Air Fleet on 28 November addressed itself to the Commander in Chief of the Luftwaffe and to Army Group Center as follows:

> In view of the strained situation, the Sixth Air Fleet finds it necessary to emphasize the importance of the airfields at Bobruysk and Orsha for the Luftwaffe. . . .
>
> It is therefore requested that the decisive importance of the airfields at Bobruysk and Orsha be considered with respect to carrying out air operations in the event that a relocation of the front lines should be under consideration.[23]

Communications sent by the Sixth Air Fleet to Goering and other available data shows clearly that the Commander in Chief of the Luftwaffe was aware of the significance of the Soviet's military power base and the massive movement of supplies and replacements to the front.[24] It would thus have been the logical thing at an early stage of affairs (as far back as late 1941 and early 1942) for him to have made urgent appeals to the Wehrmacht High Command and, especially, to Hitler, the Supreme Commander, in order to secure approval for the conduct of strategic warfare in the East. The Reichsmarschall should have pointed out the effects which strategic air warfare would have had in reducing the Soviet striking power at the front, and have made every effort to convince the Army High Command of the necessity of withdrawing some of the tactical air support on the battlefield. That he failed to express these views with the necessary emphasis, or that he failed to gain an early acceptance of them, was an error on the part of Goering which was to have fateful consequences.

Even if the Commander in Chief of the Luftwaffe had failed to win approval for the conduct of strategic warfare, it would still have been his duty to have planned and prepared for strategic operations even without the approval of higher commands. The Luftwaffe should have been kept ready at all times for commitment in strategic missions. Primary requirements in such preparation were the timely development of suitable and well-equipped operational bases and the development and procurement of appropriate aircraft. Failure to carry out this planning and preparatory work was another grave error made by Goering, and resulted primarily in a serious loss of time when the order to conduct strategic air operations was finally given in 1943.*

What must be recognized as commendable, however, was the willingness and the efforts of all concerned, the Commander in Chief of the Luftwaffe, the Sixth Air Fleet, the IV Air Corps, and the administrative area command, to do everything possible to prepare the IV Strategic Air Corps once the decision was taken to begin operations.

The basic cause of all of the serious errors and all failures to reorganize the Luftwaffe and to effect its timely reorientation was to be found at the highest level of command, in the person of Hitler, who was woefully ignorant on the subject, and who distrusted all of those around him who attempted to offer well-meant advice. He had a closed mind in certain areas, and lacked the ability to think ahead on military subjects, to place himself in the position of his opponents, or, in general, to see maps and actual facts in their proper correlation.† Hitler was nevertheless vividly interested in many individual military problems and could judge them properly, even envisioning large-scale projects, but it takes much more to make a military leader than the intuitive thought of a fortunate moment. What is needed besides pronounced ability and a well-balanced character is the long and careful training given in the Command and General Staff School and in General Staff experience, neither of which he had had.[25]

High Command Organization

It is necessary to again describe briefly the experience which had been gained and the requirements which had become necessary in 1941

---

*Editor's Note: See Richard Suchenwirth, Historical Turning Points in the German Air Force War Effort, USAF Historical Studies No. 189, Maxwell AFB, Alabama: USAF Historical Division, RSI, June 1959, pp. 76-90.

†Hitler was ignorant of the capabilities of aerial warfare and its possible impact upon the conduct of war in the various theaters of operations, which led him to freeze aircraft production at the very time when aircraft production should have been given top priority in the overall armament program. See von Manstein, Lost Victories, p. 305.

and 1942. There was a need for a really effective joint armed forces high command and real joint command organizations in the various theaters of operations and operational sectors. Despite this obvious need, the command crisis continued to smoulder under the surface, and found expression not only in small circles of desperate conspirators, who were determined to go to any extreme, but also among men like von Manstein, Milch, and Zeitzler who endeavored again and again to persuade Hitler to change the top level military command. The main objectives of these men were to persuade Hitler to (1) return the High Command of the Wehrmacht to the hands of an experienced soldier; (2) appoint a joint command for the Eastern Theater of Operations (as he had done in other theaters, in the West, Southeast, and Southwest); (3) reorganize the Wehrmacht High Command as a genuine joint general staff; (4) dismiss Generaloberst Wilhelm Keitel;* and (5) decide in favor of an elastic defense in the Eastern Theater, which would permit a great economy of forces.[26]

There was, of course, an obvious need for a clear division of the Luftwaffe into tactical units for close support of the ground forces, and into strategic forces for use in missions designed to serve the overall conduct of the war. The solution found in 1943 to activate a strategic air corps (the IV Air Corps) was not sufficiently clear. In the first place, the strategic force should have been placed directly under the Commander in Chief of the Luftwaffe, instead of the Sixth Air Fleet, which already had orders to support the Army. Thus there was always a danger that in critical situations the strategic air units would again become exhausted in close support operations for the ground forces, or, at least, that the Sixth Air Fleet would find itself obliged to neglect one of its missions in favor of the other.

Secondly, all other air forces should have been clearly organized in tactical units (divisions and corps) and in fighter divisions, and assigned the unequivocal mission of supporting the Army on the field of battle and of securing air superiority. As it was, the actual reorganization of the Luftwaffe could scarcely even be described as a halfway measure.

---

*Editor's Note: Keitel was disliked by top field commanders mainly because he failed to represent them with sufficient emphasis in his meetings with Hitler. Actually, Hitler selected Keitel, in part, because he felt that he could rely upon him to assist him in keeping the old officer corps in check, which meant abject subordination.

Operations of the Air Forces

In 1943 the truth of the principle became clearer than ever before that the smaller the size of the air forces, the greater is the necessity to concentrate them even more closely in the actual areas of main effort in order to achieve real success. This concentration of airpower should have been employed with the utmost strictness, in spite of all of the local requests for air support in sectors outside the area of main effort, even in cases in which the requests were fully justifiable.

In 1943 the focal area in the Don River bend called for the first time for a power concentration of this type in the southern sector of the Fourth Air Fleet's operational zone and, at times, in the area of Air Command Don. One sector after the other had to release aircraft in order to facilitate the required concentration and to meet the Soviet counteroffensive. The effects upon the dispositions of the Luftwaffe in Russia are evident from the following tables showing numerical strengths in numbers of aircraft:

General Area of Operation	1942 Mid-October	1942 Early December	1943 Mid-January
Leningrad	485	270	195
Moscow	425	480	380
Don River	545	700	900
Caucasus and Crimea	495	330	240[27]

Although all of the efforts to save the Sixth Army failed, in spite of the costly air operations which were undertaken for the purpose, the continuous and concentrated support by the Luftwaffe was nevertheless a major contribution to the overall defensive success in halting attacking Soviet masses and in bolstering the German ground defenses. Here, the tactics of power concentration were applied correctly and successfully.

The next area of main effort for airpower was in connection with Operation ZITADELLE and the ensuing battle for the Orel River.[28] Again forces were moved in from other areas. Hitler was also willing to commit all of his available forces without reservation in these operations. At a conference held at the Jaegerhof, near Rastenburg, East Prussia, Hitler on 1 July 1943 addressed the Commanders in Chief of the Army and the Luftwaffe, and the army and corps commanders of both services, concerning Operation ZITADELLE, informing them that he was now determined to carry out the operation, that experience had shown him that nothing could harm an army more than idleness, and that his advisors had informed him that there were indications that the Russians would soon launch an attack of their own. He then pointed out that in such a situation it would be better first to repel the Soviet attack and then to launch a counterattack, since no one could give an absolute guarantee that the Russians would act as predicted, and since in a short time the season of the year would pass in which a large-scale German attack could be launched.[29]

There was, of course, a clear danger that if the German attack was begun the Russians might attack the line in the northern sector of the Orel salient while German forces were deeply committed in their southwesterly drive at Orel. This would put the Red Army in the rear of the German attack force. In case such a situation should develop, Hitler intended to move in the last available German aircraft to stem the tide.[30]

When the large-scale Soviet attack from the northeast did materialize, there were scarcely any forces available to move in against it, since the bulk of all available airpower was already committed in the Orel-Kursk-Belgorod area. It might have been possible to have moved in air units from Combat Zone Far North, since in other sectors of the Eastern Theater the only available air forces were reconnaissance and harassing units, and it was absolutely essential to leave them where they were because of the vital nature of their missions. In the Western Theater of Operations, the Mediterranean Theater, and the Zone of the Interior, the air forces on hand were urgently required because of the critical situations in those areas.[31] A new crisis in the southern part of the Eastern Front complicated the situation still more, and the Supreme Command was compelled to draw additional units from the VIII Air Corps. As usual these were the only reserves that could be quickly moved in to halt the new and extremely dangerous Soviet offensive at the Mius River.* It is therefore useless to inquire whether it would have been at all possible, because of logistical problems, to have moved more air units in and to have concentrated them in the area around Orel and north of Kharkov for participation in Operation ZITADELLE.† The

---

*During Operation ZITADELLE the VIII Air Corps had already been compelled to release units to the 1st Air Division (Sixth Air Fleet).

†As noted previously, it would not have been possible to have based additional air forces on the airfields in the Orel-Bryansk area and to have supplied them with fuel and ammunition due to shortages of these items and serious transportation difficulties. See p. 75.

very last German aircraft could simply not have been moved in because they were needed just as badly at other critical places.

Particularly critical situations developed later at Krivoy Rog, Kiev-Shitomir, east of Orsha, and at Nevel. These crises developed almost simultaneously, so that the High Command of the Luftwaffe was no longer able to develop a clearly defined concentration of power at any single point in the East. The Luftwaffe, the "fire brigade" of the Eastern Theater of Operations, was simply no longer in a position to commit strong forces simultaneously in each of the many threatened areas.*

Individual air fleets nevertheless persevered in their efforts to employ their available forces in accordance with the principles of power concentration. They also tried to support each other whenever necessary, as was the case when the Sixth Air Fleet supported the weaker First Air Fleet in the Nevel area in October 1943. Despite these efforts, the Luftwaffe made no significant changes in its chain of command or in the tactics which it employed in 1943.

Individual Arms of the Luftwaffe

Initially there was some confusion with respect to the designation and mission of tactical support units. The term "tactical support forces" included dive-bomber, twin-engine fighter, ground-attack, fighter-bomber, and antitank air units. Equally as varied were the types of aircraft which were used in tactical support operations. These included primarily the old and tested Ju-87 "Stuka," followed by the Me-109, Me-110, Me-210, Me-410, Hs-129, Fw-190, and even the Hs-123 aircraft, which had been long ready for the museum.

Up to the summer of 1943 the theoretical and practical development of the tactical support arm, and its expansion, had been hampered by the lack of a special section to represent it on the staff of the Commander in Chief of the Luftwaffe. Dive-bombers were handled by the Bomber Inspectorate and later by the Chief of Bomber Forces, ground-attack units by the Fighter Inspectorate and later by the Chief of Fighter Forces. Officers in charge of the two inspectorates treated dive-bombers and ground-attack units as appendages of the arms they represented, and either had no time for them or lacked interest in what might be called their stepchildren.

---

*The author believes that stronger air forces could have been based and supplied in the area, provided that such arrangements were made well in advance, including the stockpiling of necessary supplies.

Soon after assuming responsibility as the new Chief of the Luftwaffe General Staff, General Korten appointed a general as chief of a new section. Originally designated Chief of Close Support Aircraft (General der Nahkampfflieger), this office was later called Chief of Tactical Support Forces.* Ground-attack and dive-bomber forces were grouped together and described uniformly as tactical support or ground-attack forces. This was a milestone on the road to a clear division in the Luftwaffe between tactical and strategic forces.

Dating back to the time of the dive-bomber,/ most of the ground-attack or tactical support units were equipped with Ju-87 aircraft, and attacked their targets, including tanks, with bombs while in a steep dive.// This form of attack was sufficiently effective during the early stages of the campaign when Soviet tanks were not heavily armored and most of the enemy aircraft were obsolete types. Col. Hans-Ulrich Rudel and a few other specialists in this type of operation became especially adept in the art of destroying tanks.** In 1943, however, the Red Army began to employ increasingly large numbers of tanks, protected by much heavier armor plate, and generally refrained from launching attacks unless there was exceedingly strong tank support to spearhead the way.[32] Antitank action now became the most important mission of the Luftwaffe, and all the more so because the ground forces suffered from an extraordinarily serious shortage of armor-piercing weapons, so that the irresistible tanks brought on a virtual "tank panic." Antitank aircraft then became the fastest and

---

*The officer appointed was Col. Dr. Ernst Kupfer, the well-qualified commander of the 2nd Dive-Bomber Wing. His successor in November 1943 was the equally experienced Generalmajor Hubertus Hitschold.

/Editor's Note: For an interesting appraisal of dive-bombing in the German Air Force see Richard Suchenwirth, Historical Turning Points in the German Air Force War Effort, USAF Historical Studies No. 189, Maxwell AFB, Alabama: USAF Historical Division, RSI, June 1959, pp. 28-31, 36-40.

//Editor's Note: Capt. David R. Mets, USAF, has written a very interesting article on the development of dive-bombing, which includes the equally interesting commentary of Maj. Gen. Orvil A. Anderson, USAF, concerning the efficacy of this type of weapon delivery. "Dive Bombing Between the Wars," The Airpower Historian, Vol. XII, No. 3, Maxwell AFB, Alabama: The Air Force Historical Foundation, July 1965.

**Hans-Ulrich Rudel was Germany's most highly decorated flyer, credited with 2,530 combat missions, the destruction of 519 tanks, and the 23,500-ton Russian battleship Marat.

most flexible available antitank weapon which, with favorable weather conditions, could be quickly sent into action upon very short notice.

Since bombing attacks were no longer sufficiently effective, the demand arose for what were called flying antitank guns, aircraft armed with tank-destroying weapons. At Rechlin, near Berlin, and later at Bryansk, an experimental antitank air detachment carried out tests with experimental aircraft types which had been used with good results in various sectors of the front.[33] The Ju-87 "Stuka," which was employed for this purpose, was even too slow for the conditions in the Eastern Theater, and, because of this lack of speed and the increasingly effective Soviet antiaircraft defenses, it became increasingly costly to carry out operations with this model. Colonel Kupfer, the new Chief of Tactical Air Support Forces, therefore insisted that his units be reequipped with Fw-190 aircraft. In September 1943 this conversion began at an accelerated pace, with the Ju-87's which were thereby released being immediately used to equip night bombing units.*

Another experimental unit had been equipped with Hs-129 planes since the end of 1942, and had been committed primarily in the Fourth Air Fleet area. As the 4th Group (composed of four squadrons) of the 9th Ground-Attack Wing, this unit remained for a time the only actual ground-attack group in existence. The small production of Hs-129 planes,/ the high vulnerability of their engines to gunfire, and their propensity to catch on fire were serious handicaps, but they were also subject to troubles from sand and dust which necessitated the use of turf-covered airfields. For these reasons Hs-129 aircraft were not used to establish additional ground-attack units or to reequip existing Ju-87 units.

Toward the end of 1943 the 1st, 2nd, 3rd, and 77th Ground-Attack (dive-bomber) Wings each received an additional tenth (antitank) squadron, composed of 12 Ju-87 aircraft armed with one or two 37-mm. cannons and 4 Ju-88 bombers. The cannon were mounted in such a way that they could be easily removed to convert the plane into a bomber in case there were no tank targets in the area.

Conversion of ground-attack units from Ju-87's to Fw-190's progressed very slowly since the mounting volume of Anglo-American massed

*The former night harassing units.

/Only seven Hs-129's were made in 1941, 221 in 1942, 411 in 1943, and 202 in 1944.

bomber attacks over the Reich forced the Luftwaffe to retain the Fw-190's as fighters in the home defense system (Reichsverteidigung). The operational status of ground-attack units equipped either with Ju-87 or Fw-190 aircraft remained remarkably high, usually between 70 and 80 percent, which was largely due to the fact that these types were easier to service than other aircraft models.

Concerning the weapons of these units it remains to be said that the development of a small-caliber shaped-charge bomb and effective rocket projectiles should have been accelerated. The development of the rocket projectiles was adversely affected by experiences with the poor quality Soviet rockets and the usually ineffective use made of them by the Russians. [34]*

The night fighter forces included harassing bomber units, later described as night ground-attack aircraft. The effectiveness of these units was first demonstrated by the Russians through the nightly operations of their U-2 units (generally called sewing machines because of the sound of their engines). In the autumn of 1942, as a result of experiences with these Soviet units, the Luftwaffe organized its own harassing squadrons, which were initially equipped with Ar-66, Go-145, Fw-58, and Fi-156 aircraft. Later they received He-45 and -46, and Hs-126 planes as well. During 1943 the German Air Command expanded these units into organizations of group size and, at the end of the year, redesignated them as night ground-attack groups. In this period of expansion, some of these squadrons were converted into Ju-87 units.

Apart from the actual material damage done by these organizations, the real value of their operations was their continually disturbing effect upon enemy troops, who were worn out from combat activities of the day and could not relax and rest properly because they knew that the enemy was still above them. [35] Actually, the casualties inflicted during harassing night raids were surprisingly small.

During 1943 additional fighter units, even in the Eastern Theater, were equipped with Fw-190 aircraft in place of the Me-109's. However,

---

*The Russians used RS-82 rocket projectiles as early as 1941, but with little success. On the German side such projectiles were first used at the turn of the year 1942-43 by the 54th Fighter Wing against ships on Lake Ladoga. No details are available, however, to indicate the extent of success in these attacks.

the conversion to FW-190's could only be carried out slowly because of the need for them in Germany and the West.* Numerically, the German fighter forces in the entire Eastern Theater were always outnumbered by their Soviet opponents, although unit operability was maintained at the relatively high level of 50 to 70 percent of the actual unit strengths.

Although the individual German airman and German aircraft types were superior to the flyers and planes of the Soviet Union, a fact which was clearly demonstrated by the confirmed number of Soviet aircraft destroyed, German fighter forces in the East gradually lost control of the air because of the steadily increasing numerical superiority of the Soviet air forces. For this reason alone they were no longer able to provide an adequately strong defense throughout the theater. Even the remarkable local successes which were achieved could not conceal this fact, and at the end of the year each of the large command areas in the East, Fourth Air Fleet sector (South), Sixth Air Fleet sector (Center), and First Air Fleet sector (North), had but a single fighter wing composed of two or three groups. On 31 December 1943 the actual total daylight fighter strength along the entire front, from the Black Sea to the arctic coast, was 385 aircraft, 306 of which were operational.[36]

What was perhaps a greater source of danger was the fact that, owing to the numerical inferiority of German fighter forces, the mutual confidence which had existed between the Army and the Luftwaffe steadily deteriorated. Ground forces, especially at the lower command levels, were unable and unwilling to understand that it was no longer possible to keep the skies free of hostile aircraft as had been the case in 1941-42. On the other hand, it was absolutely essential to frequently strip large sectors of the front of air support in order to be able to employ airpower in concentration at those places where it was most urgently needed. For security reasons it was never possible to disclose to each and every command information showing the numerical weakness of the air forces.

---

*Editor's Note: The Fw-190 was probably Germany's most successful fighter of World War II. It was highly maneuverable, well armed, and capable of speeds in excess of 400 miles per hour. The prototype was flown in mid-1939, and the first combat version went into action on the channel coast in the summer of 1941 with Fighter Wing 26 "Schlageter." Far more versatile and robust than the Me-109, it was primarily an interceptor, but was successfully modified as a fighter-bomber, fighter-dive-bomber, and even as an antitank aircraft. For details concerning the various versions of this plane see Kens and Nowarra, pp. 204-217, and Green, _War Planes of the Second World War: Fighters,_ Vol. I, pp. 93-114.

During the combat crises which became the rule of the day in 1943 German bomber forces were used primarily in direct and indirect support of the ground forces over the battlefield. Operations of this sort did not correspond at all with the capabilities of the available bomber aircraft, the He-111's and Ju-88's. These units were employed in this way only because the available number of suitable tactical support aircraft was too small to fulfill all of the Army's support demands. It was very late indeed before it became clear to the Luftwaffe and to the Army that bombers were vitally necessary for operations against the enemy's sources of power and transportation routes to the front. Large numbers of bombers were then (autumn of 1943) withdrawn from action for rehabilitation and training for strategic operations.*

Although the standard He-111 and Ju-88 aircraft had been constantly improved and modified, the minor changes made did not bring about any really decisive improvement in performance capabilities. Actually, instead of improving matters, the presence of numerous variations of these types of aircraft served only to complicate and overtax the entire supply and maintenance services throughout the Luftwaffe. An appreciable improvement in the effectiveness of bombing operations could only have been brought about by the timely conversion to four-engine bombers. Much had been expected of the He-177 "Greif,"† a model which was being developed by the Heinkel Works as early as 1938. That year the Reichs Air Ministry, obsessed with Generalmajor Ernst Udet's "Stuka" idea, insisted that even this long-range bomber had to be developed for dive-bombing performances.

The prototype made its first flight at Rechlin on 19 November 1939, and a contract was soon let for the construction of 120 aircraft in 1940. A few He-177's, equipped with various types of experimental wings, were turned out in 1940, but in June the original contract was terminated (despite

---

*See p. 226.

†Editor's Note: The He-177 version most commonly used was the A-3. This had two large power plants, one mounted on each wing. Each of these power plants consisted of two liquid-cooled engines (DB 606-A and DB 606-B) placed side by side under a single housing, developing a total horsepower of 2,700. This arrangement was an effort to avoid the lengthy and costly development of a 2,000-horsepower-class radial engine. However, there were later experimental models with four radial engines. This aircraft had a cruising speed of 257 miles per hour and a range of 2,300 miles. See Kens and Nowarra, pp. 292-299.

the wishes of the Luftwaffe General Staff) and only three planes per month were turned out. Toward the end of that year production was again commenced, but in 1941 production was stopped altogether because of structural weaknesses in the wings and the problem of engines overheating.

In 1942 the He-177 again went into serial production, and by the end of the year the Chief of Luftwaffe Supply and Administration had taken over 35 of these planes. These were first committed in the field during the fateful Stalingrad airlift operation.

The 50th Bomber Group had approximately 40 to 50 of these aircraft, which were being tested under winter conditions and were to be given a combat trial in the following spring. Of the entire group, 7 aircraft were sent to Zaporozhye under Maj. Kurt Scheede (GSC). The others had not been ready for operations or had been forced to land after taking off because of damage of one kind or another. One or two planes dropped out at Stalino because of damages, and Major Scheede proceeded on his way with the remainder of the aircraft into the Stalingrad pocket. This was the last anyone heard from the Major. The group was then taken over by Maj. Heinrich Schlosser, an experienced instructor in instrument flying, who for a short time served under the author's command while carrying out supply missions.

The 50th Bomber Group reported on 30 January 1943 that the entire group had successfully accomplished only 22 air logistical sorties to Stalingrad and only 13 combat sorties in the previous 10 days, and this with an actual strength of about 45 aircraft. The He-177 could carry a normal bomb load of six 1, 100-pound bombs, but on supply missions it carried only two 1, 100-pound and four to six 550-pound air-drop containers. The bomb racks under its wings were spaced so closely together that, although two 1, 100-pound bombs could be attached under each wing, the 1, 100-pound air-drop containers were too large to fit the racks.[37] The first operations of the He-177 in the Eastern Theater thus turned out to be complete failures, and the frequent fires resulting from the overheating of its two twin-engine power units and heavy repair requirements caused it to be withdrawn from combat employment.

Knowing that a number of modifications were being planned for this aircraft, Luftwaffe combat units continued to hope that new variations would soon appear which would be markedly improved over the previous models.[38] Luftwaffe leaders planned to incorporate the expected new versions in the IV Strategic Air Corps, but none of them appeared in the East by the end of 1943.*

Railroad interdiction operations increased during 1943, and, taking advantage of favorable weather, interdiction squadrons penetrated to the extreme limit of their ranges into Soviet operational and supply areas. These units were especially successful in attacks upon locomotives, but these were merely local achievements, having little effect upon the overall war effort. Sometimes they inflicted heavy losses upon Russian units and hampered their movements considerably, but the scope of such operations was too small to effect any lasting disruption of Soviet road or rail networks, even in specific areas.

The number of reconnaissance units which were available in the East in 1943 were usually adequate. Unit strengths were generally successfully maintained by the replacement of aircraft, although the types most commonly used for combat and other tactical reconnaissance (Hs-126 and Fw-189) were obsolete. Reconnaissance units submitted frequent urgent requests to have their aircraft replaced by later models. The only two types which had proven to be completely satisfactory were the Me-109 (for tactical reconnaissance) and the Do-217 (for night reconnaissance). The Ju-88, which was used in daylight strategic reconnaissance missions, needed immediate improvements or, if this could not be done, should have been replaced by better aircraft models. Twenty unit leaders were lost during 1943, largely because of the continued use of obsolete aircraft models. It was therefore essential to have reequipped these reconnaissance units so that they could have continued to perform their missions in a satisfactory manner.[39]

Organization of the Air Forces

In every type of air unit the speed with which its operational status declined often resulted in squadrons and groups having a surplus of

---

*Editor's Note: The problem of engine fires in the He-177 was not mastered until 1943, and the production of the aircraft was stopped altogether in 1944. Only about 200 out of the 1,094 produced by April of 1945 were ever delivered to combat units, and, at the end of the war, the British took over about 800 of them, unused and undamaged on Norwegian airfields. See Kens and Nowarra, p. 293, and Green, *Famous Bombers of the Second World War*, Vol. II, pp. 93-107.

technical and general ground service personnel for the actual number of aircraft in operation. This state of affairs should not have been allowed to continue in 1943.* Another serious weakness in air units was due to the heavy losses of unit leaders, particularly group commanders and squadron leaders and their adjutants. In many cases very young officers, who were unquestionably courageous and willing, but who had no command experience or any experience in the training of their officers, had to be assigned to positions in which they were logically bound to be failures for the foregoing reasons. Courage was not the only quality required in a unit commander, and something needed to be done to remedy the situation. The author still contends, as he did then, that the matter could have been corrected or vastly improved only by a reorganization of the Luftwaffe from wing level downward. This situation was recognized in 1942, when the author submitted the following recommendations: (1) Discontinue the group as a unit and dissolve the group staffs; (2) reorganize the wing to contain the following units:

1 headquarters squadron with 12 aircraft (command and reconnaissance "swarms")†
4 to 5 squadrons of 21 aircraft each
1 air base operations company
1 air signal platoon (radio locator)
1 replacement squadron of 21 aircraft

The author believes that this reorganization would have resulted in several advantages for the Luftwaffe. There would have been a decidedly better utilization of all types of ground service personnel. Maintenance work for the units of a wing, based on one or two airfields, could have been handled by the ground personnel normally assigned to a group, since experience had shown that on the average only about 50 percent of the aircraft of a unit were operational at a given time, and, during intensive combat, only about 33 percent. The operations of the maintenance and supply services would thereby have been consolidated and intensified.††

---

*Squadrons with a strength of 2 to 4 aircraft and groups with only 10 to 12 operational aircraft were by no means rare in the East during major battles.

†Editor's Note: A tactical formation or flight consisting of 5 or 6 aircraft.

††Very often a group commander had to pass on an operational order to a squadron leader who, besides his own plane, had only 1 or 2 operational aircraft, but still had a full complement of squadron ground personnel.

Command control and command channels would have been simpler and more direct if the intermediate command level (the group) had been eliminated, which would have done away with the intermediate transmission of orders and reporting to higher headquarters. This would have simplified the entire signal communications system, thereby also reducing the amount of communications equipment and the number of vehicles required.

Command assignments, particularly with respect to squadron leaders, would have been more permanent, because there would no longer have been any need to transfer squadron leaders so frequently to replace the large numbers of group commanders and their adjutants who were lost. The influence of wing commanders, who were invariably carefully selected and experienced senior officers, on the education of the unit officer corps would have been more immediate and effective under the reorganized plan. The handling of all matters connected with troop welfare, promotions, decorations, transfers, and similar things, would have been considerably simplified and accelerated.*

It would have been possible to have consolidated all surplus technical and general ground service personnel in newly established ground service units to be placed at the disposal of the air fleets. Such units could have been transferred to the rear to prepare for the leapfrog withdrawal of air forces during retrograde movements, or they could have been temporarily assigned to reinforce units which were committed in areas of main effort. In either case, such use of surplus ground service personnel would have been advantageous for the Luftwaffe. Last, but not least, the aforementioned modifications would have prevented the disintegration of the wings by the too frequent commitment of its groups in a number of areas, as had gradually become the rule.

Generaloberst Jeschonnek, the Chief of the Luftwaffe General Staff, rejected the author's recommendations on the ground that Goering, being so infatuated with figures, would never have allowed the change.

---

*Editor's Note: The wing (Geschwader), much like the Army regiment, was the unit in which an officer was usually rated and advanced. The Geschwader bore the traditions from the past and generally maintained fairly good unit integrity. This permitted wing commanders to make a closer evaluation of their officers, especially with respect to their leadership abilities and personal traits of character, which, in the Wehrmacht, were always considered to be as important as professional knowledge and ability.

This reason cannot be accepted, since the German public and hostile intelligence services could scarcely have deduced any alterations in German air strength--this has always been expressed in numbers of wings by numerical designations--through an internal reorganization of the wings. The only important thing was to choose a proper time and form in which to submit the recommendation. Goering could have been allowed to persist in his craze for numbers, but the actual number of available units would have been more firmly integrated and could have been employed in a simpler and more effective way. If the recommended reorganization had been adopted, only one real change would have been essential (mainly for tactical reasons). In each bomber wing the fifth squadron would have been a railroad interdiction squadron, and in each ground-attack wing the fifth squadron would have been an antitank squadron.[40]*

Flak Artillery Forces

Flak forces were a most important element in the East, as can be seen by the following table showing the percentage of available flak units committed in the various theaters of operations.

Area of Commitment	Autumn 1941	10 January 1942	Autumn 1943
Zone of the Interior	56	57	52
Western Theater of Operations	12	16	16
Southern Theater of Operations	-	-	10
Northern Theater of Operations (including Finland)	-	-	4
Eastern Theater of Operations	27	19	18[41]

*If personnel and materiel had become available to activate additional antitank squadrons, these could have been consolidated to form an antitank air wing controlled directly by the Commander in Chief of the Luftwaffe for commitment in real areas of main effort.

The flak artillery command headquarters which were committed in the Eastern Theater in 1943 were:

Under the Fourth Air Fleet (Combat Zone South)

I Flak Corps, initially under General der Flieger Otto Dessloch, from June 1943 under Generalleutnant Richard Reimann
9th Flak Division, under Generalmajor Wolfgang Pickert in the Kuban River area, and in the Crimea with the Seventeenth Army
10th Flak Division, initially under General Johann Seiffert, from August 1943 under Generalmajor Franz Engel in the Voronezh area and later Kursk
15th Flak Division, commanded by Generalmajor Eduard Muhr, in the Caucasus, and later with the new Sixth Army at the Mius and lower Dnepr Rivers
17th Flak Division, commanded by Generalmajor Karl Veith, in the communications zone of Army Group South

Under the Sixth Air Fleet (Combat Zone Center)

10th Flak Brigade, under Generalmajor Paul Pavel, then Generalmajor Schuchard, and later under Col. Adolf Wolf
12th Flak Division, under Generalmajor Ernst Buffa in the Orel area, later in Bobruysk supporting Second and Ninth Armies
18th Flak Division, under Generalmajor Richard Reimann until mid-March 1943, then under Generalmajor Heinrich, Prinz zu Reuss in the Smolensk area and later at Orsha in support of the Fourth Army*

Under the First Air Fleet (Combat Zone North)

2nd Flak Division, under Generalmajor Heine von Rantzau until September 1943, then under Generalmajor Alfons Luczny in the northern sector of Leningrad area, Novgorod, with command post at Petshanka near Siverskaya
6th Flak Division, under Generalmajor Werner Anton, in the Sixteenth Army sector[42]

*The brigade and two divisions were consolidated under the re-established II Flak Corps, under Generalleutnant Job Odebrecht, on 3 November 1943.

From the above disposition of forces it is obvious that in 1943, consonant with the main effort in ground operations, the bulk of all flak units in the East were assigned throughout the year to the Fourth Air Fleet area, in Combat Zone South.[43]

From the autumn of 1943 on, when Soviet forces launched their offensive in the center--the attack was made against the two flanks of Army Group Center--the Sixth Air Fleet, which was responsible for air support in these areas, received additional flak reinforcements besides those which were already under its command.

During this year, the main emphasis of the flak artillery mission in the Eastern Theater constantly fluctuated between air defense and ground operations. In 1941 and 1942, when there was little Soviet air activity, German flak units were often employed with outstanding success in direct-fire ground support, mainly against tanks. In fact, the results achieved against armored units by the flak artillery equalled, and in many cases exceeded, its achievements in air defense missions.[44*]

Owing to the steadily increasing Soviet armored strength, and the corresponding decline in the number of armor-piercing weapons available to the German ground forces, the Army demanded more and more flak artillery to make up for the shortage and to stave off powerful enemy attacks. But, this employment of antiaircraft artillery was really the policy of "the poor man," since flak batteries were taken away from their natural mission (air defense) at the very time when increasing protection against Soviet air attacks was needed by the ground forces because of the resurgence of enemy airpower. Moreover, increased protection became necessary for many vital installations not theretofore endangered which were exposed to aerial attack, especially airfields and supply depots, supply routes, bridges, and rail junctions.

Until the winter of 1942-43 Soviet air activities had still been relatively light. Thus, astonishing as it seems, the Russian air units did nothing to interfere with traffic on the Don River at Rostov and on the only available main highway from Bataysk to Rostov during January

---

*According to General Pickert, the 9th Flak Division had destroyed 600 aircraft and 826 tanks by 1 January 1943. In the Kuban bridgehead and in the Crimea this division reported 165 aircraft shot down and 189 tanks destroyed between 8 April and 10 May 1943. See Appendices 54 and 55 of the original German manuscript of this study. Karlsruhe Document Collection.

1943 when the German First Panzer Army and the Fourth Army were threading their way to the west from the Caucasus and the Kalmyk plains. This was a serious omission on the part of the Soviet Command.

From the summer of 1943 on, however, the air situation changed radically. Soviet air units then began for the first time with sizeable units to attack airfields, important rail junctions in the German rear areas, and concentration areas. Flak forces in the front then tried to fulfill both their air defense mission and the direct-fire ground support mission. The main enemy was the Soviet air forces, especially the ever-dangerous ground attack units. This mission was all the more important because Soviet air units had become ever bolder in their support of the Red Army as a result of the continual decline in German fighter strength. With the decline in fighter strength the need for protection by flak units was greatly increased.

Light and medium flak units were committed near the front, from the foremost lines back as far as artillery firing areas, while heavy flak batteries, also mobile, were placed in artillery firing areas and farther to the rear. The heavy batteries actually had a triple mission: (1) air defense, (2) supporting and augmenting regular artillery and providing air defense for it, and (3) direct-fire ground support against tanks which might break through the forward defenses. This illustrates the German efforts to compensate for their numerical weaknesses in antiaircraft artillery in the vast Soviet regions by achieving enough flexibility to make it possible to develop main areas of fire in critical defense sectors.

Maneuverability was not absolutely essential for the performance of the second mission, which included protecting targets in the rear areas against air attack. Here it was sufficient to move flak batteries in by means of flak transport batteries.[45]* However, it was impossible to activate enough of these transport batteries, and because of insufficient advance knowledge about the development of situations, or in case of sudden enemy breakthroughs, the time was frequently too short to include the antiaircraft pieces in the hasty withdrawals. It was then necessary to demolish the guns and all fire control instruments and devices to prevent their capture intact. Because of inadequate available transportation space, much valuable materiel had been lost during retrograde movements, most of which had to be carried out under heavy Soviet pressure.

---

*These were units in which prime movers were consolidated specifically for the movement of artillery pieces.

The inadequate output of motor vehicles by German industry compelled a separation of the flak forces into motorized and truck-drawn units in order to insure at least some degree of mobility, thereby also enhancing the chances for a quick concentration of forces in the front areas. As a rule, motorized units were committed in the front areas and truck-drawn units in the rear areas for the protection of static targets.

One basic requirement for motorized flak units was all-terrain mobility. For the light and medium guns, self-propelled mounts with protective armor similar to armored personnel carriers had proven to be the most practical, for which reason they were in great demand. For the heavy (8.8-cm.) guns, the prime movers designed for them continued to be satisfactory.

Lack of forces was the one factor which made it difficult to develop power concentrations in the air, and the necessity for a wide distribution of German air units, brought about by the increasing frequency and size of Soviet attacks against installations in rear areas, resulted in an even wider distribution of available flak batteries. In the past the rule had been to have at least one heavy flak battalion assigned for the protection of important static targets. In 1943 the number of installations requiring protection made this impossible. Thus, truck-drawn batteries in the East were reinforced with additional guns and organized into what were called twin or oversize batteries.

Flak units lacked adequate signal facilities, which, in the course of time, had made it necessary to situate all command posts interested in the air defense of airfields in close proximity. Often it was even necessary to combine a command post.

The 20-mm. flak gun was too light and lacked penetrating power. The 37-mm. gun was good and should have been set up on multiple (three or four gun) mounts. Efforts should also have been made to develop a somewhat heavier gun, with a caliber of 40 to 50 mm., especially since tests carried out with 50-mm. guns had produced such excellent results. The 8.8-cm. and the 12.8-cm. guns, which were sometimes used in defense of static installations, also proved to be satisfactory in every respect in 1943. Because of the frequent appearance of armored Soviet ground-attack aircraft it was found to be advisable to issue ammunition in mixed lots, containing both armor-piercing (shaped-charge) and regular high-explosive flak ammunition in a ratio of 1:3 or 1:4.

Heavy (motorized) flak batteries should have been issued special radio instruments so that they could have maintained contact between the battery firing positions and the artillery observers in order to keep them ready for firing at all times. An urgent need for all batteries was the issue of close-defense weapons, such as the Panzerfaust antitank rockets.*

One source of concern which remained in 1943 was the great number of motor vehicle types in use. The Wehrmacht had failed before the war to standardize its motor vehicles into a few proven types and to stockpile large amounts of spare parts for these vehicles. At the same time it took over dozens of foreign vehicle models in as many European countries, some of which were no longer being produced, and for which spare parts could scarcely be found.† German commanders attempted to remedy this situation by exchanging vehicles within their commands, aiming to reduce the vehicle types to not more than three, so as to simplify the procurement and allocation of spare parts. Usually such efforts were for naught, since nothing had been done to prevent this situation in peacetime and the problem was too widespread as the war progressed.

Flak trains should also have been created in order to permit a speedier shift of main emphasis in air defense. The individual air fleets did what they could to provide for this missing element by improvising flak trains with the means at their disposal. These were committed not only in the defense of static targets, but also frequently with great success in action against large partisan groups. In this connection it should be mentioned that it became absolutely essential to give flak units special training in close combat and ground defense in order to avoid heavy losses.[46]

On the whole the flak forces were quite successful in 1943 in both air defense and ground combat missions on the Eastern Front. In antitank action they constituted the backbone of German defenses. However, it must be said that the flak forces were numerically too weak to accomplish all of the missions they were called upon to perform, most of which were urgent necessities.

Air Signal Forces

The unsung and almost unnoticed arm of the Luftwaffe was the Air Signal Corps, which in 1943, as it had been previously, was the vital

---

*An antitank rocket launcher similar in operation and use to the U.S. "Bazooka."

†In July of 1943 the I Flak Corps reported that its units had 260 German and 120 foreign vehicle models, all in use. In some cases there were only a few vehicles of a given model in the entire corps. The procurement and repair situation was called a "nightmare."

available command instrument of the German Air Force. It gave the fullest satisfaction in the East, and it is not an exaggeration to say that, without these organic signal units a flexible control of offensive and defensive units of the Luftwaffe would have been impossible. The systematic work done (usually in advance) by air signal units did much to insure the success of Luftwaffe operations. It was due solely to the work of these organizations that power concentrations could be developed quickly and shifted from one area to another.

In some cases technical equipment was inadequate, which was a result of insufficient production, but the Air Signal Corps nevertheless mastered every situation. Its command organization and leadership were exemplary, even in the most difficult crises. Much of this achievement was due to the spirit of self-sacrifice and the untiring efforts of the air signal troops.*

The Ground Service Organization

The difficulties encountered in the field of ground service organization and in the closely related field of logistics clearly indicated the need for a timely development of airfields, command posts, maintenance workshops, and storage facilities for all types of supplies behind the front all along the line in the Eastern Theater of Operations. Only when enough of these installations were available in the rear of the combat zone of each air fleet to accommodate extra air and flak artillery units was it possible to continually shuffle units on short notice from one area to another to form power concentrations in areas of main effort. Generally speaking, all of the air fleets in the Eastern Theater and the responsible Luftwaffe administrative area commands within the various sectors accomplished this mission. This was done in a particularly exemplary manner in Combat Zone Center by the Sixth Air Fleet and the Air Administrative Area Command Moscow (later Air Administrative Area Command XXVII), under Generalleutnant Veit Fischer.

All useful Luftwaffe installations had to be destroyed upon withdrawal. This was not always properly accomplished, since it called for systematic advance preparations and for careful consideration concerning the precise time to order the demolition. This required a careful appraisal of the current situation and a close relationship with the local Army commands. Details for evacuation and demolition were set forth in what

---

*See figure 46.

Figure 46
Luftwaffe Air Signal Corps personnel at work in Russia, showing the hundreds of lines running to a main terminal from a Luftwaffe operations staff headquarters

were called evacuation and demolition schedules embodied within appropriate orders. These were executed upon receipt of a prearranged code word from air fleet headquarters. Apart from a few miscarriages, this mission was carried out in an exemplary manner.

Broadly speaking, it was still possible in 1943 to replace the sometimes exceedingly heavy losses in weapons. Occasional shortages of long duration were due to local circumstances or to transportation difficulties. In most cases the replacement of lost aircraft was carried out while the unit was being rehabilitated. A group which had lost too much of its effective strength was required to turn over its remaining aircraft to units still in the field. The personnel of the weakened units were then moved to the rear, where they were rested and supplied with aircraft of the same model or of a newer type. Generally, such rehabilitation was accomplished in a smooth functioning manner and in a relatively short time.

Difficulties were encountered in 1943 in the supply of aviation fuel. As early as 28 June 1938 the Commander in Chief of the Luftwaffe raised his demand for the stockpiling of aviation fuel from 1,500,000 tons per year to 3,000,000 tons.[47] This goal was not achieved, and at the outbreak of World War II the Luftwaffe had fuel reserves of only 200,000 tons, although by that time the Chief of Luftwaffe Supply and Administration had stipulated a need for 600,000 tons as a minimum.

The German output in natural and synthetic fuels was inadequate, and foreign supplies were vitally needed for the war effort. One of the main sources was Rumania. The quantity of mineral oil produced in Germany was insignificant, and the few small fields which were in operation, especially in Lower Saxony, played no major role in the overall fuel program. The problem of fuel supply thus remained one of Germany's most serious problems. It was only with the utmost difficulty that the Chief of Luftwaffe Supply and Administration had succeeded in having a small factory established for the production of tetraethyl lead in order to insure the production of high-quality aviation fuel.[48]

In 1941 the Luftwaffe had been compelled to take more than one quarter of its current fuel requirements from reserve stocks.[49] This was an ominous beginning. By autumn of 1943, 214,000 tons were being produced monthly, and the hope was to achieve a monthly output of 226,000 tons by the end of 1944.[50] The output of synthetic fluid fuels, which had been 4,000,000 tons per annum in 1941, was increased to 6,000,000 tons in 1943.[51]

The High Command of the Wehrmacht also ordered the build-up of its own aviation fuel reserve, from which supplies were to be released only upon requests submitted to it by the High Command of the Luftwaffe. As a result of the increased production of aviation fuel the stocks held by the Wehrmacht High Command and the High Command of the Luftwaffe increased steadily. [52]

In 1943 the manufacturing plants in Germany were generally still undamaged by air attacks. Even the increased enemy air operations against the Rumanian oil region, which in 1943 for the first time also came under attack by air forces of the Western Allies operating from their newly acquired air bases in Southern Italy, had little effect upon production. At least it can be said that the effects thereof were not decisive in 1943. Thus in an attack flown by the USAAF on 1 August 1943, the attackers achieved a moderate success but suffered heavy losses.*

In spite of all this, fuel stocks in the Eastern Theater in 1943 were by no means adequate for the uninterrupted and even increased activity of the Luftwaffe in the continual crises which erupted all along the line. What made things more difficult was the necessity of simultaneously building up fuel stocks at all airfields because the constant shift of emphasis in aerial operations required every airfield to be able at any time to receive, maintain, and supply larger numbers of aircraft than were normally stationed on them.

Transportation was another serious difficulty, due to the inadequate capacity of the already overtaxed railroads, the lack of fuel tank cars,

---

*Editor's Note: The USAAF sent out 177 aircraft in the Ploesti raid of 1 August 1943 (flown by the 44th, 93rd, 98th, 376th, and 389th Bomb Groups), losing 54 aircraft and 532 crew members. "An estimated 42 percent of Ploesti's total refining capacity was destroyed. Possibly 40 percent of the cracking capacity was knocked out for a period of from four to six months, and the production of lubricating oils was considerably reduced." W. F. Craven and J. L. Cate, eds., The Army Air Forces in World War II, Vol. II, Europe: Torch to Pointblank (August 1942 to December 1943), Chicago: University of Chicago Press, 1949, pp. 477-483. German sources indicate, as do Craven and Cate, that these results were considerably offset by the surprisingly rapid repair of the bomb damage and by placing reserve and other unused plants in operation.

and the interruption of railroad traffic by the partisans. 53* Serious fuel shortages had developed as early as the battle for Stalingrad and the retrograde movements from the Don to the area west of the Dnepr River. These difficulties had been mastered only by resorting to the most uneconomical sort of transportation, air. The Ju-52 transports, which were used for the purpose, had a fuel consumption quite disproportionate to their fuel-carrying capacity. Even during preparations for Operation ZITADELLE the difficulties encountered in procuring and moving forward the necessary aviation fuel were surmounted only with the utmost effort. 54 These fuel shortages necessarily led to the introduction of severe economic measures and compelled all Luftwaffe command staffs in the East to observe carefully planned fuel economy practices.

Personnel Matters

Most air replacement personnel were volunteers. No shortages occurred in any of the flying units in 1943, with the exception of occasional personnel shortages in strategic reconnaissance and bomber units. 55 Luftwaffe personnel replacements always arrived on time and in adequate numbers, and their training was uniformly good. Newly arrived replacement crews were first placed in the IV (Replacement) Group of each wing, where they received an orientation and familiarization with actual combat conditions. These replacement units were usually stationed in the rear areas, and were generally first employed in anti-partisan operations.

The need to rotate worn-out flak artillery units with batteries that had been hitherto deployed in quiet areas in the West was largely overlooked. Flak artillerymen thus shared the fate of the ground forces, which were literally used up in the fighting.

In view of the increasing partisan and other sabotage activities, there should have been many more regional defense units containing older age group men who could be used for guard duty. This was especially true since there were so many rear installations, which had to be widely separated because of the increasing Soviet air attacks.

Another personnel matter which should be discussed is the problem of establishing and employing Luftwaffe field divisions. From 1942 on, they had been activated in an ever increasing number, a measure which had become necessary because of the exceedingly heavy losses suffered

*At the end of 1940 only 5,200 fuel tank cars were available, despite the request of the Luftwaffe staff for 9,000 such cars.

by German ground forces in the Eastern Theater. Most of the Luftwaffe field divisions were therefore used in the East, particularly in the Nevel-Vitebsk areas, north and northwest of Smolensk. These divisions were generally organized in the field and were well equipped, but they received very brief training, so that they were, in this respect, not what they should have been. Apart from officer personnel from the flak forces, and a few other exceptions, the majority of the officers in these divisions were inexperienced and had no tactical combat training because of the exigencies of time.

The military training of the divisional commanders varied greatly. Most of them had had no experience in ground combat, and what little they had had was usually from World War I. Only a small number had ever had general staff corps training.* For these reasons, and especially because they were in some cases employed in the most crucial sectors, such as at Manych, the Don River bend area, the Donets River line, and in the Nevel area, some of these divisions suffered exceptionally heavy losses. Because of the general aggressiveness and good morale of these units, however, most of them developed into very useful defense divisions after a short period on the line.

Without question it would have been far wiser from the outset to have turned over all personnel to be used in this way to the Army. There they could have received appropriate training and have been used to bring the depleted Army divisions in the East up to strength. With these replacements from the Luftwaffe, most of whom had enthusiastically volunteered for service in ground units, the weakened divisions could undoubtedly have been turned into divisions of full combat value. Inter-service jealousies between the Commander in Chief of the Luftwaffe and the Army High Command prevented proper utilization of these men, and the heavy losses suffered by Luftwaffe field divisions because of their lack of experience and training were therefore a direct result of Goering's stubborn and selfish attitude.† The Commander in Chief of the Luftwaffe

---

*The author was among those officers who volunteered to serve in Luftwaffe field divisions, and is thus acquainted with the organization, training, and employment of these units.

†Editor's Note: Certain other high ranking Luftwaffe officers were at first also reluctant to release any men to the Army. Army commanders were, from the outset, displeased with the idea of mere tactical control over Luftwaffe field units. See various documents dealing with the matter of Luftwaffe field units. A/VI/4, Karlsruhe Document Collection.

wanted to keep control over as many of his units as possible, giving the Army only tactical control over Luftwaffe field divisions. This was similar to Goering's refusal to grant the Navy any control over air units, claiming "Everything that flies belongs to me."[56]

This senseless command system was finally changed in September 1943, when Luftwaffe field divisions were transferred to the Army and placed solely under Army control.[57] The entire episode of the Luftwaffe field divisions is a typical case of faulty organization, and the person who was unquestionably responsible for the high cost in lives was Reichsmarschall Goering.

Cooperation Between the Luftwaffe and the Army and Navy

The primary mission of the Luftwaffe in 1943 was to provide direct support in offensive and defensive operations for the ground forces. This called for extremely close cooperation between all air and ground force commands. To insure success, this relationship should not have been restricted merely to combat operations, but should also have included service operations, such as logistical functions, air-ground service work, and transportation. To secure this close cooperation, the Luftwaffe attached liaison teams to Army staffs from divisional level upward and assigned air direction teams for fighter, dive-bomber, and ground-attack operations, usually committing them in the foremost combat areas. Numerous air signal teams were also assigned to ground force units.

The closer the contact was established and maintained between the participating Army and Luftwaffe staffs, the better was the spirit of mutual confidence between the commanders of those units, and the greater was the measure of successful achievements in the course of the joint operations. The best way to secure such intimate and confident cooperation was through frequent personal discussions between the several air and ground commanders.

During operations in 1943 by units stationed at Kharkov, direct radio voice communications were to have been reestablished with the Army units, particularly panzer divisions. To test readability and work out the best system for the transmission of reports and information, a combat maneuver was conducted in collaboration with a panzer division, during which a tank battalion drove forward into the open terrain in mock attack upon a number of captured Soviet tanks placed in suitable positions for the exercise. Simultaneously, a number of German ground-attack aircraft flew over the maneuver area in support of attacking tanks. A modulated frequency radio transmitter (voice) was mounted in the commander's tank and was tuned in to the operating frequency of the air wing concerned.

The tank battalion commander was thus able to communicate directly with the aircraft and guide them to important ground targets. Pilots, in turn, were able to report immediately to the tank commander any special circumstances which they observed from the air. This two-way radio arrangement worked very well, and on occasions produced excellent results.[58]

The will of the ground forces to resist was often noticeably affected whenever this close cooperation was lacking, especially so in situations in which the ground forces had lost confidence in the will or the ability of the Luftwaffe to support them. One point must be emphasized in this regard, that it frequently became necessary to strip entire front sectors of air support in order to create the required airpower concentration in sectors of main effort. This gave the Soviet air forces freedom of action in the stripped areas, so that they naturally took advantage of the situation, occasionally inflicting heavy losses upon German ground forces.

In cases of this sort the average German soldier invariably asked the question, "Where is the Luftwaffe?" The soldier was simply unable to understand why German aircraft were not always available or in the air above him. Too often he forgot that he should and could have used his own weapons against hostile aircraft, as did the Russian soldiers, who fired at incoming German planes with everything available. The intermediate and higher Army command levels could have done a great deal more in enlightening the troops. To begin with, it was necessary for field officers themselves to understand the necessity for forming airpower concentrations and to appreciate the fact that the Luftwaffe was simply unable to provide a protective canopy over the Army at all times and in all places. Officers in leading positions also needed a thorough grounding in the use of air forces, their limitations, and their capabilities, and they should then have explained the situation to their troops and educated them to defend themselves.

All too frequently the soldier has been taught to hide instead of making good use of his available weapons. He must be taught what effect infantry small arms fire can have upon aircraft and at what ranges it is most effective.*

During air logistical operations it was found necessary and useful to utilize personnel with supply services experience to form special logistical operations staffs. These staffs were formed in the field from Army and Luftwaffe personnel under the command of Army and Luftwaffe officers of high rank, who were given special powers and command authority for the purpose of the mission.

The impact of airpower upon naval warfare is of decisive importance. It is not restricted merely to such activities as reconnaissance, escort, and combat missions in cooperation with the Navy and in protection of supply movements. It also includes combat action against enemy forces in hostile sea routes and against ports which are not the objectives of any joint air-naval operations.

It is true that the battle for naval supremacy in a given area has become contingent upon air supremacy in that area. Air supremacy over a given area results in naval supremacy in that area. The converse of this is not necessarily the case.[59] Thus, constant close cooperation between the Navy and the air forces is essential for the successful accomplishment of these missions. In the Eastern Theater of Operations this was essential in the Black Sea, the Baltic Sea, and in the arctic waters.

In the Black Sea areas land-based planes and seaplanes kept the Soviet naval bases and the Soviet Black Sea Fleet under constant surveillance. This alone enabled the weak German naval security units to operate in the area. In the Baltic, Luftwaffe operations were restricted to reconnaissance over the Gulf of Finland, since the forces available to the First Air Fleet were too weak to eliminate Allied forces at sea or Soviet naval forces by offensive operations. In northern waters the cooperation between Luftwaffe and Navy forces was generally good, and, at intermediate and lower command levels, even very good, a fact which was reflected in the successful achievements in operations against single vessels and formations of Allied ships, and in providing cover for friendly convoys.[60] Much of this success was due to the good will which existed among the top Navy and Luftwaffe commanders in the Far North.

---

*Editor's Note: Soviet troops immediately fell on their backs and fired with submachine guns, mortars, rifles, and pistols. Some of these same characteristics have been observed on the part of the Chinese Communist troops in Korea and Viet-Cong units in Vietnam.

Operations of submarines and air forces were superbly integrated, a fact which was confirmed in a letter of 30 June 1943 from Admiral Otto Schniewind of the Naval Group Command North and the Fleet Command to the Fifth Air Fleet.[61]

The Performance of the German Soldier and Airman in the East

In closing this critique of German air operations in the Eastern Theater in 1943, it is a duty and a gratification to say that the incomparable performances of the individual German soldier in combat in the East are above criticism. This applies to all ranks, from the lowest private to general officers, on the land, in the air, and on the seas. The German soldier did not make his greatest mark at the beginning of the campaign when he was marching from victory to victory, covering immense distances daily, and winning giant battles of encirclement in which enormous numbers of prisoners and vast quantities of materiel were captured, although the casualty figures show that these gains were not purchased cheaply. It was later in the campaign, when there was no longer any hope for victory, that the German soldier surpassed himself. Physically and mentally exhausted, he then clung with desperate tenacity to every inch of hostile terrain in order to keep back the Red floods from his homeland.

During the more or less orderly withdrawals, with flanks threatened and hostile forces often already in the rear areas, German troops again and again made a defiant stand to halt the advance of the overwhelmingly superior Soviet armies. In this great struggle the German troops not only had to face a numerically superior enemy, who was tough, courageous, crafty, and cruel, and whose material superiority steadily increased, but also an area with difficult terrain, mostly unsuited for large-scale movements, and in a climate which seemed at times almost too severe for human existence. This was the situation in which the German troops found themselves, probably one of the most difficult that troops have ever had to face, and most of them stood the test with honor.

Closing Remarks

At the end of 1943 German forces in the Eastern Theater of Operations were involved in gravely crucial defensive battles all along the front. Bleeding from numerous wounds and badly weakened through personnel and materiel losses, the German Army of the East had withdrawn as best it could from one position to another under great pressure by vastly superior Soviet forces. The focal points of action in the bitter fighting around the end of the year were Nikopol, Krivoy Rog, Kremenchug, the area west of Kiev, Gomel, the sector east of Orsha, and the areas of Nevel and Leningrad.

In every area the threat of new Soviet offensives loomed ominously, and the weak air forces available were daily committed to action in support of the hard-pressed German armies as well as in constant battles against an overwhelmingly superior air enemy. Although it had been clearly obvious, and had been admitted by everyone concerned, that all major and tactical achievements in the past years of warfare, in both attack and defense, had been largely due to the superiority and to the effective operations of the Luftwaffe, the German Supreme Command had not taken this fact into account in the overall armament program. Without air support there was no possibility of bringing to a successful conclusion any large-scale offensive or defensive operation on land or at sea.

Furthermore, it was quite obvious, without considering land and naval warfare, that the only way to bring about conditions for final victory in a modern war was to secure air superiority through the action of a superior air force and through the operations of this air force in destroying the enemy's sources of power. Total warfare had only really become possible because of the rise of airpower.

The only logical conclusion, and one which the Supreme Command should definitely have drawn, was that the strength or weakness of the Luftwaffe would influence the outcome of the war more than any other factor or factors, in fact, that it was the major determining issue between victory and defeat. With a proper understanding of this lesson, Hitler and the High Command of the Wehrmacht should have awarded the Luftwaffe first priority in funds, raw materials, manpower, and all fields of armament and manufacturing. The nations at war with Germany at the time had drawn this logical conclusion at an early stage and had adapted their armament planning to it; whereas German air armament, so far as the requirements evolving from the obvious lessons of the war were concerned, had remained in practically the same stage of development which it had been in before the war. Apart from numerous minor improvements, many of which were nothing at all but improvisations, the striking power of the Luftwaffe had not increased decisively from a standpoint of numerical strength or technical performance.

The normal attrition of war had worn down the substance of the Luftwaffe incessantly, and the process had been speeded up by the wasteful commitment of its forces in numerous senseless missions. The output of the German industry was insufficient to fulfill the requirements of the time or to increase the strength of its fighting forces. The fault for these conditions was to be sought in the illogical pattern of overall planning in which the German Air Force was not accorded that position in the overall national potential which it should have had, considering its significance as a factor capable of influencing, and even deciding, the outcome of the war. The German Supreme Command was at fault in its estimate and evaluation of the three weighty factors in war: time, needed to meet the requirements of research and development and for production; space, which had assumed global dimensions; and strength, as expressed in numbers and equipment.

Thus, while the heavy burden of responsibility rests upon the supreme military, economic, and political leadership--primarily upon Hitler--it is also shared by the Fuehrer's closest political, economic, and military leaders and advisors, therefore also by the Commander in Chief of the Luftwaffe.

Numerically far too weak to carry out its mission, the Luftwaffe had thus become clearly inferior in strength to its Soviet opponents, who were growing steadily stronger, in the continuously severe and crucial defensive battles of 1943. The German Luftwaffe's numerous local successes were due to the high quality of its personnel and their commanders, and in no way obscures the aforementioned fact. With the small number of units available to it, the Luftwaffe was no longer able to meet all of the demands made upon it in the gigantic spaces of the East in 1943. It was thus inevitable that it gradually become weaker and weaker on the way to its unavoidable and final downfall.

The Conclusion of the War in the East, 1944-1945*

From 1943 on, German forces in the East were fighting for their lives in a series of desperate withdrawal battles and defensive battles, on

---

*Note by the Chief, USAF Historical Division: This closing section is contributed by the editor, Mr. Harry R. Fletcher. General Plocher's studies of GAF operations in the Eastern Theater of Operations were originally intended to cover the years 1944 and 1945, but his recall in March of 1957 to duty in the new Bundeswehr prevented the realization of the complete project. Consequently, only the years 1941, 1942, and 1943 are covered in the Plocher series. Unfortunately, the German Air Force Monograph Project had to be brought to an end before a new author could be found to write the story for 1944 and 1945. Mr. Fletcher's contribution, together with other studies in the GAF Monograph Project which deal with the Eastern Front, helps to fill this gap.

land, on sea, and in the air. The same situation prevailed, although with perhaps a lesser spirit of urgency, in the Western and Southern Theaters of Operation. Crucial failures in industrial, logistical, and military planning began to exert a serious effect upon Germany's prosecution of the war, and it was too late to rectify them. In every field of activity the ingenuity and inventiveness of the German nation was taxed to the utmost, but the numerous improvisations of all kinds which were tried could never offset the initial failures to plan and prepare for contingencies. This problem was also increasingly complicated by Allied strategic bombing, which for frequency and intensity had already reached levels hitherto unknown in warfare. Because of these attacks, the High Command of the Luftwaffe was compelled to concentrate large numbers of fighters and interceptors, invariably those of the latest type, in home defense areas.

Although seldom seen in its true perspective, but of immense importance, was the Mediterranean Theater of Operations and its impact upon the Wehrmacht, especially the Luftwaffe. Commitments in this area deprived the Eastern Theater of large numbers of aircraft and highly trained personnel which were critically needed in the unequal contest in Russia. Losses of both men and planes in the Mediterranean were heavy in 1942 and 1943, and since the Allies on all fronts gave the German Command no respite, there was no possibility of altering the deteriorating situation. Air superiority had clearly passed to the Allies on all fronts.

Hampering the Wehrmacht's efforts still further was the fact that its strongest asset, its capable and well-trained officer corps, had become increasingly frustrated and helpless in the face of Hitler's continual direct interference in combat operations. Thus, as the war reached its most crucial stages, the Fuehrer became ever more unwilling to accept advice, or to face the grim realities of the current situations, and withdrew more and more into a world of fantasy. Making this bad situation worse, Goering, who had repeatedly failed to make good on his exaggerated promises, had lost the confidence of his leader, and the Luftwaffe suffered accordingly.

Measures taken by top-level Luftwaffe leaders, who were loath to delegate authority, made it impossible for their subordinates, even those in high command positions, to work with initiative and a spirit of independence. For example, in July of 1944, Generaloberst Hans-Juergen Stumpff, Commander of Air Fleet Reich, complained to the Chief of the General Staff of the Luftwaffe that he could not issue any orders on his own, and pointed out that he was not even permitted to move a single piece of flak artillery without orders from above.[62]

Also of decisive importance for the conduct of Germany's air war was the handling of personnel matters in high-level command agencies. The principle prevailing in the closing years of the war, whereby bravery in action was a sufficient recommendation for a key position regardless of the man's intellectual or command capabilities or his comprehension of complex problems in the conduct of aerial warfare, was neither appropriate nor successful. Perhaps such a crippling state of affairs in command and leadership might have been bearable early in the war, but by 1944 it was intolerable.

In the winter of 1943-44 the Red Army opened attacks all along the front, with especially powerful thrusts in the boundary area between Army Groups Center (Busch) and South (v. Manstein), but with by far the greatest weight falling upon the front of Army Group South. Simultaneous drives by the Second Ukrainian Army Group (Marshal Ivan Koniev), supported by the Third Ukrainian Army Group (Marshal Rodion Y. Malinovsky), forced back the front of the Eighth Army of Army Group Center and the First Panzer Army of Army Group "A" (v. Kleist), while the First Baltic Army Group (Marshal Ivan Bagramyan) struck the left wing of Army Group Center and the right (southern) wing of Army Group North (Model)* between Vitebsk and Velikiye Luki. In these encounters the Luftwaffe's failure to develop a really adequate "tank-buster" aircraft began to be manifest. Various types of fighter and dive-bomber aircraft were modified for this role, but this effort was too weak and impractical to be of much help.

By early 1944 the Luftwaffe still had plenty of fight and was occasionally capable of sending out 1,000 sorties a day on the Eastern Front. It was then in a situation of almost ridiculous air inferiority and might have been utterly destroyed in the East, except for the fact that the Russians did not normally employ their air forces independently, but continued to use them almost entirely in an offensive role in support of the Army.

In 1941 the Luftwaffe had sent about 3,000 first-line combat aircraft into action against Russia, but by 1944 it was unable to muster more than 2,000 planes at best, and even this figure was highly deceptive, since, after late 1942, many of the aircraft listed as combat types in the Eastern Theater were biplanes of the 1930's and other obsolete models. The striking force of the Luftwaffe was therefore not even two-thirds of what it had been in 1941 but was less than one-half. This fact was clear to

---

*General der Panzertruppe Walter Model assumed command of Army Group North on 9 January 1944.

most combat air commanders, who carefully shepherded their forces for fear of losing their few operational aircraft. Large numbers of German bombers were committed as air transports for weeks at a time in efforts to supply encircled Army units. The result was a heavy loss of combat aircraft and highly trained aircrews, many of which could not be replaced. As the war progressed, bomber forces, like fighter units, became more and more linked with the operations of the ground forces.

Dive-bomber units probably fared the best, since they were able throughout the war to remain primarily in the mission for which they were designed, although as the Luftwaffe lost its air superiority, and especially after the dive-bomber arm was strengthened by the addition of obsolete biplane types, fighter cover was necessary for the accomplishment of their assignments.[63]

By 15 January 1944 Soviet forces had broken through the German lines north of the Dvina River, forcing back the Third Panzer Army into the area west of Nevel, and had penetrated deep into the Pripyat Marshes, reaching the old Polish boundary west of Sarny. The center of Army Group South recoiled under heavy attacks and withdrew far to the southwest of Kazatin and Zhitomir. Units of Army Group "A" along the Dnepr River were forced to make a hasty retreat to Kirov and Krivoy Rog, leaving the Sixth Army holding a salient that projected to the east from Krivoy Rog to the area east of Nikopol and along the lower Dnepr to Kherson. During these drives the Red Army captured large quantities of German heavy equipment and materiel, mostly from the Army. The Luftwaffe did an admirable job in destroying its facilities as it withdrew, and succeeded in taking out all of its essential equipment so that it could continue operations despite adversities. The improvisations and ingenuity exercised by German Air Force commanders in the field were quite commendable.[64]

In mid-January Russian forces moving southward from Fastov met Soviet units moving westward from the vicinity of Kremenchug, enveloping seven divisions of the German Eighth Army west of Cherkassy. Here, the VIII Air Corps distinguished itself by delivering approximately 250 tons of food and supplies daily to the surrounded group until it was able to make its breakout on 15 February. Of the 50,000 men in the pocket, 32,000 managed to reach the safety of their own lines to the west.[65]

In the North, despite meager air support, German losses were not as heavy as elsewhere on the Eastern Front up to 1944, which permitted Army Group North to carry out more methodical defensive measures. In February, powerful Soviet forces drove back the Sixteenth and Eighteenth Armies of Army Group North, thereby completing the liberation of

Leningrad. But by hanging on to certain key positions the Wehrmacht was able to establish a new line extending from the area west of Nevel to the vicinity of Opochka and Pekov to Lake Peipus and Narva, where German forces staved off early Soviet attempts to drive into Latvia and Estonia.[66]

From March to June of 1944 the front changed very little from the Gulf of Finland southward to the Pripyat Marshes, in part because of the mud season, but chiefly because the Soviet Command had shifted its offensive to the fronts of Army Groups South and "A." In March both of these groups reeled back from the Pripyat to the Crimea under the heavy blows of superior Russian forces,* retreating first to the Bug River and then, by April, behind the Dniester River in a line running from just east of Odessa to north of Tiraspol to the Prut River north of Iaşi, Rumania, and thence roughly northward, passing to the west of Cernauti, Tarnopol, Dubno, and Lutsk, to the Kovel area.[67] On 24 March, five Soviet armored corps, followed by massed infantry forces, of Marshal Georgi Zhukov's First Ukrainian Army Group, crossed the Dniester River due south of Tarnopol and linked up with the divisions of Marshal Ivan Koniev, which had crossed the Dniester earlier several miles to the east. The German First Panzer Army (General der Panzertruppe Hans Hube) was thereby encircled in a large arc north of the Dniester near Kamenets-Podolski.

Here again Hitler ordered a static defense, but Hube opted to conduct a withdrawal of the entire pocket toward the West.† After concentrating his forces, shortening his lines, and disposing of unnecessary heavy equipment, Hube began his operation. Soviet forces surrounding the pocket had overextended their supply lines, which First Panzer Army units were able to sever, and, before the Russians realized what was happening, the First Panzer Army had moved almost to the German lines.

---

*The Soviet Command normally planned upon a six to one numerical advantage in launching an offensive, and considered a four to one advantage to be the bare minimum necessary for success. See Raymond L. Garthoff, Soviet Military Doctrine, Glencoe, Illinois: The Free Press, 1953, pp. 127-129.

†The Soviet Commander had given General Hube an ultimatum to surrender at once or all who surrendered later would be shot. This helped Hube in his resolve to withdraw his forces. This operation is mentioned here because it is a unique tactical movement of an entire encircled force, holding its perimeters, toward friendly lines, which is quite different from a breakout operation. In this case it succeeded remarkably well.

Soviet forces then attacked, as expected, the northern and eastern perimeters of the pocket, but all of these efforts were warded off.

Although the nearest German airfield was 125 miles away, the Luftwaffe carried out daily air logistical missions for the panzer army. During these operations Luftwaffe units delivered both food and supplies to Hube's forces, changing airfields daily in accordance with the fluid situation, and finally being forced to air-drop supplies because of an absence of landing fields. While these deliveries never amounted to more than a part of the required tonnage for the maintenance of the encircled force, they were welcomed, since thawing snows had ruled out any early relief operations or supply by ground routes. By 5 April the First Panzer Army had not only moved far enough west to meet the current German front, but, in the meantime, had even managed to envelop some small Russian units, destroying 357 tanks and 280 pieces of artillery in the operation. The German losses were surprisingly light.[68]

In the Crimea a castrophe comparable in size to the loss of the Sixth Army at Stalingrad was narrowly averted by quick and resourceful action on the part of the German Seventeenth Army and its allied units. These forces had been isolated from the rest of the German front since 1 November 1943 and had frequently been in danger of annihilation. Left to defend themselves against powerful enemy thrusts from the north across the isthmus of Perekop, from the east and northeast across the Kerch Peninsula and the Sivash Sea, it had surmounted its problems better than had been expected. However, irresistible pressures from the north and east in early April of 1944 forced it to retreat toward Sevastopol. Between 17 April and 12 May the Seventeenth Army evacuated its forces by air and water from the Crimea to the western shores of the Black Sea, an operation which was carried out under incredible difficulties, and resulted in heavy German losses.*

The Luftwaffe rendered invaluable service in these evacuation operations, although forced to work in a situation of great air inferiority. The few available German fighters were scarcely able to provide more than local cover.[69]

From late June until mid-August the German line in the south held fast along the lower Dniester River to the area west of Cernauti, but

---

*The reader's attention is directed to the numerous documents located in the Karlsruhe Document Collection concerning the preparations for and the actual withdrawal operations in the Crimea.

north of this Koniev's First Ukrainian Army Group, driving toward Brody and Lvov, threw back German forces nearly to the Carpathian Mountains. On 27 July Lvov fell to the Red Army and by the first week in August, Russian troops had reached the San and upper Vistula Rivers. *

By attack and infiltration Soviet forces gradually cleaned out the Pripyat Marsh area, taking Brest-Litovsk on 28 July and Siedlce and the Vistula River south of Warsaw by 7 August. North of the marsh area the Russians made their greatest gains, pushing the Wehrmacht back across the Beresina River, and driving as far as Wilna, Lithuania, and the middle Niemen River by 10 July.[70]

On 12 July the First Baltic Army Group of Marshal Ivan Bagramyan, the Second Baltic Army Group of Marshal Andrei I. Yeremenko, and the Third Baltic Army Group of Marshal I. I. Maslennikov opened an offensive all along the line from the Gulf of Finland to the area west of Nevel. The left wing of Bagramyan's army group seized the upper course of the Dvina River and drove in a northwesterly arc deep into the interior of eastern Lithuania, while the right wing advanced westward out of Nevel toward the middle course of the Dvina. At the same time, forces of Yeremenko and Maslennikov pushed back the German front from the area east of Opochka to the Narva area, making larger gains in the south against the German Sixteenth Army, which was immediately forced to withdraw to avoid envelopment.[71] Heavy fighting characterized all of the actions in the Baltic region, the control of which was essential to the defense of the Reich. The populace in this area, which had just achieved independence from Russia in 1918, and had had extremely unpleasant experiences at the hands of the Soviet Union in 1940-41, had no especial love for the Germans, but hated and feared the Russians much more.† Defeat to them meant absorption by the Soviet Union.[72]

Dispersal of its forces was the cardinal weakness of the Luftwaffe in these operations. No longer did German air units go ahead of the advancing ground forces. Instead, they were rapidly shifted from side to side wherever a crisis developed, often arriving too late to alleviate

---

*The Soviet June offensive began on the 22nd, and included 100 fresh divisions and 2,000 of the latest type aircraft. About 300,000 Germans were killed during these operations. See G/VI/b, Karlsruhe Document Collection.

†Many Latvian and Estonian men served in combat units established by the Reich as foreign SS units. These units fought well until the end of the war, but the SS designation was to hamper the subsequent employment and emigration of personnel from such organizations when they became displaced persons.

the danger. This continual transferring of air units was a result of numerical weakness in German air strength and the Luftwaffe's consequent inability to accomplish its missions all along an extended front. The Wehrmacht's strength and overall fighting power declined rapidly after 1943, but the strongest air forces remained in the West. Ground forces strength, despite continued deterioration, remained greater in the East until the end.

While German forces were engaged in crucial struggles, the Wehrmacht was severely shaken by an attempted assassination of Hitler on 20 July 1944. Actively involved were a number of the most respected names in the German Army, as well as several prominent civilians. The failure of the plot resulted in the execution of dozens of high-ranking officers, the retirement of others, and the resignations of still others. This retaliatory action by Hitler removed hundreds of capable officers from command positions. Among those who died as a result of the bomb explosion was Generaloberst Guenther Korten, Chief of Staff of the Luftwaffe.[73]

At the end of the first week in August, Bialystok, a point which had long been important as a center of German air activity, had fallen. The forces of Marshal Chernyakovsky's Third White Russian Army Group seized Kaunas, Lithuania, while Bagramyan's troops, driving northwest out of the area northeast of Wilna, penetrated into southern Latvia and almost reached the Gulf of Riga before German and allied forces brought them to a halt at Jelgava. Soviet forces also drove back the front from the Dvina to Pskov, clearing most of eastern Latvia. The Eighteenth Army, however, held its front in Estonia quite well throughout July and early August.

In the Far North the situation began to deteriorate on 9 June when the Red Army opened a massive barrage against the weak Finnish forces along the Karelian Front, and on the following day, with strong armored and infantry forces which outnumbered the Finns about 9 to 1, broke through the front and quickly penetrated deep into the Karelian interior. Finnish troops had proven to be superior to the Germans in forest fighting, and had long been critical of them in their battles against massed armor and infantry in the great open spaces of Russia. This time, the Germans had the dubious pleasure of noting that the Finns did not do as well as the Wehrmacht in this first taste of Soviet power in the open. The unique experiences of operations in the Far North, and the earlier, localized, fighting of the Winter War of 1939-40, had led the Finns to seriously underestimate the Soviet enemy.[74]

The Finnish Karelian Army was virtually uncovered as the Soviet Command launched about 1,000 air sorties daily against it. Luftwaffe reserves which were hastened to the area had little effect, since the German Air Force had an effective combat strength in the Far North of only about 100 aircraft.[75] Weakness was again the reason for a pathetic response.

August of 1944 was a black month for the Wehrmacht in the southern part of the Eastern Theater. The Russian Second and Third Ukrainian Army Groups, mounting immense power, had succeeded in throwing German forces back as far as Focsani and Galati in Rumania, spreading panic and disorder throughout the country. The Soviet attack upon the Dniester River line had completely demoralized the Rumanian Army Group, which then quickly dissolved. On the 23rd, King Michael, who had sought to reestablish himself with the Allies in order to save his throne, summoned Field Marshal Ion Antonescu, the foremost Rumanian leader, to his presence. Upon Russian insistence, he then arrested Antonescu and turned him over to Soviet authorities.* At the same time, Michael declared an end of hostilities. Angered by the defection of his ally, Hitler on 25 August ordered the aerial bombardment of Bucharest, which resulted in an immediate Rumanian declaration of war against Germany. Only a few Rumanians then remained in service with the Germans, while many went over to the Red Army.

By the end of the month, although the Soviet Command suffered one of its most serious reverses along the Vistula on the Warsaw front,/ Red forces had captured Ploesti and the greater part of the surrounding Rumanian oil region and driven deep into Bulgaria. The ring formed by the Carpathian and Transylvanian Mountains might have afforded an excellent defensive ring for German units, had the Russians not quickly gained access to many passes and to the heights of the Transylvanian Alps, thereby opening the way into Rumania and the Hungarian plain.[76]//

On 2 September the Finnish government, which had faced an almost unbroken series of reverses on the fighting front, offered to declare a cease-fire and to request the withdrawal of German forces from its territory. Two days later the armistice went into effect, although the Red

---

*Shot by the Soviet authorities in May 1946.

/This defensive achievement was made almost without air support.

//Once beyond the Transylvanian Alps the way into the Reich was open via the Danube valley.

Army continued to fire upon Finnish positions for an additional 24 hours. On 10 September the Finnish delegation in Moscow signed the armistice, which guaranteed the Soviet Union all that it had seized in 1939-40, as well as certain other strategic concessions and reparation payments. The German Twentieth Mountain Army then took action to defend itself and to withdraw into Norway.

By mid-September the Red Army had made small, but important, gains all along the front from the Gulf of Finland to the Carpathians, especially along the Sixteenth and Eighteenth Army fronts in Combat Zone North. There it concentrated its forces for a further offensive which carried it through Tallinn (Reval), Estonia, and to the Baltic islands of Hiiumaa and Saaremaa. Units of the Leningrad Army Group and the Third Baltic Army Group then turned southwestward, driving German and allied forces out of Estonia and deep into Latvia, while Yeremenko's forces advanced from the east, seizing Riga and the surrounding area. Bagramyan's forces then continued in their westerly course from the vicinity of Siaulia, breaking through the front of Army Group North and driving to the Baltic Sea north of Memel. This isolated the remaining forces of Army Group North* in the Latvian province of Kurland, where it successfully held out until the end of the war, although it was no longer able to exercise any effect upon the conflict.

Meanwhile, Germany's air forces, especially those in the East, grew weaker and more obsolete. This was doubly serious because Soviet industry had made gigantic strides in the production of newer and better models, such as the improved "Stormovik" fighter-bombers, the Yaks, and the Lagg fighters, and because the Soviet Command had accumulated a large number of the latest type Allied fighters and medium bombers. The Luftwaffe used every possible expedient to make more efficient use of its dwindling air units in helping to "check the dike" at various points. In so doing, however, it lost its independence and sense of mission. Only briefly did German air units regain the initiative in the air, once in early March of 1943 in the retaking of Kharkov, and the other time in July during the fighting in the Kursk area. Thereafter they were utterly entrapped in a circle of events from which there was no escape.

South of Memel, Soviet forces drove across the German border into East Prussia, and by 19 January 1945 had reached Tilsit. Here, as in other parts of Germany's eastern provinces, the fighting was especially

---

*After 25 July under Field Marshal Walter Model, redesignated 25 January 1945 as Army Group Kurland.

sharp and bitter, involving house to house combat, and frequent "last ditch" stands by small detachments. Floods of refugees were churned to a mass on the roads by Soviet armored columns, while thousands of others were summarily rounded up and liquidated. Whatever the Germans had done to civilians in the East was being repaid a thousandfold. In the areas south of the Baltic everyone capable of bearing arms or doing anything for the German war effort was summoned to the front, their determination fanned by warnings from Goebbels' Propaganda Ministry that Germany's eastern areas would be given to Russia and Poland in the event of an Allied victory.* To the south of East Prussia, Red Army forces crossed the Narev River and by 12 January 1945 had reached Warsaw, breaking up the German central front, while other units drove as far as Budapest and Lake Balaton in Hungary.[77]

As the month of January drew to a close, Russian units had already reached the Silesian industrial area, had driven almost to the upper reaches of the Oder River, had taken Tannenberg and Allenstein in East Prussia, and were preparing for the investment of Koenigsberg. On 15 February, Breslau was surrounded and an 11-week battle ensued, with fighting from house to house and from cellar to cellar until the city finally fell. Determined efforts by the Luftwaffe enabled the defenders to hold out as long as they did. Resolute stands were also made by the Wehrmacht all along the Baltic and in southern Pomerania, where Red forces were held up for some time. On 30 March Danzig fell, permitting the final conquest of the Pomeranian coastal area.

During the month of February 1945 the Luftwaffe lent all the support at its disposal to the ground forces in an effort to stop the Russians at the lower Oder River, especially at the important crossing points of Stettin, Kuestrin, Frankfurt on the Oder, and just south of Guben. With the beginning of the general withdrawal on all fronts the Luftwaffe was also called upon to air supply countless units which had become enveloped while fulfilling Hitler's orders "not to retreat a step." A number of cities were declared "fortresses" and defended for considerable periods of time. Many of these, like Posen, Budapest, Schneidemuehl, Elbing, and Breslau, were supplied as well as possible by air until their capitulations. Often only 2 to 6 aircraft were available to carry out these transport missions.

---

*By early 1945 the acquisition of Allied documents confirmed the statements of the Reichs Propaganda Ministry that a permanent division of Germany was envisioned by the Allies, which included population transfers. A statement to this effect had also been made on 14 December 1944 by Winston Churchill in the House of Commons.

The attrition rate was heavy and few aircraft returned to base undamaged. Fighter cover could scarcely be provided in many instances, and when fighters were on hand they were heavily outnumbered by Russian aircraft. In the closing months of the war the Soviet air forces carried out as many as 10,000 sorties daily against the pathetically weak German units.

Some flyers, especially experienced aviators like Col. Hans-Ulrich Rudel, intent on doing everything possible to stop the irresistible Red Armies, flew combat missions until the very end of the war. Rudel accounted for more than 500 Soviet tanks, while Erich Hartmann scored 352 aerial victories against Soviet forces. Spectacular and excellent as their efforts were, they were but a small aspect of the total war and had virtually no effect upon the overall campaign.

The Russians capitalized upon German weaknesses and errors, many of the latter being the results of weakness. In almost four years of war the Red Army had learned a great deal about military operations from the Germans, and by 1945 its air units made a serious impact upon both German ground and air units. The German Command found itself caught in a vicious circle, in which each attempt to solve a problem meant neglect of another problem of almost equal urgency. Although it was treasonous in the Third Reich to say so, many of the more sage minds realized long before the war's end that the cause was lost. Armament Minister Dr. Albert Speer openly acknowledged that Germany's strength had reached its end when its synthetic gasoline plants were destroyed by Allied air forces. Yet, even after American and Soviet troops had met at the Elbe River, elements of the Wehrmacht were still fighting. As Professor Gerhard Ritter of Freiburg once noted, "The German Army continued to march as long as the music played."[78]

In the last months of the war lieutenants usually commanded companies, and often battalions, while under-age, over-age, limited-service, Hitler Youth, and Volkssturm personnel were thrown into the breach in an effort to hold off the inevitable end. Whole divisions and armies were ground down and redesignated, while entire air fleets were created from the residue of wings, groups, and even squadrons. Some units existed only on paper or in the clouded mind of the Fuehrer, who had retired with his closest admirers to the security of his bunker in Berlin.

The Commander in Chief of the Luftwaffe, whose stock with the Fuehrer had sunk to a cipher, made the grave mistake in April of 1945 of suggesting that he (Goering) assume the leadership of the Reich from his headquarters in Bavaria. Blind with rage, Hitler retaliated at once. On the 23rd, Goering was stripped of all of his offices and placed under arrest by the SS. The Reichsmarschall was able, however, to summon an Air Signal Troop unit, which rescued him from the SS guards and escorted him to freedom.* Robert Ritter von Greim, who was promoted to Field Marshal 25 April 1945, then assumed command of the Luftwaffe. This had no effect upon the outcome of the war, since von Greim could do nothing to improve the already disastrous situation. Moreover, he had been wounded while being flown to the Fuehrer's bunker in Berlin.

The Western Allies based the conduct of their air warfare upon entirely different principles from those of the Luftwaffe, while the Soviet Air Force, like that of Germany, was closely linked to air support operations. In the West, the Allies had been forced from the beginning of the war into the defensive, and had then carefully examined the Luftwaffe's use of airpower in 1939 and 1940 and concluded, quite correctly, that a strong air force would be the key to victory in World War II. The Soviet Union, which had lost most of its air force in the German attacks of 1941, came to similar conclusions, even though it laid no stress upon development of a strategic air force. Thus, in the West and the East the Allies concentrated upon building and establishing strong and modern air arms, which they were able to do because of their vast economic and industrial potentials and the almost total absence of enemy interference. Hitler, on the other hand, a man who was inordinately "Army minded," failed to attach the proper significance to the employment of airpower, and neglected to inaugurate far-reaching policies with respect to the conduct of aerial warfare. The High Command likewise failed to establish the required air armament program at a sufficiently early date, and to provide for a powerful air defense system.

Probably what was demonstrated more than anything else in the war is that it is impossible in the long run for a small European nation, even with captured resources at its disposal, to presume to offer continuous effective resistance to the combined strength of two continents. Two huge countries, with their industrial areas intact, and with a virtually untouched aircraft and armament industry, could arm themselves at top speed. Germany, which had neglected the very things which might have helped to offset these advantages, was therefore unable to match the strength disparity which was bound to set it.

Many Germans, taking note of the scientific developments in their country, hoped that these would turn the tables in their favor. The remarkable increase in fighter production, despite heavy Allied bombings, the

*Goering surrendered soon after to American forces.

continuation and vast improvement in the air armament program, and the development of the _Vergeltungs_ (_V_ or retaliation) weapons, tended to strengthen these hopes, which were in any case more akin to wishful thinking than to reality. Actually, these tremendous efforts late in the war only pointed up more emphatically the extent to which Germany had neglected long-range planning in its air armament program and in the conduct of aerial warfare. Moreover, the use made of jet aircraft and V-weapons indicated that the German High Command continued to think in tactical rather than in strategic terms.

In the closing months of World War II there was no way by which the Luftwaffe could alter the overall situation. It had lost its air superiority in 1943, and since then had found itself increasingly on the defensive. Its few attempts to carry out strategic operations during the war had been spasmodic and ineffective, and from the second year of the war in the East, German air units had become simply "fire brigades" for the ground forces. They were thus bound to a mission comparable to that of the Red Air Force, which had surpassed the Luftwaffe in strength and was rapidly gaining in efficiency of operation. Eventually, the Luftwaffe could not even carry out its support missions satisfactorily, and tied to the Army, it was unable to become a really determining force. Its fortunes then fell with those of the ground forces, whose complete defeat decided the fate of the Wehrmacht in the East.

FOOTNOTES

Chapter 1

1. Grossadmiral Erich Raeder, testimony taken between July and August 1945, Trial of the Major War Criminals Before the International Military Tribunal, Nuernberg, Vol. XXXIX, Washington: U.S. Government Printing Office, 1948, pp. 521-523, 560. See also Alan Bullock, Hitler: A Study in Tyranny, New York: Harper & Row, 1954, p. 358.

2. General der Infanterie Kurt von Tippelskirch, Geschichte des Zweiten Weltkriegs (History of the Second World War), Bonn: Athenaeum Verlag, 1951, pp. 241-242. Cited hereafter as Tippelskirch, Second World War. See also General der Infanterie Guenther Blumentritt, "Die Ueberwindung der Krise vor Moskau im Winter 1941/42" ("The Mastery of the Crisis Before Moscow in the Winter of 1941-42"), Wehrwissenschaftliche Rundschau (Military Science Review), Vol. 4, Darmstadt: E. S. Mittler & Sohn, 1954, p. 112.

3. Generalfeldmarschall Erich von Manstein, Verlorene Siege (Lost Victories), Bonn: Athenaeum Verlag, 1955, pp. 290-292. Cited hereafter as Manstein, Lost Victories.

4. Walter Goerlitz, Der Zweite Weltkrieg 1939-1945 (The Second World War 1939-1945), Vol. II, Stuttgart: Steingrueben Verlag, pp. 410-413. Cited hereafter as Goerlitz, Second World War, II. See also Generalleutnant Hermann Plocher (Ret.), The German Air Force versus Russia, 1942, USAF Historical Studies No. 154, Maxwell AFB, Alabama: USAF Historical Division, ASI, pp. 306-329. Cited hereafter as Plocher, GAF versus Russia, 1942.

5. Manstein, Lost Victories, p. 421.

6. I. Flakkorps, Ia Op 2, Korpshauptquartier, den 21.2.1943, "Verzeichnis der Dienststellenleiter und Stellenbesetzung der Kommando-Behoerden im Kampfraum Sued" (Corps Headquarters, I Flak Corps, Operations Division, 21 February 1943, "Directory of Officials and Assignments of Command Officials in Combat Zone South"), G/VI/5a, Karlsruhe Document Collection. Cited hereafter as Command Assignments, 1943.

7. Manstein, *Lost Victories*, p. 417.

8. *Ibid.*, p. 419.

9. *Ibid.*, pp. 408-409.

10. *Ibid.*, p. 412.

11. Tippelskirch, *Second World War*, p. 322.

12. Generalleutnant Wolfgang Pickert (Ret.), *Vom Kuban-Brueckenkopf bis Sewastopol* (*From the Kuban Bridgehead to Sevastopol*), Heidelberg: Kurt Vowinckel Verlag, 1955, pp. 13-17. Cited hereafter as Pickert, *Kuban Bridgehead*.

13. Manstein, *Lost Victories*, p. 429.

14. *Ibid.*, pp. 432, 436-437. See also Plocher, *GAF versus Russia, 1942*, pp. 328-329. See also Generalfeldmarschall Erhard Milch, Kriegstagebuch (Field Marshal Erhard Milch, War Diary), 28 January-4 February 1943, G/VI/4d, Karlsruhe Document Collection. Cited hereafter as Milch Diary.

15. Manstein, *Lost Victories*, p. 450.

16. Pickert, *Kuban Bridgehead*, pp. 16-17. See also Manstein, *Lost Victories*, pp. 435-436.

17. *Command Assignments, 1943.*

18. Manstein, *Lost Victories*, pp. 467-468, 472.

19. Luftflottenkommando 4., Ia, "Einsatz der Luftflotte 4. im Kampfraum Sued der Ostfront vom 1. 1. 1943 bis zum 12. 9. 1943" (Fourth Air Fleet Command, Operations, "Operations of the Fourth Air Fleet in Combat Zone South of the Eastern Front from 1 January 1943 to 12 September 1943"), G/VI/5a, Karlsruhe Document Collection. Cited hereafter as *Operations, Fourth Air Fleet.*

20. "Militaerischer Werdegang der fuehrenden deutschen Luftwaffen-Offiziere an der Ostfront," a document probably drawn from official Luftwaffe personnel records, with which it closely agrees. Anlage 3 zu USAF Studie 155 ("Military Careers of the Leading German Luftwaffe Officers on the Eastern Front," Appendix 3 to USAF Study 155, original German manuscript), Karlsruhe Document Collection. Cited hereafter as *Military Careers*.

21. *Ibid.*, p. 9.

22. Luftflottenkommando 4., Kriegstagebuch und persoenliche Aufzeichnungen des Ob. der Luftflotte 4., vom 1. 1. 43 - 21. 3. 43 (Fourth Air Fleet Command, War Diary and Personal Notations of the Commander in Chief of the Fourth Air Fleet, from 1 January to 21 March 1943), Karlsruhe Document Collection. Cited hereafter as *War Diary, Fourth Air Fleet* (I).

23. OKL, Luftwaffen-fuehrungsstab Ia, "Befehls-und Unterstellungsverhaeltnisse Luftwaffe-Heer im Osten, 1943" (High Command of the Luftwaffe, Operations Staff, "Command and Subordinate Relationships Air Force-Army in the East, 1943"), a chart showing these relationships by areas within the Eastern Theater of Operations, G/VI/5b, Karlsruhe Document Collection.

24. Karlheinz Rieker, *Ein Mann verliert einen Weltkrieg* (*One Man Loses a World War*), Frankfurt a/Main: Fridericus Verlag (publication date not given), p. 195. Cited hereafter as Rieker, *One Man Loses a World War*.

25. *Ibid.*, p. 221.

26. *Ibid.*, p. 228.

27. *Operations, Fourth Air Fleet,* 16, 18, 20 February 1943.

28. Map of the Kuban Bridgehead of uncertain origin, but in all probability drawn from official Luftwaffe sources, Appendix 9a to the original German manuscript "Der Einsatz der deutschen Luftwaffe im Osten 1943" ("The Employment of the German Air Force in the East 1943"), Karlsruhe Document Collection. Cited hereafter as Map, Kuban Bridgehead.

29. Kampfgeschwader 4., Geschichte des Kampfgeschwaders "General Wever" Nr. 4, III. /K. G.4 im Osten, 1943 (Bomber Wing 4, History of the Bomber Wing "General Wever" No. 4, 3rd Group, Bomber Wing 4 in the East, 1943), Karlsruhe Document Collection. Cited hereafter as <u>4th Bomber Wing History</u>.

30. Manstein, <u>Lost Victories</u>, p. 462.

31. <u>War Diary, Fourth Air Fleet</u> (I).

32. General der Flieger Rudolf Meister (Ret.) and Lt. Col. Kurt von Greiff (GSC, Ret.), "Erfahrungen mit Panzerjaegerstaffeln," Auszug aus dem Bericht des Generals der Jagdflieger Nr. 673/3 geh., vom 5. 3. 1943 ("Experiences with Antitank Squadrons," excerpt from the Report of the General of Fighters No. 673/3, Secret, of 5 March 1943), Karlsruhe Document Collection.

33. <u>Operations, Fourth Air Fleet</u>, 1-15 March 1943. See also <u>War Diary, Fourth Air Fleet</u> (I), 27 February-15 March 1943. See also Manstein, <u>Lost Victories</u>, pp. 462-463.

34. Manstein, <u>Lost Victories</u>, p. 464.

35. <u>War Diary, Fourth Air Fleet</u> (I), 6 March 1943.

36. <u>Ibid.</u>, 10-11 March 1943.

37. <u>Ibid.</u>, 11-12 March 1943.

38. <u>Ibid.</u>, 12 March 1943.

39. <u>Ibid.</u>, 14-15 March 1943.

40. <u>Ibid.</u>, 16-18 March 1943. See also <u>Operations, Fourth Air Fleet</u>, 16-18 March 1943.

41. Wing Commander Asher Lee, <u>The German Air Force</u>, New York: Harper & Brothers Publishers, 1946, p. 159.

42. <u>Ibid.</u>, pp. 159-161. See also Great Britain, The Air Ministry (A. C. A. S. [I]), <u>The Rise and Fall of the German Air Force (1933 to 1945)</u>, Air Ministry Pamphlet No. 248, London: The Air Ministry, 1948, p. 231. Cited hereafter as British Air Ministry, <u>Rise and Fall of the GAF</u>.

43. OKL, Chef des Generalstabes der Luftwaffe, 8. (kriegswissenschaftliche) Abt., "Die deutschen Luftangriffe auf sowjetische Ruestungsindustrie-Ziele im Jahr 1943" (High Command of the Luftwaffe, Chief of the General Staff of the Luftwaffe, 8th [Military Science] Branch, "The German Air Attacks upon Soviet Armament Industry Targets in the Year 1943"), a document drawn from Foreign Documents Group 4406, Karlsruhe Document Collection. Cited hereafter as OKL, Attacks on Soviet Industry.

44. Operations, Fourth Air Fleet, 14-20 March 1943. See also Manstein, Lost Victories, p. 467. See also British Air Ministry, Rise and Fall of the GAF, p. 232. See also OKL, Chef des Generalstabes der Luftwaffe, 8. (kriegswissenschaftliche) Abt., "Einsatz der Luftflotte 4. gegen die sowjetischen Eisenbahnen im Kampfraum Sued, 1943" (High Command of the Luftwaffe, Chief of the General Staff of the Luftwaffe, 8th [Military Science] Branch, "Employment of the Fourth Air Fleet Against the Soviet Railroads in Combat Zone South, 1943"), a chart showing the operations of the Fourth Air Fleet against Soviet rail installations throughout 1943, Karlsruhe Document Collection. Cited hereafter as OKL, Operations Against Soviet Railroads.

45. OKL, Operations Against Soviet Railroads.

Chapter 2

1. Manstein, Lost Victories, pp. 408-411.

2. Ibid., p. 412.

3. 4th Bomber Wing History. See also Maps Nos. 1, 5, and 6, this study.

4. Ibid.

5. Map, Kuban Bridgehead.

6. War Diary, Fourth Air Fleet (I), 9-11 February 1943.

7. Rieker, One Man Loses a World War, p. 281.

8. OKL, Operations Against Soviet Railroads.

9. *War Diary, Fourth Air Fleet,* Appendix 3 of 13 March 1943.

10. Pickert, *Kuban Bridgehead,* p. 19.

11. *Ibid.*, p. 20.

12. *Ibid.*, pp. 20-21.

13. 9. Flakdivision, Div. Stab, la, "Gliderung der 9. Flakdivision Anfang Maerz 1943" (9th Flak Division, Division Staff, Operations, "Organizational Structure of the 9th Flak Division, Beginning of March 1943"), Karlsruhe Document Collection.

14. Pickert, *Kuban Bridgehead,* pp. 21-22.

15. __________, "Das I. Flieger-Korps im Kuban-Brueckenkopf und auf der Krim bei der Unterstuetzung der Heeresgruppe A (17. Armee) bei den Verteidigungsoperationen vom 24. Juni bis 15. November 1943" ("The 1st Air Corps in the Kuban Bridgehead and in the Crimea in Support of Army Group A [Seventeenth Army] in the Defensive Operations from 24 June to 15 November 1943"), written in POW camp in 1946, in all probability by Generalleutnant Karl Angerstein, Karlsruhe Document Collection. Cited hereafter as 1st Air Corps, Kuban Bridgehead.

16. Fliegerfuehrer Sued, "Staerke und Dislokation der sowjetischen Schwarzmeer-Flotte" (Air Commander South, "Strength and Disposition of the Soviet Black Sea Fleet"), Karlsruhe Document Collection.

17. Generalmajor Fritz Morzik (Ret.), Major Hans-Juergen Willers (Ret.), and Captain Huelsmann (Ret.), "Zur Luftversorgung des Kuban-Brueckenkopfes 1943" ("On the Air Supply of the Kuban Bridgehead 1943"), Karlsruhe Document Collection.

18. *Operations, Fourth Air Fleet,* 9 March 1943.

19. Rieker, *One Man Loses a World War,* pp. 282-283.

20. *Operations, Fourth Air Fleet,* 21 February-12 March 1943. See also Pickert, *Kuban Bridgehead,* pp. 35-36.

21. *War Diary, Fourth Air Fleet,* 13-14 March 1943.

22. British Air Ministry, Rise and Fall of the GAF, pp. 228-231. See also Manstein, Lost Victories, pp. 464-467.

23. Military Careers.

24. War Diary, Fourth Air Fleet, 14-15 April 1943.

25. Rieker, One Man Loses a World War, pp. 283-284.

26. Stuka-Geschwader 2., "Kriegstagebuch des Stuka-Geschwaders 2.," II. Teil (Dive-Bomber Wing 2, "War Diary of the 2nd Dive-Bomber Wing," Part II), reports of 17 April 1943, Karlsruhe Document Collection. Cited hereafter as War Diary, 2nd Dive-Bomber Wing.

27. Ibid., 18 April 1943.

28. Ibid., 19 April 1943.

29. Ibid., 20 April 1943.

30. Ibid., 20-21 April 1943.

31. Rieker, One Man Loses a World War, p. 285. See also Operations, Fourth Air Fleet, 20-24 April 1943. See also War Diary, 2nd Dive-Bomber Wing, 20-24 April 1943.

32. Operations, Fourth Air Fleet, 29, 30 April, 3, 7 May 1943.

33. Rieker, One Man Loses a World War, p. 285.

34. Ibid., p. 286.

35. Ibid., p. 287.

36. 1st Air Corps, Kuban Bridgehead, Section 5, A.

37. Col. Hans-Ulrich Rudel, Trotzdem (Nevertheless), Waiblingen/Wuertemberg: Verlag Lothar Leberecht, 1950, p. 76. Cited hereafter as Rudel, Nevertheless. See also Antitank Squadrons.

38. Ibid., pp. 84-85.

39. Rieker, One Man Loses a World War, p. 287.

40. 1st Air Corps, Kuban Bridgehead, Section 3. See also Pickert, Kuban Bridgehead, p. 43.

41. 1st Air Corps, Kuban Bridgehead, Section 3.

42. 9. Flakdivision, Ia, "Erfahrungsbericht der 9. Flakartillerie vom 23. Juli 1943" (9th Flak Division, Operations, "Experience Report of 23 July 1943 of the 9th Flak Artillery"), Karlsruhe Document Collection.

43. Pickert, Kuban Bridgehead, p. 45.

44. 1st Air Corps, Kuban Bridgehead. See also Pickert, Kuban Bridgehead, pp. 45-46.

45. 1st Air Corps, Kuban Bridgehead.

46. Rieker, One Man Loses a World War, pp. 288-289.

47. 1st Air Corps, Kuban Bridgehead, Section 5, C.

48. Operations, Fourth Air Fleet, 10-11 September 1943.

49. Pickert, Kuban Bridgehead, pp. 49-50.

50. Axel, Buchner, "Kuban-Brueckenkopf - Fels in der Brandung," Die Deutsche Soldatenzeitung, 1953, Nr. 23-27 ("Kuban Bridgehead - Cliffs in the Breakers," The German Soldiers' Newspaper).

Chapter 3

1. Tippelskirch, Second World War, pp. 328-331.

2. Generalleutnant Oldwig von Natzmer, "Operations of Encircled Forces," MS No. T-12, 1951, EUCOM: EUCOM Historical Division, OCMH, U.S. Army. See also Tippelskirch, Second World War, pp. 327-328.

3. Generalmajor Hans-Detlef Herhudt von Rohden (Ret.), "The Russian War in 1943," Document No. 19 of the von Rohden Collection (a study which includes operational data taken directly from the 8th Military Science Branch of the Luftwaffe), Operations in the East from 2-15 February 1943. Cited hereafter as Von Rohden Study.

4. *Ibid.*, Operations in the East, 20-27 February 1943.

5. *Ibid.*, Operations in the East, 28 February 1943.

6. *Ibid.*, Operations in the East, 18-23 March 1943.

7. *Ibid.*, Operations in the East, 24-31 March 1943.

8. 14. "Muenchhausen" Fernaufklaerungsstaffel, Luftwaffenkommando Ost, *Chronik der (F) 14. "Muenchhausen"* (14th "Muenchhausen" Strategic Reconnaissance Squadron, Air Command East, *Chronicles of the 4th Squadron [Strategic] 14th Reconnaissance Wing, "Muenchhausen"*), Frankfurt am Main/Griesheim: Hermes-Druck, no date of publication, pp. 9-10.

9. Generalleutnant Hermann Plocher (Ret.), "Staerke und Gliederung der deutschen fliegenden Verbaende 1943 im Osten" ("Strength and Organization of German Flying Units in the East 1943"), G/VI/5, Karlsruhe Document Collection. Cited hereafter as Plocher, *Luftwaffe Strength and Organization (East)*.

10. *Ibid.*

11. *OKL, Attacks on Soviet Industry.* See also *OKL, Operations Against Soviet Railroads.*

12. Fritz Freiherr von Siegler, *Die hoeheren Dienststellen der deutschen Wehrmacht 1933-1945 (The Higher Positions of the German Armed Forces 1933-1945)*, Muenchen: Institute fuer Zeitgeschichte, 1953, pp. 52, 53, 57.

13. Luftflottenkommando 6., Fuehrungsabteilung Ia, B.Nr. 7807/43, geheim, H.Qu., den 9.10.43, "Taetigkeitsbericht des Luftflottenkommandos 6. fuer die Zeit vom 1.-30. Juni 1943," (Sixth Air Fleet Command, Operations Branch, Operations Officer, Report No. 7807 of 1943, Secret, Sixth Air Fleet Headquarters, 9 October 1943, "Activity Report of the Sixth Air Fleet for the Period 1-30 June 1943"), p. 6. Cited hereafter as Activity Report, Sixth Air Fleet. See also Von Rohden Study, Operations in the East, 12 May 1943.

14. OKL, Luftwaffenfuehrungsstab Ic, "Die deutschen Luftangriffe auf sowjetische Ruestungsindustrie-Ziele im Jahr 1943" (High Command of the Luftwaffe, Luftwaffe Operations Staff, Intelligence, "The German Air Attacks upon Soviet Armament Industry Targets in the Year 1943"), extracts from a number of documents pertaining to these operations between 2 June and 31 July 1943, G/VI/5b, Karlsruhe Document Collection. Cited hereafter as *OKL, Intelligence, Attacks on Soviet Industry*.

15. Maj. Friedrich Lang (Ret.), "Der Einsatz der III. Sturzkampfgeschwader 1. in der Zeit vom 1. 4. 43 bist 1. 5. 1944" ("The Employment of the 3rd Squadron, 1st Dive-Bomber Wing, in the Period from 1 April 1943 to 1 May 1944"), G/VI/5b, Karlsruhe Document Collection. Cited hereafter as Lang, *Employment of 1st Dive-Bomber Wing.*

16. *Activity Report, Sixth Air Fleet.*

17. Lang, *Employment of 1st Dive-Bomber Wing.*

18. Col. Hasso Neitzel (Ret.), "Sicherung der rueckwaertigen Verbindung in Russland," Auszuege aus einer Studie der EUCOM Historical Division, MS No. T-19, pp. 44-52 ("Security of Rear Communications in Russia," excerpts from a study of the EUCOM Historical Division, MS #T-19), G/VI/5b, Karlsuhe Document Collection.

19. ________, "Einsatz der deutschen Luftwaffe gegen sowjetische Industrieziele und Aufmarschbewegungen" ("Employment of the German Air Force Against Soviet Industrial Targets and Concentration Movements"), a map, probably of High Command of the Luftwaffe origin, G/VI/5b, Karlsruhe Document Collection.

20. Manstein, *Lost Victories*, p. 473. See also Tippelskirch, *Second World War*, p. 378. See also Goerlitz, *Second World War, II*, p. 179.

21. Goerlitz, *Second World War, II*, p. 194.

22. *Ibid.*, p. 183.

23. Tippelskirch, *Second World War*, p. 381.

24. Manstein, *Lost Victories*, p. 497.

25. Generalleutnant Hermann Plocher (Ret.), *The German Air Force versus Russia, 1941,* USAF Historical Studies No. 153, Maxwell AFB, Alabama: USAF Historical Division, ASI, July 1965, pp. 7-8. Cited hereafter as Plocher, *GAF versus Russia, 1941.*

26. Manstein, *Lost Victories,* pp. 483-484.

27. OKW, Chef der Wehrmachtfuehrungsstab Ia Op., "Die Lage an der Ostfront September 1943," Auszug aus dem Vortrag des Chefs des Wehrmachtfuehrungsstabes, Generaloberst Alfred Jodl, am 7. 11. 1943 (High Command of the Wehrmacht, Chief of the Wehrmacht Operations Staff, Operations Officer, "The Situation on the Eastern Front September 1943," excerpt from the speech of the Chief of the Wehrmacht Operations Staff, Generaloberst Alfred Jodl on 7 November 1943), G/VI/5b, Karlsruhe Document Collection.

28. Manstein, *Lost Victories,* p. 485. See also Goerlitz, *Second World War, II,* p. 200.

29. Manstein, *Lost Victories,* p. 486.

30. *Ibid.*, p. 488.

31. Generalfeldmarschall a. D. Albert Kesselring, Reichsfinanzminister Lutz Graf Schwerin von Krosigk, u. a. *Bilanz des Zweiten Weltkriegs: Erkenntnisse und Verpflichtungen fuer die Zukunft (Balance Sheet of the Second World War: Insights and Obligations for the Future),* Hamburg: Gerhard Stalling Verlag, 1953, p. 58. Cited hereafter as Kesselring, *et al.*, *Balance Sheet of Operations.*

32. Manstein, *Lost Victories,* p. 491. See also Generalmajor Fritz Kless (Ret.), "Bericht ueber den Einsatz der Luftflotte 6. waehrend 'Zitadelle' und in der Schlacht im Orelbogen" ("Report on the Employment of the Sixth Air Fleet During 'Zitadelle' and in the Battle in the Orel Salient"), G/VI/5a, Karlsruhe Document Collection. Cited hereafter as Kless, *Sixth Air Fleet Operations During Zitadelle.* See also General der Flieger Hans Seidemann (Ret.), "Das VIII. Flieger-Korps im Einsatz waehrend der Operation 'Zitadelle'" ("The VIII Air Corps in Action During the Operation 'Zitadelle'"), G/VI/5a, Karlsruhe Document Collection. Cited hereafter as Seidemann, *VIII Air Corps During Zitadelle.*

33. Manstein, Lost Victories, p. 495. Kesselring et al., Balance Sheet of Operations.

34. Manstein, Lost Victories, p. 496. See also Military Careers. See also Seidemann, VIII Air Corps During Zitadelle. See also Plocher, Luftwaffe Strength and Organization (East).

35. Kless, Sixth Air Fleet Operations During Zitadelle.

36. Ibid. See also Col. Hermann Teske (Ret.), "Partisanen gegen die Eisenbahnen," Wehrwissenschaftliche-Rundschau, 3. Jahrgang, Okt. 1953 ("Partisans Against the Railroads," Military Science Review, 3rd Year, October 1953), Vol. 10, Darmstadt: E. S. Mittler & Sohn, G. m. b. H., 1953. Cited hereafter as Teske, Partisan Attacks.

37. Kless, Sixth Air Fleet Operations During Zitadelle.

38. Ibid. See also Seidemann, VIII Air Corps During Zitadelle.

39. Manstein, Lost Victories, p. 497. See also Seidemann, VIII Air Corps During Zitadelle. See also Kless, Sixth Air Fleet Operations During Zitadelle.

40. Plocher, Luftwaffe Strength and Organization (East).

41. 4th Bomber Wing History.

42. Lang, Employment of 1st Dive-Bomber Wing.

43. Plocher, Luftwaffe Strength and Organization (East).

44. Kless, Sixth Air Fleet Operations During Zitadelle.

45. Ibid.

46. Tippelskirch, Second World War, p. 381.

47. Goerlitz, Second World War, II, pp. 203-204.

48. Manstein, Lost Victories, p. 500. See also Kless, Sixth Air Fleet Operations During Zitadelle. See also Rudel, Nevertheless, p. 85.

49. __________, "Einsatz der IV. Pz. /S.G. 9 am 8. Juli 1943 bei Bjelgorod" ("Employment of the 9th Dive-Bomber Wing and the IV Panzer Corps on the 8th of July near Belgorod"), a map drawn from official Luftwaffe situation maps, G/VI/4b, Karlsruhe Document Collection. Cited hereafter as Map, IV Panzer Corps Near Belgorod.

50. Rudel, Nevertheless, pp. 91-92.

51. Ibid., p. 93.

52. Ibid., pp. 93-94.

53. Ibid., p. 94.

54. Map, IV Panzer Corps Near Belgorod.

55. Seidemann, VIII Air Corps During Zitadelle.

56. Armeeoberkommando 9., Abt. Ia, "Gefechtsbericht der 9. Armee und der 2. Panzerarmee ueber die Schlacht im Orelbogen vom 5. Juli bis 18. August 1943" (Headquarters, Ninth Army, Operations Branch, "Combat Report of the Ninth Army and the Second Panzer Army Concerning the Battle in the Orel Salient from 5 July to 18 August 1943"), G/VI/4c, Karlsruhe Document Collection. Cited hereafter as Ninth Army Operations Report.

Chapter 4

1. Ninth Army Operations Report (see maps therein).

2. Plocher, Luftwaffe Strength and Organization (East). See also 4th Bomber Wing History.

3. Kless, Sixth Air Fleet Operations During Zitadelle.

4. Manstein, Lost Victories, p. 489. See also Seidemann, VIII Air Corps During Zitadelle.

5. Manstein, Lost Victories, pp. 503-506. See also OKL, 8. (kriegswissenschaftliche) Abt., "Luftwaffe verhindert waehrend der Schlacht im Orelbogen die Einschliessung von zwei Armeen, 19-21 Juli 1943" (High Command of the Luftwaffe, 8th [Military Science] Branch, "The Luftwaffe Prevents the Envelopment of Two Armies During the Battle in the Orel Salient, 19-21 July 1943"), a situation map showing the course of action during the period 19-21 July 1943, G/VI/4c, Karlsruhe Document Collection.

6. Kless, Sixth Air Fleet Operations During Zitadelle.

7. Ninth Army Operations Report, p. 4.

8. General der Flieger Paul Deichmann (Ret.), "Bericht ueber eine Besprechung bei Hitler ueber Zitadelle" ("Report Concerning a Conversation with Hitler on Zitadelle"), 1956, G/VI/4d, Karlsruhe Document Collection. Cited hereafter as Deichmann, Report on Zitadelle.

9. Kless, Sixth Air Fleet Operations During Zitadelle.

10. Manstein, Lost Victories, p. 501.

11. Tippelskirch, Second World War, p. 382.

12. Ninth Army Operations Report, p. 7. See also maps 7-11 (appendices) to the German original manuscript of this study.

13. Kless, Sixth Air Fleet Operations During Zitadelle.

14. Ibid. See also Ninth Army Operations Report.

15. Rieker, One Man Loses a World War, p. 267.

16. Ninth Army Operations Report, p. 11, and map No. 11 thereof. See also Kless, Sixth Air Fleet Operations During Zitadelle.

17. Ninth Army Operations Report, pp. 11-12.

18. Rieker, One Man Loses a World War, pp. 267-268.

19. Kless, Sixth Air Fleet Operations During Zitadelle. See also Tippelskirch, Second World War, p. 383. See also Ninth Army Operations Report, maps 8-11.

20. Kless, Sixth Air Fleet Operations During Zitadelle. See also Ninth Army Operations Report, map 11.

21. Tippelskirch, Second World War, p. 383.

22. Military Careers.

23. Tippelskirch, Second World War, p. 400.

24. OKL, Luftwaffenfuehrungsstab Ic, "Einsaetze der Luftwaffe im Osten in der Zeit vom 10. 10. - 31. 10. 1943" (High Command of the Luftwaffe, Luftwaffe Operations Staff [Intelligence], "Employment of the Luftwaffe in the East in the Period from 10 October to 31 October 1943"), a document taken from daily situation reports from the various air fleet commands, pp. 28-29, G/VI/5d, Karlsruhe Document Collection. Cited hereafter as October Air Operations.

25. Ibid., p. 29.

26. Ibid., p. 30.

27. Ibid., pp. 30-31.

28. Ibid., p. 31.

29. Ibid., pp. 31-32.

30. 4th Bomber Wing History, p. 23. See also October Air Operations, pp. 28-32.

31. General der Flakartillerie Otto von Renz (Ret.), "Flakeinsatz an den einzelnen Fronten 1939-1945" ("Employment of Flak Artillery on the Individual Fronts 1939-1945"), and "Einsatz der Flak bei den einzelnen Luftflotten usw" ("Employment of Flak Artillery with the Individual Air Fleets, etc."), 1955, F/VI/1, Karlsruhe Document Collection. Cited hereafter as Von Renz, Flak Artillery in Air Fleet Commands.

32. Military Careers.

33. __________, "Die Lage im Mittelabschnitt der Ostfront Juli bis Ende 1943" ("The Situation in the Central Sector of the Eastern Front, July to the End of 1943"), a map, probably drawn from official Luftwaffe maps in the 8th (Military Science) Branch, G/VI/5a, Karlsruhe Document Collection. Cited hereafter as Map, Situation Combat Zone Center. See also __________, "Zum Einsatz der Flak 1943 im Osten" ("For the Employment of Flak in the East 1943"), a chart taken from High Command of the Luftwaffe materials in the 8th (Military Science) Branch, F/VI/1, Karlsruhe Document Collection. Cited hereafter as Employment of Flak Artillery.

34. Tippelskirch, Second World War, p. 398.

35. Plocher, Luftwaffe Strength and Organization (East).

36. Tippelskirch, Second World War, p. 398. See also 4th Bomber Wing History. See also Employment of Flak Artillery.

37. Manstein, Lost Victories, p. 503. See also Plocher, Luftwaffe Strength and Organization (East).

38. Operations, Fourth Air Fleet, reports from 17-21 July 1943.

39. Ibid., 19-20 July 1943.

40. Ibid., 30-31 July 1943.

41. Ibid., 1-3 August 1943.

42. General der Flieger Hans Seidemann (Ret.), "Das VIII. Flieger-Korps im Kampfraum zwischen Donez und Dnjepr-Kampfraum Charkow - 15. Juli - Ende September 1943" ("The VIII Air Corps in the Combat Area Between the Donets and the Dnepr and Kharkov - 15 July to the End of September 1943"), dated November 1956, G/VI/5a, Karlsruhe Document Collection. Cited hereafter as Seidemann, VIII Air Corps, Donets-Kharkov.

43. Operations, Fourth Air Fleet. See also United States Department of the Army, German Defense Tactics Against Russian Breakthroughs, Department of the Army Pamphlet No. 20-233, a study written by Generaloberst Erhard Raus (Ret.), Washington: OCMH, EUCOM Historical Division, October 1951, pp. 64-65. Cited hereafter as DA Pam. 20-233.

44. Operations, Fourth Air Fleet, 4 August 1943.

45. Ibid., 5 August 1943.

46. Ibid., 6-16 August 1943. See also DA Pam. 20-233, pp. 65-67.

47. Manstein, Lost Victories, pp. 517-518. See also Generaloberst Erhard Raus (Ret.) et al., "Peculiarities of Russian Warfare," MS No. T-22, Heidelberg: EUCOM Historical Division, June 1949. See also DA Pam. 20-233, pp. 68-69. See also Operations, Fourth Air Fleet, 16 August 1943.

48. Operations, Fourth Air Fleet, 20 August 1943.

49. Seidemann, VIII Air Corps, Donets-Kharkov.

50. Seidemann, VIII Air Corps During Zitadelle.

51. Manstein, Lost Victories, pp. 519-525, 528-529.

52. Ibid., pp. 539-540.

53. Ibid., pp. 536-538.

54. Maj. Frank Neubert (Ret.), "Beispiele der dauernden Verlegung von Lw. Verbaenden je nach Schwerpunkt (Feuerwehr-Taktik)" ("Examples of Continual Shifting of Luftwaffe Units According to the Point of Main Effort [Fire-fighting Tactics]"), a document found in appendix 27 of the original German manuscript of this study, Karlsruhe Document Collection.

55. Rudel, Nevertheless, pp. 102-104.

56. Col. Hans Christian Kobe (Ret.) "Raeumung und Zerstoerung von Flugplaetzen im Osten" ("Evacuation and Destruction of Airfields in the East"), G/VI/5a, Karlsruhe Document Collection. See also Manstein, Lost Victories. p. 545.

57. Manstein, Lost Victories, pp. 545-546.

58. Brigadegeneral (Bundeswehr) Hellmuth Reinhardt, "Russische Luftlande-Operationen" ("Russian Airborne Operations"), G/VI/5a, Karlsruhe Document Collection.

59. Raymond L. Garthoff, Soviet Military Doctrine, Glencoe, Illinois: The Free Press, 1953, p. 355. Cited hereafter as Garthoff, Soviet Military Doctrine.

60. General der Flieger Hans Seidemann, "Die Kaempfe bei Kiew und der Einsatz des VIII. Flieger-Korps (Ende September 1943 - Anfang November 1943)" ("The Battles Near Kiev and the Employment of the VIII Air Corps, End of September to the Beginning of November 1943"), G/VI/5bb, Karlsruhe Document Collection. Cited hereafter as Seidemann, VIII Air Corps, September-November 1943.

61. Manstein, Lost Victories, pp. 546-547. See also Seidemann, VIII Air Corps, September-November 1943.

62. Seidemann, VIII Air Corps, September-November 1943.

63. Garthoff, Soviet Military Doctrine. See also Seidemann, VIII Air Corps, September-November 1943.

64. October Air Operations, 10 October 1943.

65. Ibid., 11-27 October 1943.

66. Tippelskirch, Second World War, p. 395.

67. Ibid., pp. 395-396.

68. Rudel, Nevertheless, pp. 107-108.

69. Tippelskirch, Second World War, p. 396.

70. Goerlitz, Second World War, II, pp. 229-230.

71. Map, Situation Combat Zone Center.

72. Goerlitz, Second World War, II, pp. 230-231.

73. General der Flieger Rudolf Meister (Ret.), "Einsatz der Luftflotte 4. in Russland 1943" ("Employment of the Fourth Air Fleet in Russia 1943"), G/VI/5a, Karlsruhe Document Collection.

74. Goerlitz, Second World War, II, p. 231. See also Military Careers, references to Generalleutnant Karl Angerstein.

75. Map, Situation Combat Zone Center. Goerlitz, Second World War, II, pp. 230-231.

76. Goerlitz, Second World War, II, p. 231.

77. Manstein, Lost Victories, pp. 564-565.

Chapter 5

1. Pickert, Kuban Bridgehead, pp. 54-55.

2. Plocher, Luftwaffe Strength and Organization (East). See also Generalleutnant Karl Angerstein (Ret.), "Das I. Fliegerkorps am Kuban-Brueckenkopf und auf der Krim bei der Unterstuetzung der Heeresgruppe A (17. Armee) bei den Verteidigungs-operationen vom 24. 6. bis 15. 11. 1943" ("The 1st Air Corps in the Kuban Bridgehead and in the Crimea in Support of Army Group A [Seventeenth Army] in the Defensive Operations from 24 June to 15 November 1943"), 1946, G/VI/5d, Karlsruhe Document Collection. Cited hereafter as Angerstein, Kuban and Crimea.

3. Angerstein, Kuban and Crimea.

4. Pickert, Kuban Bridgehead, pp. 68-69.

5. Ibid., pp. 69-70.

6. Angerstein, Kuban and Crimea. See also Pickert, Kuban Bridgehead, p. 69.

7. Pickert, Kuban Bridgehead, pp. 69-71. See also Angerstein, Kuban and Crimea. See also remarks of Field Marshal Ewald v. Kleist in personnel records of Generaloberst Jaenicke (copies of German Army 201 files), Karlsruhe Document Collection.

8. USAAF, Assistant Chief of Air Staff, "Iran-USSR: ATC Serves Lend-Lease," Impact, Vol. 1, No. 7, October 1943, Washington: USAAF, Office of the Assistant Chief of Air Staff, Intelligence, 1943, p. 35. Cited hereafter as Impact, October 1943. See also OKL, Luftwaffenfuehrungsstab Ic, geheim, vom 6. 8. 43., "Suedroute der angelsaechsischen Einfuhr nach der SU" (High Command of the Luftwaffe, Luftwaffe Operations Staff, Intelligence, Secret, of 6 August 1943, "South Route of the Anglo-Saxon Deliveries to the Soviet Union"). Cited hereafter as OKL, Deliveries to Russia.

9. *Impact*, October 1943, pp. 35-36.

10. *OKL, Deliveries to Russia.* See also *Impact*, October 1943, p. 35.

11. Col. Freiherr von Weitershausen (GSC, Ret), "Verteidigung und Raeumung von Sewastopol im Mai 1944," *Wehrwissenschaftliche Rundschau*, 4. Jahrgang, Heft 5, Mai 1945 ("Defense and Evacuation of Sevastopol in May 1944," *Military Science Review*, 4th Year, Vol. 5, May 1945), Darmstadt: E. S. Mittler & Sohn, G. m. b. H., 1945. Cited hereafter as Weitershausen, *Defense and Evacuation of Sevastopol.*

12. Goerlitz, *Second World War, II*, p. 238. See also Manstein, *Lost Victories*, p. 511.

13. Manstein, *Lost Victories*, p. 571.

14. Pickert, *Kuban Bridgehead*, p. 68. See also Angerstein, *Kuban and Crimea.*

15. Angerstein, *Kuban and Crimea.*

16. Pickert, *Kuban Bridgehead*, p. 72.

17. *Ibid.*, pp. 72-73.

18. Angerstein, *Kuban and Crimea.*

19. Pickert, *Kuban Bridgehead*, p. 77.

20. Angerstein, *Kuban and Crimea.*

21. Pickert, *Kuban Bridgehead*, p. 79.

22. Angerstein, *Kuban and Crimea.* See also Weitershausen, *Defense and Evacuation of Sevastopol.* See also Pickert, *Kuban Bridgehead*, p. 79.

23. Pickert, *Kuban Bridgehead*, p. 88.

24. Weitershausen, *Defense and Evacuation of Sevastopol.* See also Pickert, *Kuban Bridgehead*, p. 88, map p. 89.

25. Pickert, *Kuban Bridgehead*, p. 84.

26. __________, "Flieger und Flak im Kampf um die Krim (Okt. -Dez. 1943)" ("Flyers and Flak Forces in the Battle for the Crimea Oct. - Dec. 1943"), a map drawn from official Luftwaffe records, G/VI/ 5d, Karlsruhe Document Collection. Cited hereafter as Map, Air and Flak in the Crimea. See also Military Careers. See also General der Flieger Paul Deichmann (Ret.), Statement of General Deichmann to the Author, 9 January 1957, G/VI, Karlsruhe Document Collection. Cited hereafter as Deichmann Report.

27. Deichmann Report.

28. General der Flieger Paul Deichmann (Ret.), "Kurzbericht ueber den Einsatz des I. Fliegerkorps im Sueden der Ostfront von Dezember 1943 - Kriegsende," ("Short Report on the Employment of the 1st Air Corps in the Southern Part of the Eastern Front from December 1943 to the War's End"), G/VI/6a, Karlsruhe Document Collection. Cited hereafter as Deichmann, Report on 1st Air Corps.

29. Pickert, Kuban Bridgehead, p. 88. See also Deichmann, Report on 1st Air Corps.

Chapter 6

1. Military Careers. See also Luftwaffe Strength and Organization (East).

2. Lt. Col. (Bundeswehr) Rudolf Jenett, "Beitrag zum Thema Russland Feldzug 1943," vom 5. 11. 1956 ("Contribution to the Topic Russian Campaign 1943," of 5 November 1956), Karlsruhe Document Collection. Cited hereafter as Jenett, Northern Operations.

3. Ibid., pp. 1-3.

4. Personal Recollections of the Author.

5. Tippelskirch, Second World War, pp. 329-330.

6. Jenett, Northern Operations.

7. 4th Bomber Wing History.

8. Manstein, Lost Victories, pp. 487-492.

9. Military Careers.

10. Tippelskirch, Second World War, p. 441.

11. Ibid., p. 402.

12. Jenett, Northern Operations.

13. Luftwaffe Strength and Organization (East). See also October Air Operations, pp. 1-7.

14. Tippelskirch, Second World War, pp. 439-441. See Map No. 14.

15. October Air Operations, pp. 1-7. See also OKL, Fuehrungsstab Ia Nr. 8634/43, g. Kdos. Chefsache (Op 2) vom 24. 8. 43, "Einsatz der Luftverteidigung, Flakartillerie, Luftflotte 5, Stand: 24. 8. 43" (High Command of the Luftwaffe, Operations Staff No. 8634 of 1943, Top Secret Command Matter [Operations] of 24 August 1943, "Employment of Air Defenses, Flak Artillery, Fifth Air Fleet, Situation as of: 24 August 1943"), a map showing full dispositions in the Northern-Far Northern areas on that date, Karlsruhe Document Collection.

16. Generalleutnant Andreas Nielsen (Ret.), "Beitrag zum Thema, Kampf im Norden 1943" ("Contribution to the Topic, Battle in the North 1943"), Karlsruhe Document Collection. Cited hereafter as Nielsen, Battle in the North, 1943. See also General der Infanterie Waldemar Erfurth (Ret.), Der Finnische Krieg 1941-1944 (The Finnish War 1941-1944), Wiesbaden: Limes Verlag, 1950, p. 153. Cited hereafter as Erfurth, The Finnish War.

17. Nielsen, Battle in the North, 1943.

18. Generalleutnant Hermann Hoelter (Ret.), Armee in der Arktis (Army in the Arctic), Bad Nauheim: Hans-Henning Podzun Verlag, 1953, pp. 18-19. Cited hereafter as Hoelter, Army in the Arctic.

19. Erfurth, The Finnish War, pp. 137-141, 191.

20. Ibid., p. 143.

21. Military Careers.

22. Erfurth, The Finnish War, p. 191.

23. *Ibid.*, pp. 152-153. See also Tippelskirch, *Second World War*, p. 445.

24. Hoelter, *Army in the Arctic*, p. 18. See also Erfurth, *The Finnish War*, p. 142.

25. Goerlitz, *Second World War*, II, pp. 449-450.

26. Erfurth, *The Finnish War*, p. 154. See also General der Infanterie Waldemar Erfurth (Ret.), "The Last Finnish War 1941-44," MS #C-073, Heidelberg: EUCOM Historical Division, 1949.

27. General der Infanterie Waldemar Erfurth (Ret.), Schreiben an Generalleutnant a.D. Hermann Plocher, vom 2.10.56 (Letter from General Erfurth to General Plocher, dated 2 October 1946), Karlsruhe Document Collection.

28. Generalleutnant Andreas Nielsen (Ret.), Brief an Generalleutnant a.D. Hermann Plocher, vom 1.11.56 (Letter from General Nielsen to Generalleutnant Plocher (Ret.), dated 1 November 1956).

29. Nielsen, *Battle in the North, 1943*.

30. Erfurth, *The Finnish War*, pp. 148-150. See also Nielsen, *Battle in the North, 1943*.

31. Der Fuehrer und Oberste Befehlshaber der Wehrmacht, OKW/WFSt Nr. 662375/43, g.Kdos. Chefsache, F.HQu., den 28.9.43, *Weisung Nr. 50* (The Fuehrer and Supreme Commander of the Wehrmacht, High Command of the Wehrmacht, Wehrmacht Operations Staff No. 662375 of 1943, Top Secret Command Matter, the Fuehrer's Headquarters, 28 September 1943, *Directive No. 50*). Cited hereafter as *Directive No. 50*. See also Hoelter, *Army in the Arctic*, pp. 21-22.

32. Erfurth, *The Finnish War*, pp. 153-156. See also Hoelter, *Army in the Arctic*, pp. 21-23.

33. Hoelter, *Army in the Arctic*. pp. 22-24. See also *Directive No. 50*.

34. Col. Karl Mittmann, "Russlandfeldzug 1943, Verlauf der Operationen im Jahre 1943" ("Russian Campaign 1943, Course of Operations in the Year 1943"), a study prepared for the 8th (Military Science) Branch of the Luftwaffe, 1944, G/VI/5a, Karlsruhe Document Collection. See also Col. Karl Mittmann, "Die Luftlage an der Ostfront in der Zeit von Ende April-September 1943" ("The Air Situation on the Eastern Front in the Period from the End of April to September 1943"), a study prepared for the 8th (Military Science) Branch of the Luftwaffe, 1944, G/VI/5d, Karlsruhe Document Collection.

35. Generalleutnant Ernst-August Roth (Ret.), "Einsatz der Luftflotte 5. an der Ostfront 1943" ("Employment of the Fifth Air Fleet on the Eastern Front 1943"), Karlsruhe Document Collection. Cited hereafter as Roth, *Fifth Air Fleet 1943.* See also Generalleutnant Hermann Plocher (Ret.), "Einsaetze und Erfolge der ueber dem Eismeer und an der Murmansk-Front eingesetzten Verbaende der Luftflotte 5" ("Missions and Results of Units of the Fifth Air Fleet Employed over the Arctic Seas and the Murmansk Front"), G/VI/5b, Karlsruhe Document Collection. Cited hereafter as Plocher, *Employment of the Fifth Air Fleet.*

36. Roth, *Fifth Air Fleet,* 1943.

37. OKM, Admiral Nordmeer, Br.B.Nr. 299, g.Kdos., Chefsache, vom 14.5.1943, "Zusammenarbeit Luftwaffe-Kriegsmarine im Nordmeer 1943" (High Command of the Navy, Admiral Norwegian Sea, Letter Book No. 299, Top Secret Command Matter, of 14 May 1943, "Cooperation Between Luftwaffe and Navy in the Norwegian Sea Area 1943"), an official letter written by Admiral Otto Schniewind, Admiral, Norwegian Sea. Cited hereafter as Admiral Norwegian Sea, *Navy-Luftwaffe Cooperation.*

38. Winston S. Churchill, *The Second World War*: Vol. 5, *Closing the Ring,* Boston: Houghton Mifflin Company, 1951, pp. 256-257. (Also published in German under the title *Der Zweite Weltkrieg*: Band V, *Der Ring Schliesst Sich.*)

39. *Ibid.*, p. 261.

40. *Ibid.*, p. 263.

41. *Ibid.*, p. 264.

42. *Ibid.*, p. 267.

43. *Ibid.*, pp. 274-275.

44. Plocher, *Employment of the Fifth Air Fleet.* See also records for German Navy operations through 4 November 1943 in the Navy Project Karlsruhe.

45. Generaloberst Hans-Juergen Stumpff (Ret.), "Gedanken zum Kampf der deutschen Luftwaffe im Gebiet noerdlich des Polarkreises" ("Thoughts on the Battle of the German Air Force in the Area North of the Arctic Circle"), Karlsruhe Document Collection. Cited hereafter as Stumpff, *Air Warfare in the Arctic.*

46. Documents concerning these operations in the Navy Project Karlsruhe. See also Stumpff, *Air Warfare in the Arctic.*

47. *October Air Operations,* pp. 21-27. See also Roth, *Fifth Air Fleet, 1943.*

48. Stumpff, *Air Warfare in the Arctic.*

49. Nielsen, *Battle in the North, 1943.*

50. Stumpff, *Air Warfare in the Arctic.*

51. Plocher, *Employment of the Fifth Air Fleet.* See also Stumpff, *Air Warfare in the Arctic.*

52. Nielsen, *Battle in the North, 1943.*

53. Col. Dr. Ernst Kuehl (Ret.), Letter from Col. Dr. Ernst Kuehl (Ret.) to Generalleutnant Hermann Plocher (Ret.), dated 28 November 1956.

54. Plocher, *Luftwaffe Strength and Organization (East).* See also Plocher, *Employment of the Fifth Air Fleet.*

55. Col. Ludwig Wahl (Ret.), "Beitrag zum Thema: Seenotdienst" ("Contribution to the Topic: Sea Rescue Service"), Karlsruhe Document Collection. Cited hereafter as Wahl, *Air-Sea Rescue.*

56. Nielsen, *Battle in the North, 1943.* See also Wahl, *Air-Sea Rescue.*

57. Military Careers.

58. Nielsen, Battle in the North, 1943.

59. Erfurth, The Finnish War, p. 147.

Chapter 7

1. Luftdivision 16., "Bericht des Luftdivisions 16.," Ziffer 10. u. 17. (Air Division 16, "Report of the Air Division 16," Ciphers 10 and 17), G/VI/5b, Karlsruhe Document Collection. Cited hereafter as Air Division 16, Report.

2. Ibid., Cipher 31.

3. Generalleutnant Hermann Plocher (Ret.), "Die Bilanz des Luftwaffen Einsatzes, 1941" ("The Balance Sheet of the Luftwaffe Operations, 1941"), Karlsruhe Document Collection.

4. OKL, Luftwaffenfuehrungsstab, Ic/IV, GL/A Nr. 11258/43, Geheim (Rue) vom 4. 6. 43, "Entscheidende Angriffsziele in der sowjetrussischen Kriegswirtschaft" (High Command of the Luftwaffe, Luftwaffe Operations Staff. Intelligence, Branch 4, Chief of Special Supply and Procurement, No. 11258 of 1943, Secret (Armament) of 4 June 1943, "Decisive Attack Targets in the Soviet Union's War Economy"), G/VI/4d, Karlsruhe Document Collection. Cited hereafter as OKL, Decisive Targets.

5. OKL, Intelligence, Attacks on Soviet Industry.

6. Der Chef der Luftflotte 6., Br. B. Nr. 241/43, G. Kdos. Chefs H. Qu., den 12. 6. 43, "Bekaempfung der sowjetrussischen Kriegswirtschaft" (The Chief of the Sixth Air Fleet, Book No. 241 of 1943, Top Secret Command Matter, Corps Headquarters, 12 June 1943, "Combating the Soviet Russian War Economy"), G/VI/5b, Karlsruhe Document Collection.

7. Ibid., Part III.

8. OKH, Generalstab des Heeres, Ia, Nr. 10038/43, g. Kdos. Chefs (High Command of the Army, General Staff of the Army, Operations Branch, No. 10038 of 1943, Top Secret Command Matter), a document which appears in the collection without the date of issue, Karlsruhe Document Collection.

9. Activity Report, Sixth Air Fleet, Part III, p. 15.

10. Plocher, Luftwaffe Strength and Organization (East).

11. Generalleutnant Hermann Plocher (Ret.), "Vorschlag der Neugliederung der Fuehrungsorganisation der Luftwaffe" ("Recommendation for a Reorganization of the Leadership [Command Apparatus] of the Luftwaffe"), chart, Karlsruhe Document Collection.

12. Military Careers.

13. British Air Ministry, Rise and Fall of the GAF.

14. Walter Goerlitz, Der Zweite Weltkrieg 1939-1945 (The Second World War 1939-1945), Vol. I, Stuttgart: Steingrueben Verlag, 1951, pp. 446-447. Cited hereafter as Goerlitz, Second World War, I.

15. Air Division 16, Report, Cipher 10.

16. OKL, Luftwaffenfuehrungsstab, 8. (kriegswissenschaftliche) Abt., "Ueberblick ueber die deutsche Luftkriegfuehrung" (High Command of the Luftwaffe, Luftwaffe Operations Staff, 8th [Military Science] Branch, "Overview of the German Air War Leadership"), G/VI/5a, Karlsruhe Document Collection.

17. OKL, Luftwaffenfuehrungsstab, Ia, op. Nr. 8865/43, g.Kdos. Chefs den 9.11.43, "Kurze Studie Kampf gegen die russische Ruestungsindustrie" (High Command of the Luftwaffe, Luftwaffe Operations Staff, Op. No. 8865 of 1943, Top Secret Command Matter, 9 November 1943, "Short Study of the Battle Against the Russian Armament Industry"), G/VI/5b, Karlsruhe Document Collection. Cited hereafter as OKL, Russian Armament Industry.

18. Goerlitz, Second World War, II, p. 223.

19. Rieker, One Man Loses a World War, pp. 295-296.

20. General der Artillerie Alfred Jodl, "Bericht eines Besprechungs in Muenchen ueber die Lage im Osten, 7.1.43" ("Report of a Meeting in Munich on the Situation in the East, 7 January 1943"), G/VI/5d, Karlsruhe Document Collection.

21. General der Artillerie Alfred Jodl, "Auszug aus Vortrag des Chefs des Wehrmachtfuehrungsstabes vom 7. 11. 43" ("Excerpt from a Report of the Chief of the Wehrmacht Operations Staff of 7 November 1943"), G/VI/5b, Karlsruhe Document Collection.

22. OKL, *Russian Armament Industry*.

23. OKL, Luftwaffenfuehrungsstab, Ia, vom 26. 11. 43, "Befehle und Anordnungen fuer Aufstellung und Einsatz des IV. (Fernkampf) Fliegerkorps, 1943" (High Command of the Luftwaffe, Luftwaffe Operations Staff, of 26 November 1943, "Orders and Disposition for Establishing and Employing the IV [Strategic] Air Corps, 1943"), G/VI/5a, Karlsruhe Document Collection.

24. OKL, *Decisive Targets*.

25. Goerlitz, *Second World War*, *II*, p. 185.

26. Manstein, *Lost Victories*, p. 317. See also Milch Diary, 8 February 1943, 10-11 February 1943.

27. British Air Ministry, *Rise and Fall of the GAF*.

28. Plocher, *Luftwaffe Strength and Organization (East)*.

29. Deichmann, *Report on Zitadelle*.

30. *Ibid.*

31. Plocher, *Luftwaffe Strength and Organization (East)*.

32. General der Artillerie Alfred Jodl, "Auszug aus Vortrag des Chefs des Wehrmachtfuehrungsstabes vom 1. 10. 43" ("Excerpt from a Report of the Chief of the Wehrmacht Operations Staff of 1 October 1943"), G/VI/5b, Karlsruhe Document Collection.

33. Rudel, *Nevertheless*, p. 16.

34. Col. Dr. Ernst Kupfer, "Vortrag des Generals der Schlachtflieger, Oberst Dr. Kupfer am 10. 9. 43 ueber Schlachtflieger, Panzerbekaempfungsflieger, Stoer (Nachtschlacht) Flieger, anlaesslich einer Generalluftzeugmeister-Besprechung unter Vorsitz von Generalfeldmarschall Milch" ("Verbal Report of the General of Fighter-Bombers, Col. Dr. Kupfer, on 10 September 1943, Concerning Fighter-Bomber Fliers, Antitank Fliers, Destroyer [Night Fighter-Bomber] Fliers, on the Occasion of a Meeting of the Chief of Luftwaffe Supply and Procurement under the Chairmanship of Field Marshal Milch"), G/VI/4d, Karlsruhe Document Collection.

35. Ibid., p. 23.

36. Plocher, Luftwaffe Strength and Organization (East).

37. Maj. Hans-Juergen Willers, "Bericht ueber die He-177" ("Report on the He-177"), C/IV/2cc, Karlsruhe Document Collection.

38. Field Marshal Erhard Milch, "Auszug aus einer Besprechung beim Reichsmarschall Goering am 30. 4. 43" ("Excerpt from a Meeting with Reichsmarschall Goering on 30 April 1943"), Karlsruhe Document Collection.

39. General der Aufklaeruhgeflieger, "Auszug aus einer Generalluftzeugmeister-Besprechung am 15. 6. 43" (General of the Reconnaissance Fliers, "Excerpt from a Meeting of the Chief of Luftwaffe Supply and Procurement on 15 June 1943"), Karlsruhe Document Collection.

40. Personal Recollections of the Author.

41. Von Renz, Flak Artillery in Air Fleet Commands.

42. Employment of Flak Artillery.

43. Von Renz, Flak Artillery in Air Fleet Commands.

44. General der Flakartillerie Wolfgang Pickert (Ret.), "Auszuege aus Berichten der 9. Flak Div. 1. 1. 43 bis 10. 5. 43, Krim und Kuban" ("Excerpts from Reports of the 9th Flak Division, 1 January to 10 May 1943"), G/VI/5d, Karlsruhe Document Collection.

45. General der Flakartillerie Walter von Axthelm, "Entwicklung der Flak-Raketen: Auszug aus einem Schreiben vom 16. 9. 54" ("Development of Antiaircraft Rockets: Excerpt from a Letter of 16 September 1954"), Karlsruhe Document Collection.

46. Flakkorps, "Bericht des I. Flak-Korps vom Juli 1943" ("Report of the I Flak Corps from July 1943"), a report drawn from the official war diary of the I Flak Corps, Karlsruhe Document Collection.

47. OKL, Gen. Qu. der Luftwaffe, "Besprechung ueber Bevorratung der deutschen Luftwaffe mit Flugbetriebstoff" ("Meeting on Stocking of Aviation Fuel for the German Luftwaffe"), C/I/5, Karlsruhe Document Collection.

48. Goerlitz, *Second World War*, *I*, p. 411.

49. Chester Wilmot, *The Struggle for Europe*, New York: Harper & Bros., 1952, p. 94. Cited hereafter as Wilmot, *Struggle for Europe*.

50. Major Dereser, Reichs Air Ministry, "Bericht vom 12. 6. 44 ueber Flugbetriebsstoffversorgung" ("Report of 12 June 1944 Concerning the Supplying of Aviation Fuel"), C/I/5, Karlsruhe Document Collection.

51. Wilmot, *Struggle for Europe*, pp. 94-95.

52. OKL, Gen. Qu., 6. Abt., vom 25. 5. 45, "Entwicklung der Flugbetriebsstofflage der deutschen Luftwaffe" (High Command of the Luftwaffe, Quartermaster General, 6th Branch, of 25 May 1945, "Development of the Aviation Fuel Situation of the German Luftwaffe"), C/I/5, Karlsruhe Document Collection.

53. Teske, *Partisan Attacks*.

54. Kless, *Sixth Air Fleet Operations During Zitadelle*.

55. Plocher, *Luftwaffe Strength and Organization (East)*.

56. Vizeadmiral Friedrich Ruge, *Der Seekrieg 1939-1945 (The Sea War 1939-1945)*, Stuttgart: K. F. Koehler Verlag, 1954, pp. 36-38.

57. Seidemann, VIII Air Corps, Donets-Kharkov.

58. Capt. Cristoph Wolf (Ret.), "Die Luftnachrichten bei den Schlachtflieger-Verbaende" ("The Air Signal Troops with the Fighter-Bomber Units"), Karlsruhe Document Collection.

59. OKM, Admiral Nordmeer, Br. B. Nr. 298, g. Kdos. Chefs vom 14. 5. 43, "Operative Grundlagen und Ueberlegungen zum Einsatz der Ueberwasserstreitkraefte gegen England-Russland Geleitzuege" (High Command of the Navy, Admiral Norwegian Sea, Letter Book No. 298, Top Secret Command Matter of 14 May 1943, "Strategic Foundations and Considerations for the Employment of Surface Forces Against England to Russia Convoys"), G/VI/5d, Karlsruhe Document Collection. See also Admiral Norwegian Sea, Navy-Luftwaffe Cooperation.

60. Admiral Norwegian Sea, Navy-Luftwaffe Cooperation. See also OKM, Ia, Br.B. Nr. 640/43, g. Kdos. Chefs vom 30. 6. 43 (High Command of the Navy, Operations, Letter Book No. 640 of 1943, Top Secret Command Matter, of 30 June 1943), G/VI/5d, Karlsruhe Document Collection.

61. Konteradmiral Wilhelm Moessel, Ia Kriegsmarine bei OKL (Verb. Offz.) am 24. 11. 43, "Zusammenwirken der Luftwaffe mit der Kriegsmarine" (Operations Officer of the Navy with the High Command of the Luftwaffe [Liaison Officer] on 24 November 1943 [Statement], "Cooperation of the Luftwaffe with the Navy"), F/IV/3, Karlsruhe Document Collection.

62. OKL, Generalstab der Luftwaffe, Chef des Luftwaffenfuehrungsstabes, Ia (High Command of the Luftwaffe, General Staff of the Luftwaffe, Chief of the Luftwaffe Operations Staff, Op.), a document dated 17 July 1944, reviewing Luftwaffe operations in 1943-44, Karlsruhe Document Collection.

63. Generalleutnant Walter Schwabedissen (Ret.), "Mehrfrontenluftkrieg: Probleme der deutschen Luftwaffe waehrend des Zweiten Weltkriegs" ("Multi-Front Air War: Problems of the German Luftwaffe During the Second World War"), pp. 94-97, a monograph in draft form written for the USAF Historical Division, Karlsruhe Document Collection.

64. General der Flakartillerie Wolfgang Pickert (Ret.), "Flakartillerie im Verband des Heeres" ("Flak Artillery in Army Units"), a study dated 1954, Karlsruhe Document Collection.

65. United States Department of the Army, Operations of Encircled Forces: German Experiences in Russia, DA Pamphlet No. 20-234, a study written by Generalleutnant Oldwig von Natzmer, Washington: Office of the Chief of Military History, EUCOM Historical Division, January 1952, pp. 37-41. Cited hereafter as DA Pam. No. 20-234. See also Goerlitz, Second World War, II, pp. 242-243. See also Tippelskirch, Second World War, pp. 428-430.

66. Tippelskirch, Second World War, pp. 328-329. See also Percy E. Schramm and Hans O. H. Stange, compilers, Geschichte des Zweiten Weltkriegs, Erste Auflag (History of the Second World War, First Edition), Bielefeld: A. G. Ploetz Verlagsbuchhandlung, 1951, p. 47. A historical chronology of World War II. Cited hereafter as Schramm and Stange, Second World War.

67. Schramm and Stange, Second World War, pp. 46-48. See also Tippelskirch, Second World War, pp. 448-450, 530-535.

68. DA Pam. 20-234, pp. 43-45, 48-51.

69. Tippelskirch, Second World War, pp. 437-438. See also Schramm and Stange, Second World War, p. 47.

70. Goerlitz, Second World War, II, pp. 453-455. See also Schramm and Stange, Second World War, p. 48. See also Tippelskirch, Second World War, pp. 544-545.

71. Goerlitz, Second World War, II, pp. 454-455.

72. Tippelskirch, Second World War, pp. 548-549.

73. Goerlitz, Second World War, II, pp. 300-338. See also the remarks on the 20 July 1944 plot in General der Infanterie Dietrich von Choltitz (Ret.), Soldat unter Soldaten (Soldier Among Soldiers), Zuerich: Europa Verlag, 1951, pp. 219-246, 303-305.

74. Earl F. Ziemke, The German Northern Theater of Operations 1940-1945, DA Pamphlet No. 20-271, Washington: Office of the Chief of Military History, Department of the Army, 15 December 1959, pp. 278-279. Cited hereafter as Ziemke, Northern Theater of Operations. See also Erfurth, The Finnish War, pp. 227-230.

75. British Air Ministry, Rise and Fall of the GAF, p. 358. See also Ziemke, Northern Theater of Operations, pp. 279-280. See also Erfurth, The Finnish War, p. 228.

76. Schramm and Stange, Second World War, pp. 49-50.

77. Erfurth, The Finnish War, pp. 269-270. See also Schramm and Stange, Second World War, pp. 52-53, 61.

78. Comment made to the writer by Prof. Dr. Gerhard Ritter of the University of Freiburg during a visit to the German Club, University of Wisconsin, 1952.

APPENDIX I

BIOGRAPHICAL SECTION

Generalleutnant Karl Angerstein

Born in 1890; entered Inf. Regt. No. 87, September 1911; transferred, 2 June 1914, to Flying Corps; served in fighter, bomber units during World War I; served in Air Police units in Prussia, Saxony, 1919-1933; 1934, headed Air Office, Air Administrative Area V in Munich as Major of Police. Transferred, 1935, to Luftwaffe; associated with bomber, dive-bomber forces; awarded Knight's Cross, 1940; 15 June 1943, took command of 1st Air Corps. Later, Luftwaffe Liaison Officer with the Army and Judge on National Military Court. Survived the war.

Marshal of the Soviet Union Ivan K. Bagramyan

Born in Armenia in 1897; volunteered for war service, 1917, and fought on Turkish front; 1918-1920, fought in Red Army in Civil War; General by 1940; 1941, Deputy Chief, Southwestern Front in Battle of Kiev; served later under Timoshenko and Budenny; 1944, Commander, First Baltic Front (Army Group) in Orel, White Russian, East Prussian campaigns. After World War II repressed resistance and opposition groups in Baltic States. Member Latvian Communist Party, 1954; Marshal of Soviet Union, 1955, and Hero, USSR; dubbed by colleagues a strict, rude, unpopular commander.

Field Marshal Ernst Busch

World War I officer; served in 1920's and 30's in Reichswehr. Commanded Sixteenth Army in the West, October 1939-end of March 1941, moving with Sixteenth Army to the East at the end of May. October 1943, relinquished command of Sixteenth Army, assumed command of Army Group Center. Took command of German Forces in the North (Western Front), 15 April 1944. Long suffering from a heart ailment, died in British custody in 1945.

Generaladmiral Rolf Carls

Served with distinction in German Imperial Navy during World War I. By 1936 was Admiral of the Fleet, serving in 1936 and 1937 in Spanish waters. On 1 November 1938 took command of Naval Station Baltic. Assumed command, 21 September 1940, of Naval Command North, which he held until 1 March 1943. Generaladmiral, 19 July 1940. Killed in April 1945 in an Allied air attack on Germany.

General der Flieger Paul Deichmann

Infantry officer and aerial observer, World War I; later Reichswehr officer. Transferred, 1934, to Reichs Air Ministry as technical advisor. Chief of Staff, II Air Corps in the West and in Russia, World War II. August 1942-June 1943, Chief of Staff, Wehrmacht Command South under Field Marshal Kesselring. Subsequently held other important Luftwaffe posts, including command of IV Air Administrative Command (Austria). Recipient of the Knight's Cross. Lent invaluable assistance to USAF Historical Division's GAF Monograph Project in Karlsruhe and to the Fuehrungsakademie of the Bundeswehr. In 1964, he became the first foreigner to receive the Air University Award.

Generaloberst Otto Dessloch

A senior officer, born in Posen, 1889; entered military service, 1910. Commissioned before World War I, and served as pilot and observer throughout the war. Served in the Reichswehr between wars, taking flying training in Russia in 1926 when flying was forbidden in Germany. Generalmajor, 1939, and Commander, Air Division 6. In invasion of Russia commanded I Flak Corps in the East; later served as Commander of Fourth and Sixth Air Fleets. Promoted to Generaloberst, 1 March 1944. Won the Knight's Cross. Survived the war.

Generaloberst Eduard Dietl

In the Bavarian Army in World War I, remaining in service in the new Reichswehr after 1918. Active in the formation of the German Mountain Troop organization. In 1941, after a successful campaign around Narvik, took command of XIX Mountain Corps in northern Norway and Finland. January 1942, assumed command of German Army Command Lapland; June 1942, of the Twentieth Mountain Army. Killed in an air accident, 25 June 1944.

General der Infanterie Waldemar Erfurth

One of the senior German Army officers. Born in 1879; entered Prussian Army in 1897; appointed in 1911 to the Great General Staff, in which he served during World War I. Served in the Reichswehr after the war, became a General by 1927, and retired in 1931 as Generalleutnant of Infantry. Recalled, 1935, and assigned to the Army General Staff; 12 June 1941-11 September 1944, served as German General attached to the Finnish Supreme Command. An officer with great tact and diplomacy, he ended his career as General for Special Assignments with the German High Command.

Generaloberst Nikolaus von Falkenhorst

World War I veteran. Commanded XXI Army Group in Norwegian Campaign, 1940. In April 1941 assumed command of Army Command Norway in Norway and Finland. January 1942, Commander of all Wehrmacht Forces in Norway, a post he held until December 1944. Sentenced to death by a joint British-Norwegian court after World War II, his sentence was commuted to life, then to ten years, and on 23 July 1953 was remitted.

Generalmajor Sigismund Freiherr von Falkenstein

Born in 1903, he enlisted 1 October 1922 in Cavalry Regiment 11 in Erfurt; commissioned in 1925. Took flying, communications training, 1930-33. Transferred, 1933, to Inspectorate of Flying Schools of the Luftwaffe. After additional training, became, 1 October 1936, Chief of a Group of the 3rd Branch, Luftwaffe General Staff. In 1938 commanded the 8th Group, 355th Bomber Wing, and in 1939, the 1st Group, 27th Bomber Wing. On 25 February became Chief of Staff, X Air Corps, and on 6 January 1944, of Air Fleet Reich. He ended his service career as Commander, 3rd Air Division.

General der Infanterie Friedrich Fangohr

A Prussian, born in 1893, he entered the Service in 1916 and served throughout World War I. Served in the Reichswehr, becoming a Captain by 1933. On 10 September 1939 became Operations Officer, 13th Division, and by 1 June 1942 had become Chief of Staff, Fourth Panzer Army. On 15 June 1944 he was transferred to the Fuehrer Reserve. Later served with Army Group North Ukraine, and as Commanding General, 122nd Infantry Division. In 1945 was Commandant of the OKW Liaison Staff at Eisenhower's Headquarters. A strong personality, "with a perceptive view," who was "unshaken in crises."

General der Flieger Martin Fiebig

Trained in the Soviet Union in the late 1920's when flying was proscribed in Germany. A specialist in close support operations. Commanded Air Division 1, and the VIII Air Corps, succeeding von Richthofen. He then bore the heavy responsibility of trying to support Army Group Don and supply the Sixth Army at Stalingrad. December 1942, awarded Oak Leaf to his Knight's Cross. Later led II Air Corps, and ended his wartime service as Commander in Chief of Luftwaffe Command Northeast.

General der Flieger Veit Fischer

Born in Landshut, Bavaria, in 1890, he began his career in 1909 and served in World War I. Between wars he served in the Reichswehr, and took part in flying activities during the time when these were banned by the Versailles Treaty. By 1936 he was a Colonel in the new Luftwaffe, and by 1939, Generalmajor. Talented staff and administrative officer, was in 1941 Chief of Staff for Special Assignments, Air Administrative Area Command 2, and in 1942 Commander of Air Administrative Command, Moscow. Assumed command, 1943, of Field Air Administrative Area Headquarters XXVIII, and at the end of the war was in the Sixth Air Fleet Reserve. He survived the war.

Generalmajor Robert Fuchs

Born in 1895 in Berlin-Reinickendorf; entered Uhlan Regt. No. 1, 6 August 1914, as a war volunteer; commissioned, 7 August 1915. Commanded machine-gun company in the war and remained in the Reichswehr after 1918. In 1926 began flying training and course work for engineering degree. Transferred, 1933, as engineer to the Luftwaffe Technical Office, Testing Branch, Reichs Air Ministry. Commander of the 3rd Group, 153rd Bomber Wing in 1936, he served with the K/88 Group of "Legion Condor" in Spain until 15 August 1937; assumed command of Fighter Wing 26, 29 September 1939 and transferred to the Third Air Fleet Command in 1940. Later was Commander, Fighter Regt. 33, Commanding General of the 22nd Luftwaffe Field Division, and finally Commander of the 1st Air Division.

General der Artillerie Maximilian Fretter-Pico

Born in Karlsruhe in 1892; entered the military service in 1910 and was commissioned 27 January 1912. He served in General Staff and command positions during World War I. Between wars served in the Reichswehr Ministry and in artillery commands. In 1939 served as Chief of Staff, XXIV Corps; April 1941, took command of the 97th Infantry Division. In 1942 he commanded the XXX Corps; General der Artillerie, 1 June 1942. Assumed command of the Sixth Army, 18 August 1944. Mackensen called him "a very good commanding general, swift in decision, clear and sure in his orders, an optimist." Suffered hearing trouble late in the war, was cured and returned to duty as an outstanding commander. Recipient of the Knight's Cross with Oak Leaf and German Cross in Gold.

Reichsmarschall Hermann Wilhelm Goering

Credited with 20 aerial victories in World War I; last Commander of the famous Fighter Wing "Freiherr von Richthofen" No. 1. After the war promoted aviation ventures in Germany and Sweden, avidly supporting the Nazi Party. Wounded and fled to Sweden after Hitler's abortive 1923 "Putsch" in Munich; returned to the Reich and soon became a leading political figure. Commander in Chief of the Luftwaffe; promoted, 1938, to Field Marshal. July 1940, became the only Reichsmarschall in Germany. Removed from his post, 23 April 1945, and only escaped his Fuehrer's wrath by the intervention of his own troops. Tried and sentenced at Nuremberg; took his own life 15 October 1946.

Field Marshal Robert Ritter von Greim

World War I flyer who won 28 aerial victories and received a hereditary title from the King of Bavaria. Helped organize Chiang Kai-shek's Chinese Air Force in the 1920's, and organized the German Commercial Pilots' School in Wuerzburg. Reentered the Service, 1934, as a Major in command of Fighter Wing "Richthofen." In 1939, commanded Air Division 5; 1940-43, commanded the V Air Corps. July 1943, Commander of Luftwaffe Command East (later redesignated Sixth Air Fleet). Field Marshal, 25 April 1945; given Goering's post as Commander in Chief of the (then almost nonexistent) Luftwaffe. Knight's Cross winner. Took his own life in 1945 shortly after his capture by American forces.

Generaloberst Josef Harpe

Harpe had World War I and Reichswehr service, later specializing in armored warfare. In 1935, commanded 3rd Panzer Regiment; by 1 September 1939 was on the staff of the 1st Panzer Brigade, which he commanded later that year. Assumed command, October 1940, of 12th Panzer Division; January 1942, of XXXXI Panzer Corps. Became Commander, 4 November 1943, of the Ninth Army; May 1944, of the Fourth Panzer Army; and August 1944, of Army Group North Ukraine. September 1944, took command of Army Group "A," until transferred 17 January 1945 to the Fuehrer Reserve. Model described him as "an outstanding, well-proven commanding general, . . . equal to any situation."

Obergruppenfuehrer und Generaloberst der Waffen SS Paul Hausser

A veteran of World War I, he remained in the Army during the 1920's, and by 1927 had risen to Colonel in the 10th Saxon Infantry Regiment. In the early 1930's left the Reichswehr and joined the SS.

By 1936, as a Brigadefuehrer, commanded the SS Verfuegungsdivision (later called "Das Reich"). During 1943 commanded the II SS Panzer Corps in the battle for Kharkov and in Combat Zone South. Subsequently commanded the Seventh Army, Army Group Upper Rhine, and Army Group "C." Hausser, the recipient of the Knight's Cross with Oak Leaf and Swords, was an outstanding exception to the rule that SS officers were better politicians than soldiers.

Generaloberst Alexander Holle

Enlisted, November 1915, in Infantry Regiment No. 13, and served in World War I. Later served in the 100,000-Man Army in the 16th Infantry Regiment. Attended the War Academy, 1931. April 1934, assigned to the Luftwaffe; by March 1938 had command of the 1st Group, 3rd Dive-Bomber Wing "Immelmann." January 1940, Chief of Staff, IV Air Corps. Served thereafter as Commander, 26th Bomber Wing; Chief of Staff, Air Commander North (East); Chief of the Luftwaffe Staff in Greece; Commander, X Air Corps, Fourth Air Fleet, and Luftwaffe Command West. From December 1944 until the war's end, Holle commanded the German Luftwaffe (IV Air Corps) in Denmark.

Generaloberst Karl Hollidt

Born, 1891, in Speyer, he entered the Service in 1909 and served during World War I and between wars as an infantry officer. By 1938 he was a Generalmajor. September 1939, commanded the 52nd Infantry Division, and later was Chief of Staff, V Corps; Commander in Chief, East, Ninth Army; and Commander of the 50th Division. In 1942, commanded the XVII Corps and Army Force Hollidt. March 1943, took command of the Sixth Army, then went to the Fuehrer Reserve until 1945, when he was recalled for service with Reichsleiter Bormann as Representative of the Gauleiter of Rhineland-Westphalia. Manstein called him a "solid personality, in whom one could place confidence."

Generaloberst Hermann Hoth

A World War I veteran who participated in the Polish and Western campaigns early in World War II, and on 22 June 1941 commanded the Third Panzer Army in Russia. October 1941, assumed command of Seventeenth Army; June 1942, took charge of the Fourth Panzer Army (Eastern Front). November 1943, Commander of German Forces Erzgebirge (Ore Mountains) in Bohemia. Tried in Nuremberg and sentenced to 15 years' imprisonment at Landsberg.

Generaloberst Erwin Jaenecke

A World War I veteran who served after 1918 in the Reichswehr. By 1939 a Generalmajor. Then served in various staff positions until 1 February 1942, when he took command of the 389th Infantry Division. In November he assumed command of the IV Corps; 1 April 1943, of the LXXXVI Corps; and 3 June, of the Seventh Army, which he commanded until sent to the Fuehrer Reserve, 1 May 1944. A letter to Hitler, describing Germany's adverse position, led to his discharge from the Army in January 1945. General Schoerner noted in 1944, "For a long time now he [Jaenecke] has not had the necessary faith that he could successfully accomplish his difficult tasks."

Generaloberst Hans Jeschonnek

Served in World War I; between wars, served in the Reichswehr and promoted aviation groups. September 1933, transferred to the Luftwaffe as a Captain. By February 1939 had become Chief of the Luftwaffe General Staff. Although a protégé of General Wever, Jeschonnek remained basically an opponent of strategic airpower. Differed at times with Goering, and sometimes even with Hitler, whom he considered to be a genius. His appointment as Chief of the Luftwaffe General Staff represents the first clear break with the older traditions of the Reichswehr. The circumstances surrounding his suicide, 19 August 1943, provide an interesting insight into command and policy problems in the Luftwaffe.

Generaloberst Alfred Jodl

Born in 1890 and served in World War I in the artillery. Remained in Bavarian artillery units in the Reichswehr until 1929, when he began to carry out staff assignments. A Generalmajor, 1 April 1939, he became Chief of the Wehrmacht Operations Staff, 19 July 1940, a position he held until the war's end. Generaloberst, 30 January 1944. He was tried in the OKW trials in Nuremberg and hanged, 16 October 1946.

General der Flieger Josef Kammhuber

Born in 1896 in Upper Bavaria, he began his military career in 1914 and served in World War I. Following the war, served until 1929 as an infantry officer, then transferring to the flying service. May to September 1930, took special training in Russia when flying was outlawed in Germany by the Versailles Treaty. In 1931 again took flying training in Russia, and in 1933 transferred to the Luftwaffe. Rising rapidly, he was Chief of Staff, 2nd Air Wing by 1939; in 1940, Commander of the 51st Bomber Wing, and in July, of the 1st Bomber Wing. July 1940, took command of the 1st Night Fighter Division; 15 September 1943, of all night fighters; and January 1944, of the Fifth Air Fleet. At the war's end commanded all jet units. Recipient of the Knight's Cross. General der Flieger, 30 January 1943. Served after World War II as the first Commander (Inspector) of the West German Air Force, retiring in 1962.

Field Marshal Wilhelm Keitel

Service prior to and during World War I; remained in service in the new Reichswehr. By September 1939, had risen to the post of Chief of the High Command of the Wehrmacht, an office he held until the end of World War II. Hitler found him useful chiefly because he could rely upon him to be a "Yes man," and one who might help to keep the old Reichswehr officers in line; held in low esteem by many of the professional officer corps. Tried and convicted in the OKW trials at Nuremberg, and executed on 16 October 1946.

Generaloberst Alfred Keller

Won the highest decorations during World War I as Commander of Bomber Wing I, and was an "old eagle," having flown before 1914. Advanced civil aviation enterprises in the 1920's; in 1934 returned to the Army as a Major. March 1935, transferred to the Luftwaffe; March 1939, took command of the IV Air Corps; and from 22 June 1941 to 28 July 1943 commanded the First Air Fleet in Russia. Thereafter until the war's end, served as Corps Leader of the National Socialist Flying Corps (NSFK). Survived the war.

General der Panzertruppe Franz Werner Kempf

Born in Koenigsberg in 1886, Kempf began his military career before World War I; served in that war and in the Reichswehr in the 1920's and 1930's. September 1939, commanded Panzer Division Kempf; in November, the 6th Panzer Division; January 1941, the XXXXVIII Corps; and on 20 February 1943, assumed command of Army Force Kempf, which he led until 14 August, when he was retired from active service. Winner of the Knight's Cross with Oak Leaf. Manstein described him as a better corps commander than an army commander.

Field Marshal Ewald von Kleist

Member of a famous Prussian family, 31 of whom had won the coveted Pour le Mérite. Served in World War I; transferred from cavalry forces to armored units after the war. Retired, 28 February 1938. Recalled as Commander of the XXII Army Corps, 1 September 1939. Served in the West and in the Balkans in armored units. Took part in the invasion of Russia at the head of the 1st Panzer Group; November 1942, assumed command of Army Group "A" (East), with which he served until March 1944. Kleist was delivered to Tito's government in 1946 by the Americans, and in 1948 to the Soviet Union, where he is reported to have died in a Russian prison.

Field Marshal Guenther von Kluge

Mountain artillery officer, World War I. Between wars served in the Reichswehr. Commanded the Fourth Army in Poland, in the West, and along the German-Soviet border. December 1941, Commander of Army Group Center, which post he held until his transfer in October 1943 to the Fuehrer Reserve. From July 1944 to August 1944, commanded Army Groups "B" and "D" in the West. An avowed enemy of Hitler, he participated in the 20 July 1944 plot. Summoned to appear in Berlin, obviously for Gestapo interrogation, von Kluge took poison on 19 August 1944.

General der Flieger Karl Koller

Born in 1898 in Bavaria, he entered the Bavarian Army in 1914 and served throughout World War I, part of the time in the flying service. Left the service in 1919 and served in Bavarian State Police (air units). Transferred in 1935 to Luftwaffe; by 1938 was Chief of Operations Branch, Luftwaffe Group 3; and in January 1941 became Chief of Staff, Third Air Fleet. September 1943, became Chief of Luftwaffe Operations Staff. Promoted 1 August 1944 to General der Flieger, he became on 27 November 1944 Chief of the General Staff of the Luftwaffe, which position he held until the war's end. Survived the war.

Marshal of the Soviet Union Ivan Koniev

Born in 1897 in Kirov area of peasant stock, he worked in revolutionary activities from 1914 through World War I, helping to suppress anti-Red peasants in 1918, and was Commissar of Armored Train No. 102 during the Civil War. After attending various military schools and holding important posts, he commanded, December 1941, the Kalinin

Front and helped throw back German forces before Moscow. From the summer of 1942 to the spring of 1943, commanded army forces in Velikiye Luki and Rzhev areas, halted German drives across the Don in 1943, and led counterattacks in 1943 at Kharkov and Belgorod. February 1944, commanded Second Ukrainian Front; participated in the drive to the Oder at Breslau, and to Torgau on the Elbe, where he met U. S. forces. In 1955, commanded armed forces of Warsaw Pact States. A great favorite of Stalin and twice Hero of the Soviet Union.

Generaloberst Guenther Korten

Served in the First World War. By 1939 was one of the leading personalities in the Luftwaffe. September and October 1939, served as Chief of Staff of the Fourth Air Fleet in Poland; early 1940 to July 1940, Chief of the General Staff of the Third Air Fleet (West); April 1941, Chief of the General Staff of the Fourth Air Fleet (Balkans), later in Russia. From July 1942, he held the commands of the I Air Corps, Air Force Command Don, First Air Fleet; August 1943, became Chief of the General Staff, Luftwaffe, a post he held until 22 July 1944. Seriously wounded in Count von Stauffenberg's bomb attempt on Hitler's life, July 1944, and died two days later.

General der Flieger Werner Kreipe

A Hanoverian, born in 1904, who entered the military service in December 1925. One of the youngest of World War II generals. Took part in Hitler's "Putsch" of 1923. Temporarily released from the Army in 1930 for flying training in Bavaria. Transferred in October 1934 to the Luftwaffe as a Captain; began climb through staffs of Reichs Air Ministry and Luftwaffe General Staff. Liaison officer, 1936, to Italian Air Force; 1937, to Belgain Air Force; visited Britain with State Secretary Milch. Commanded 2nd Bomber Wing in France, 1940. November 1941, became Chief of Staff, 1st Air Corps; 24 April 1942, of Air Command Don;. July 1943, of Commander of Training. On 1 August 1944 became Chief of Staff of the Luftwaffe; 5 December became Commandant of Air War College, Berlin. After World War II served with Federal Ministry of Traffic, Bonn.

Field Marshal Georg von Kuechler

Served in World War I and in the Reichswehr, and held various administrative posts until World War II. Commanded Third Army in Poland, Eighteenth Army in the West; directed the Eighteenth Army in the invasion of the Soviet Union in 1941. January 1942 until January 1944,

Commander of Army Group North. Sentenced to 20 years' imprisonment at Nuremberg; freed, February 1955.

Colonel Dr. Ernst Kuehl

Born in Breslau in 1888; served in artillery in World War I. Active in flying between wars. Transferred in 1935 as reserve officer to Luftwaffe. Squadron officer and Operations Officer, 55th Bomber Wing in Poland, France, Battle of Britain, 1939-1941; Commander, II Group, 55th Bomber Wing, spring 1941; Commander, 55th Bomber Wing, September 1942; Commander Air Command Norwegian Sea, September 1943; February 1944, took command of 3rd Air Division; June-July 1944, with 4th Air Brigade, experimenting with strategic operations (He-177's); August 1944, Air Commander Trondheim; January 1945, Commander, 5th Air Division (Narvik area). Surrendered to British at war's end.

Colonel (Reserve) Dr. Ernst Kupfer

Born on 2 July 1907, he was one of the younger generation of senior officers of the Luftwaffe in 1942-43. Winner of the Knight's Cross with Oak Leaf. He was killed in action on 6 November 1943 while commanding Fighter-Bomber Forces (East).

General der Gebirgstruppe Hubert Lanz

Born in 1896 in Wuerttemberg, Lanz served in the cavalry during World War I and in the Reichswehr between the wars. At the outbreak of World War II he was Chief of Staff, V Corps. February 1940, became Chief of Staff, XVIII Corps, and in October, Commander, 1st Mountain Division. On 3 February 1943 took command of Army Group Lanz; on 25 June 1943, of Army Group "A" (during commander's leave); and on 25 August, XXII Mountain Corps. Recipient of the Knight's Cross with Oak Leaf. Generaloberst Ruoff describes him as, "Clever, swift, and brave officer."

Generaloberst Georg Lindemann

World War I veteran and of the 100,000-Man Army. After holding numerous important staff and command positions, on 19 January 1942 assumed command of the Eighteenth Army and Army Group North (Eastern Front), which position he held until 3 July 1944. January 1945 until the end of World War II was Commander in Chief of the Wehrmacht in Denmark (renamed 6 May 1945 as Army Force Lindemann).

Generaloberst Eberhard von Mackensen

Born in Bromberg in 1889, son of the famous German Field Marshal August von Mackensen. A veteran of service before and during World War I. In the first year of World War II he became Chief of Staff of the Twelfth Army. On 15 January 1941 assumed command of the III Corps, and on 21 November 1942 took command of the First Panzer Army. Generaloberst, 6 July 1943; November 1943, Commander of the Fourteenth Army in northern Italy until 5 June 1944. Sentenced to death by a British court in 1947, then to life, and on 2 October 1952 was freed.

General der Flieger Alfred Mahnke

With service dating back to 1908, he was one of the "old eagles," having flown prior to 1914. Served in World War I as a flyer, and in the air arm of the Prussian State Police after 1918. Transferred, 1935, to the Luftwaffe in grade of Colonel. Mainly connected with Air Administrative Commands during World War II, he assumed command on 3 November 1942 of the Fourth Air Fleet in Russia, and on 15 February 1943 of Air Division Donets. Later served in the Air Administrative Command South, and with the Luftwaffe Reception Staff North. General der Flieger, 1 September 1943. Survived the war.

Field Marshal Carl Gustav Freiherr Mannerheim

Finnish statesman and military leader. One of the top cavalry officers in the Russian Imperial Army prior to and during World War I, and was a member of the Imperial War Council. December 1917, left the Czar's service and took command of the Finnish Army of Liberation; joined by German units, drove the Russians from Finnish soil. Doctor of Philosophy; made substantial contributions in the field of geography. Commander in Chief of Finnish Armed Forces during Russo-Finnish War of 1939-40 and World War II. Later, President of Finland.

Field Marshal Fritz Erich von Manstein

Served in World War I. Chief of Staff, Army Group South (von Rundstedt), 1939; September 1941, assumed command of the Eleventh Army in the East; November 1942, Commander, Army Group Don, and February 1943, of Army Group South. Rated by many as the best strategist in the German Army during World War II. On 30 March 1944, following a final disagreement with the Fuehrer, Manstein resigned. His Verlorene Siege (Lost Victories) is one of the best military histories of German operations in World War II.

General der Panzertruppe Hasso von Manteuffel

One of the most highly decorated German ground force officers in World War II. Born in 1897 in Brandenburg. Served in World War I and the Reichswehr. After 1941 he was, generally, on the Eastern Front. Earned an enviable reputation as commander of panzer and panzer grenadier units. Took command on 13 July 1942 of the 7th Panzer Grenadier Brigade, and on 20 August of the 7th Panzer Division. Also commanded Panzer Grenadier Division "Gross Deutschland," 20 January to 4 September 1944, when he took command of the Fifth Panzer Army. March 1945, became Commander, Third Panzer Army. Winner of the Knight's Cross with Oak Leaf, Swords, and Diamonds. Generaloberst Reinhardt called him, "A most outstanding command personality in every respect, and a brave soldier." Survived the war.

General der Flieger Rudolf Meister

Aerial observer during World War I; served in Field Flying Detachment 420 of the Free Corps (Freikorps) after the war. Trained in the Soviet Union in military aviation, 1928-1930. Served with various schools and in the General Staff of the Luftwaffe. December 1939, Chief of the General Staff, I Air Corps; October 1940, Chief of Staff of the VIII Air Corps; September 1943, Commander, IV Air Corps. Became Commander of Luftwaffe Forces in Denmark, October 1944, and finished his service as Chief of the Luftwaffe Personnel Office.

Field Marshal Erhard Milch

Served during World War I as a member of Fighter Group 6. After the war, left the service and entered private aviation business. February 1933, appointed State Secretary of Aviation with rank of Colonel in the Luftwaffe. Field Marshal, July 1940. A competent technical officer with great talent in this field, and a person of boundless energy. Until his dismissal by Hitler over the use of jet aircraft, was the number two man in the German Air Force. Survived the war and lives in retirement.

Field Marshal Walter Model

Served in World War I and in the Reichswehr. September 1939, Chief of Staff, IV Corps; October 1939, Chief of Staff of the Sixteenth Army; November 1939, commanded the 3rd Panzer Division; October 1941, commanded XXXXI Corps; January 1942, the Ninth Army (with the Second Panzer Army as well as of July 1942); January 1944, commanded Army Group North in Russia; March 1944, Army Group North Ukraine;

and June 1944, Army Group Center. Holder of Knight's Cross with Oak Leaf, Swords, and Diamonds. An ardent Nazi. August 1944 until end of the war, Commander, Army Groups "B" and "D" in the West.

Generalleutnant Andreas Nielsen

A veteran of World War I and Reichswehr service; participated in the Hitler "Putsch" in Munich, November 1923; 1928, went to Russia for flight training; 1939, to Spain as a bomber group commander in "Legion Condor." October 1940, became Chief of Staff, Fifth Air Fleet (Norway and Finland); December 1943, German Luftwaffe Commander Denmark. May 1944, Chief of Staff, Air Fleet Reich; assisted in demobilization of Luftwaffe in northern Germany, 1945. After two years of British imprisonment, was released and became one of the principal contributors to the USAF Historical Division's GAF Monograph Project. Died in April 1957.

General der Flakartillerie Paul Pavel

Flak officer with broad experience in the South, Southeast, and the East. Commanded the 2nd Battalion, 3rd Flak Regiment, at Weimar in 1938, and went into the war with that unit. Later commanded Flak regiments and brigades, including in 1943 command of X Flak Brigade of the 12th Flak Division. January 1944 to May 1945, commanded 19th Flak Division.

General der Flieger Kurt Plfugbeil

World War I flyer; in the Reichswehr in 1920. March 1928, went to Russia to receive bombing training. Early 1930's, served in Germany and Italy; 1935, officially transferred to the Luftwaffe. August 1939, Commander of the VIII Air Corps; January to August 1940, directed the Air Administrative Command which served Luftwaffe units in France and Belgium. Thereafter, until September 1943, commanded the IV Air Corps, much of which time he served in the East. Completed his service as Commander, First Air Fleet. Died May 1955.

Generalleutnant Wolfgang Pickert

Served on both Eastern and Western Fronts during World War I; with the Reichswehr after 1918. Held various command and staff positions during 1920's and early 30's. Joined the Flak Artillery arm of the Luftwaffe, 1935, and by 1937 was Inspector of Flak Forces of the Reichs Air Ministry. From 1939 to April 1940, commanded Rhine-Ruhr Air

Defense District. In French Campaign was Chief of Staff, I Flak Corps. Served as Chief of Staff, Air Fleet Reich, until May 1942, when he took command of the 9th Flak Division (Stalingrad, Kuban Bridgehead, Crimea). Commander, III Flak Corps (Normandy, Ardennes, Rhine), 1944; Commanding General of Flak Forces, Luftwaffe High Command, March 1945; and in April was present at capitulation negotiations of Army Group Italy. Winner of Knight's Cross, Pickert contributed after the war to the USAF Historical Division's GAF Monograph Project.

Generalleutnant Hermann Plocher

See "About the Author" in the front section of this study.

General of the Red Army Markian M. Popov

Veteran of Red Army service during the Civil War, and in the Russo-Finnish War of 1939-40. Commanded rifle division at the outbreak of war with Germany, 1941. Commander of the Bryansk Front after the summer of 1943 in collaboration with Sokolovski's Western Front, leading to the capture of Orel and Bryansk. In 1944-45 fought in White Russian and East Prussian operations. Later served with Ministry of Defense in Moscow. Member of the Supreme Soviet, 1954.

Generaloberst Erhard Raus

Born in 1889; entered the Army in 1905; served during World War I and later in the 100,000-Man Army. In 1939, Chief of Staff and Deputy Commander, XVII Corps; July 1940, Commander of Infantry Regiment 243; May 1941, Commander, 6th Rifle Brigade; November 1941, Commander, 6th Panzer Division; February to July 1943 in Fuehrer Reserve. In July 1943 took command of the II Corps; 5 November, of the XXXXVII Panzer Corps; 10 December 1943, Commander of Fourth Panzer Army; April 1944, Commander, First Panzer Army (East); and from August 1944 until the war's end commanded the Third Panzer Army (East). Survived the war.

General der Flakartillerie Richard Reimann

Served during the First World War. September 1939, Commander of Flak Regiment 8; commanding officer of the Luftwaffe Flak School, 1940; Commander of the I Flak Corps, 1941; Commander of the 18th Flak Division (Motorized), 1942; early 1943, Inspector of Flak Artillery Forces in the Eastern Theater of Operations. In 1943, again took command of the

I Flak Corps. One of the most talented antiaircraft officers in the Wehrmacht, and winner of the Knight's Cross.

Generaloberst Hans Reinhardt

Service during World War I and the Reichswehr. By October 1941 he had become Commander of the Third Panzer Army, which he led until August 1944. Served until 1 January 1945 as Commander of Army Group Center. January 1945, assumed command of Army Group North, a post he held just two days. Sentenced in 1948 at Nuremberg to 15 years' imprisonment; July 1952, pardoned and released.

Generalmajor Franz Reuss

Born, 1904, in Augsburg. Began his service in the 1920's with the Bavarian State Police; transferred, 1935, to the Army, serving in the cavalry. Attended the War Academy in Berlin, 1936-38; transferred, autumn 1938, to the Luftwaffe; took flying training. In 1939, commanded squadron in Fighter Wing 51; January 1940, assumed command of the 2nd Group, 76th Bomber Wing; wounded in France; August 1940 to February 1941, audited courses at Air War College, Berlin; June 1941, became Operations Officer, IV Air Corps; December 1942, Chief of Staff of the II Luftwaffe Field Corps (East). After September 1943, commanded 4th Air Division until capitulation. Generalmajor, 1 June 1944.

Field Marshal Dr. Ing. Wolfram Freiherr von Richthofen

Cousin of the famous Baron Manfred Richthofen, Wolfram also served in Fighter Wing No. 1 during World War I and scored 8 aerial victories. Served in the Reichswehr; during 1920's earned his doctorate in engineering at Hanover. In Spain with "Legion Condor," which he commanded, 1938-39. Served in Polish and Western Campaigns. June 1941, Commander, VIII Air Corps in the East; July 1942, assumed command of Fourth Air Fleet. In 1943 took command of the Second Air Fleet. Promoted to Field Marshal, February 1943. Once an enemy of dive bombing, but later became a staunch advocate of such operations, which he carried out so effectively in southern Russia. Died of a lingering illness in Austria, July 1945.

Generalleutnant Herbert J. Rieckhoff

World War I veteran, born just before the turn of the century. Active in police air units in the 1920's and early 1930's. Transferred to the Luftwaffe, and by 1939 was Lt. Colonel and Operations Officer of the

Second Air Fleet, Braunschweig; 1940, Commander, 30th Bomber Wing; later, Commander of 2nd Bomber Wing. In 1941 became Chief of Staff, First Air Fleet (Koenigsberg), and served with unit in the East, acting also as air commander. In 1943 became Commander, 3rd Air Division (East) and later student at Air War Academy; Deputy Commander, Air War Academy, Berlin-Gatow, 1944; ended his service as Air Commander, Air Administrative Area V.

Generalmajor Hans-Detlef Herhudt von Rohden

Began his service before World War I, and was trained after the war in General Staff work. In 1935, transferred to the Luftwaffe, serving with the Reichs Air Ministry; 1939, commanded bomber group in Schwerin; later Chief of Staff, IX Air Corps in West. For three months in 1941 was Chief of Staff, First Air Fleet (East); 1942, Chief of the General Staff, Fourth Air Fleet. He served in 1943 as instructor in the Air War Academy, and in 1944-45 as Chief of the 8th (Military Science) Branch of the General Staff of the Luftwaffe. Known afterward for some of his historical contributions to the history of airpower, much of his work was unfinished. Died, 17 December 1952, in the Taunus Mountains.

Generalleutnant Ernst-August Roth

Born in Potsdam in 1898 and served in World War I in the German Imperial Navy, part of the time as a flyer. Remained in the Navy after the war, visiting a number of countries, and was on duty at the Disarmament Conference at Geneva, 1924 to 1927; 1927-28 served aboard the battleship *Schlesien*; later served with Reichs Air Ministry until his transfer to the Luftwaffe, 1935; September 1939, commanded Coastal Flying Group 106 Norderney; 1940, served in Norwegian Campaign as Air Transport Chief and Commander, Bomber Wing 40; Commander, 40th Bomber Wing in Russia, 1941. Between 1941 and 1944 served as Air Commander Sicily, Air Commander Lofoten Islands, and Air Commander Kirkenes; 1944-45 was Commanding General of the Luftwaffe in Norway. Generalleutnant, January 1945.

Colonel Hans-Ulrich Rudel

A Silesian Pastor's son who began his service in 1936. Commissioned in 1938, he was assigned to a dive-bomber group; strategic reconnaissance pilot in Polish Campaign; also served in the West. On 22 June 1941, again a dive-bomber pilot, he won Germany's highest decorations. Colonel, 1 January 1945. He flew 2,530 combat missions over the most critical areas of the front, destroyed 519 tanks (enough for an armored corps), numerous fortifications, the 23, 500-ton Soviet battleship Marat, and many smaller vessels. In the East, 1941-45, he was wounded five times, losing a leg the last time, but returned to action. Already the recipient of the Knight's Cross with Oak Leaf, Swords, and Diamonds, Hitler devised for him the unique award of the Golden Oak Leaf. Rudel survived the war and went to Argentina, where he works for an aircraft firm.

Generaloberst Richard Ruoff

A Wuerttemberger, born in 1883, his service was continuous from 1903 to 1943. At the outbreak of war in September 1939, commanded the V Corps. On 12 January 1941 assumed command of the Fourth Panzer Army; May 1942, of the Seventeenth Army, which he commanded until transferred for health reasons to the Fuehrer Reserve, 25 June 1943. Generaloberst, 1 April 1942. Held the Knight's Cross.

Admiral Hubert Schmundt

Began his service in the German Imperial Navy, 1908, and served continuously until 1945. August 1939, Chief of Staff, Naval Group Command East and, concurrently, Commander, Naval Forces in Bay of Danzig. April 1940, Commander, Naval Reconnaissance Forces; August 1940, Commander of Cruisers; November 1941, Commander, Naval Command Norwegian Sea in operations against Anglo-American convoys bound for Murmansk and Arkhangelsk and Allied raiding parties striking at German positions in Norway. September 1942, Chief of Naval Ordnance Office; March 1943, Commander, Naval Command Baltic; and June 1944, Special Purposes Officer for the Navy. Won Knight's Cross, 1940.

Generaladmiral Otto Schniewind

Entered German Imperial Navy, 1907; served in both world wars and between wars. October 1938 to June 1941, Chief of Staff of Naval Operations; October 1938 to June 1939, also held post of Chief, Naval Command Office; June 1941 to July 1944, Fleet Admiral, and March 1943 to May 1944, also Commander, Naval Group Command North; August 1944, sent to Fuehrer Reserve, from which he was recalled to active duty in April 1945. Recipient of Knight's Cross. Tried at Nuremberg and freed, October 1948.

Generalleutnant Adalbert Schulz

World War I veteran who remained in the Reichswehr during the 1920's and early 30's. Held various command and staff positions in the Wehrmacht, mainly in armored units. Demonstrated outstanding leadership ability in action, for which he was decorated with the Knight's Cross and the Oak Leaf to that award. Killed in action in 1943 while in command of the 7th Panzer Division.

General der Flieger Hans Seidemann

Barely missed World War I service, having entered the Cadet School before the end of the war. Later served in infantry units in Potsdam and Munich. Transferred to the Luftwaffe, 1935; served in the General Staff. From 1 December 1938 to 30 June 1939 was Chief of Staff of "Legion Condor" in Spain; 1939, Chief of Staff, VIII Air Corps; August 1940, Chief of Staff, Second Air Fleet; 1943-44, Air Commander Africa and Commander, Luftwaffe Forces Tunis; 1945, commanded the VIII Air Corps. Knight's Cross winner. Promoted to General der Flieger in March 1945.

Generalleutnant Rainer Stahel

One of the most remarkable ground combat leaders of the war. Born in 1892, he served in World War I, the latter part as commander of a machine-gun company in the Royal Prussian Light Infantry Regiment No. 27, a volunteer unit that helped the Finns achieve their independence from Russia. Enlisted in Finnish Army and by 1933 was Chief of Finnish Defense Forces. Returned to Germany in 1934 as Flak officer in the Luftwaffe; became specialist in "breakout" operations in the East; distinguished himself many times, including at Wilna, Warsaw, and Bucharest; also trouble-shooter in Rome and Sicily during the war. Broadly educated, especially gifted in Scandinavian languages, but was never used in that area during World War II. Won Knight's Cross with Oak Leaf and Swords. Captured by the Russians in 1945, and reported by them to have died just prior to his scheduled release in 1956.

Generalleutnant (Reserve) Hyazinth Count Strachwitz von Gross-Zauche und Camminetz

A Silesian, born in 1893, with service in World War I and the Reichswehr. Fought in Polish and French Campaigns. Received Knight's Cross in Russia, 1941; 1942, received Oak Leaf to this award. January

1943, assumed command of Panzer Regiment "Gross Deutschland." General Hube said of him in 1942, "A spirited person with exceptional leadership ability for a reserve officer." June 1943, General Balck described him as, "A self-confident person, with exemplary character as an officer, industrious, with much initiative, generous, outstandingly brave, and with a clear view for operational possibilities." Late 1944, suffered pulmonary embolism, was in critical condition, but recovered and returned to action. January 1945, commanded panzer forces, Army Group Center. Survived the war.

Generaloberst Hans-Juergen Stumpff

Military service prior to and during World War I, and a General Staff officer in the Reichswehr. Transferred, 1933, to the Luftwaffe as Chief of the Personnel Office, Reichs Air Ministry. June 1937 to January 1939, Chief of the General Staff of the Luftwaffe. During the first part of 1940, commanded the First Air Fleet. May 1940, Commander, Fifth Air Fleet (Norway and Finland) until November 1943. Later commanded defense units of the Reich until the capitulation.

General der Flieger Bernhard Waber

Born in Austria in 1884, served in World War I, and integrated into the German Luftwaffe, 1938. August 1939 to October 1941, Commander of Air Administrative Area VIII (Polish area); March 1942, promoted to General der Flieger; commanded Air Administrative Command Kiev, 1942-43; 1944, German Luftwaffe Northern Balkans. Court-martialled for having permitted illegal black market and other activities to go on within his command, as well as for personally engaging in large-scale looting and other similar activities, for which he was sentenced and executed by firing squad, 6 February 1945.

General der Artillerie Walter Warlimont

Served in the German Army in World War I and in the Reichswehr. In 1929 was Liaison Officer on duty with the U. S. Army in the United States; 1936, went to Spain at outbreak of Civil War to head up Hitler's assistance program to Franco, which he handled with great skill and dispatch; 1937, held command positions; November 1938, appointed Chief, National Defense Branch, High Command of the Wehrmacht and Deputy Commissioner for the Chief of the Wehrmacht Operations Office; January 1939, became Deputy Chief of the Wehrmacht Operations Staff under Jodl, a position he held until released for health reasons, 6 September 1944.

Said to have been the mind behind the Wehrmacht Operations Staff and the vehicle through whom Jodl reached the ear of Hitler. Sentenced to life imprisonment in the OKW trials at Nuremberg. This was later commuted to 18 years, and remitted in the 1950's.

Marshal of the Soviet Union Andrei I. Yeremenko

Born in 1893 in the Ukraine. Fought in World War I, defecting to revolutionaries later in the war; continued in Red Army Service through the Civil War. In 1941 commanded an army on the Western Front under Zhukov; autumn 1942, Commander in Chief, Stalingrad Front; 1943 (after fall of Stalingrad), commanded the Smolensk Front, and later in year Second Baltic Front; 1944, commanded forces in the Black Sea area; 1945, Commander, Fourth Ukrainian Front, ending war in Czechoslovakia. One of the senior commanders of the Red Army and Minister of Defense, U.S.S.R. in the 1950's. Member of Supreme Soviet, 1946, 1950, 1954.

Generaloberst Kurt Zeitzler

An infantryman, born in 1895, with service from 1914 to 1945. September 1939 was Chief of Staff, XXII Corps and also the First Panzer Army; April 1942, Chief of Staff, Army Group West; September 1942 became Chief of Staff of the German Army, in which capacity he served until his transfer to the Fuehrer Reserve, August 1944. Kleist characterizes him as a "strong personality, with a will of iron and incredible industry." Often out of accord with Hitler, he was discharged from service, 31 January 1945.

General der Panzertruppe Hans v. Zorn

A veteran of World War I service in the Bavarian Army, he served in the Reichswehr between wars. By 1928 he was on the staff of the 7th Bavarian Infantry Division. Rising in staff and command positions, he climaxed his career as Commanding General, XXXXVI Panzer Corps (Eastern Front), in the course of which duty he was killed in action, 2 August 1943. Knight's Cross winner.

APPENDIX II

LIST OF GAF MONOGRAPH PROJECT STUDIES

I. Published

Study No.	Title
153	The German Air Force versus Russia, 1941
154	The German Air Force versus Russia, 1942
155	The German Air Force versus Russia, 1943
163	German Air Force Operations in Support of the Army
167	German Air Force Airlift Operations
173	The German Air Force General Staff
175	The Russian Air Force in the Eyes of German Commanders
176	Russian Reactions to German Air Power
177	Airpower and Russian Partisan Warfare
189	Historical Turning Points in the German Air Force War Effort

II. To Be Published (in approximately the following order)

174	Command and Leadership in the German Air Force (Goering, Milch, Jeschonnek, Udet, Weber)
161	The German Air Force versus the Allies in the Mediterranean
158	The German Air Force versus the Allies in the West (1)

Study No.	Title
159	The German Air Force versus the Allies in the West (2)
178	Problems of Fighting a Three-Front Air War
164	German Air Force Air Defense Operations
185	Effects of Allied Air Attacks on German Air Force Bases and Installations

III. Not To Be Published but Will Be Made Available to Researchers in the Historical Division Archives

Study No.	Title
150	The German Air Force in the Spanish War
151	The German Air Force in Poland
152	The German Air Force in France and the Low Countries
156	The Battle of Britain
157	Operation Sea Lion
162	The Battle of Crete
165	German Air Force Air Interdiction Operations
166	German Air Force Counter Air Operations
168	German Air Force Air-Sea Rescue Operations
169	Training in the German Air Force
170	Procurement in the German Air Force
171	Intelligence in the German Air Force
172	German Air Force Medicine

Study No.	Title
179	Problems of Waging a Day and Night Defensive Air War
180	The Problem of the Long-Range Night Intruder Bomber
181	The Problem of Air Superiority in the Battle with Allied Strategic Air Forces
182	Fighter-Bomber Operations in Situations of Air Inferiority
183	Analysis of Specialized Anglo-American Techniques
184	Effects of Allied Air Attacks on German Divisional and Army Organizations on the Battle Fronts
186	The German Air Force System of Target Analysis
187	The German Air Force System of Weapons Selection
188	German Civil Air Defense
190	The Organization of the German Air Force High Command and Higher Echelon Headquarters Within the German Air Force
194	Development of German Antiaircraft Weapons and Equipment up to 1945
Extra Study	The Radio Intercept Service of the German Air Force

LIST OF MAPS

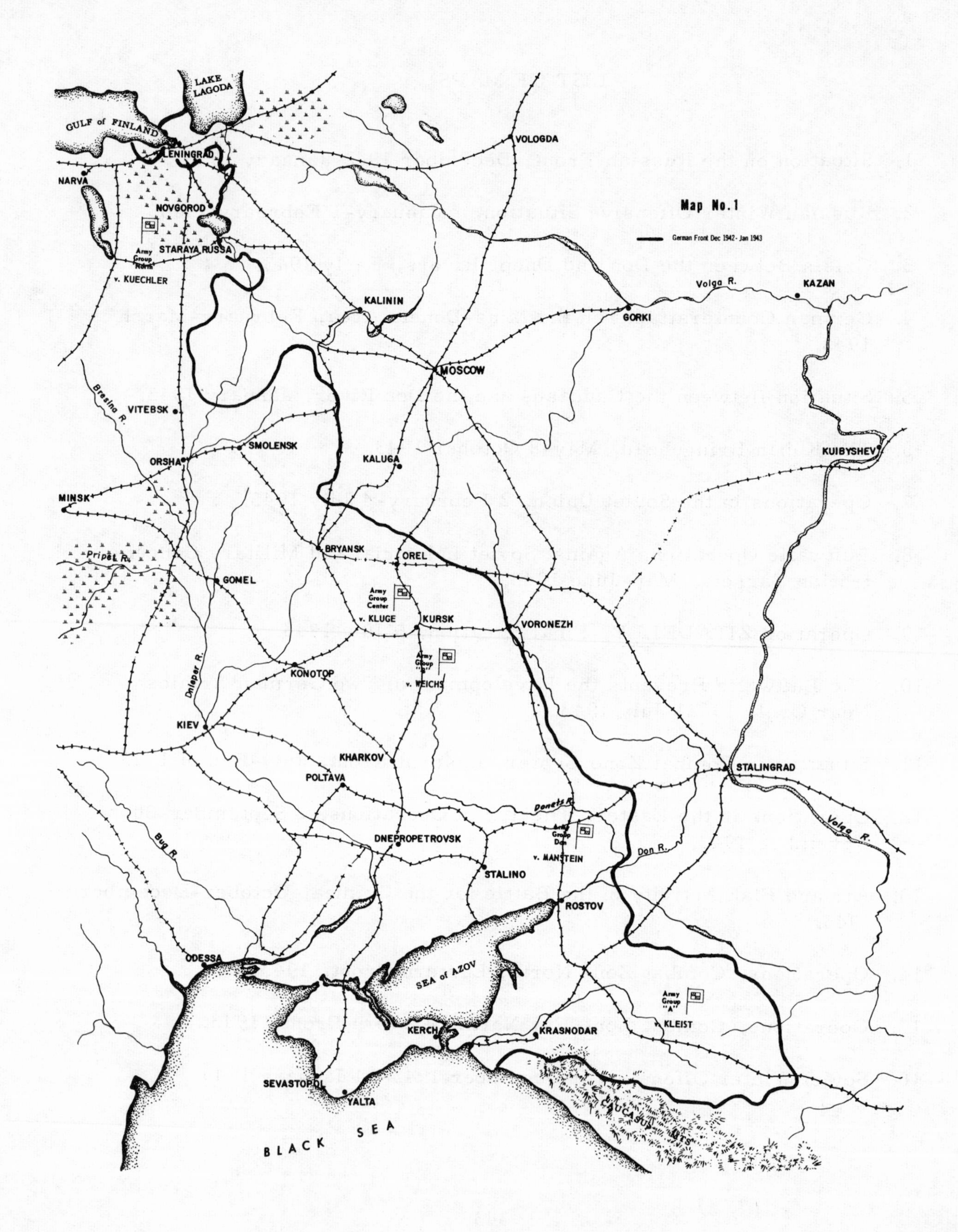
Map No. 1
German Front Dec 1942 - Jan 1943
LAKE LAGODA
GULF of FINLAND
LENINGRAD
NARVA
NOVGOROD
Army Group North
STARAYA RUSSA
v. KUECHLER
VOLOGDA
KALININ
GORKI
Volga R.
KAZAN
MOSCOW
Bresina R.
VITEBSK
SMOLENSK
ORSHA
KALUGA
KUIBYSHEV
MINSK
BRYANSK
OREL
Pripet R.
GOMEL
Army Group Center
v. KLUGE
KURSK
VORONEZH
KONOTOP
v. WEICHS
Dnieper R.
KIEV
KHARKOV
POLTAVA
STALINGRAD
Donets R.
Army Group Don
v. MANSTEIN
Bug R.
DNEPROPETROVSK
STALINO
Don R.
Volga R.
ROSTOV
ODESSA
SEA of AZOV
Army Group "A"
v. KLEIST
KERCH
KRASNODAR
SEVASTOPOL
YALTA
CAUCASUS MTS
BLACK SEA

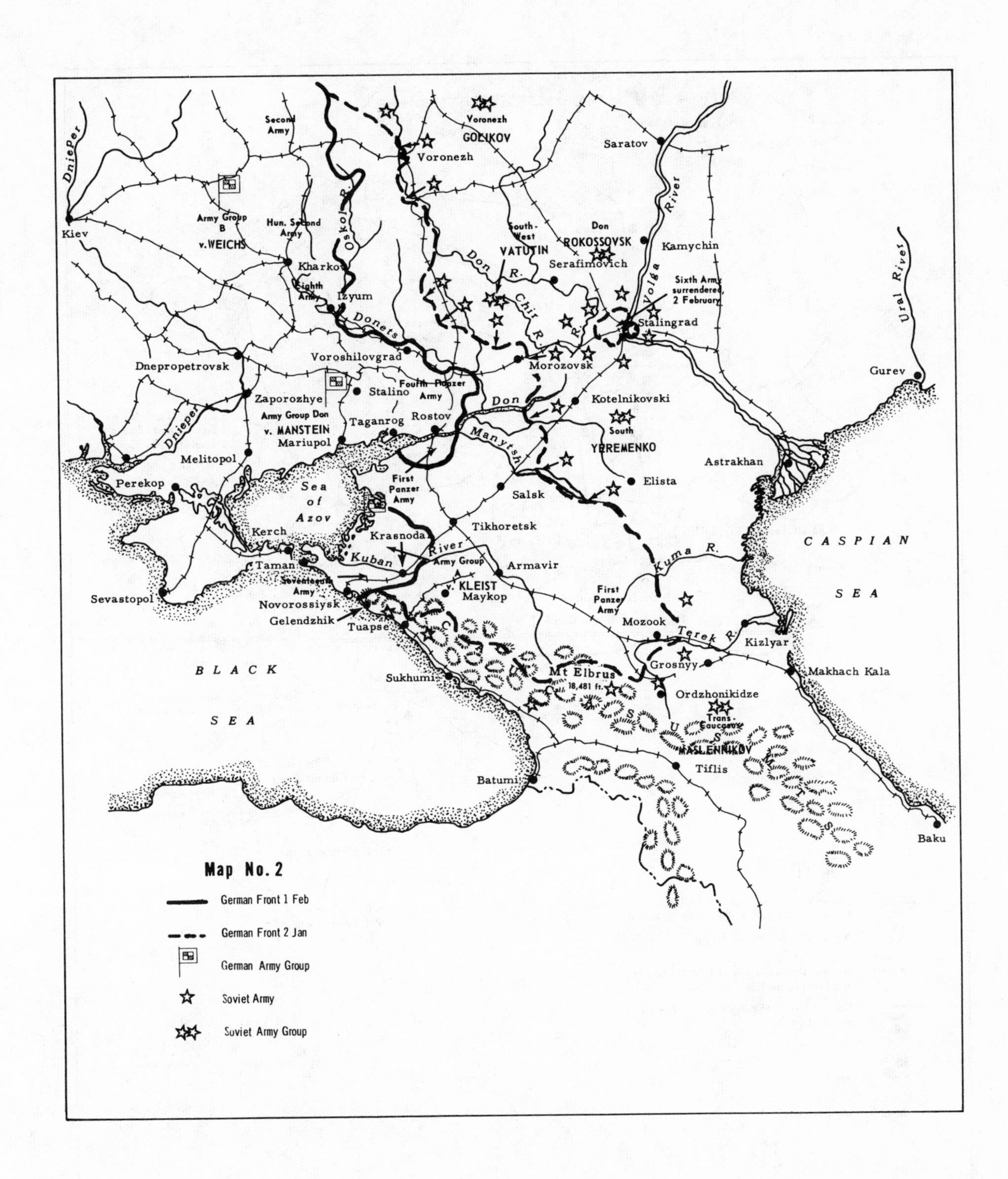
Map No. 2
German Front 1 Feb
German Front 2 Jan
German Army Group
Soviet Army
Soviet Army Group
Dnieper
Kiev
Second Army
Army Group B
v. WEICHS
Hun. Second Army
Kharkov
Eighth Army
Izyum
Oskol R.
Voronezh
GOLIKOV
Saratov
Volga River
Kamychin
Ural River
South-West
VATUTIN
Don
ROKOSSOVSK
Serafimovich
Don R.
Chir R.
Sixth Army surrendered, 2 February
Stalingrad
Donets
Voroshilovgrad
Morozovsk
Dnepropetrovsk
Stalino
Fourth Panzer Army
Zaporozhye
Army Group Don
v. MANSTEIN
Taganrog
Rostov
Mariupol
Kotelnikovski
South
YEREMENKO
Manytsh
Gurev
Melitopol
Perekop
Sea of Azov
First Panzer Army
Salsk
Elista
Astrakhan
Kerch
Krasnodar
Tikhoretsk
Kuban River
Army Group A
v. KLEIST
Armavir
Kuma R.
CASPIAN SEA
Taman
Seventeenth Army
Sevastopol
Novorossiysk
Maykop
First Panzer Army
Gelendzhik
Tuapse
Mozook
Terek R.
Kizlyar
BLACK SEA
Mt Elbrus
18,481 ft.
Grosnyy
Makhach Kala
Sukhumi
Ordzhonikidze
Trans-Caucasus
MASLENNIKOV
Tiflis
Batumi
Baku

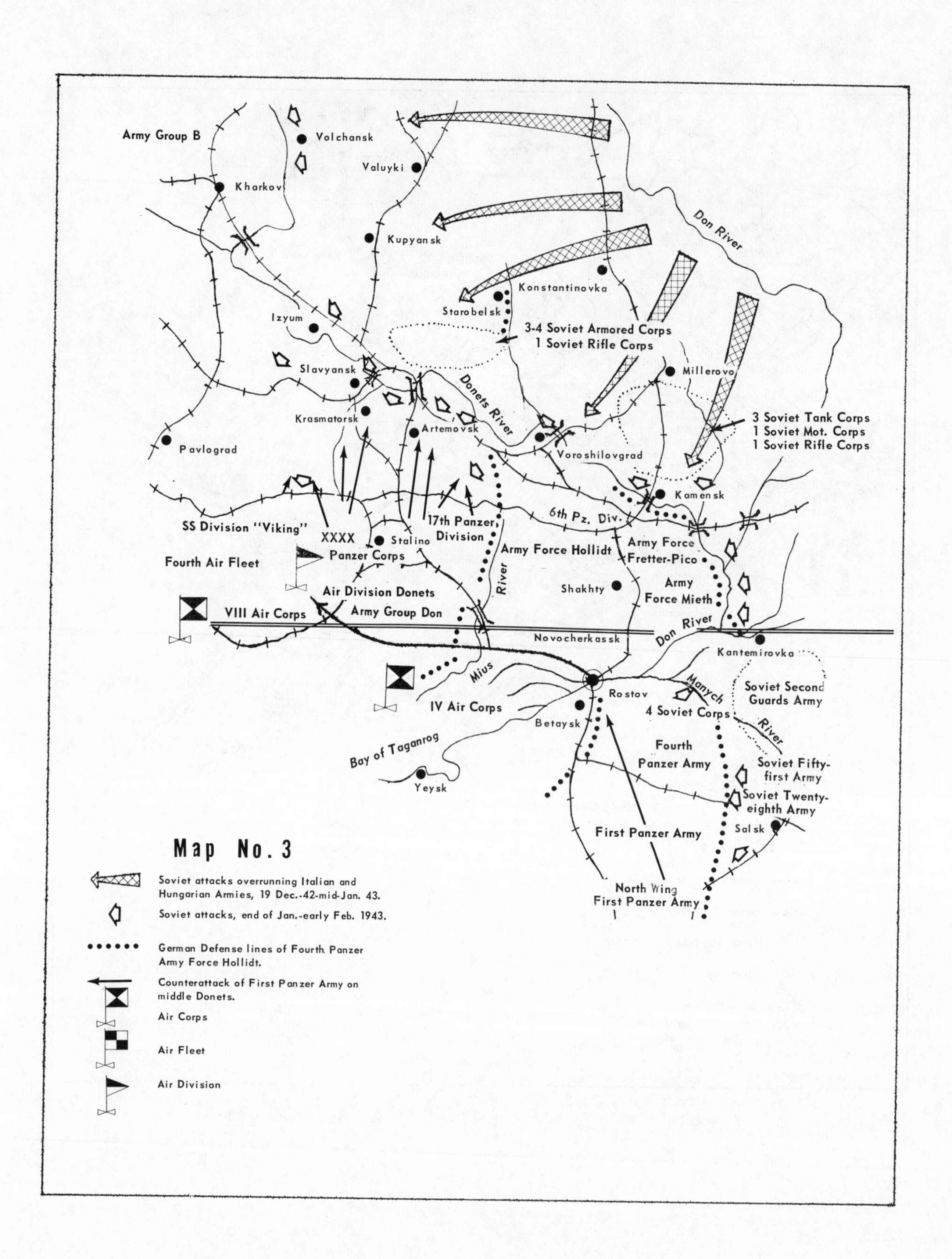
Army Group B
Volchansk
Valuyki
Kharkov
Kupyansk
Don River
Konstantinovka
Starobelsk
Izyum
3-4 Soviet Armored Corps
1 Soviet Rifle Corps
Millerovo
Slavyansk
Krasmatorsk
Artemovsk
Donets River
3 Soviet Tank Corps
1 Soviet Mot. Corps
1 Soviet Rifle Corps
Pavlograd
Voroshilovgrad
Kamensk
6th Pz. Div.
SS Division "Viking"
XXXX
Panzer Corps
Stalino
17th Panzer Division
Army Force Hollidt
Army Force Fretter-Pico
Fourth Air Fleet
Shakhty
Army Force Mieth
River
Air Division Donets
VIII Air Corps
Army Group Don
Novocherkassk
Don River
Kantemirovka
Mius
Rostov
Manych
Soviet Second Guards Army
IV Air Corps
Betaysk
4 Soviet Corps
River
Bay of Taganrog
Fourth Panzer Army
Soviet Fifty-first Army
Yeysk
Soviet Twenty-eighth Army
Salsk
First Panzer Army
Map No. 3
North Wing First Panzer Army
Soviet attacks overrunning Italian and Hungarian Armies, 19 Dec.-42-mid-Jan. 43.
Soviet attacks, end of Jan.-early Feb. 1943.
German Defense lines of Fourth Panzer Army Force Hollidt.
Counterattack of First Panzer Army on middle Donets.
Air Corps
Air Fleet
Air Division

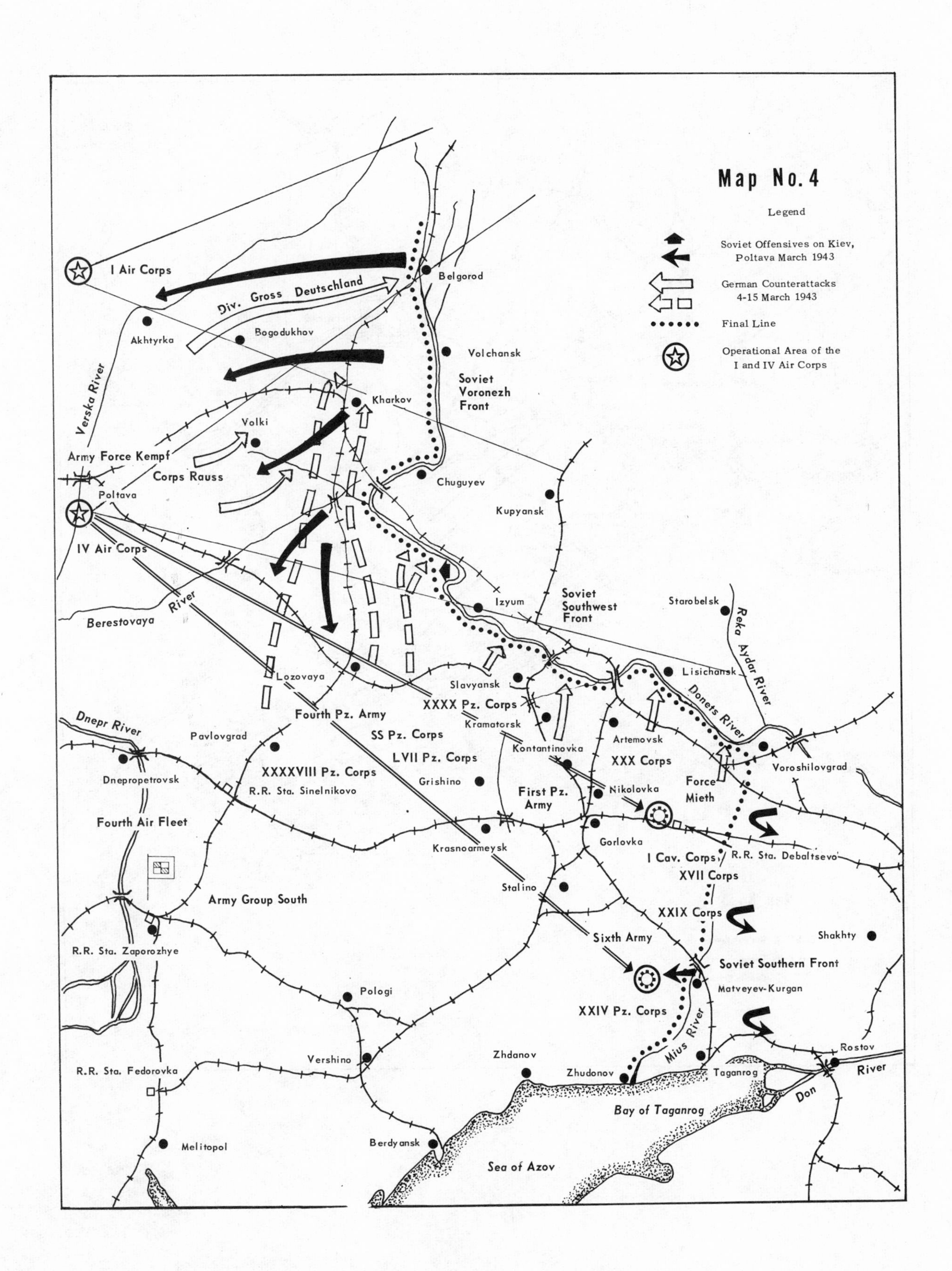
Map No. 4
Legend
Soviet Offensives on Kiev, Poltava March 1943
German Counterattacks 4-15 March 1943
Final Line
Operational Area of the I and IV Air Corps
I Air Corps
Div. Gross Deutschland
Belgorod
Akhtyrka
Bogodukhov
Volchansk
Soviet Voronezh Front
Verska River
Kharkov
Volki
Army Force Kempf
Corps Rauss
Chuguyev
Poltava
Kupyansk
IV Air Corps
Izyum
Soviet Southwest Front
Starobelsk
Reka Aydar River
Berestovaya River
Lozovaya
Slavyansk
Lisichansk
Donets River
Fourth Pz. Army
XXXX Pz. Corps
Kramatorsk
Dnepr River
Pavlovgrad
SS Pz. Corps
Artemovsk
Kontantinovka
LVII Pz. Corps
XXX Corps
Voroshilovgrad
Dnepropetrovsk
XXXXVIII Pz. Corps
R.R. Sta. Sinelnikovo
Grishino
First Pz. Army
Nikolovka
Force Mieth
Fourth Air Fleet
Gorlovka
Krasnoarmeysk
I Cav. Corps
R.R. Sta. Debaltsevo
XVII Corps
Stalino
Army Group South
XXIX Corps
Shakhty
Sixth Army
R.R. Sta. Zaporozhye
Soviet Southern Front
Matveyev-Kurgan
Pologi
XXIV Pz. Corps
Mius River
Rostov
Vershino
Zhdanov
Zhudonov
Taganrog
River
R.R. Sta. Fedorovka
Don
Bay of Taganrog
Melitopol
Berdyansk
Sea of Azov

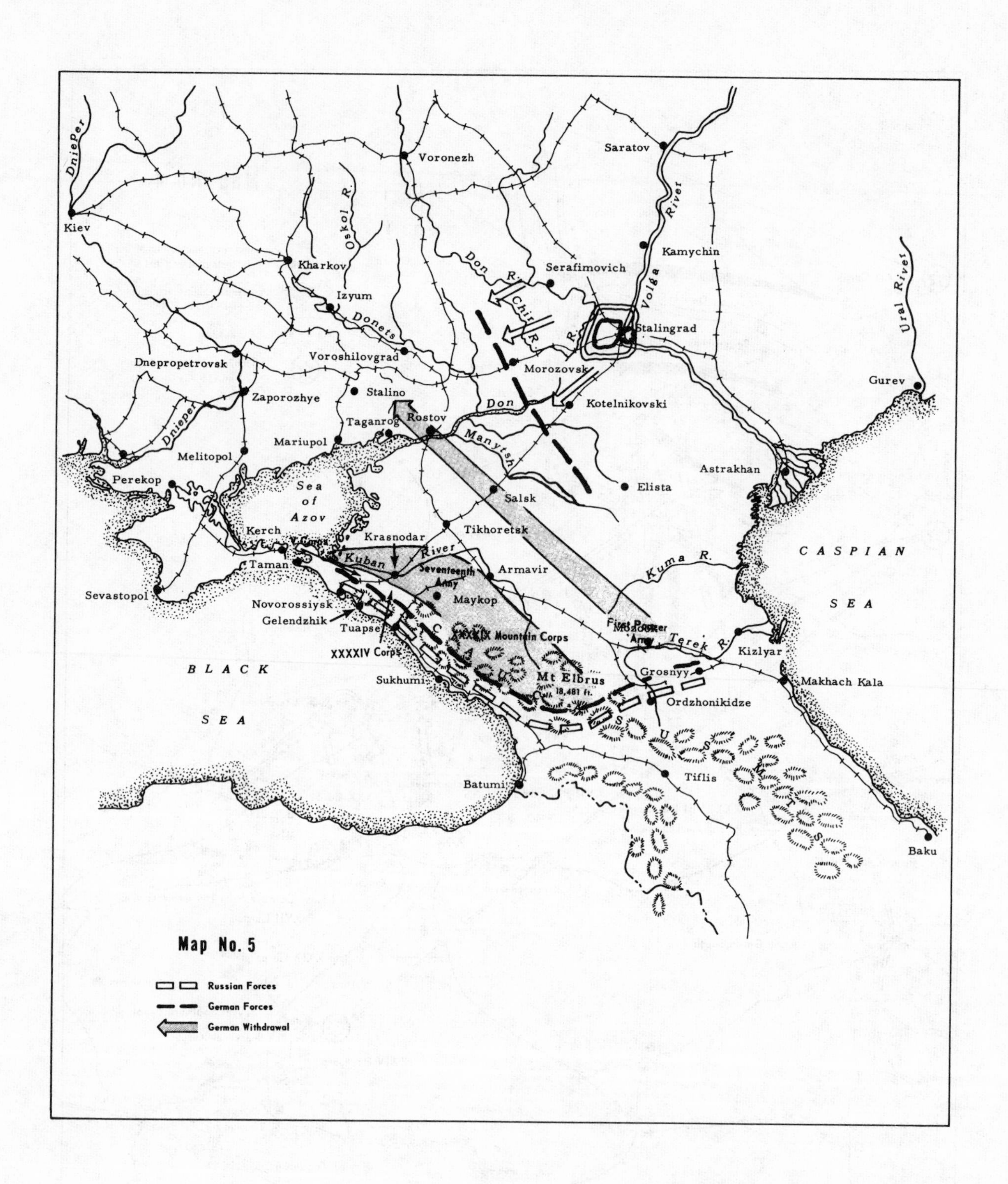

Dnieper
Kiev
Voronezh
Saratov
Oskol R.
Kharkov
Izyum
Donets
Don R.
Chir R.
Serafimovich
Kamychin
Volga River
Stalingrad
Ural River
Dnepropetrovsk
Voroshilovgrad
Morozovsk
Stalino
Zaporozhye
Dnieper
Kotelnikovski
Don
Gurev
Taganrog
Rostov
Mariupol
Melitopol
Manytsh
Perekop
Sea of Azov
Salsk
Elista
Astrakhan
Kerch
V Corps
Krasnodar
Tikhoretsk
Kuban River
Taman
Seventeenth Army
Armavir
Kuma R.
CASPIAN SEA
Sevastopol
Maykop
Novorossiysk
Gelendzhik
Tuapse
XXXXIX Mountain Corps
First Panzer Army
Mozdok
Terek R.
XXXXIV Corps
Kizlyar
BLACK SEA
Sukhumi
Mt Elbrus
18,481 ft.
Grosnyy
Makhach Kala
Ordzhonikidze
Batumi
Tiflis
Baku
Map No. 5
Russian Forces
German Forces
German Withdrawal

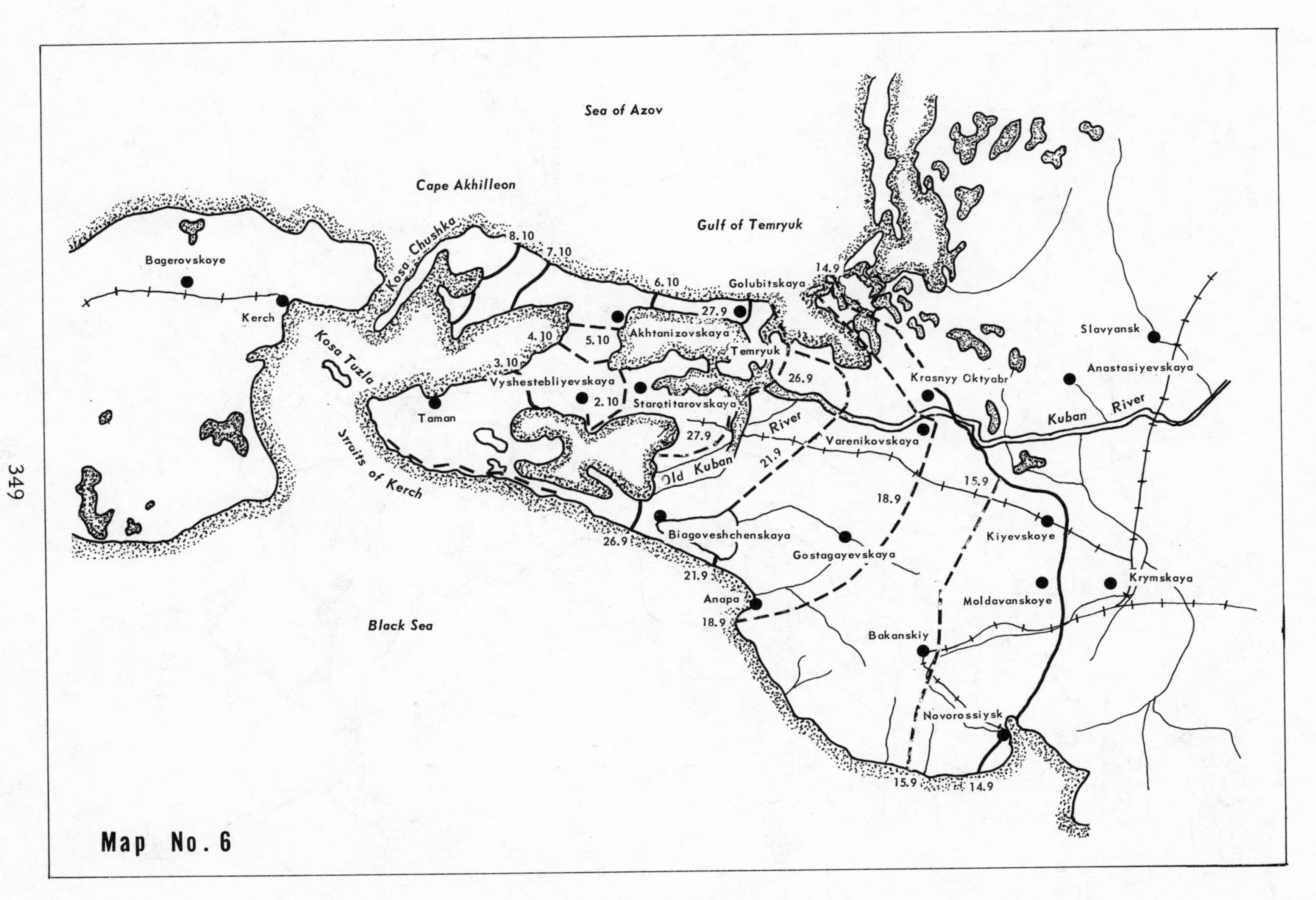
Sea of Azov
Cape Akhilleon
Gulf of Temryuk
Kosa Chushka
Bagerovskoye
Kerch
Kosa Tuzla
Straits of Kerch
Taman
Vyshestebliyevskaya
Akhtanizovskaya
Starotitarovskaya
Golubitskaya
Temryuk
Old Kuban
River
Kuban River
Krasnyy Oktyabr
Slavyansk
Anastasiyevskaya
Varenikovskaya
Biagoveshchenskaya
Gostagayevskaya
Anapa
Black Sea
Kiyevskoye
Krymskaya
Moldavanskoye
Bakanskiy
Novorossiysk
8.10
7.10
6.10
5.10
4.10
3.10
2.10
27.9
27.9
26.9
26.9
21.9
21.9
18.9
18.9
15.9
15.9
14.9
14.9
Map No. 6

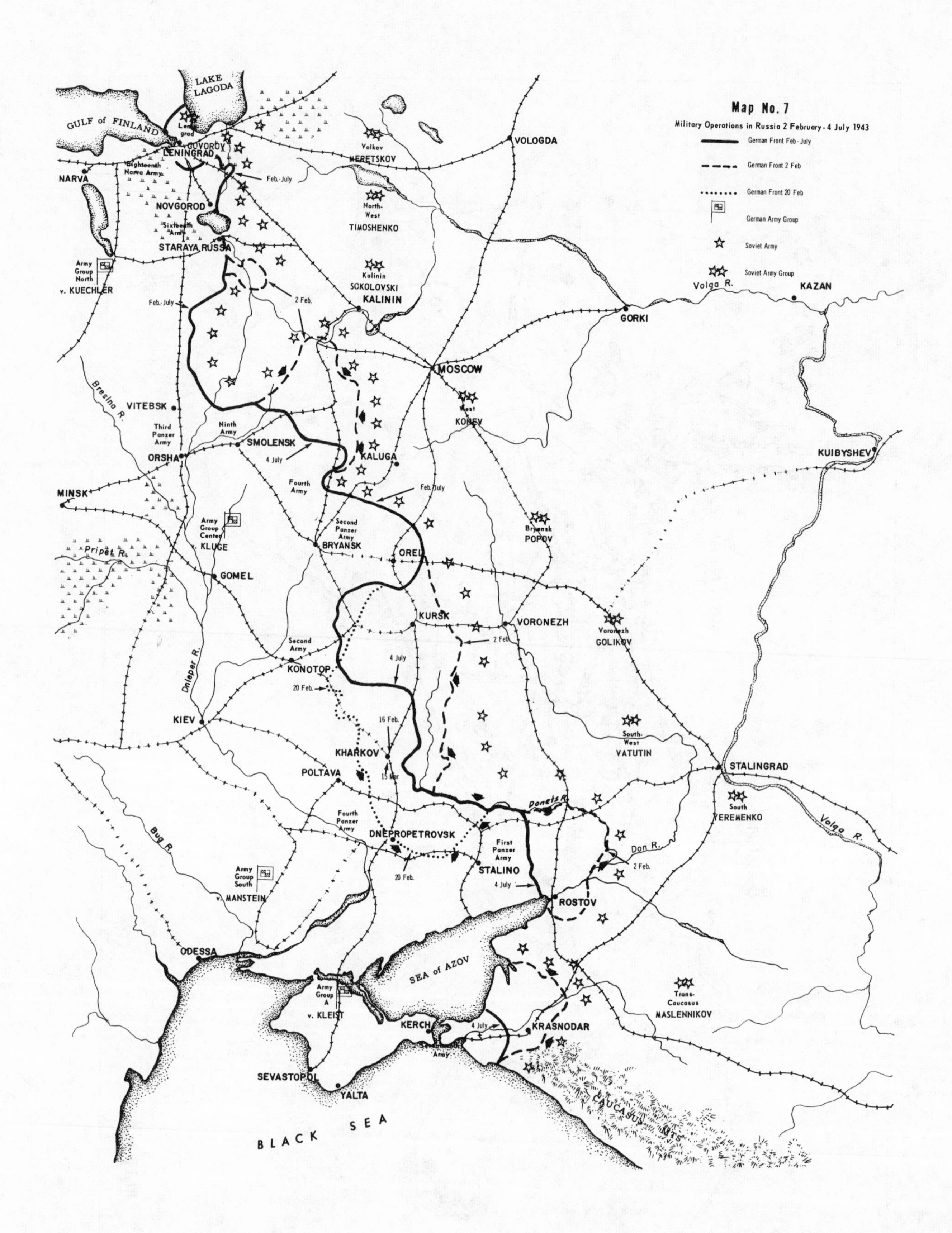
Map No. 7
Military Operations in Russia 2 February - 4 July 1943
German Front Feb - July
German Front 2 Feb
German Front 20 Feb
German Army Group
Soviet Army
Soviet Army Group
LAKE LAGODA
GULF of FINLAND
LENINGRAD
GOVOROV
NARVA
Eighteenth Narva Army
NOVGOROD
Sixteenth Army
STARAYA RUSSA
Army Group North
v. KUECHLER
Volkov
MERETSKOV
North-West
TIMOSHENKO
Kalinin
SOKOLOVSKI
KALININ
VOLOGDA
Volga R.
KAZAN
GORKI
MOSCOW
West
KONEV
Bresina R.
VITEBSK
Third Panzer Army
Ninth Army
SMOLENSK
ORSHA
KALUGA
KUIBYSHEV
MINSK
Fourth Army
Army Group Center
v. KLUGE
Second Panzer Army
BRYANSK
OREL
Bryansk
POPOV
Pripet R.
GOMEL
KURSK
VORONEZH
Voronezh
GOLIKOV
Second Army
KONOTOP
Dnieper R.
KIEV
South-West
VATUTIN
KHARKOV
POLTAVA
STALINGRAD
Donets R.
South
YEREMENKO
Fourth Panzer Army
DNEPROPETROVSK
First Panzer Army
STALINO
Don R.
Bug R.
Army Group South
v. MANSTEIN
ROSTOV
Volga R.
ODESSA
SEA of AZOV
Army Group A
v. KLEIST
Trans-Caucasus
MASLENNIKOV
KERCH
KRASNODAR
SEVASTOPOL
YALTA
CAUCASUS MTS
BLACK SEA
Feb.-July
2 Feb.
4 July
20 Feb.
16 Feb.
15 Mar

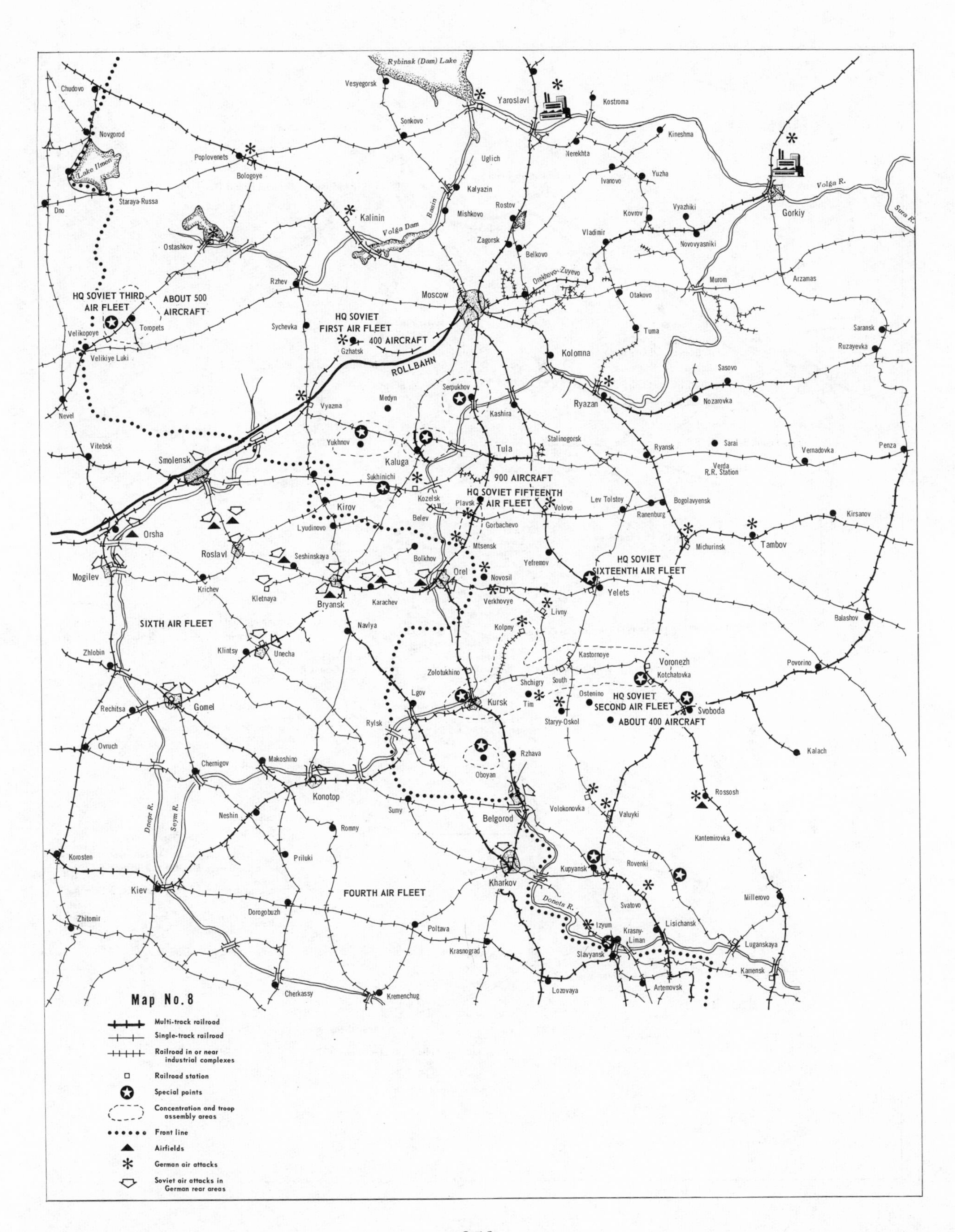
Rybinsk (Dam) Lake
Chudovo
Vesyegorsk
Yaroslavl
Kostroma
Novgorod
Sonkovo
Kineshma
Lake Ilmen
Poplovenets
Bologoye
Uglich
Nerekhta
Ivanovo
Yuzha
Staraya-Russa
Kalyazin
Volga R.
Dno
Kalinin
Mishkovo
Rostov
Kovrov
Vyazhiki
Gorkiy
Volga Dam Basin
Zagorsk
Vladimir
Novovyasniki
Ostashkov
Belkovo
Sura R.
Orekhovo-Zuyevo
Rzhev
Murom
Arzamas
HQ SOVIET THIRD AIR FLEET
ABOUT 500 AIRCRAFT
Moscow
Otakovo
Toropets
HQ SOVIET FIRST AIR FLEET
Sychevka
400 AIRCRAFT
Saransk
Velikopoye
Tuma
Gzhatsk
Ruzayevka
Velikiye Luki
Kolomna
ROLLBAHN
Sasovo
Serpukhov
Nevel
Vyazma
Medyn
Ryazan
Nozarovka
Kashira
Yukhnov
Vitebsk
Stalinogorsk
Tula
Ryansk
Sarai
Vernadovka
Penza
Smolensk
Kaluga
Verda R.R. Station
900 AIRCRAFT
Sukhinichi
HQ SOVIET FIFTEENTH AIR FLEET
Kozelsk
Plavsk
Lev Tolstoy
Bogolavyensk
Kirov
Volovo
Ranenburg
Belev
Lyudinovo
Gorbachevo
Kirsanov
Orsha
Mtsensk
Michurinsk
Tambov
Roslavl
Seshinskaya
Bolkhov
Yefremov
HQ SOVIET SIXTEENTH AIR FLEET
Mogilev
Orel
Novosil
Krichev
Kletnaya
Bryansk
Karachev
Verkhovye
Yelets
Livny
SIXTH AIR FLEET
Navlya
Balashov
Kolpny
Zhlobin
Klintsy
Unecha
Kastornoye
Voronezh
Povorino
Kotchatovka
Zolotukhino
Shchigry
South
Ostenino
HQ SOVIET SECOND AIR FLEET
Rechitsa
Gomel
Lgov
Kursk
Tim
Svoboda
Staryy-Oskol
ABOUT 400 AIRCRAFT
Rylsk
Ovruch
Rzhava
Kalach
Chernigov
Makoshino
Oboyan
Konotop
Rossosh
Neshin
Sumy
Volokonovka
Belgorod
Valuyki
Dnepr R.
Seym R.
Romny
Kantemirovka
Korosten
Priluki
Rovenki
Kupyansk
Kiev
FOURTH AIR FLEET
Kharkov
Millerovo
Donets R.
Svatovo
Dorogobuzh
Zhitomir
Izyum
Lisichansk
Poltava
Krasny-Liman
Krasnograd
Slavyansk
Luganskaya
Kamensk
Cherkassy
Kremenchug
Lozovaya
Artemovsk
Map No. 8
Multi-track railroad
Single-track railroad
Railroad in or near industrial complexes
Railroad station
Special points
Concentration and troop assembly areas
Front line
Airfields
German air attacks
Soviet air attacks in German rear areas

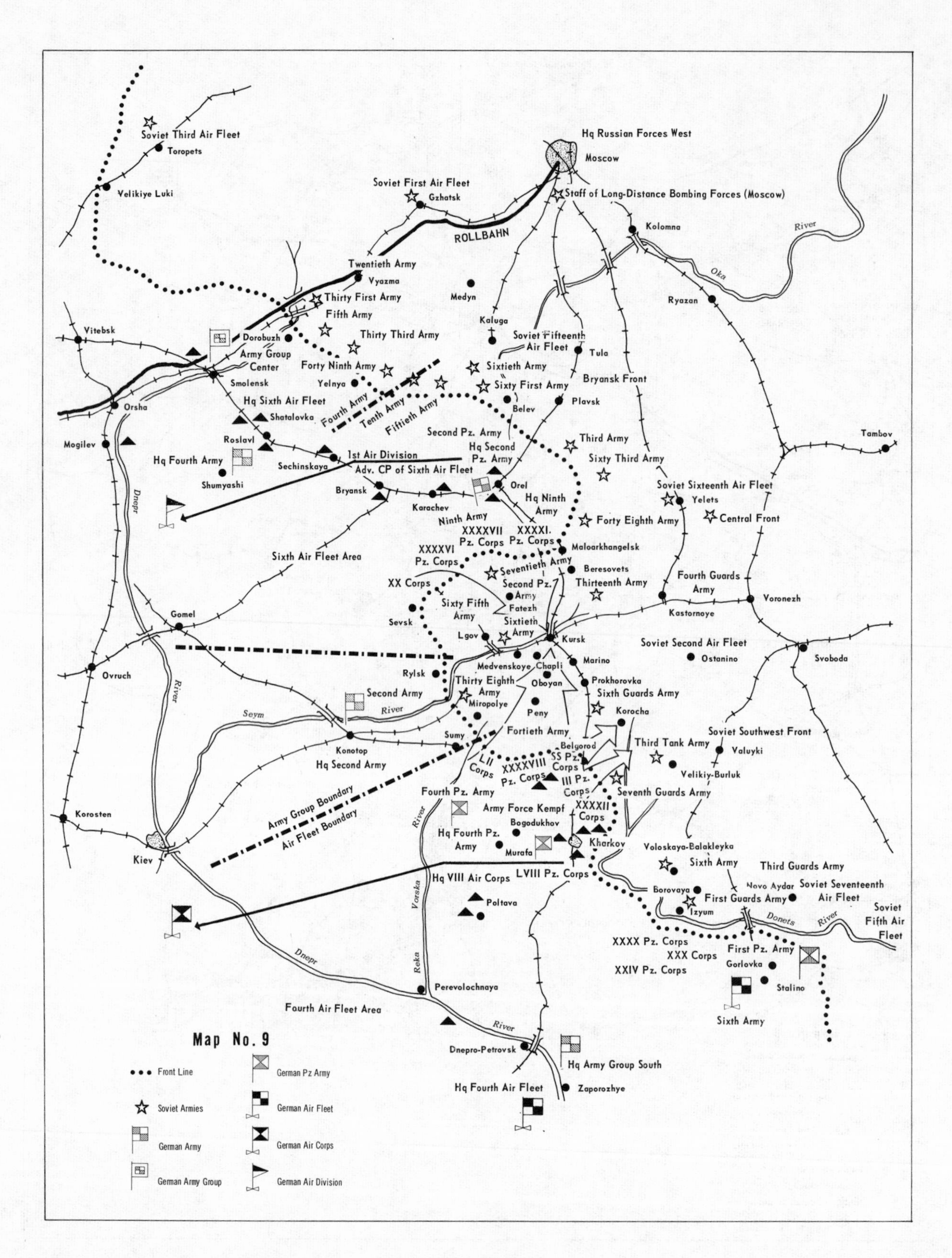
Map No. 9
Front Line
Soviet Armies
German Army
German Army Group
German Pz Army
German Air Fleet
German Air Corps
German Air Division
Soviet Third Air Fleet
Toropets
Velikiye Luki
Hq Russian Forces West
Moscow
Soviet First Air Fleet
Gzhatsk
Staff of Long-Distance Bombing Forces (Moscow)
ROLLBAHN
Kolomna
Oka
River
Twentieth Army
Vyazma
Thirty First Army
Fifth Army
Thirty Third Army
Medyn
Ryazan
Vitebsk
Dorobuzh
Army Group Center
Smolensk
Kaluga
Soviet Fifteenth Air Fleet
Tula
Forty Ninth Army
Sixtieth Army
Sixty First Army
Yelnya
Orsha
Hq Sixth Air Fleet
Shatalovka
Fourth Army
Tenth Army
Fiftieth Army
Belev
Plavsk
Bryansk Front
Mogilev
Roslavl
Hq Fourth Army
Shumyashi
Sechinskaya
1st Air Division
Adv. CP of Sixth Air Fleet
Second Pz. Army
Hq Second Pz. Army
Third Army
Sixty Third Army
Tambov
Orel
Bryansk
Karachev
Hq Ninth Army
Soviet Sixteenth Air Fleet
Yelets
Central Front
Dnepr
Ninth Army
XXXXVII Pz. Corps
XXXXI. Pz. Corps
Forty Eighth Army
XXXXVI Pz. Corps
Maloarkhangelsk
Sixth Air Fleet Area
Seventieth Army
Beresovets
Second Pz. Army
Thirteenth Army
Fourth Guards Army
XX Corps
Sixty Fifth Army
Fatezh
Voronezh
Kastornoye
Gomel
Sevsk
Sixtieth Army
Lgov
Kursk
Soviet Second Air Fleet
Ostanino
Svoboda
Ovruch
Medvenskoye
Chapli
Marino
Rylsk
Thirty Eighth Army
Oboyan
Prokhorovka
Sixth Guards Army
Second Army
Seym
River
Miropolye
Peny
Korocha
Fortieth Army
Sumy
Konotop
Hq Second Army
Belgorod
SS Pz. Corps
LII Corps
XXXXVIII Pz. Corps
III Pz. Corps
Third Tank Army
Soviet Southwest Front
Valuyki
Velikiy-Burluk
Seventh Guards Army
Fourth Pz. Army
Army Force Kempf
Army Group Boundary
Air Fleet Boundary
XXXXII Corps
Korosten
Hq Fourth Pz. Army
Bogodukhov
Murafa
Kharkov
Voloskaya-Balakleyka
Sixth Army
Third Guards Army
Kiev
Hq VIII Air Corps
LVIII Pz. Corps
Borovaya
Novo Aydar
Soviet Seventeenth Air Fleet
First Guards Army
Izyum
Poltava
Vorska
Donets
River
Soviet Fifth Air Fleet
XXXX Pz. Corps
XXX Corps
First Pz. Army
XXIV Pz. Corps
Gorlovka
Stalino
Reka
Perevolochnaya
Sixth Army
Fourth Air Fleet Area
River
Dnepro-Petrovsk
Hq Army Group South
Hq Fourth Air Fleet
Zaporozhye

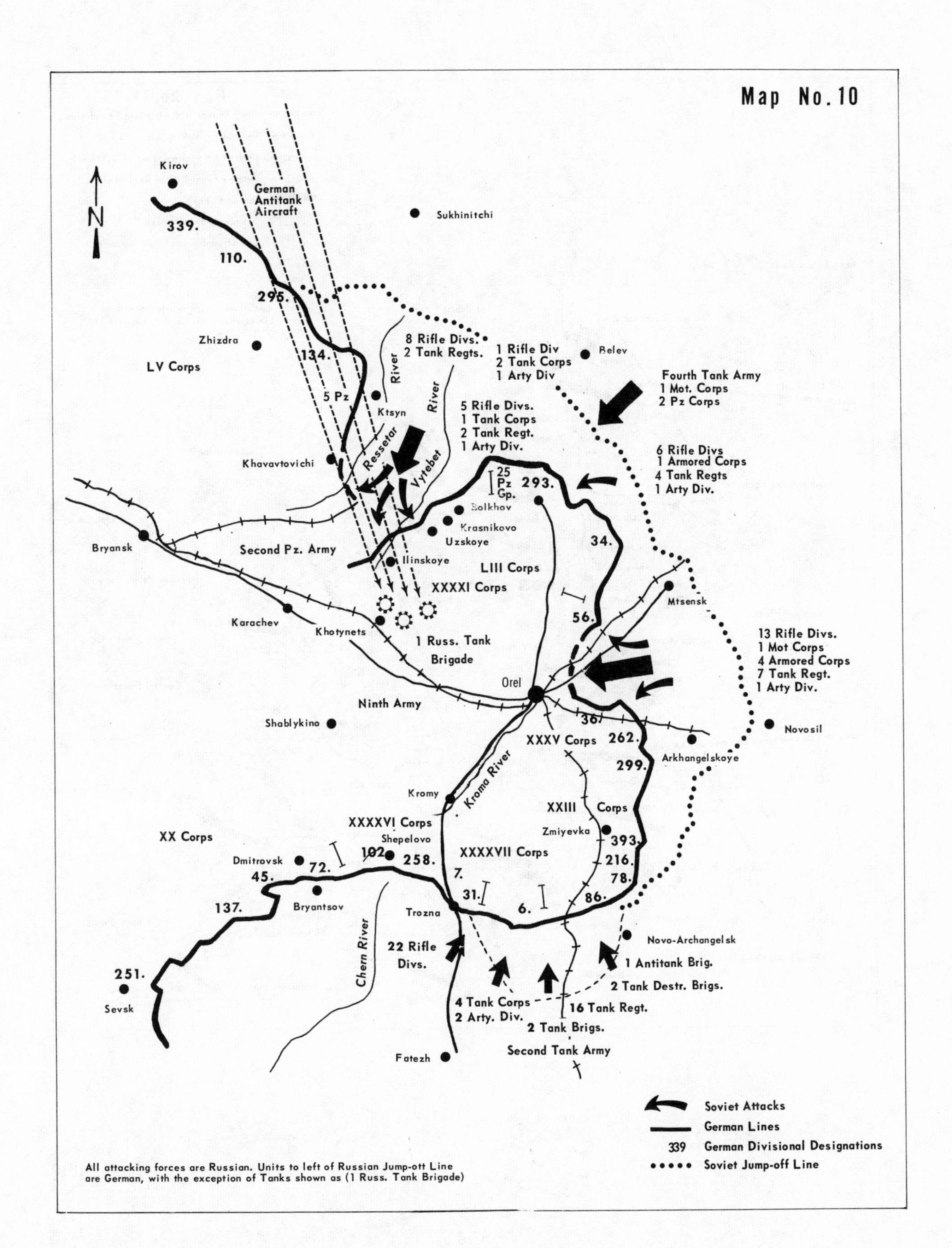
Map No. 10
Kirov
German
Antitank
Aircraft
Sukhinitchi
N
339.
110.
295.
Zhizdra
134.
LV Corps
8 Rifle Divs.
2 Tank Regts.
1 Rifle Div
2 Tank Corps
1 Arty Div
Belev
Fourth Tank Army
1 Mot. Corps
2 Pz Corps
5 Pz
Ktsyn
River
River
Ressetar
Vytebet
5 Rifle Divs.
1 Tank Corps
2 Tank Regt.
1 Arty Div.
Khavavtovichi
6 Rifle Divs
1 Armored Corps
4 Tank Regts
1 Arty Div.
25
Pz
Gp.
293.
Bolkhov
Krasnikovo
Uzskoye
34.
Bryansk
Second Pz. Army
Ilinskoye
LIII Corps
XXXXI Corps
Mtsensk
Karachev
Khotynets
1 Russ. Tank
Brigade
56.
13 Rifle Divs.
1 Mot Corps
4 Armored Corps
7 Tank Regt.
1 Arty Div.
Orel
Ninth Army
Shablykino
36
Novosil
XXXV Corps
262.
Arkhangelskoye
299.
Kroma River
Kromy
XXIII Corps
XXXXVI Corps
Zmiyevka
XX Corps
Shepelovo
393.
XXXXVII Corps
Dmitrovsk
72.
102
258.
216.
45.
7.
78.
Bryantsov
31.
6.
86.
137.
Trozna
Novo-Archangelsk
Chern River
22 Rifle
Divs.
1 Antitank Brig.
251.
2 Tank Destr. Brigs.
Sevsk
4 Tank Corps
2 Arty. Div.
16 Tank Regt.
2 Tank Brigs.
Second Tank Army
Fatezh
Soviet Attacks
German Lines
339 German Divisional Designations
Soviet Jump-off Line
All attacking forces are Russian. Units to left of Russian Jump-ott Line
are German, with the exception of Tanks shown as (1 Russ. Tank Brigade)

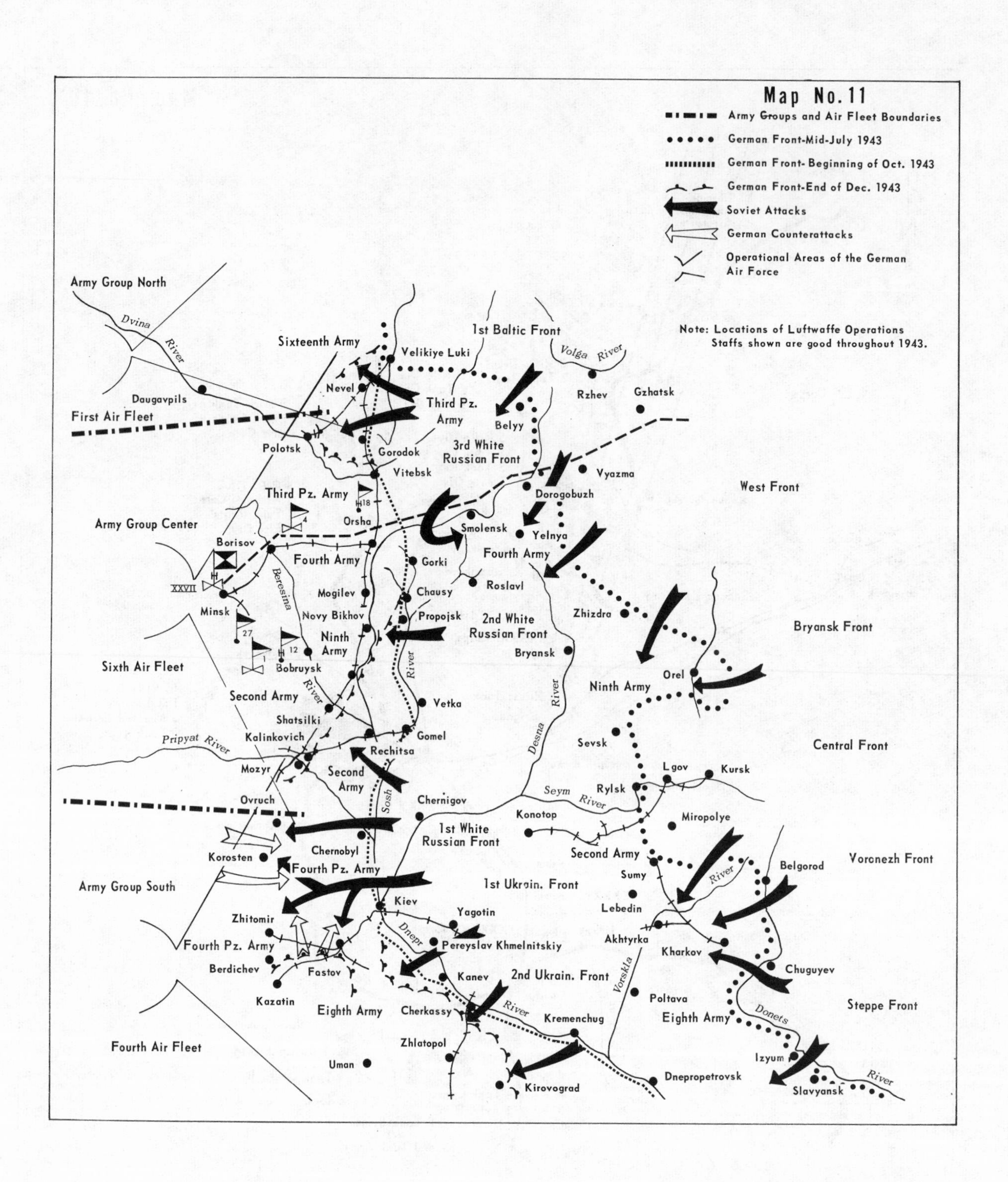

Map No. 11
Army Groups and Air Fleet Boundaries
German Front-Mid-July 1943
German Front-Beginning of Oct. 1943
German Front-End of Dec. 1943
Soviet Attacks
German Counterattacks
Operational Areas of the German Air Force
Note: Locations of Luftwaffe Operations Staffs shown are good throughout 1943.
Army Group North
Dvina River
Sixteenth Army
Velikiye Luki
1st Baltic Front
Volga River
Rzhev
Gzhatsk
Daugavpils
Nevel
Third Pz. Army
Belyy
First Air Fleet
Polotsk
Gorodok
3rd White Russian Front
Vitebsk
Vyazma
Dorogobuzh
West Front
Third Pz. Army
Orsha
Smolensk
Yelnya
Army Group Center
Borisov
Fourth Army
Fourth Army
Gorki
XXVII
Beresina
Roslavl
Minsk
Mogilev
Chausy
Novy Bikhov
Propojsk
Zhizdra
2nd White Russian Front
Bryansk Front
Ninth Army
Bryansk
Sixth Air Fleet
Bobruysk
Ninth Army
Orel
Second Army
River
Vetka
Desna River
Shatsilki
Kalinkovich
Gomel
Sevsk
Central Front
Pripyat River
Rechitsa
Mozyr
Second Army
Lgov
Kursk
Rylsk
Seym River
Ovruch
Sosh River
Chernigov
Konotop
Miropolye
1st White Russian Front
Chernobyl
Korosten
Second Army
Fourth Pz. Army
Belgorod
Voronezh Front
Sumy
Army Group South
1st Ukrain. Front
Kiev
Lebedin
Zhitomir
Yagotin
Akhtyrka
Fourth Pz. Army
Dnepr
Pereyslav Khmelnitskiy
Kharkov
Berdichev
Fastov
Kanev
2nd Ukrain. Front
Vorskla
Chuguyev
Kazatin
Eighth Army
Cherkassy
Poltava
Steppe Front
River
Kremenchug
Eighth Army
Donets
Fourth Air Fleet
Zhlatopol
Izyum
Uman
Dnepropetrovsk
Kirovograd
Slavyansk
River

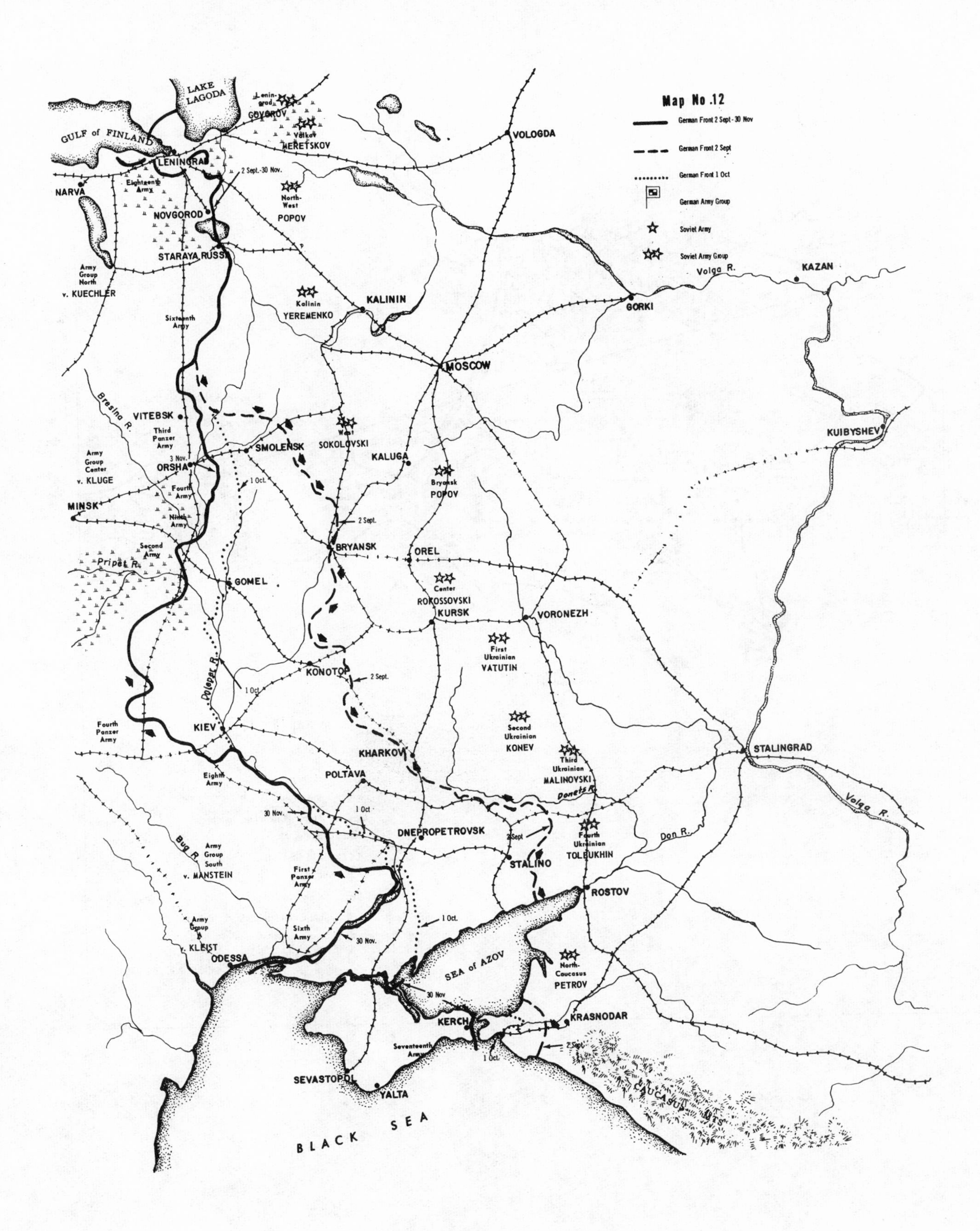

Map No. 12
German Front 2 Sept - 30 Nov
German Front 2 Sept
German Front 1 Oct
German Army Group
Soviet Army
Soviet Army Group
LAKE LAGODA
GULF of FINLAND
LENINGRAD
Leningrad GOVOROV
Volkov MERETSKOV
VOLOGDA
NARVA
Eighteenth Army
2 Sept.-30 Nov.
North-West POPOV
NOVGOROD
STARAYA RUSSA
Army Group North v. KUECHLER
KAZAN
Volga R.
Kalinin YEREMENKO
KALININ
GORKI
Sixteenth Army
MOSCOW
Bresina R.
VITEBSK
Third Panzer Army
SMOLENSK
West SOKOLOVSKI
KUIBYSHEV
Army Group Center v. KLUGE
3 Nov.
ORSHA
KALUGA
Bryansk POPOV
1 Oct.
Fourth Army
MINSK
Ninth Army
2 Sept.
BRYANSK
OREL
Second Army
Pripet R.
GOMEL
Center ROKOSSOVSKI
KURSK
VORONEZH
First Ukrainian VATUTIN
Dnieper R.
KONOTOP
2 Sept.
1 Oct.
Second Ukrainian KONEV
Fourth Panzer Army
KIEV
KHARKOV
Third Ukrainian MALINOVSKI
STALINGRAD
POLTAVA
Eighth Army
Donets R.
30 Nov.
1 Oct.
DNEPROPETROVSK
2 Sept.
Fourth Ukrainian TOLBUKHIN
Don R.
Volga R.
Bug R.
Army Group South v. MANSTEIN
First Panzer Army
STALINO
ROSTOV
Army Group A v. KLEIST
Sixth Army
1 Oct.
30 Nov.
ODESSA
SEA of AZOV
North-Caucasus PETROV
30 Nov.
KRASNODAR
KERCH
2 Sept.
1 Oct.
Seventeenth Army
SEVASTOPOL
YALTA
CAUCASUS MTS
BLACK SEA

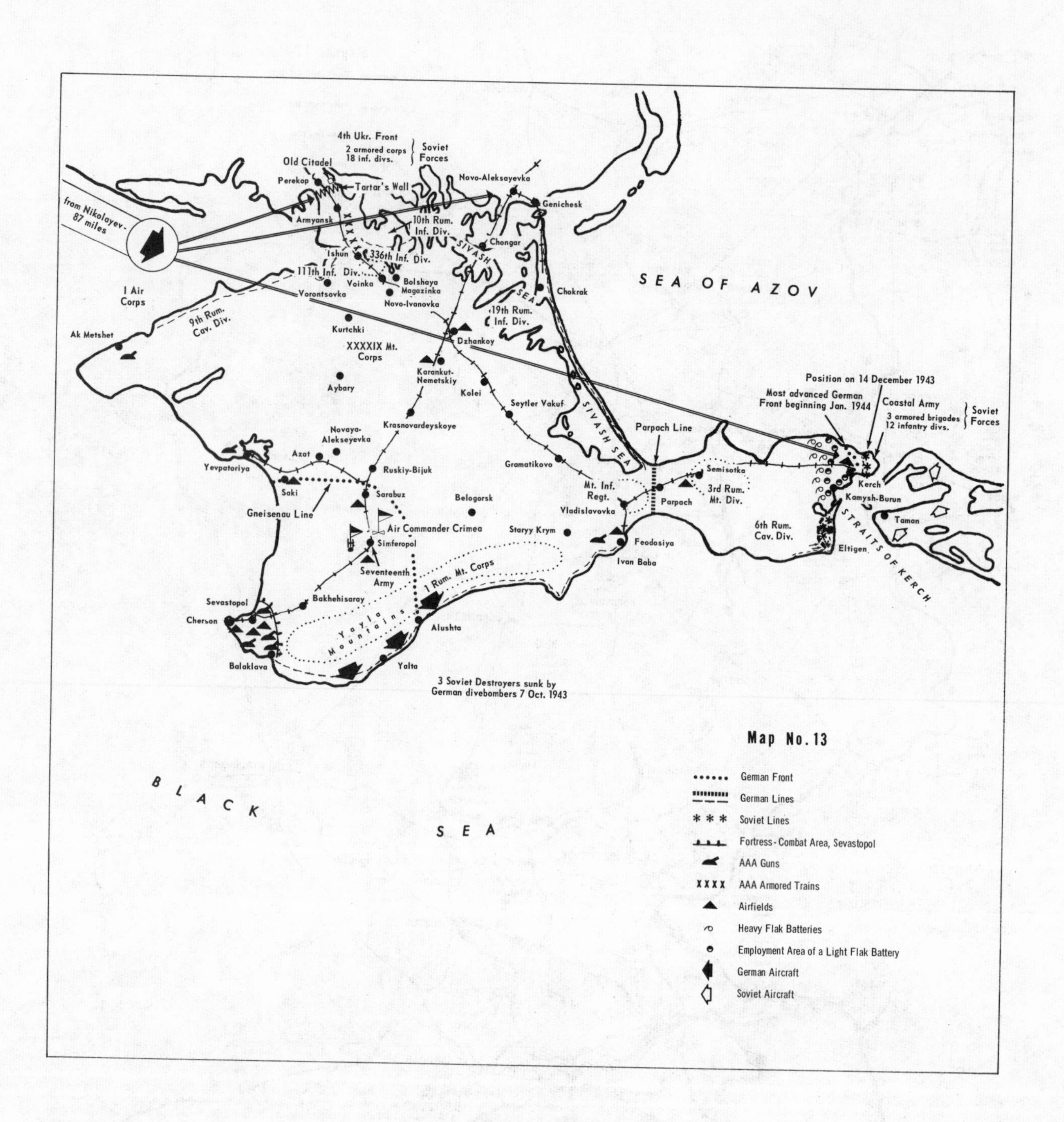
4th Ukr. Front
2 armored corps
18 inf. divs.
Soviet Forces
Old Citadel
Perekop
Tartar's Wall
Novo-Aleksayevka
Genichesk
from Nikolayev-87 miles
Armyansk
10th Rum. Inf. Div.
Chongar
Ishun
336th Inf. Div.
SIVASH
111th Inf. Div.
Voinka
Bolshaya Magazinka
SEA
Chokrak
SEA OF AZOV
1 Air Corps
Vorontsovka
Novo-Ivanovka
9th Rum. Cav. Div.
19th Rum. Inf. Div.
Kurtchki
Dzhankoy
Ak Metshet
XXXXIX Mt. Corps
Karankut-Nemetskiy
Aybary
Kolei
Position on 14 December 1943
Most advanced German Front beginning Jan. 1944
Coastal Army
3 armored brigades
12 infantry divs.
Soviet Forces
Seytler Vakuf
SIVASH SEA
Krasnovardeyskoye
Parpach Line
Novaya-Alekseyevka
Azot
Gramatikovo
Yevpatoriya
Ruskiy-Bijuk
Semisotka
Saki
Mt. Inf. Regt.
3rd Rum. Mt. Div.
Kerch
Sarabuz
Belogorsk
Parpach
Kamysh-Burun
Gneisenau Line
Vladislavovka
Taman
Air Commander Crimea
Staryy Krym
6th Rum. Cav. Div.
Simferopol
Feodosiya
Ivan Baba
Eltigen
STRAITS OF KERCH
Seventeenth Army
1 Rum. Mt. Corps
Sevastopol
Bakhchisaray
Cherson
Yayla Mountains
Alushta
Balaklava
Yalta
3 Soviet Destroyers sunk by German divebombers 7 Oct. 1943
BLACK SEA
Map No. 13
German Front
German Lines
Soviet Lines
Fortress-Combat Area, Sevastopol
AAA Guns
AAA Armored Trains
Airfields
Heavy Flak Batteries
Employment Area of a Light Flak Battery
German Aircraft
Soviet Aircraft

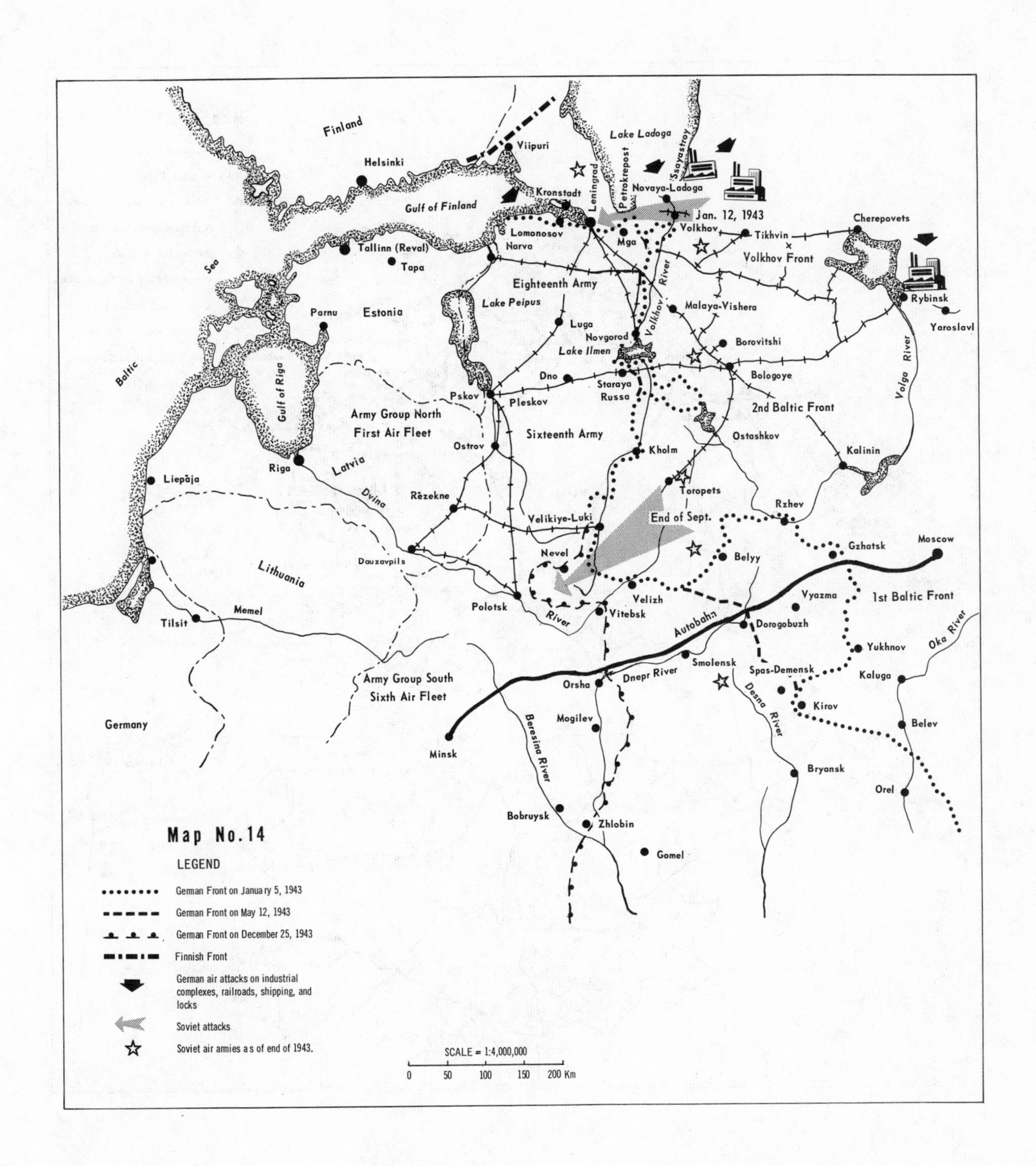

Finland
Helsinki
Viipuri
Lake Ladoga
Kronstadt
Leningrad
Petrokrepost
Novaya-Ladoga
Gulf of Finland
Jan. 12, 1943
Lomonosov
Narva
Mga
Volkhov
Tikhvin
Cherepovets
Volkhov Front
Tallinn (Reval)
Tapa
Sea
Eighteenth Army
Lake Peipus
Rybinsk
Yaroslavl
Parnu
Estonia
Luga
Malaya-Vishera
Novgorod
Borovitshi
Lake Ilmen
Volkhov River
Volga River
Baltic
Gulf of Riga
Dno
Staraya Russa
Bologoye
Pskov
Pleskov
2nd Baltic Front
Army Group North
First Air Fleet
Sixteenth Army
Ostashkov
Ostrov
Kalinin
Riga
Latvia
Kholm
Liepāja
Toropets
Dvina
Rēzekne
Rzhev
Velikiye-Luki
End of Sept.
Gzhatsk
Moscow
Nevel
Belyy
Dauzavpils
Lithuania
Velizh
Vyazma
1st Baltic Front
Polotsk
River
Vitebsk
Autobahn
Dorogobuzh
Tilsit
Memel
Yukhnov
Oka River
Smolensk
Spas-Demensk
Kaluga
Army Group South
Sixth Air Fleet
Orsha
Dnepr River
Desna River
Kirov
Germany
Mogilev
Belev
Minsk
Beresina River
Bryansk
Orel
Bobruysk
Zhlobin
Gomel
Map No. 14
LEGEND
German Front on January 5, 1943
German Front on May 12, 1943
German Front on December 25, 1943
Finnish Front
German air attacks on industrial complexes, railroads, shipping, and locks
Soviet attacks
Soviet air armies as of end of 1943.
SCALE = 1:4,000,000
0 50 100 150 200 Km

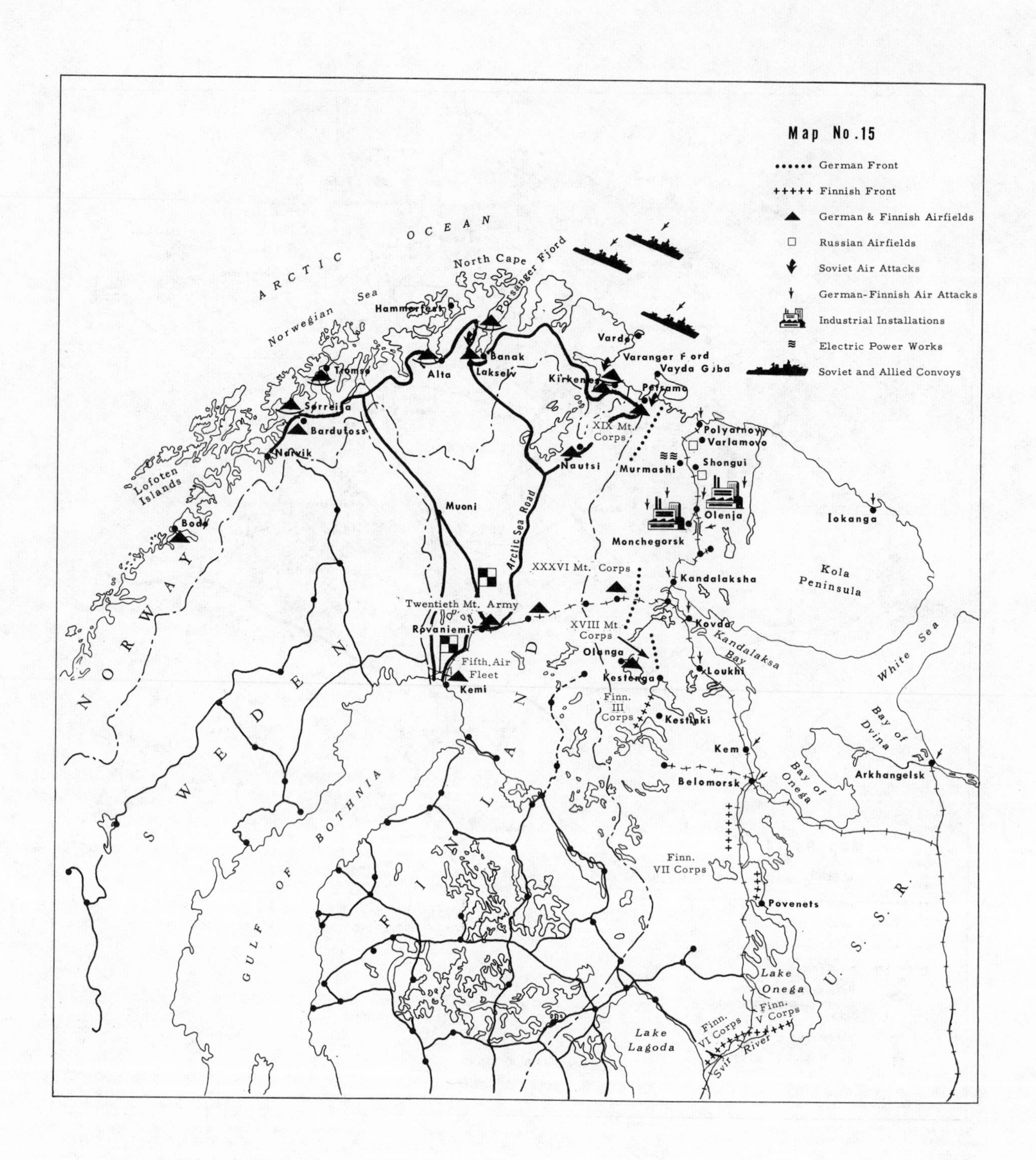

Map No.15
German Front
Finnish Front
German & Finnish Airfields
Russian Airfields
Soviet Air Attacks
German-Finnish Air Attacks
Industrial Installations
Electric Power Works
Soviet and Allied Convoys
ARCTIC OCEAN
Norwegian Sea
North Cape
Porsanger Fjord
Hammerfest
Alta
Banak
Lakselv
Vardø
Varanger Ford
Vayda Guba
Kirkenes
Petsamo
Tromsø
Sørreisa
Bardufoss
Narvik
Lofoten Islands
Bodø
XIX Mt. Corps
Nautsi
Murmashi
Polyarnoye
Varlamovo
Shongui
Olenja
Monchegorsk
Iokanga
Muoni
Arctic Sea Road
XXXVI Mt. Corps
Kandalaksha
Kola Peninsula
Twentieth Mt. Army
Rovaniemi
XVIII Mt. Corps
Kovda
Kandalaksa Bay
White Sea
Fifth Air Fleet
Kemi
Olanga
Kestenga
Loukhi
Finn. III Corps
Kestinki
Kem
Bay of Dvina
Arkhangelsk
Belomorsk
Bay of Onega
NORWAY
SWEDEN
GULF OF BOTHNIA
FINLAND
Finn. VII Corps
Povenets
U.S.S.R.
Lake Onega
Finn. V Corps
Finn. VI Corps
Svir River
Lake Lagoda

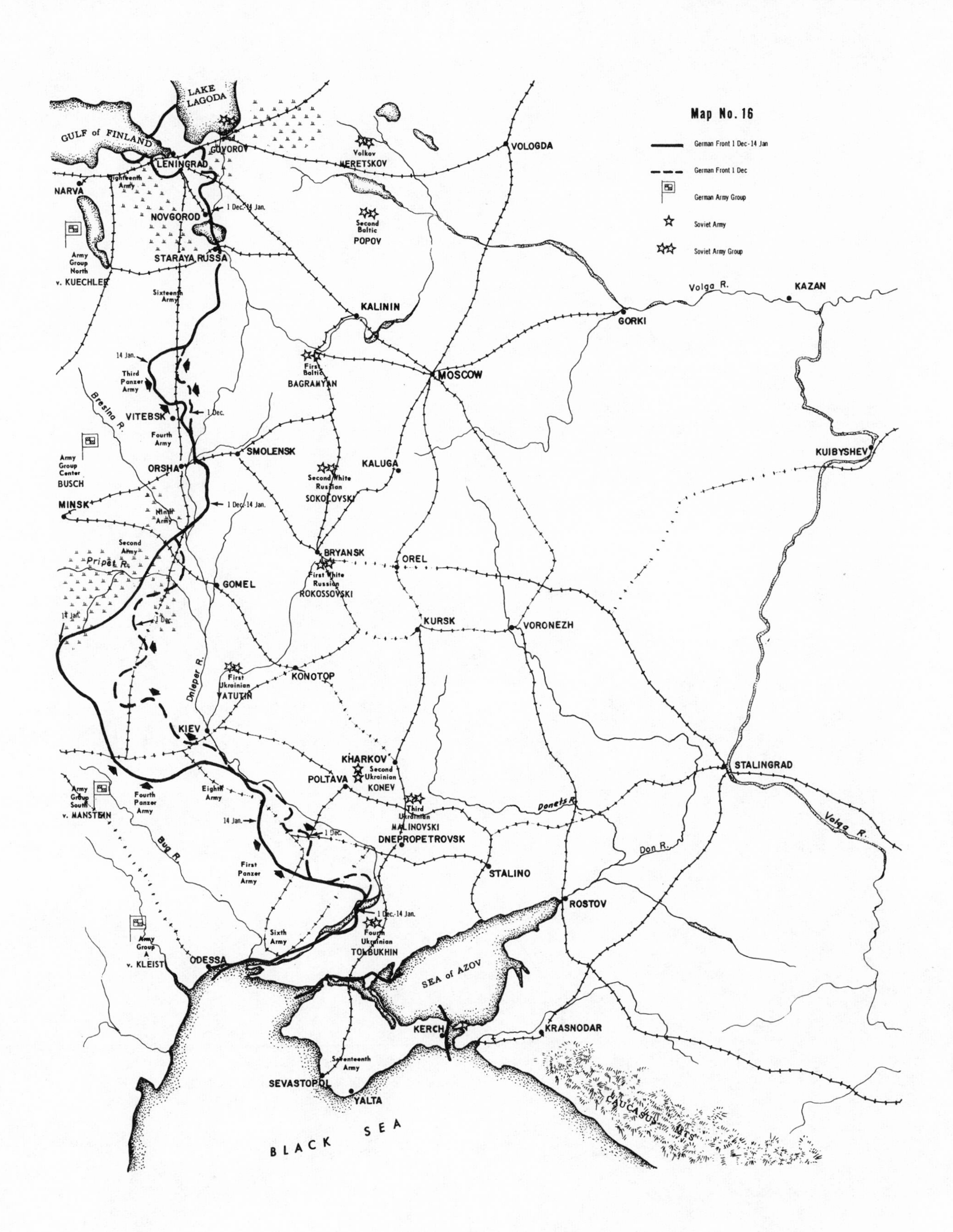

Map No. 16
German Front 1 Dec-14 Jan
German Front 1 Dec
German Army Group
Soviet Army
Soviet Army Group
LAKE LAGODA
GULF of FINLAND
LENINGRAD
GOVOROV
NARVA
Eighteenth Army
NOVGOROD
1 Dec-14 Jan.
Army Group North
v. KUECHLER
STARAYA RUSSA
Volkov
MERETSKOV
VOLOGDA
Second Baltic
POPOV
Volga R.
KAZAN
GORKI
KALININ
Sixteenth Army
14 Jan.
Third Panzer Army
First Baltic
BAGRAMYAN
MOSCOW
Bresina R.
1 Dec.
VITEBSK
Fourth Army
SMOLENSK
KALUGA
Army Group Center
BUSCH
ORSHA
Second White Russian
SOKOLOVSKI
KUIBYSHEV
MINSK
1 Dec-14 Jan.
Ninth Army
Second Army
Pripet R.
BRYANSK
OREL
First White Russian
ROKOSSOVSKI
GOMEL
14 Jan.
1 Dec.
KURSK
VORONEZH
Dnieper R.
First Ukrainian
VATUTIN
KONOTOP
KIEV
KHARKOV
Second Ukrainian
KONEV
POLTAVA
STALINGRAD
Army Group South
v. MANSTEIN
Fourth Panzer Army
Eighth Army
Third Ukrainian
MALINOVSKI
Donets R.
14 Jan.
1 Dec.
DNEPROPETROVSK
Volga R.
Bug R.
Don R.
First Panzer Army
STALINO
ROSTOV
1 Dec.-14 Jan.
Sixth Army
Fourth Ukrainian
TOLBUKHIN
Army Group A
v. KLEIST
ODESSA
SEA of AZOV
KERCH
KRASNODAR
Seventeenth Army
SEVASTOPOL
YALTA
CAUCASUS MTS
BLACK SEA

LIST OF CHARTS

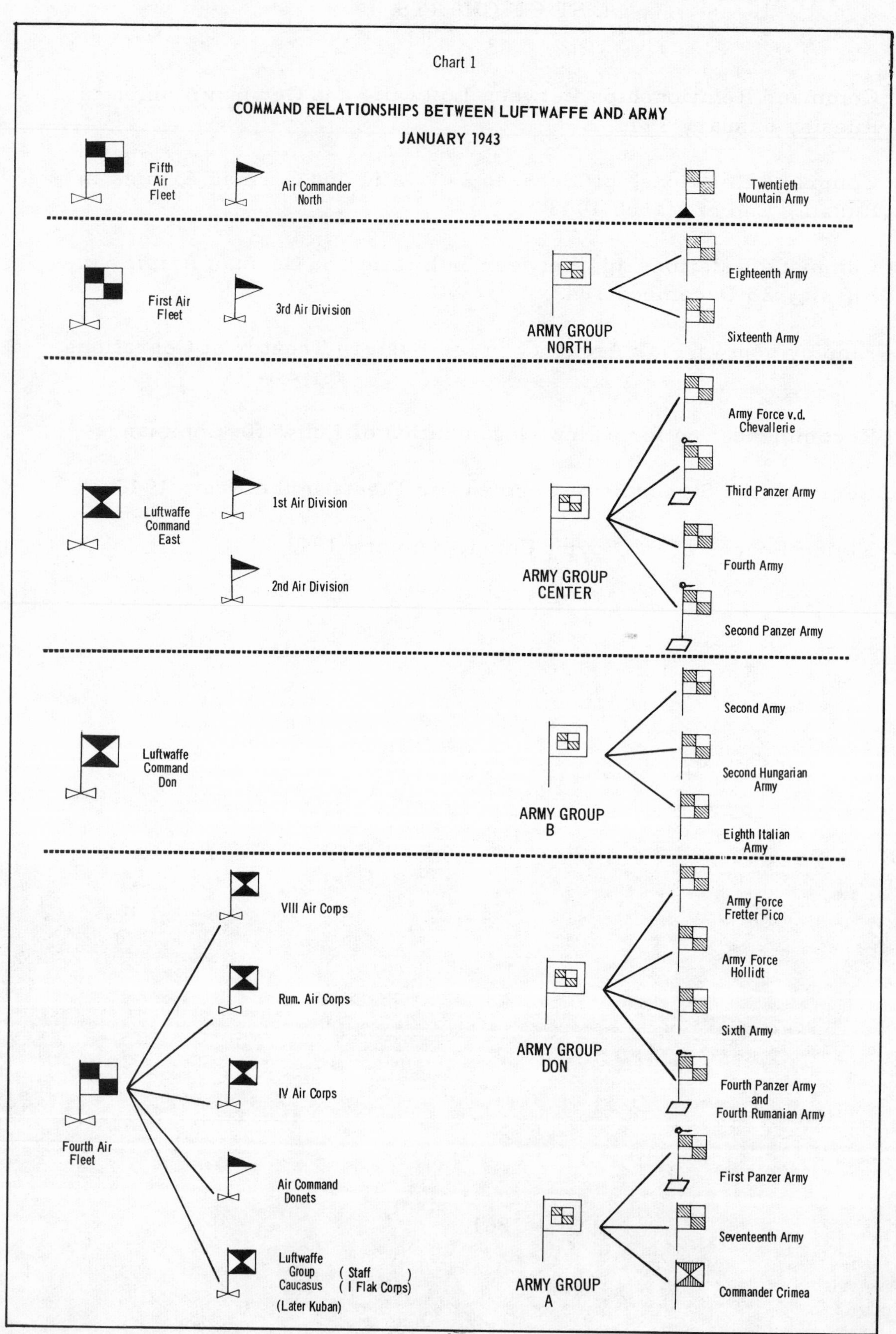

Chart 1
COMMAND RELATIONSHIPS BETWEEN LUFTWAFFE AND ARMY
JANUARY 1943
Fifth Air Fleet
Air Commander North
Twentieth Mountain Army
First Air Fleet
3rd Air Division
ARMY GROUP NORTH
Eighteenth Army
Sixteenth Army
Luftwaffe Command East
1st Air Division
2nd Air Division
ARMY GROUP CENTER
Army Force v.d. Chevallerie
Third Panzer Army
Fourth Army
Second Panzer Army
Luftwaffe Command Don
ARMY GROUP B
Second Army
Second Hungarian Army
Eighth Italian Army
Fourth Air Fleet
VIII Air Corps
Rum. Air Corps
IV Air Corps
Air Command Donets
Luftwaffe Group Caucasus
(Staff)
(I Flak Corps)
(Later Kuban)
ARMY GROUP DON
Army Force Fretter Pico
Army Force Hollidt
Sixth Army
Fourth Panzer Army and Fourth Rumanian Army
ARMY GROUP A
First Panzer Army
Seventeenth Army
Commander Crimea

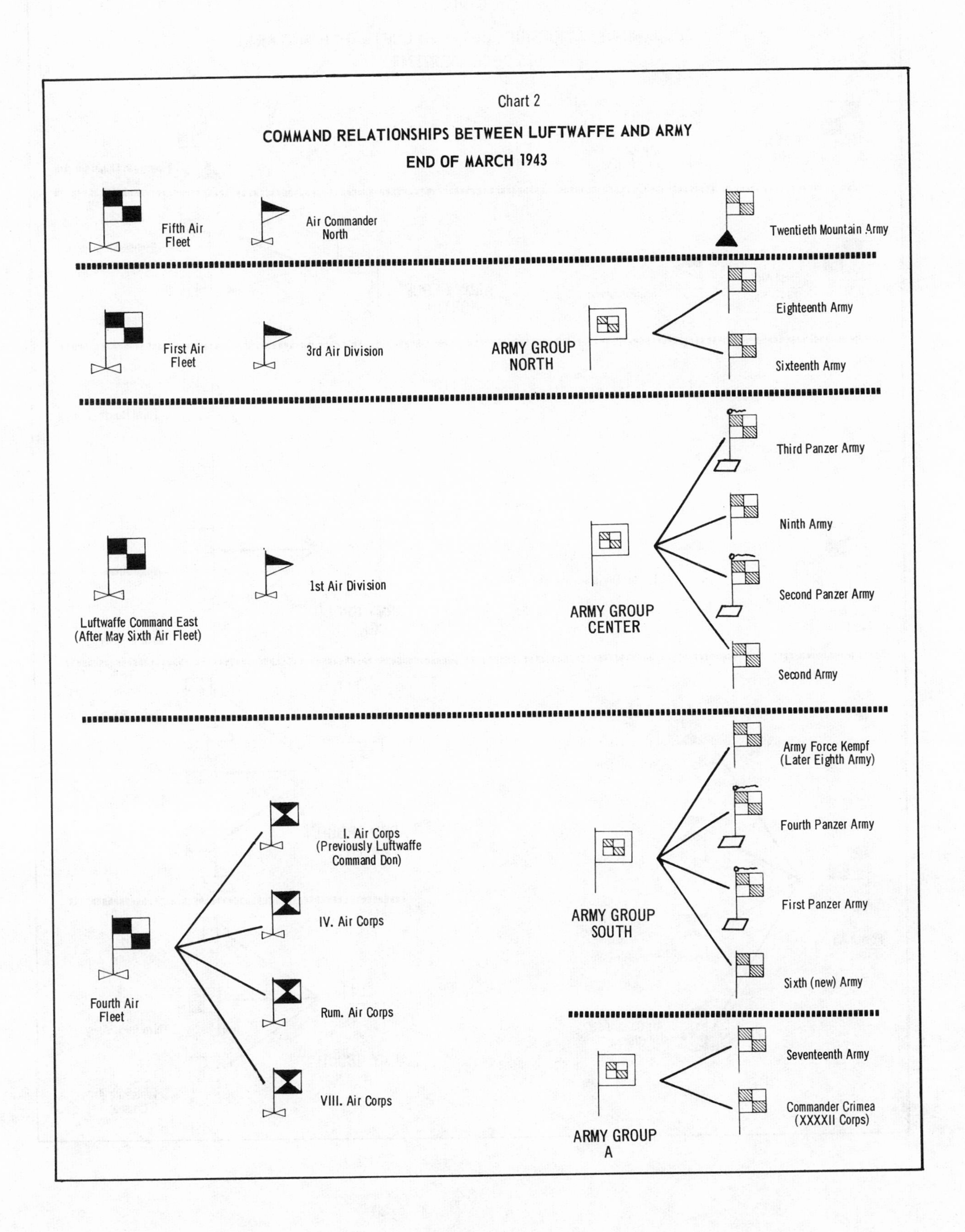
Chart 2
COMMAND RELATIONSHIPS BETWEEN LUFTWAFFE AND ARMY
END OF MARCH 1943
Fifth Air Fleet
Air Commander North
Twentieth Mountain Army
First Air Fleet
3rd Air Division
ARMY GROUP NORTH
Eighteenth Army
Sixteenth Army
Luftwaffe Command East
(After May Sixth Air Fleet)
1st Air Division
ARMY GROUP CENTER
Third Panzer Army
Ninth Army
Second Panzer Army
Second Army
Fourth Air Fleet
I. Air Corps
(Previously Luftwaffe Command Don)
IV. Air Corps
Rum. Air Corps
VIII. Air Corps
ARMY GROUP SOUTH
Army Force Kempf
(Later Eighth Army)
Fourth Panzer Army
First Panzer Army
Sixth (new) Army
ARMY GROUP A
Seventeenth Army
Commander Crimea
(XXXXII Corps)

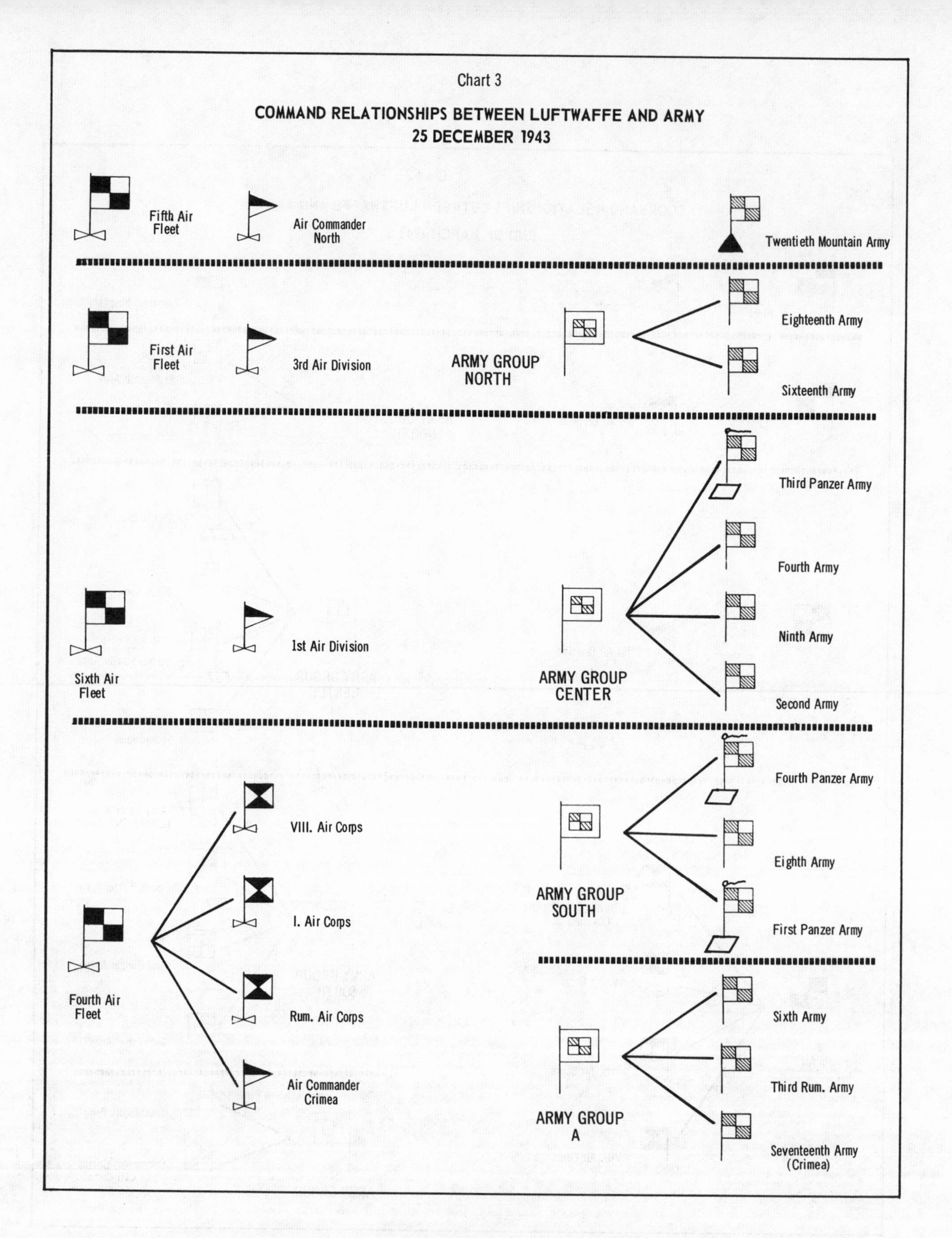
Chart 3
COMMAND RELATIONSHIPS BETWEEN LUFTWAFFE AND ARMY
25 DECEMBER 1943
Fifth Air Fleet
Air Commander North
Twentieth Mountain Army
First Air Fleet
3rd Air Division
ARMY GROUP NORTH
Eighteenth Army
Sixteenth Army
Sixth Air Fleet
1st Air Division
ARMY GROUP CENTER
Third Panzer Army
Fourth Army
Ninth Army
Second Army
Fourth Air Fleet
VIII. Air Corps
I. Air Corps
Rum. Air Corps
Air Commander Crimea
ARMY GROUP SOUTH
Fourth Panzer Army
Eighth Army
First Panzer Army
ARMY GROUP A
Sixth Army
Third Rum. Army
Seventeenth Army (Crimea)

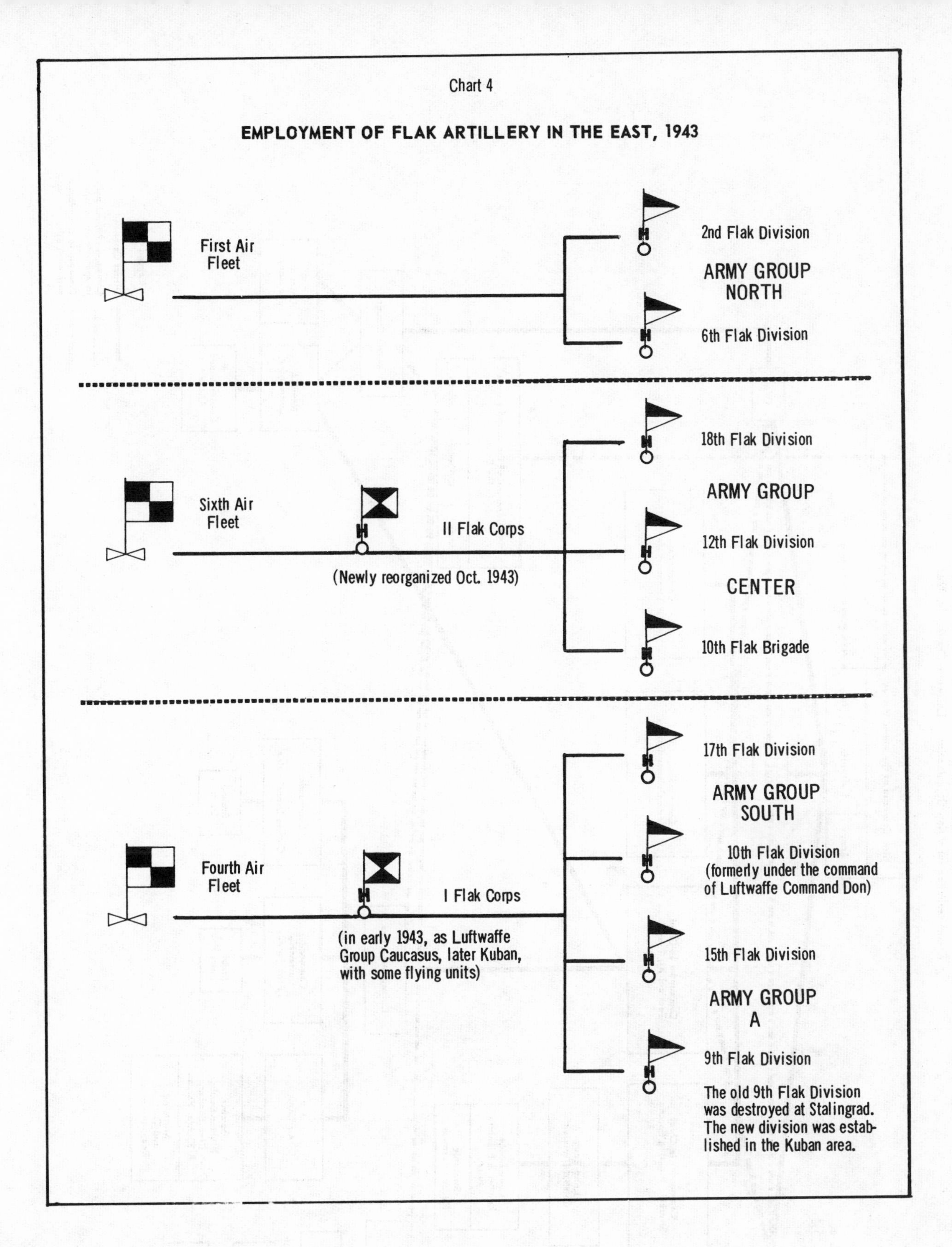
Chart 4
EMPLOYMENT OF FLAK ARTILLERY IN THE EAST, 1943
First Air Fleet
2nd Flak Division
ARMY GROUP NORTH
6th Flak Division
Sixth Air Fleet
II Flak Corps
(Newly reorganized Oct. 1943)
18th Flak Division
ARMY GROUP
12th Flak Division
CENTER
10th Flak Brigade
Fourth Air Fleet
I Flak Corps
(in early 1943, as Luftwaffe Group Caucasus, later Kuban, with some flying units)
17th Flak Division
ARMY GROUP SOUTH
10th Flak Division (formerly under the command of Luftwaffe Command Don)
15th Flak Division
ARMY GROUP A
9th Flak Division
The old 9th Flak Division was destroyed at Stalingrad. The new division was established in the Kuban area.

Recommendation for a New Organization of Luftwaffe Commands, 1943

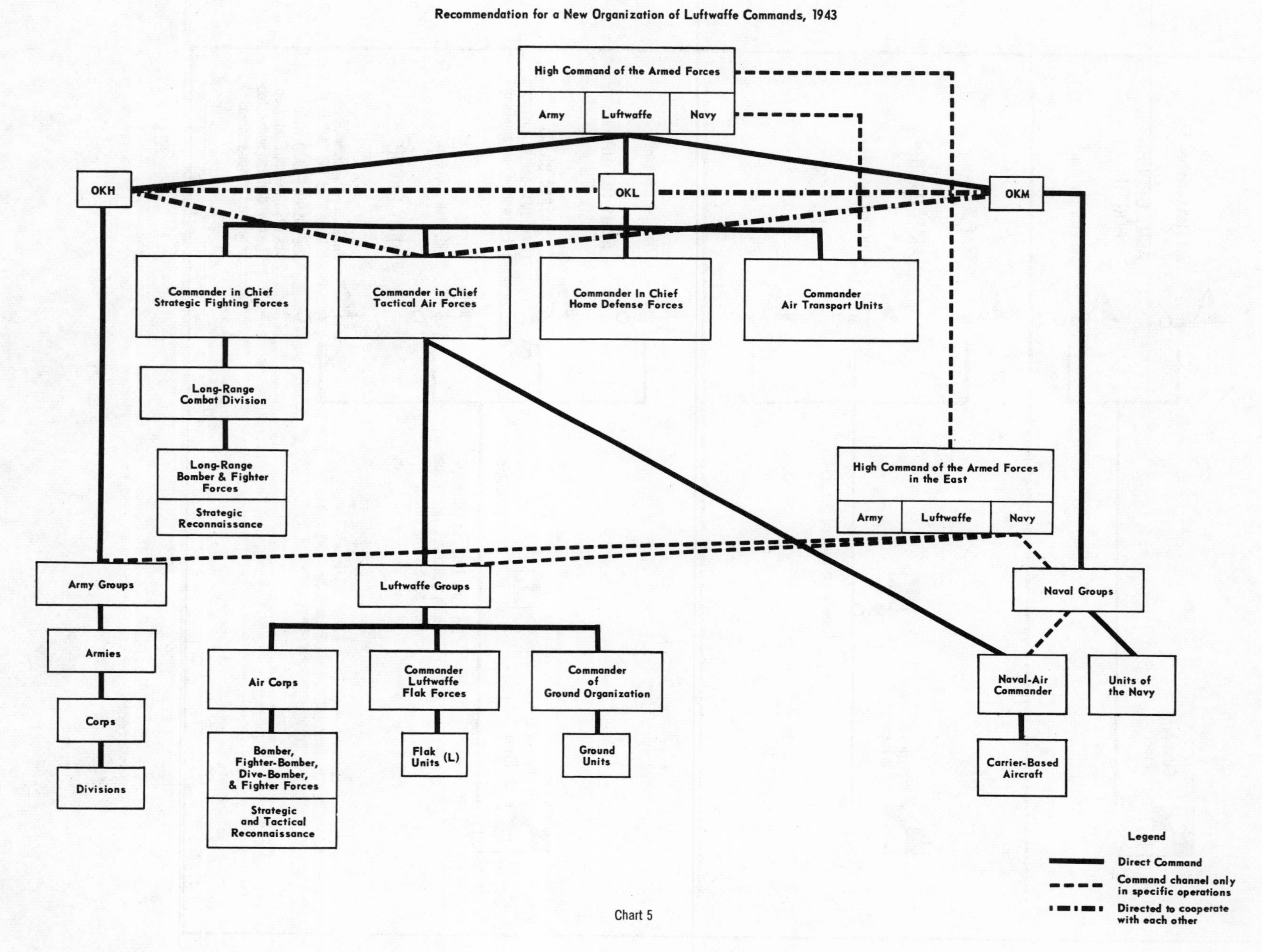

Chart 5

AIR FLEET	31 January 1943						20 February 1943					10 March 1943					10 April 1943	
	Fourth	Don	East	First	Fifth	South	Fourth	East	First	Fifth	South	Fourth	East	First	Fifth	South		
Tact. Recon (Squadrons)	11	3	9	4	1	28	5 Gps.	4 Gps.	2 Gps.	1	11 1/3	11	11	4	1	27	No data available for the individual Air Fleets.	
Strat. Recon (Squadrons)	5	3	5	4	2 1/3	19 1/3	8	6	4	2	20	6	6	4	2	18		
Fighters (Groups)	2	1	1 1/3	1	2	7 1/3	4	2 1/3	2 2/3	2	11	4*	3 1/3	3 1/3	2 1/3	13		1 Group was in the Ploesti area
Destroyers (Groups)	2	1/3 (Pz)	-	-	-	2 1/3	1 1/3	-	-	1/3	1 2/3	1	-	-	1/3	1 1/3		
Ftr-Bomber (Groups)	2	-	-	-	-	2	1 2/3	-	-	-	1 1/3	2 2/3	-	-	1/3	3		
Bomber (Groups)	8 1/3	3 1/3	1	2	1	15 2/3	11 2/3	1	2	1 1/3	16	11 2/3	1	1	1	14 2/3		
Dive-Bomber (Groups)	3	1	1 1/3*	1	-	6 1/3	6	-	1 2/3	1/3	8	5	2*	-	-	7		*1 Group attached to First Air Fleet for Operations.
Sea-Air (Squadrons)	1	-	-	-	-	1	1	-	-	-	1	- - -	- - -	- - -	- - -	- - -		

Flying Forces of the Soviet Union, Summer 1943

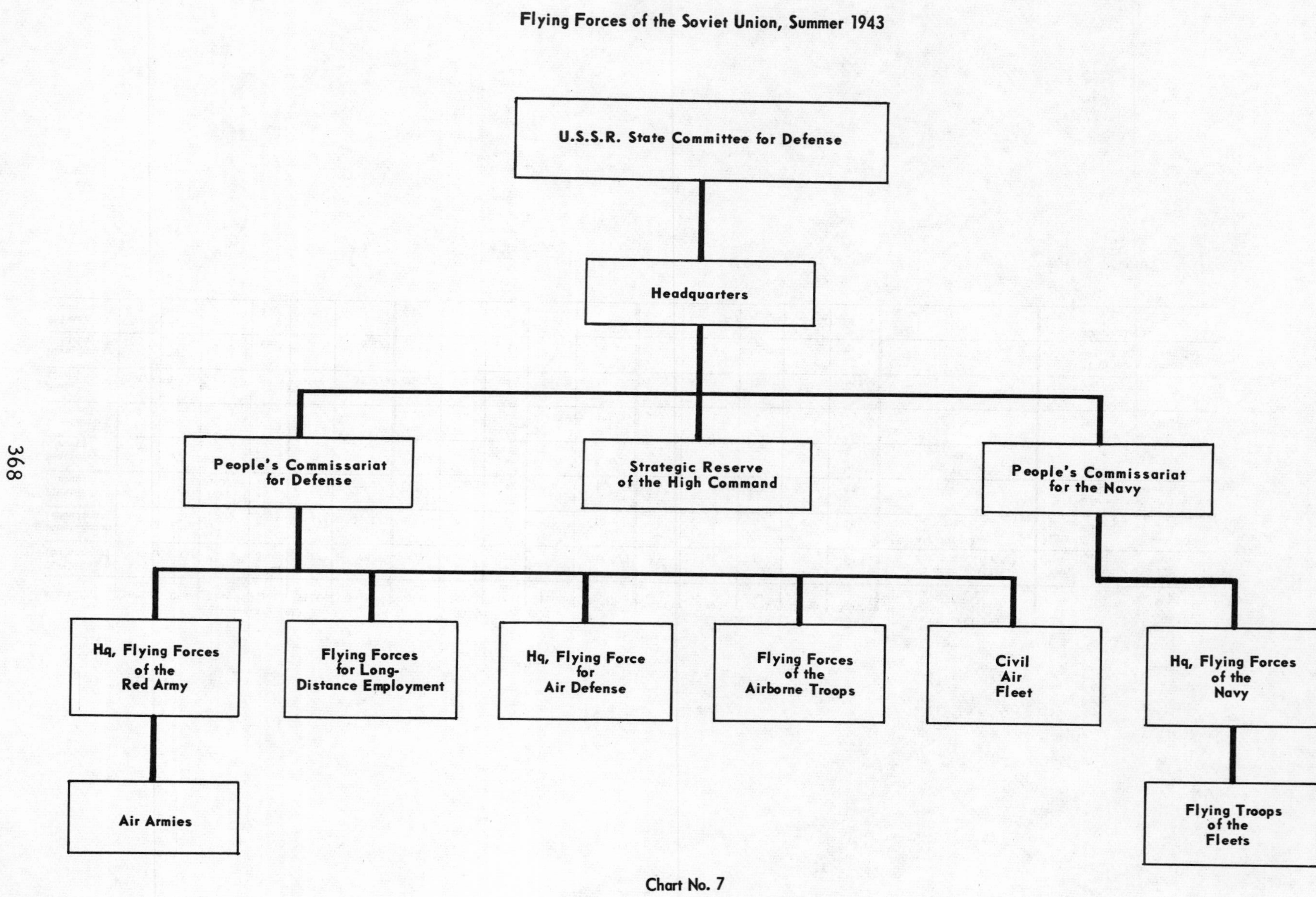

Chart No. 7